CREATIVE KEYBOARD'S

COMPLETE CHORD CLASSICS

S0-ATC-952

for Keyboard

A collection
of classical music
arrangements employing
chord symbols and simple
accompaniment patterns for the
intermediate-level pianist.

Dedicated to my students
who inspired and assisted me
in refining these arrangements.

Frank Levin 1992

Creative Keyboard Publications

Arranged by Frank Levin

Contents

Introduction

If you have just a modest level of technical skill at the piano, this manual can help you learn many of the most well known classics in surprisingly full-sounding but relatively simple arrangements. The system uses a lead-sheet format like that used by jazz and pop musicians as a starting point for improvisations.

However, these lead sheets are different because they don't require the performer to improvise anything. They are in fact complete arrangements. In addition to the standard melody and chord symbols, they contain new symbols developed specifically for this volume. These symbols indicate the accompaniment patterns to be used and where the chords are to be played on the keyboard. Detailed instructions are provided. Directions for playing all the chords found on the lead sheets are also included.

The instructions are sufficiently complete for pianists with intermediate skills to master the material on their own.

Pop and jazz musicians, including bands accustomed to working from lead sheets, will find the collection an excellent means of supplementing their repertoire and filling requests for popular classics. The work of about fifty composers is presented, including favorites by such masters as Beethoven, Chopin, Mendelssohn, Mozart, Schubert, Schumann, and Tschaikovsky.

Teachers may use the book in a variety of ways. It can serve as an introduction to the art of playing from lead sheets. It can be used as a general introduction to the classics. It can be used for teaching theory, including chord structures, standard progressions and harmonic analysis. Finally, because the arrangements involve repetitious accompaniment patterns, they can help students feel underlying rhythmic patterns and gain facility in counting and playing in time.

Pieces are grouped according to the six accompaniment patterns used. The accompaniment patterns move from easiest to most difficult; so do the selections within each pattern.

Appendix A is an alphabetic index by title; Appendix B, by composer. Appendix C is a complete chord reference chart. Appendix D covers practicing hints, and Appendix E presents sample arrangements with the accompaniments included.

How To Use This Book on a Self-Study Basis

If you are working on your own and have had little or no training in improvising techniques, I would recommend that you approach the study of the material in this volume in the following way:

Begin by studying the introductory material carefully. If you don't already know them, try to commit to memory such basic chords as C, F, and G major; D, E, and A minor; and G, D, A, and E 7th. This will permit you to play most of the chords in the first few pieces in each group.

Start with the *Block Chord* group and learn the first two or three pieces, then go on to the *Waltz Pattern Group* and do the same. Continue in sequence through the remaining groups except the last. This procedure will teach you to play the basic chords and accompaniment patterns.

Remember to count. You'll sound a lot better, and it's particularly easy in the first pieces; it will also prepare you for the more difficult rhythmic interplay between hands as you progress through more challenging material. You may also find it helpful to pencil in the *ooms*, *pahs*, or other symbols above their appropriate positions in the bar, e.g.:

Nocturne in E♭ Major

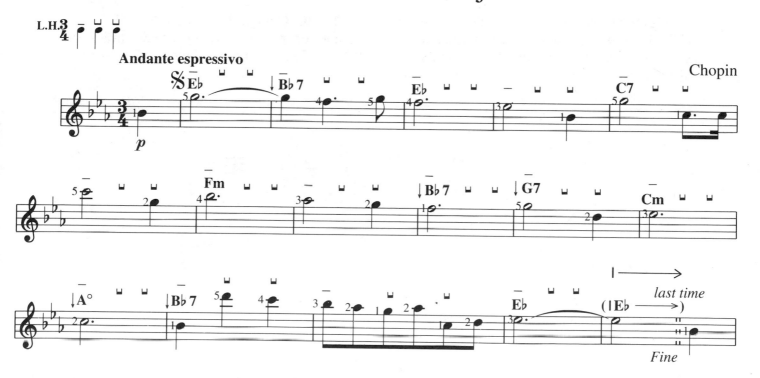

Once you've learned the basic chords and patterns, study the next few pieces in each group to add to your chord repertoire and ability to handle more difficult rhythms. After that, you'll find you're able to move relatively freely throughout the book. In fact, many students, as they become more comfortable with the chords and accompaniment patterns, find that they're able to play all but the most difficult selections almost at sight.

Finally, you may like to try some of the "challenge" pieces in the last section. Most students on their own learn to use the knowledge they obtain working with this material to create simple arrangements of popular songs found in fakebooks or chorded sheet music. You may even be challenged to make your own arrangements from original editions as this author has done! Appendix D provides other useful practicing hints.

Reading Chord Symbols

To play the accompaniment patterns, you first need to learn the chords from which they are derived. We start with major triads which provide the basis for all other chords.

Major Triads

Put the fifth finger of your left hand on the C below middle C and play five successive notes to the right. Lift the second and fourth fingers; you're left with C, E, and G. Play the three notes together. They produce a bright harmonious sound. This is a major triad. The lowest note, which is called the root, gives the triad its name: C major. The middle note of the triad, E, under the third finger, is the third; the top note, G, under the thumb, is the fifth. Between the root and the third are four half-steps, and between the third and the fifth are three half-steps. All major triads have this interval pattern.

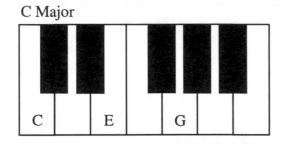

Triads are always spelled with alternate-letter names. Thus the C major triad is spelled C E G, not C F♭ G. Note also that triads are written on successive lines or spaces of the staff. Major triads are symbolized by capital letters based on the root of the chord. The examples below will test your understanding.

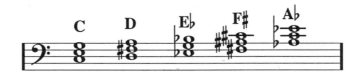

Minor Triads

A minor triad is formed by flatting the third of the major triad. Minor triads are symbolized by a lower-case m after the capital—Cm, Dm, E♭m, F♯m etc.

Diminished Triads

A diminished triad is formed by flatting both the third and the fifth of the major triad. Diminished triads are symbolized by a small circle after the capital—Co, Do, E♭o, F♯o, etc.

Augmented Triads

An augmented triad is formed by sharping the fifth of the major triad. Augmented triads are symbolized by a plus sign after the capital—C+, D+, etc.

Sixth Chords

A sixth chord is a major or minor triad with the note a whole step[1] above the fifth (i.e., the sixth above the root) added to the triad. Sixth chords are symbolized by a 6 next to the major or minor chord symbol.

[1]Two half-steps equal a whole step—G to A, A to B, B♭ to C, etc.

Seventh Chords

Seventh chords contain four notes; the fourth note is seven letters up from the root. A seventh chord is written on four consecutive lines or spaces. There are six kinds of seventh chords found in these arrangements: major, minor, diminished, half-diminished (also referred to as minor seven flat fives), augmented, and dominant sevenths. Some are rarely found. Dominant and minor sevenths occur most frequently. The table summarizes the key features of the seventh chords.

Type	Symbol	Formation	Examples
Dominant	7	Add the note a whole step below the root to the top of the major triad.	
Minor	m7	Add the note a whole step below the root to the top of the minor triad.	
Half Diminished (minor 7 flat 5)	m7♭5	Add the note a whole step below the root to the top of the diminished triad.	
Augmented	+7	Add the note a whole step below the root to the top of the augmented triad.	
Major	△7	Add the note a *half step* below the root to the top of the major triad.	
Diminished	o7	Add the note *three half steps* below the root to the top of the diminished triad.	

Note: Most 7th Chords are formed by adding the note, a whole step below the root, to the top of the base triad. The Major and the Diminished 7th are the two exceptions.

Suspensions

A suspension is formed by replacing the third of a major triad with the note a half-step higher; this note is written as a fourth above the root. Suspensions are symbolized by the abbreviation "sus" after the capital—Csus, Dsus.

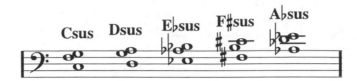

Suspensions may also be found on dominant seventh chords.

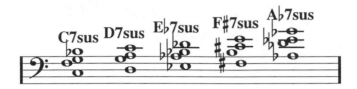

Altered Chords

An altered chord is formed by flatting the fifth of the major triad or dominant seventh chord. Rarely found in these arrangements, altered chords are identified by a bracketed ♭5 after the major or dominant seventh symbol.

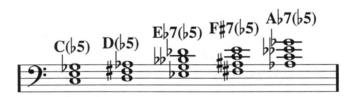

Inversions

The rearrangement of the notes of a chord so that the third, fifth, or seventh is in the bass is called an inversion. It's used to achieve a smoother connection between chords. The chord is symbolized first, followed by a slash and the note that is in the bass:

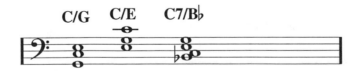

Occasionally non-chord notes may also be used as bass notes, as Em/A. Specific instructions for playing these chords are provided in the selections in which they're found.

In the simplest arrangements at the beginning of each accompaniment pattern group, inversions are rarely used because students just learning chords find them difficult to remember. In more advanced selections however, inversions are employed to re-create, as far as possible, the movement of the original bass line and be in accord with traditional voice leading practices.

Left Hand Accompaniment Patterns

The primary purpose of an accompaniment is to provide the harmonic and rhythmic background for the melody. The key word is *background*. An accompaniment must be played more softly than the melody line so that it doesn't overshadow the melody. And it must be played in relatively strict time to provide an underlying rhythmic pulse. Remember that the first beat is slightly accented.

Practice the accompaniment separately until you can play it comfortably in time. Then practice playing it softly; that will help you control the balance between hands.

The six accompaniment patterns used in this manual are described below, as are the symbols that will be used for them at the top left corner of each piece.

Block Chord Pattern

This accompaniment pattern is indicated with vertical lines. All chords are played as block chords and in the rhythm indicated by the "time value" notes found below the vertical lines. The pattern instructions indicate the number of block chords per bar. L.H. represents left hand.

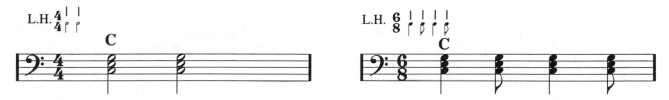

Rests and staccato markings may also be featured in the pattern profile.

Occasionally a bar may contain extra block chords. Where their time value is not obvious from their alignment with the melody notes, time value notes are included with the chord symbols to indicate the accompaniment rhythm to be played.

A horizontal arrow → (duration arrow) is used to represent a chord held longer than the pattern. The point of the arrow indicates the beat at which the chord is released.

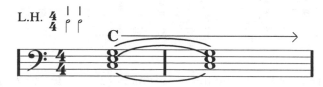

9

For harmonic reasons or to keep out of the way of the melody line, a note may be dropped from the chord. This is found in other accompaniment patterns as well.

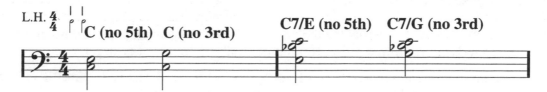

When a block chord is used in a selection with another accompaniment pattern, a vertical line to the left of the chord symbol identifies a chord to be played as a block chord: ⏐C, ⏐A, ⏐Em, etc.

Most pianists first attempting block chords will find triads fairly easy, but four-note seventh chords can be awkward. Try this approach in practicing: Slowly play one note at a time from bottom to top until all are down. Hold the chord for about five seconds before repeating the exercise. Repeat several times. By practicing this way, you will develop the finger strength to play the block sevenths.

Waltz Pattern

This accompaniment pattern is symbolized by — ⊔ ⊔ , (oom, pah, pah). The *oom* represents the bass note of the chord and the *pahs*, all chord notes above the bass. The pattern is accompanied by time value notes below each symbol.

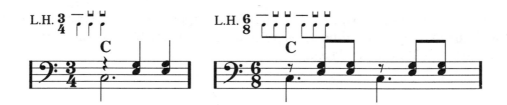

The bass note may be held through the bar at the performer's discretion.

Waltz pattern pieces may contain bars with block (⏐) or rolled chords (⸾), rests (R), duration arrows (→), or some combination of *ooms* (—), and *pahs* (⊔). Time value notes as described above would accompany these symbols when their placement with respect to the melody is not clear.

The waltz pattern covers mazurkas, minuets, and many other selections in 3/4 or 6/8 time, as well as waltzes.

March Pattern

This pattern is symbolized by — ⊔ (oom, pah) or — ⊔ — ⊔ (oom, pah, oom, pah).

As with the waltz, the bass note may be held through the pattern. Staccato markings and chords with missing notes are also featured.

Music with this accompaniment pattern tends to be bright and up tempo; however, it is occasionally used in slow selections.

Ballad Pattern

This pattern is symbolized by — ⊔ R ⊔ (oom, pah, rest, pah).

It is often used with slow, songful melodies. Again the bass note may be held throughout the pattern or released, according to taste.

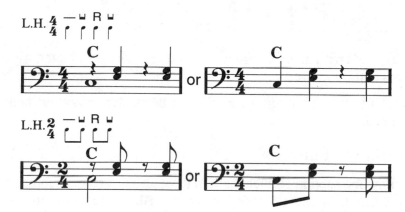

It is frequently used in conjunction with the march pattern when a chord change occurs in the middle of the bar:

Alberti Bass and Related Patterns

These patterns are symbolized with some combination of the the initials B, M, and T, where B represents the bass note of the chord, M the middle note, and T the top note. When seventh chords are used, the third or fifth is omitted as specified on the sheet music.

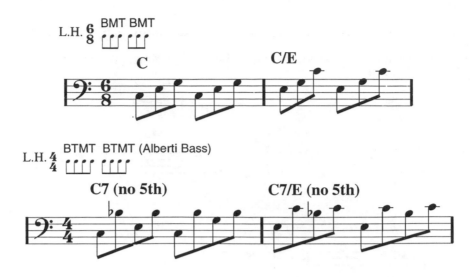

Rolled Chord Pattern

This pattern is symbolized by wavy vertical lines with rhythm noted by appropriate time value notes. The bass note of the chord is played first, followed as quickly and evenly as possible by succeeding notes from lowest to highest. All notes are held for the duration of the chord:

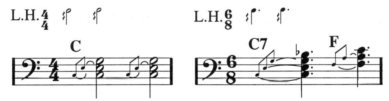

Duration arrows (→), extra chords with time value notes, and other devices characteristic of the *Block Chord Pattern* apply to this pattern as well.

Rolled chords, often difficult for the inexperienced pianist, can be mastered by slow, heavy practice, with gradual increase in speed.

Combining Accompaniment Patterns

Although most pieces employ one accompaniment pattern throughout, a few combine patterns. The *Ballad Pattern*, as previously noted, uses the *March Pattern* when there are two chord changes in the bar. Several arrangements change pattern in their B sections. Changes in pattern are always clearly marked in the music and the pieces are grouped according to the opening pattern. The symbols used are the same ones employed in identifying the various accompaniment patterns.

Other Patterns

At the end of the book is a collection of generally more difficult pieces employing multiple patterns and patterns not found elsewhere in the book. These should challenge the enthusiast and provide a hint of directions to be explored in possible future editions.

Endings

Providing a satisfactory ending for a piece often requires breaking the pattern to produce a block or broken chord, a single bass note, or some other concluding sound. Such endings are always clearly marked by using the accompaniment pattern symbols described above.

Most *Waltz Pattern* pieces, for example, end with a block chord designated by a vertical line next to the last chord symbol, followed by a horizontal arrow indicating how long the block chord should be sustained. Some pieces end with a rolled chord, indicated by a wavy line to the left of the chord symbol, or a specific pattern of *ooms* and *pahs* is written out, designating the ending pattern. The simple sustained bass note ending without a chord is described below under (N.C.) directions.

Other Symbols and Instructions

Chord Symbols

A chord symbol remains in effect until the next chord symbol appears.

Chords not specifically defined in the *Introduction* are spelled out in the arrangements, and always from bottom to top.

Hand Placement Arrows

Arrows are used to identify the appropriate position for a chord on the keyboard. No arrow next to a chord symbol indicates that the bass note of the chord is to be played in the seven notes just below middle C—from low C to B below middle C. A downward arrow ↓ indicates that the bass note of the chord is to be played between the C and B of the next octave down. Two downward arrows ↓↓ indicate that the bass note is to be played between the C and B of the octave below that. An upward arrow ↑ next to the chord symbol indicates that the bass note of the chord should fall in the octave between middle C and the B seven notes above. Two upward arrows ↑↑ indicate that the bass note is to be played in the octave above that.

N.C.

(N.C.) means that no chord is to be played. This direction remains in effect until the next chord symbol appears on the music. If the (N.C.) is preceded by a capital, as C (N.C.), the bass note is to be played alone, without a chord. This frequently occurs at the end of a piece and is often accompanied by hand placement and duration arrows such as ↓ E♭ (N.C.) →.

Tempo, Expression, and Related Markings

The use of tempo and expression markings, dynamic symbols, and repeat and related structural signs is consistent with that of the standard classical repertoire. For students unfamiliar with these terms and symbols, there are many inexpensive guides available. The *Student's Musical Dictionary*, published by Mel Bay Publications, Inc., is one such example.

When 8va markings are used, they shift only the melody part(s), not the accompaniment, up an octave.

Phrasing

As phrasing is not indicated, use your judgment and musical sense in shaping melodic lines. Singing often helps to identify the underlying phrasing or the possible breaks in legato fingering.

Dynamics

Although dynamic markings are provided, remember that an upward moving melodic line implies a crescendo, and a downward moving melodic line implies a diminuendo. The dynamic high point is usually at or near the end of the piece. Carefully thought out dynamic variation can be a great benefit in making a performance interesting.

Other Reference Material

A good music reference covering the lives of the composers, historical trends, styles, and other background information is invaluable for the enthusiast.

Acknowledgments

Thanks to Tony Arioli for encouraging me to produce this book and for providing music drafting supplies, to Jim Heisterkampf for assistance with the design of the pilot edition, to Steve Yuan and Ed and Eleanore Perkins for text editing and word-processing assistance, to Hal Young for help with music copying, and to Kathy Hirzel for technical expertise in printing the pilot edition.

Thanks, too, to the following students and friends for their useful suggestions in refining these arrangements: Lynda Beigel, Lorraine Blue, Larry Blair, Lucky Choi, Nellie Keate, Dexter Fong, Lillian Klein, Tom Knox, Evaline Landahl, Rigmor Larsen, George Lynch, Rick Winget, Tina Tan, and Gladys Woodd.

Finally, thanks to my teachers, Garry Remal, Jim Grantham, and especially Dr. Sol Joseph, of the San Francisco Conservatory of Music, for their invaluable instruction and support.

Your comments and suggestions are welcome. Please send them to me in care of the publisher.

Frank Levin

Block Chord Pattern Pieces
Ode To Joy

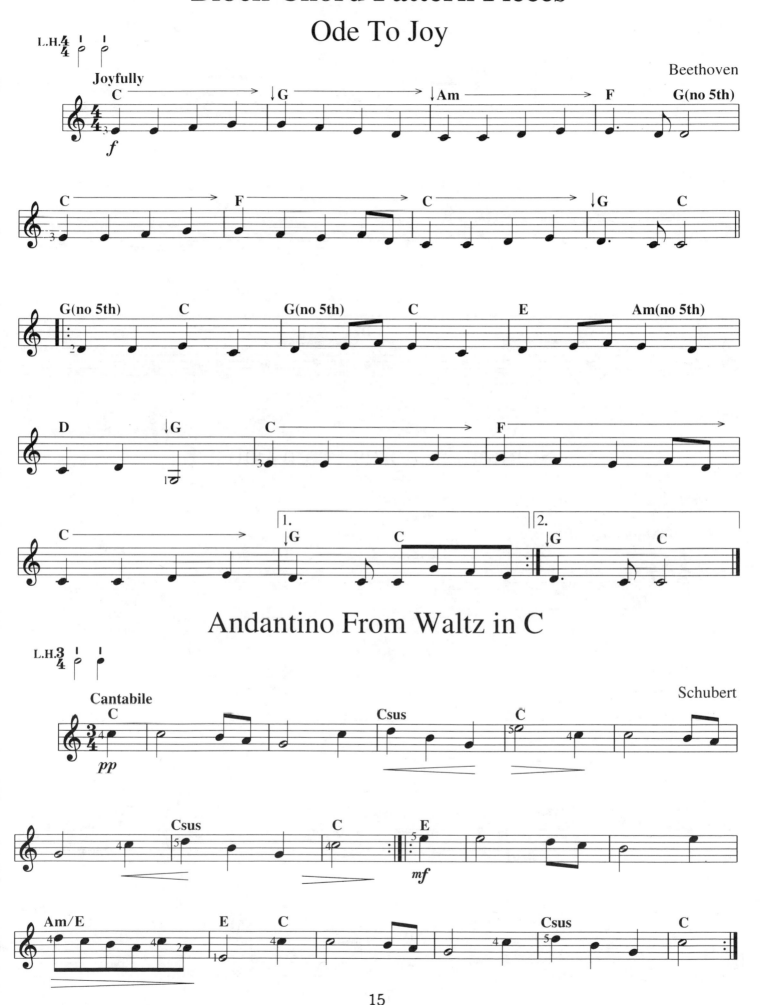

Andantino From Waltz in C

Grand March from Aida

Verdi

Soldiers' Chorus From Faust

Gounod

Pomp and Circumstance March No 1.

Elgar

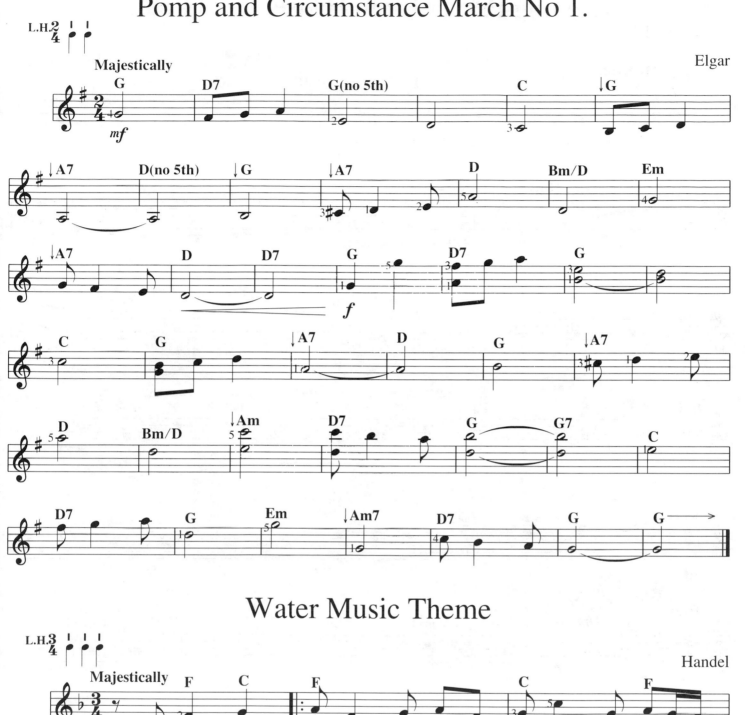

Water Music Theme

Handel

Evening Prayer From Hansel and Gretel

Humperdinck

Arabesque

The Wild Horseman

Wedding March

Coronation March From The Prophet

The Star-Spangled Banner

Smith

America (God Save the Queen)

Carey

Funeral March of a Marionette

Gounod

Prelude in C Minor

Chopin

Nocturne in G Minor
for Right or Left Hand Alone *

Chopin

Jig

Martini

Tambourin

Rameau

Jesu, Joy Of Man's Desiring

J.S. Bach

To A Wild Rose

Largo

Handel

Largo From The New World Symphony

Bridal Chorus from Lohengrin

Wagner

Waltz Pattern Pieces
The Skaters

Waldteufel

Lullaby

Brahms

Emperor Waltz

Strauss

Over the Waves

Rosas

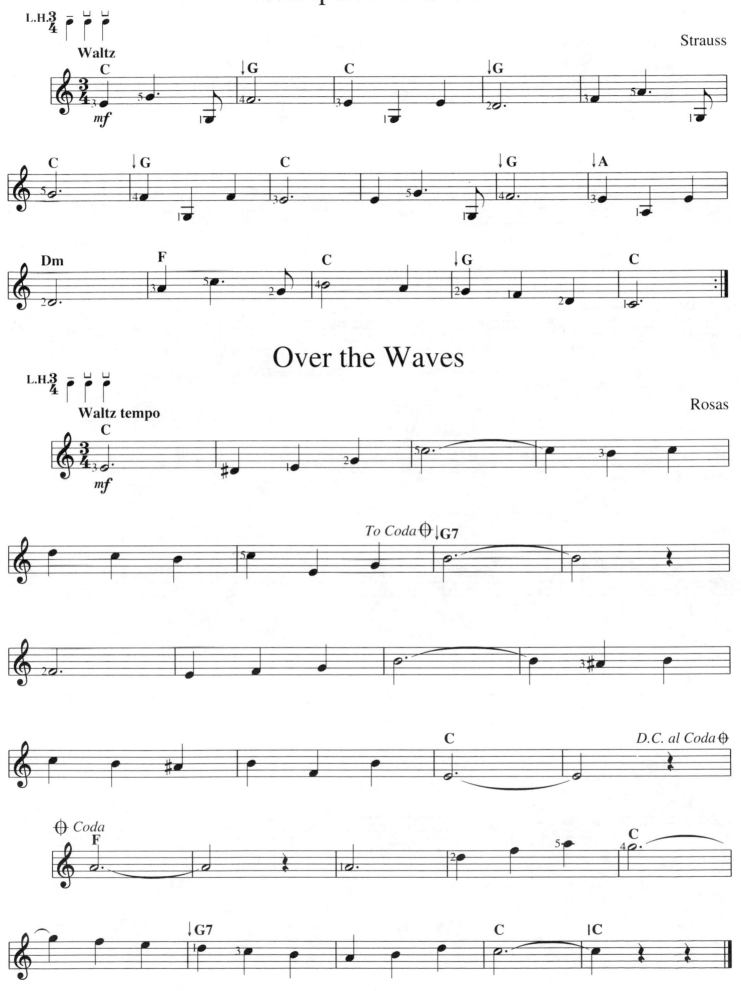

Waves Of The Danube

Ivanovici

Blue Danube Waltz

J. Strauss Jr.

Evening Star

Wagner

Landler in A Minor

Schubert

Minuet from Don Giovanni

Mozart

La Donna e Mobile from Rigoletto

Verdi

Sleeping Beauty Waltz

Tchaikovsky

Celeste Aida

Verdi

Romanze from the Sonatina in G

Beethoven

Minuet in G Major

Serenade

Schubert

* Melody but not chords are played 8va.

Nocturne in E♭ Major

Mazurka in B♭ Major

Chopin

Musetta's Waltz from La Bohéme

Puccini

41

Waltz in A♭ Major

The Disappointed Serenader

Brahms

March Pattern Pieces
The Can Can

Offenbach

Radetzky March

J. Strauss

Give Me Thy Hand from Don Giovanni

Mozart

Narcissus

Nevin

Humoresque

Anvil Chorus From Il Trovatore

Verdi

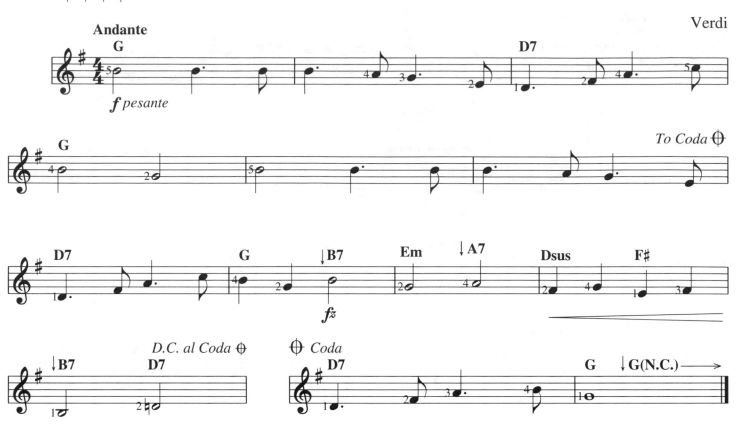

Aria From The Marriage of Figaro

Mozart

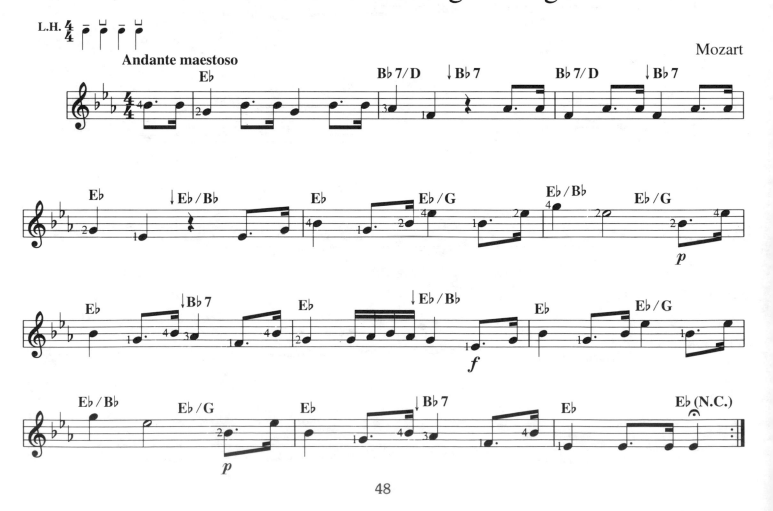

Norwegian Dance

Grieg

Allegretto tranquillo e grazioso
2nd time 8va 8 bars.

Hungarian Dance No. 5

Brahms

Allegro passionato

poco rit.

49

June Barcarolle

Tchaikovsky

Vesti La Giubba

Leoncavallo

Gymnopedie No. 1 in D Major

Satie

Air in F

Trumpet Air

53

Golliwogg's Cake Walk

Debussy

Dance of the Sugar Plum Fairy

Tchaikovsky

Delicato
R.H. 8va throughout

Ballad Pattern Pieces
Intermezzo From Rosamond

Schubert

The Stars and Stripes Forever

Sousa

Arrival of the Swans from Swan Lake

Tchaikovsky

The Fifers

Dandrieu

Songs My Mother Taught Me

Dvořák

Say Ye Who Borrow from The Marriage of Figaro

Mozart

Salut D'Amour

Elgar

Old French Song

Tchaikovsky

None But the Lonely Heart

Tchaikovsky

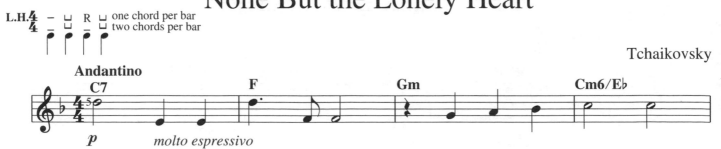

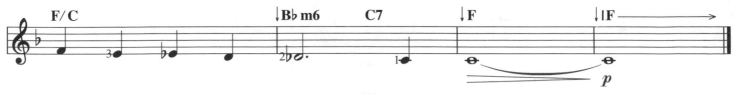

Melody in F Major

Rubinstein

At The Fireside

Schumann

Love At Thy Sweet Voice From Samson and Delilah

Saint- Saens

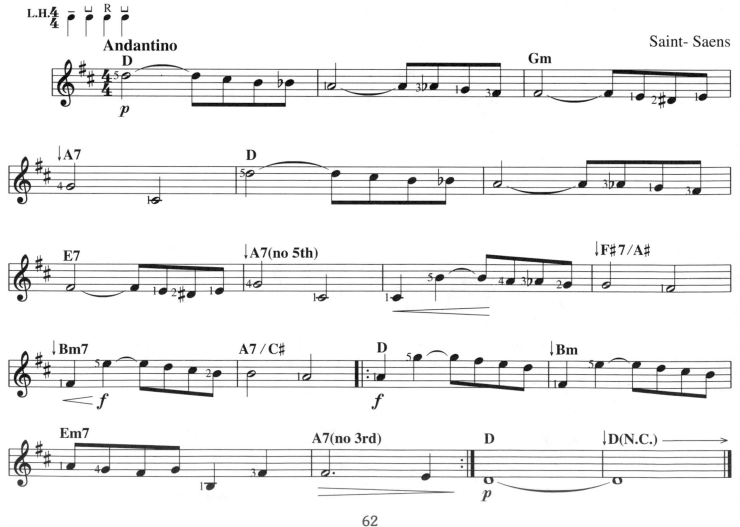

Lost Happiness

Symphony No. 6: Love Theme

Tchaikovsky

Etude in E Major

Alberti Bass and Related Pattern Pieces

Sonatina in C Major

Haydn

Carnival Scene

Couperin

Andante from The Surprise Symphony

Haydn

Allegretto from Tempest Sonata

Beethoven

Little Cradle - Song

Schumann

68

Gavotte From The Third English Suite

J. S. Bach

About Strange Lands and People

Schumann

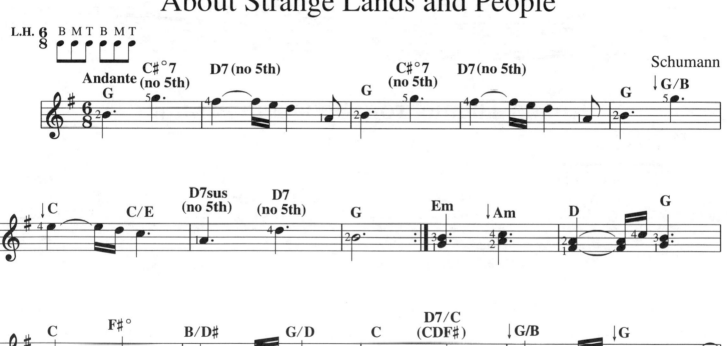

Opening Theme from Violin Concerto

Mendelssohn

Rondo Theme from Sonata in A Major

Schubert

Shepherd's Song From Pastoral Symphony

The Swan from Carnival of the Animals

Saint - Saëns

Panis Angelicus

Ave Maria

Schubert

For players unable to execute the two against three rhythm all triplets should be played as follows:

Canon in D Major

Venetian Boat Song in F# Minor

Mendelssohn

Arabesque

Rolled Chord Pattern Pieces
Minuet

On Wings of Song

That Sheep May Safely Graze

J.S. Bach

Amaryllis

Louis XIII

Barcarolle

Offenbach

Norwegian Folk Song in G Major

Grieg

Opening Theme from Sonata No. 19

Beethoven

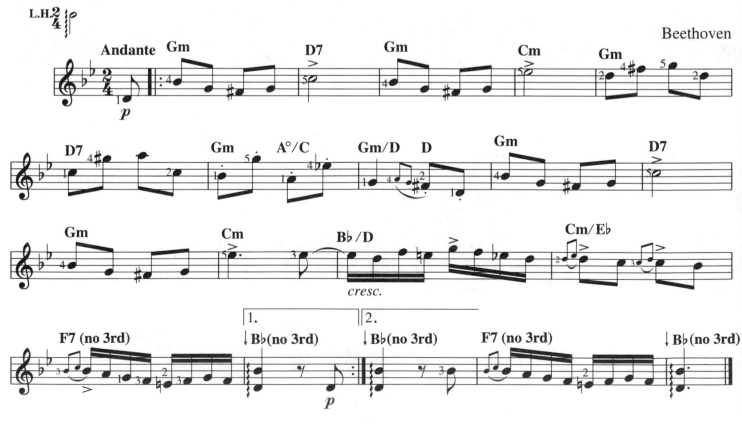

Pomp and Circumstance March No. 4.

Elgar

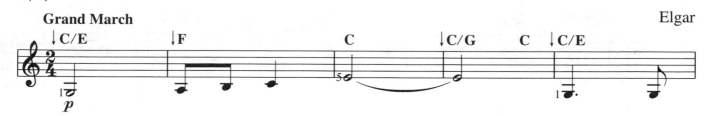

Nocturne

Schumann

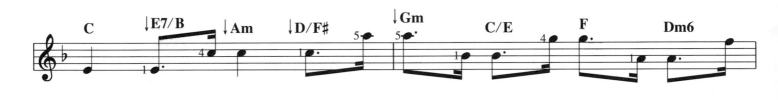

84

Slumber Song

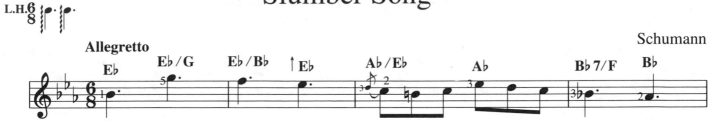

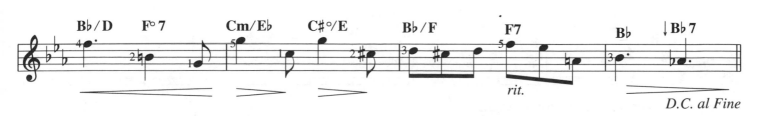

Song Of The Moldau

Smetana

* Lower melody note may be omitted throughout.

Elegy

Miscellaneous
Alla Turca

Mozart

Arioso

J.S. Bach

89

Adagio from Clarinet Concerto

Mozart

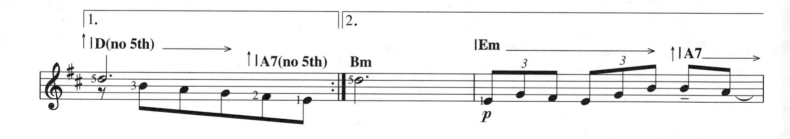

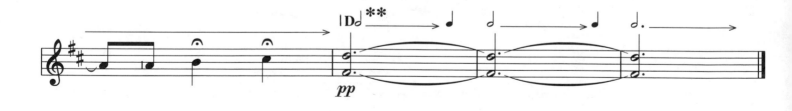

Für Elise

91

Tango in D Major

Albeniz

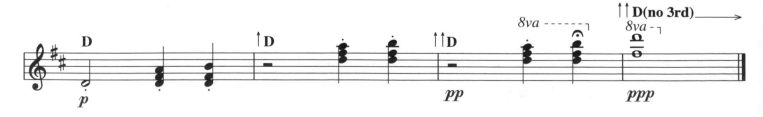

Innig from Davidsbundler Tanze

En Bateau

Debussy

Ballade in G Minor

Chopin

Appendix A: Index by Title

Appendix B: Index by Composer

Appendix C: Chord Reference Chart

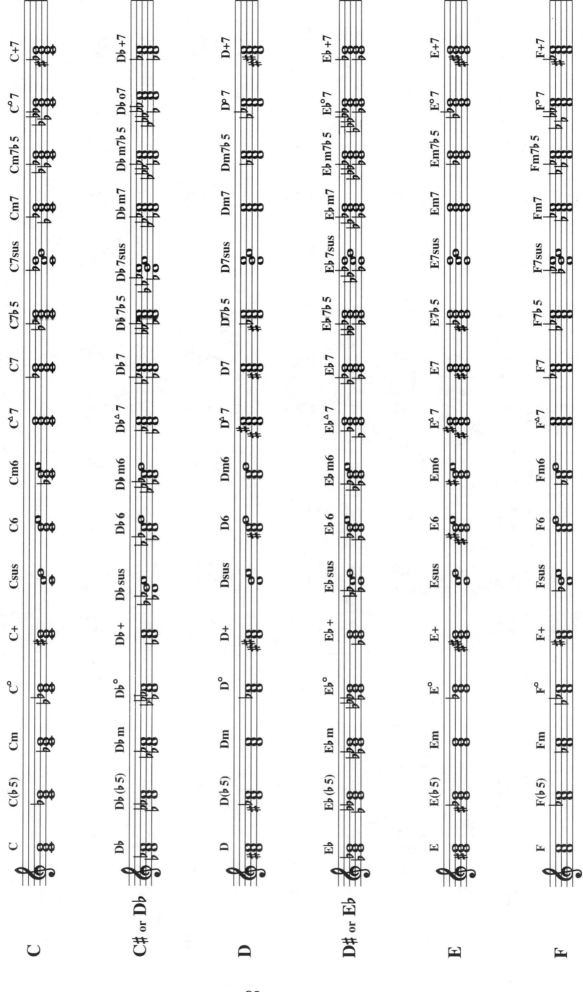

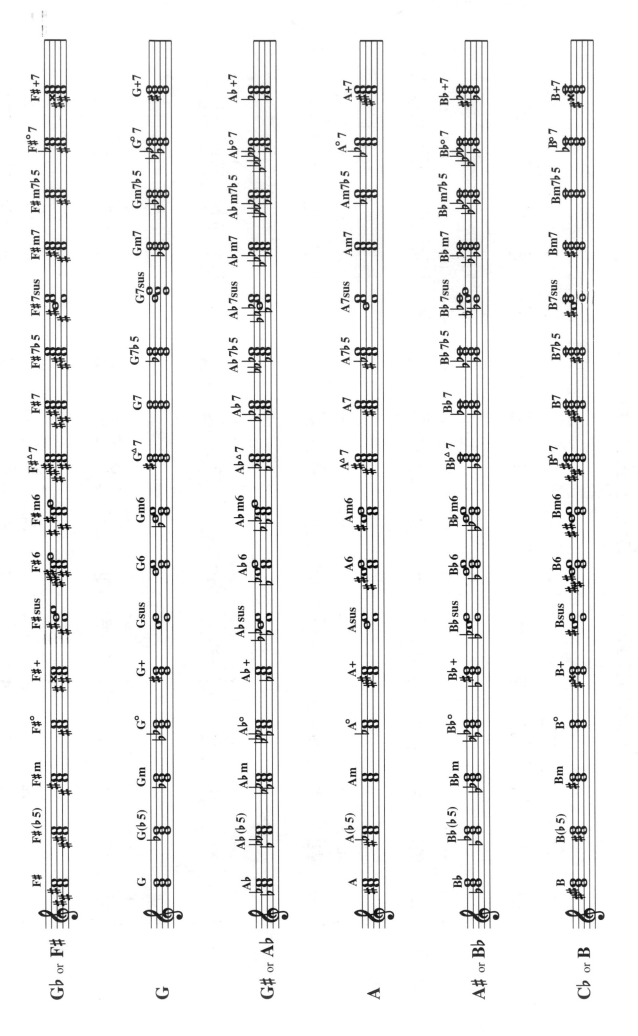

Appendix D: General Practicing Hints

There are prodigies who can sit down at the piano and learn effortlessly, but most students must practice diligently to play well. Often students frustrate themselves by trying to do too much at once. Attempting to handle notes, fingering, timing, and expression in both hands at the same time can be overwhelming. However, by dividing the practicing process into a number of manageable sub-steps, you can progress more readily with a minimum of frustration. Below is a method I've found most effective in accomplishing this end.

First, divide the piece into practice sections, following as much as possible the phrasing and natural breaks in the music. If the music is relatively easy for you, these sections may be eight to sixteen bars long. If the music is particularly difficult, two to four bar sections may be more appropriate.

Begin in the first section with the right hand. Play the notes firmly, with the correct fingering. If fingering is not provided, write it in if necessary to guarantee you use the same fingering each time, since learning is facilitated by exact repetition.

Don't rush. Pick a tempo that enables you to play comfortably and accurately. Remember, if you play a note wrong once, you'll tend to make the same mistake again. Repeat the notes in the section until you can play them effortlessly and without stumbling. Saying the names of the notes out loud as you play tends to increase concentration and speeds learning.

Once you've mastered the notes and fingering, go over the section again, focusing on playing in time. Repeat the section several times until you can play it correctly. Then go on to the next and succeeding sections, treating each in the same way, until you finish the piece. This is concentrated work. You may want to stretch this process out over several practice sessions.

The left hand part also should be practiced separately. Begin again in the first practice section by playing the chords in block formation in their given sequence. Go over any difficult chord connections until they can be executed comfortably. You may want t o verify the notes of chords you are not certain about by consulting the chord reference chart in Appendix C. Once you've mastered the chords in the first practice section, move on to succeeding practice sections, repeating the process until you've learned all the chords and chord connections. Next apply the accompaniment pattern to the chords, again practice section by practice section.

Don't attempt to put the hands together until you can play each part independently, comfortably, and in time. Practice sections should be employed in putting the hands together. It is often helpful to alternately play the right and left hand parts several times independently before attempting to coordinate them. Counting at this stage is essential to ensure that the parts come together correctly. It's also important to repeat the section several times once the hands are together to consolidate the learning and ensure that there will be a minimum of "learning loss" between practice sessions. This frustrating but common phenomenon can be reduced by maintaining a frequent practice schedule.

Pieces should be taken up to tempo very gradually; rushing the process leads to mistakes that are easily learned and difficult to correct.

Finally, focus on dynamics, phrasing, and other performance details to achieve a polished effect.

Sometimes, in spite of careful practicing, you may find yourself stumbling at a certain point in the music. If you examine the situation, you'll usually find you're making the same mistake each time—like forgetting to play a sharp, putting one in that's not there, missing fingering, or playing a phrase consistently out of time. I've found the best way to deal with such trouble spots is first to identify exactly what you're doing wrong. Then go carefully over the bar or phrase containing the trouble spot several times, reminding yourself as you approach it exactly what you must do to correct the problem, such as "play G not A" or "count two not three." As you follow this procedure, you'll tend to memorize the correct version and transform it into one of the securest parts of your performance.

To play convincingly, the performer must get beyond the notes and attempt to convey the spirit of the music. In doing so, several factors should be considered: the work's title, tempo and expression markings; knowledge of the composer's life, times, and the performance practices of the day; and most importantly, the performer's own imagination. Imagining dancers will make your waltz more life-like, as thinking of a loved one will render a love song more convincing. The more knowledge and imagination you can bring to your performance, the more effective and communicative will be your style.

Appendix E: Sample Arrangements with Accompaniments Included

Andantino from Waltz in C Major

Schubert

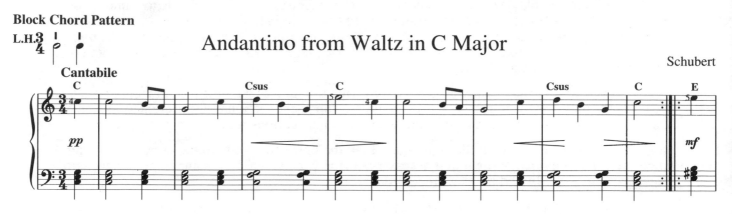

Emperor Waltz

Strauss Jr.

March Pattern

Give Me Thy Hand From Don Giovanni

Mozart

Ballad Pattern

Intermezzo From Rosamond

Schubert

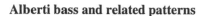

Surprise Symphony: Andante Theme

Haydn

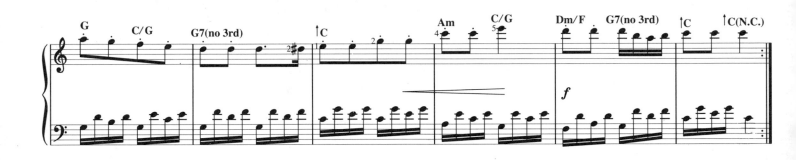

Rolled chord pattern

Minuet

Purcell

Microsoft®
PowerPoint® 2013:
Essentials

ALEC FEHL
Asheville-Buncombe Technical Community College

LABYRINTH
LEARNING™

Berkeley, CA

Microsoft PowerPoint 2013: Essentials

LABYRINTH
LEARNING™

Labyrinth Learning
2560 9th Street, Suite 320
Berkeley, California 94710
800.522.9746
On the web at lablearning.com

President:
Brian Favro

Product Development Manager:
Jason Favro

Managing Editor:
Laura Popelka

Production Editor:
Margaret Young

Production Manager:
Rad Proctor

eLearning Production Manager:
Arl S. Nadel

eLearning Development:
Judy Mardar and Andrew Vaughnley

Developmental Editors:
Trisha Conlon and Sandra Rittman

Indexing:
Joanne Sprott

Cover Design:
Mick Koller, SuperLab Design

Interior Design:
Mark Ong, Side-by-Side Studio

ITEM: 1-59136-484-1
ISBN-13: 978-1-59136-484-9

Manufactured in the United States of America.

10 9 8 7 6 5 4 3 2 1

Contents in Brief

Table of Contents

POWERPOINT 2013 LESSON 3: ADDING GRAPHICS, ANIMATION, AND SOUND

POWERPOINT 2013 LESSON 4: INSERTING CHARTS

POWERPOINT 2013 LESSON 12: INTEGRATING WITH OTHER OFFICE PROGRAMS

Quick Reference Tables

PRESENTING TASKS

TABLE TASKS

Preface

In today's digital world, knowing how to use the most popular suite of desktop software applications is critical. Our goal is to teach new users how to take advantage of this technology and to help experienced users understand how the applications have changed from previous versions. We begin with fundamental concepts and take learners through a systematic progression of exercises, resulting in skill mastery.

An online student resource center accompanies this book. It contains Concepts Review quizzes, student exercise files, and other learning tools. The URL for the student resource center is printed on the inside front cover of this textbook.

Supplemental Options

Video Tutorials: Our easy-to-follow instructional design is complemented with hundreds of videos that demonstrate the concepts and skills covered in this textbook. All videos can be accessed online with a single license key. Videos are an option for all learners. Keys can be purchased at http://lablearning.com/Store/Shop-Videos.

eLab Course Management System: eLab is a web-based learning systems that integrates seamlessly with this textbook. eLab is an option for students enrolled in instructor-led courses that have adopted eLab as part of their course curriculum.

Visual Conventions

This book uses visual and typographic cues to guide students through the lessons. Some of these cues are described below.

Type this text	Text you type at the keyboard is printed in this typeface.
Action words	The important action words in exercise steps are presented in boldface.
Ribbon	Glossary terms are presented in black text with a blue background.
⚠ TIP	Tips, notes, and warnings are called out with special icons.
Command→ Command→ Command→ Command	Commands to execute from the Ribbon are presented like this: Ribbon Tab→Command Group→Command→Subcommand.
FROM THE KEYBOARD Ctrl + S to save	These margin notes present shortcut keys for executing certain tasks.
FROM THE RIBBON File→Save	These margin notes show Ribbon paths for executing certain tasks.

It is recommended that students set their screen resolutions to 1024 x 768. This will help ensure that their screens most closely match the printed illustrations. Multiple factors, including screen resolution, DPI setting, monitor size, and window size, can affect the appearance of the Microsoft Ribbon. In this book, screen captures were taken with a screen resolution of 1024 x 768.

Acknowledgements

This textbook has benefited greatly from the reviews and suggestions of the following instructors.

Ann Blackman, *Parkland College*

Lori Collins, *Pike-Lincoln Technical Center*

Rhonda Davis, *Isothermal Community College*

Miriam Foronda, *University of New Mexico – Taos*

Teresita Galvizo, *South East High School*

Joan Johnson, *Lake Sumter Community College*

John Mims, *Central New Mexico Community College Workforce Training Center*

Kay Nelson, *The Lifelong Learning Center, Missoula County Public Schools*

Monika Olsen, *Acalanes Adult Education*

Kari Phillips, *Davis Applied Technology College*

Mary Jo Slater, *Community College of Beaver County*

Cynthia Wade, *CierraTEC*

Microsoft®
PowerPoint 2013:
Essentials

Creating and Delivering a Presentation

In this lesson, you will create a PowerPoint presentation for the iJams music distribution company. Throughout the lesson, you will be using many PowerPoint features to develop the presentation. You will be working with document themes, text layout styles, and Microsoft Word outlines. By the end of the lesson, your presentation will be ready for delivery. Equipped with the tips and techniques for a successful presentation, you will practice its delivery to the JamWorks trade show.

LESSON OUTLINE

Presenting PowerPoint

Using Document Themes

Creating a Basic Presentation

Delivering the Slide Show

Getting Help

Concepts Review

Reinforce Your Skills

Apply Your Skills

Extend Your Skills

Transfer Your Skills

LEARNING OBJECTIVES

After studying this lesson, you will be able to:

- Apply a document theme to a new presentation
- Insert new slides
- Add text to a slide
- View a slide show
- Present a slide show

Creating a Presentation

iJams is an online music distribution company that sells physical CDs in addition to downloadable music. Unsigned musicians send in an existing CD or MP3 files of their original material, and then iJams duplicates the CDs on demand as orders come in and makes the MP3s available for immediate purchase or download. Musicians can also send in digital files of CD artwork, and iJams will print full-color CD inserts and other supporting materials. Additionally, iJams sells promotional items such as T-shirts, stickers, and mouse pads branded for artists.

As an employee of iJams, you have been asked to make a presentation representing the company to the JamWorks trade show. Your goal is to introduce iJams to trade show attendees and entice them with a promotional offer. You decide to use PowerPoint with a new netbook computer and video projection system to develop and deliver your presentation. You choose PowerPoint because it is easy to learn and seamlessly integrates with other Microsoft Office applications.

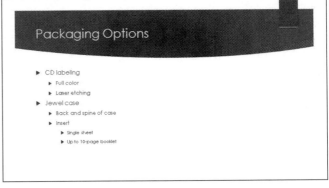

Slides from the iJams presentation

Presenting PowerPoint

Video Library http://labyrinthelab.com/videos   Video Number: PP13-V0101

PowerPoint 2013 is an intuitive, powerful presentation graphics program that enables you to create dynamic, multimedia presentations for a variety of functions. Whether you are developing a one-on-one presentation for your manager or a sophisticated presentation for a large group, PowerPoint provides the tools to make your presentation a success. PowerPoint allows you to project your presentation in a variety of ways. Most presentations are delivered via a computer projection display attached to a notebook computer. There are also other ways to deliver presentations. For example, you can deliver a presentation as an online broadcast over the Internet or save it as a video to be emailed or distributed on CD.

PowerPoint provides easy-to-use tools that let you concentrate on the content of your presentation instead of focusing on the design details. Using PowerPoint's built-in document themes, you can rapidly create highly effective professional presentations.

Starting PowerPoint

To create a new presentation, use one of the following methods.

- In Windows 7, click the Start button then choose All Programs→Microsoft Office 2013→PowerPoint 2013.

- In Windows 8, scroll to the right of the Start screen then click the PowerPoint 2013 tile.

After the PowerPoint program has started, click Blank Presentation to create a new blank presentation. To open an existing presentation:

- Start PowerPoint, choose File→Open and click a recent presentation, or navigate to the presentation file and double-click it.

- In either version of Windows, navigate to the desired presentation by using Windows Explorer or Computer and double-click the presentation.

PowerPoint 2013

Start PowerPoint

In this exercise, you will start PowerPoint.

1. Follow these steps for the version of Windows you are running to open the PowerPoint 2013 program:

Windows 7

Ⓐ Click **Start**.

Ⓑ Point to **All Programs**.

Ⓒ Scroll down if necessary.

Ⓓ Click **Microsoft Office 2013**.

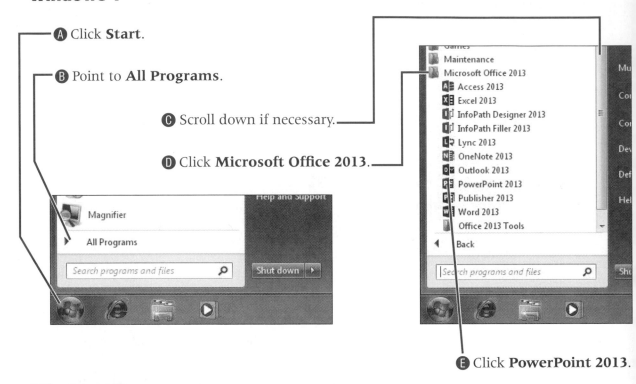

Ⓔ Click **PowerPoint 2013**.

Windows 8

Ⓐ Tap the [Windows] key, if necessary, to show the **Start screen**.

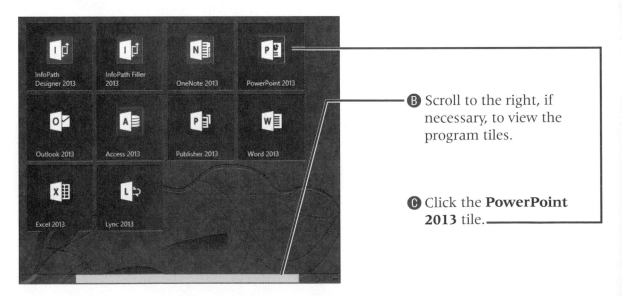

Ⓑ Scroll to the right, if necessary, to view the program tiles.

Ⓒ Click the **PowerPoint 2013** tile.

Creating a New Presentation

Video Library   http://labyrinthelab.com/videos   Video Number: PP13-V0102

When PowerPoint 2013 starts, it displays a Start screen that offers a variety of templates from which to choose. If your computer is connected to the Internet, PowerPoint will automatically display additional templates downloaded from the Microsoft web site. A template is a blank presentation that is preformatted with matching graphics, colors, and fonts. If you are not connected to the Internet, PowerPoint will display its default templates. A blank presentation option also is always available on the Start screen. Using the blank presentation template creates a blank, unformatted presentation to which you can add graphics, colors, and special fonts later.

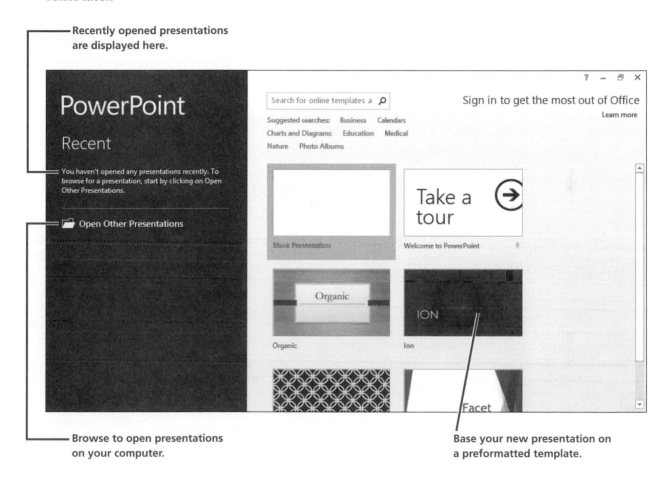

Recently opened presentations are displayed here.

Browse to open presentations on your computer.

Base your new presentation on a preformatted template.

DEVELOP YOUR SKILLS PP01-D02
Create a Blank Presentation

In this exercise, you will create a new, blank presentation.

1. Click the **Blank Presentation** template on the PowerPoint Start screen.

   A new, blank presentation appears. You will develop it throughout this lesson.

Navigating the PowerPoint Window

The PowerPoint 2013 program window, like other Microsoft Office programs, groups commands on the Ribbon. The following illustration provides an overview of the program window.

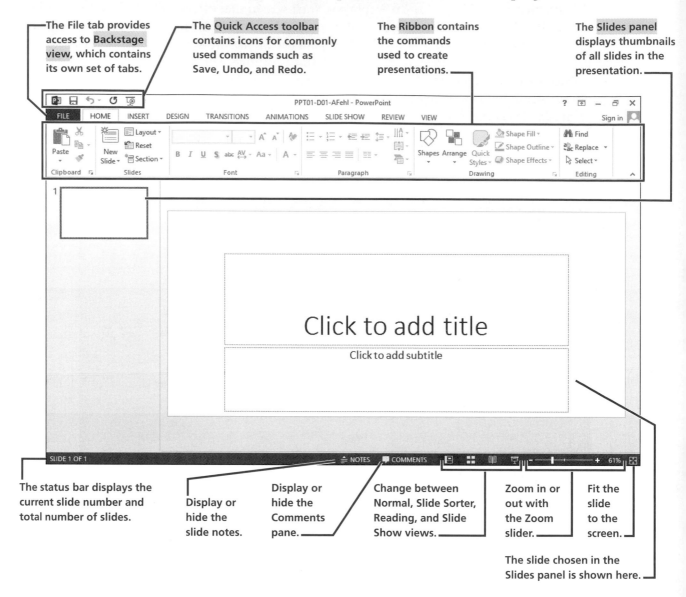

The File tab provides access to Backstage view, which contains its own set of tabs.

The Quick Access toolbar contains icons for commonly used commands such as Save, Undo, and Redo.

The Ribbon contains the commands used to create presentations.

The Slides panel displays thumbnails of all slides in the presentation.

The status bar displays the current slide number and total number of slides.

Display or hide the slide notes.

Display or hide the Comments pane.

Change between Normal, Slide Sorter, Reading, and Slide Show views.

Zoom in or out with the Zoom slider.

Fit the slide to the screen.

The slide chosen in the Slides panel is shown here.

Saving the Presentation

Video Library http://labyrinthelab.com/videos Video Number: PP13-V0103

The byword in PowerPoint is to save early and save often. You can use the Save button on the Quick Access toolbar or in Backstage view. If it's the first time a presentation has been saved, the Save As dialog box will appear because the file will need a name and location on your computer. You can also use the Save As dialog box to make a copy of a presentation by saving it under a new name or to a different location. If the file has already been saved, PowerPoint replaces the previous version with the new, edited version.

FROM THE KEYBOARD
Ctrl+S to save

FROM THE RIBBON
File→Save

Save the Presentation

In this exercise, you will save the presentation by giving it a name and a location on your computer.

Before You Begin: Navigate to the student resource center to download the student exercise files for this book.

1. Click the **Save** 🖫 button on the Quick Access toolbar.

   PowerPoint displays the Save As dialog box because this presentation has not yet been given a filename.

2. Follow these steps to save the presentation to your file storage location:

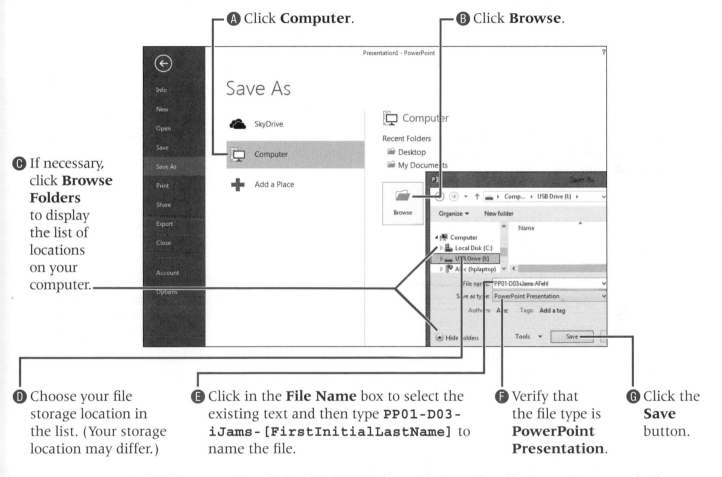

Ⓐ Click **Computer**.

Ⓑ Click **Browse**.

Ⓒ If necessary, click **Browse Folders** to display the list of locations on your computer.

Ⓓ Choose your file storage location in the list. (Your storage location may differ.)

Ⓔ Click in the **File Name** box to select the existing text and then type **PP01-D03-iJams-[FirstInitialLastName]** to name the file.

Ⓕ Verify that the file type is **PowerPoint Presentation**.

Ⓖ Click the **Save** button.

In the filename, replace the bracketed text with your first initial and last name. For example, the author's filename would look like this: PP01-D03-iJams-AFehl.

PowerPoint saves the presentation.

Save as Video

PowerPoint 2013 also allows you to save your presentation as a video. This is helpful if you want to distribute your presentation to others without requiring them to have PowerPoint or other special software. The video files are saved in the MPEG-4 (.mp4) format and are playable on any computer. When saving as a video, be patient as it takes some time to convert your presentation to the video format.

The status bar at the bottom of the PowerPoint window shows the video conversion progress.

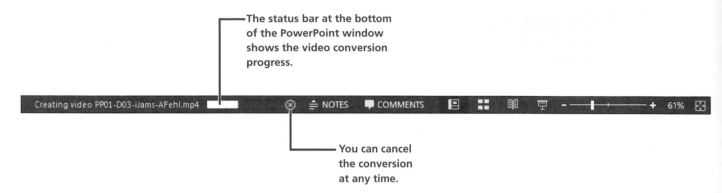

Creating video PP01-D03-iJams-AFehl.mp4   ⊗   ≜ NOTES   💬 COMMENTS   🄴   🄳   🕮   🖵   — ╪   +   61%   ⛶

You can cancel the conversion at any time.

The video version of a presentation can be 15 times larger than the original PowerPoint file. Be aware of the file size before you try to email a video to someone.

FROM THE RIBBON
File→Export→Create a Video

Inserting Text

Video Library   http://labyrinthelab.com/videos   Video Number: PP13-V0104

PowerPoint slides have placeholders set up for you to type in. For example, the title slide currently visible on the screen has placeholders for a title and subtitle. You click in the desired placeholder to enter text on a slide. For example, to enter the title on a slide, you click in the title placeholder and then type the text. Do not press the [Enter] key; the placeholders are already formatted with word wrap. The placeholders also are already formatted with font and paragraph settings to make a cohesive presentation. As you will see shortly, it's easy to make changes to the formatting of slides by applying a theme.

Type a Title Slide

In this exercise, you will enter a title and subtitle for the presentation.

1. Choose **File→Save As** and save your file as **PP01-D04-iJams-[FirstInitialLastName]**.

2. Follow these steps to add a title and subtitle:

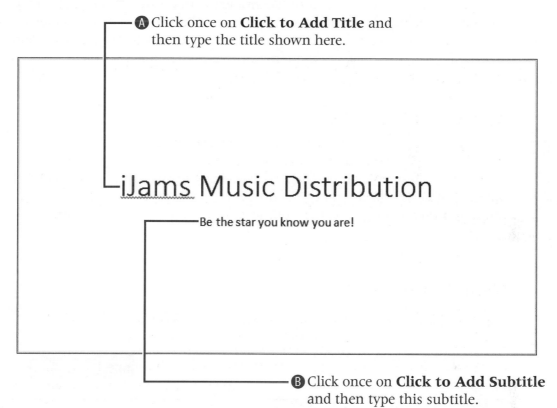

Ⓐ Click once on **Click to Add Title** and then type the title shown here.

iJams Music Distribution

Be the star you know you are!

Ⓑ Click once on **Click to Add Subtitle** and then type this subtitle.

PowerPoint enters the titles. At this point, you have a title slide, but it looks rather plain. This is about to change.

3. Save the presentation and leave it open; you will modify it throughout the lesson.

Using Document Themes

Video Library   http://labyrinthelab.com/videos   Video Number: PP13-V0105

You can use PowerPoint's built-in document themes, which provide a ready-made backdrop for your presentations, to easily format all slides in a presentation. When you use a document theme, your presentation automatically includes an attractive color scheme, consistent font style and size, and bulleted lists to synchronize with the design and style of the presentation. Document themes also position placeholders on slides for titles, text, bulleted lists, graphics, and other objects. By using document themes, you can focus on content by simply filling in the blanks as you create the presentation. You access document themes from the Themes group on the Design tab.

Choosing a Theme

Nine document themes are included with PowerPoint 2013. Additionally, each theme has four variations. A theme variation uses different colors and sometimes a different background. PowerPoint automatically downloads additional themes and adds them to the Themes gallery on the Ribbon if your computer is connected to the Internet. Match the theme to the type of presentation you are giving. Keep the design appropriate to the function and the audience.

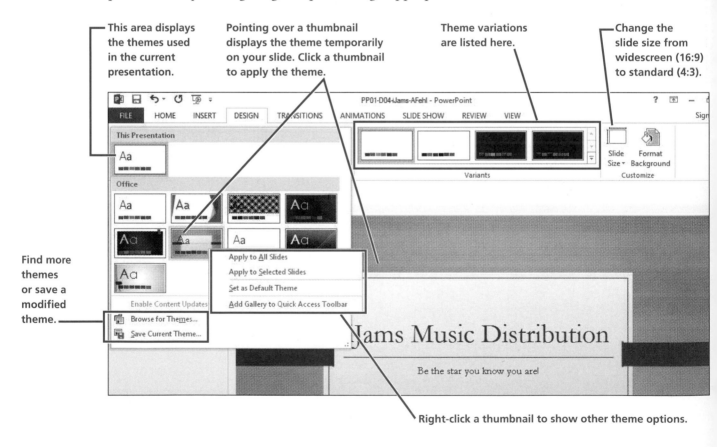

This area displays the themes used in the current presentation.

Pointing over a thumbnail displays the theme temporarily on your slide. Click a thumbnail to apply the theme.

Theme variations are listed here.

Change the slide size from widescreen (16:9) to standard (4:3).

Find more themes or save a modified theme.

Right-click a thumbnail to show other theme options.

Finding Additional Themes

New themes are sent to Microsoft daily, so if you just can't find the right one, browse the Microsoft Office Online website for new themes. You can also search for new themes from the PowerPoint Start screen.

Using the PowerPoint Ribbon

The PowerPoint Ribbon is organized into nine default tabs: File, Home, Insert, Design, Transitions, Animations, Slide Show, Review, and View. As in other Office 2013 applications, additional tabs appear when certain elements on a slide are selected. These additional tabs, called contextual tabs, offer commands specific to the selected element; for example, selecting a picture on a slide results in the Picture Tools Format tab being shown. Deselecting the picture returns the Ribbon to its original state with the nine default tabs.

FROM THE RIBBON
Design→Themes

Each tab contains many commands, which are organized in groups called command groups. Each group is labeled across the bottom and contains a variety of buttons or button menus.

The Home tab displays several groups of buttons.

Some groups contain a small icon in the bottom-right corner that, when clicked, displays a dialog box or a task pane.

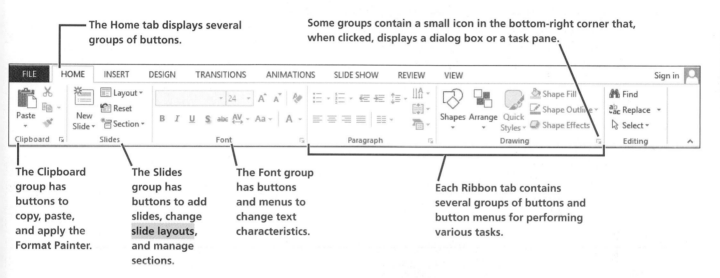

The Clipboard group has buttons to copy, paste, and apply the Format Painter.

The Slides group has buttons to add slides, change slide layouts, and manage sections.

The Font group has buttons and menus to change text characteristics.

Each Ribbon tab contains several groups of buttons and button menus for performing various tasks.

PowerPoint 2013

Apply a Document Theme

In this exercise, you will choose a document theme and apply it to the presentation.

1. Choose **File→Save As** and save your file as `PP01-D05-iJams-[FirstInitialLastName]`.

2. Follow these steps to choose a theme for the presentation:

   Depending on your monitor resolution, you may see a different number of thumbnails in the Themes group.

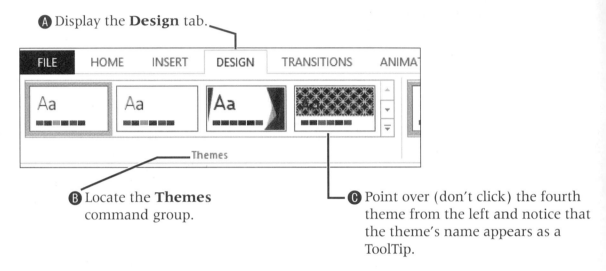

Ⓐ Display the **Design** tab.

Ⓑ Locate the **Themes** command group.

Ⓒ Point over (don't click) the fourth theme from the left and notice that the theme's name appears as a ToolTip.

PowerPoint displays a Live Preview of the theme on your title slide. This gives you a good idea of the overall design of the theme. Notice that the fonts and locations have changed for the title and subtitle. A different theme can radically redesign your presentation.

Throughout this book, the preceding command will be written as follows: Choose Design→Themes→[Theme command].

3. Point over (don't click) several more theme thumbnails.

   You see a Live Preview of each theme on the actual slide. The themes visible on the Ribbon are just a small portion of those available, however.

4. Follow these steps to choose a theme:

A Choose **Design→Themes→More**.   **B** Point to preview the **Organic** theme.

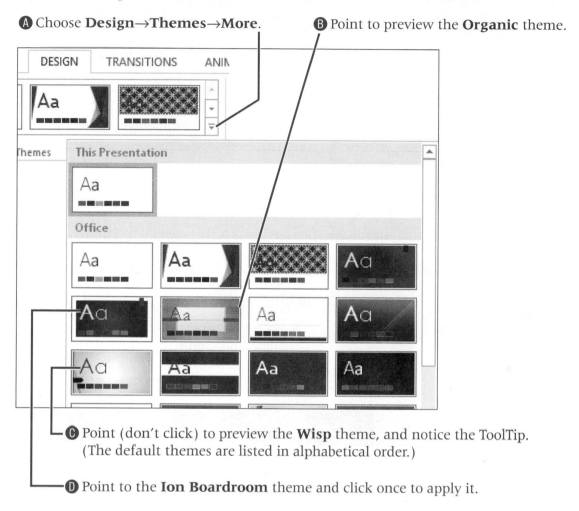

C Point (don't click) to preview the **Wisp** theme, and notice the ToolTip. (The default themes are listed in alphabetical order.)

D Point to the **Ion Boardroom** theme and click once to apply it.

PowerPoint applies the theme to your presentation.

5. Save the presentation and leave it open for the next exercise.

Choosing Slide Sizes

Video Library   http://labyrinthelab.com/videos   Video Number: PP13-V0106

By default, PowerPoint creates slides for widescreen format with a 16:9 ratio. This maximizes the use of space on the slide by taking advantage of the widescreen format on most modern computers. In fact, many of the new PowerPoint 2013 themes were designed specifically for widescreen use. You can easily switch to standard (4:3) format from the Ribbon if you need a narrower slide or have a non-widescreen computer monitor.

> **FROM THE RIBBON**
>
> Design→Customize →Slide Size to change the slide size

DEVELOP YOUR SKILLS PP01-D06
Apply a Theme Variation

In this exercise, you will experiment with slide sizes and choose a document theme variation.

1. Save your file as **PP01-D06-iJams-[FirstInitialLastName]**.

2. Follow these steps to change the slide size:

Ⓐ Display the **Design** tab.   Ⓑ Locate the **Customize** command group.   Ⓒ Click the **Slide Size** button.

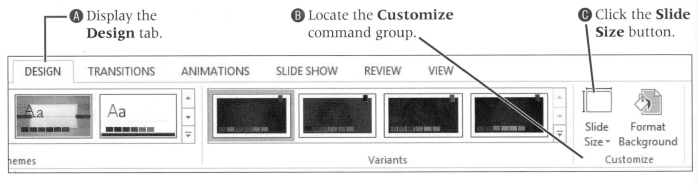

Ⓓ Click **Standard (4:3)**.

Ⓔ Click **Ensure Fit**.

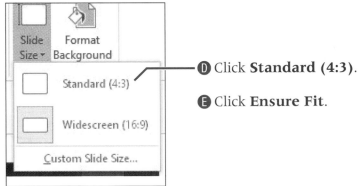

The slide is resized, and the slide title shifts to wrap across two lines.

3. Choose **Design→Customize→Slide Size→Widescreen (16:9)** to return the slide to widescreen format.

4. Locate the **Design→Variants** group on the Ribbon.

5. Point to several theme variations to view the Live Preview on the slide.

6. Click the **second variation** (with the green background) to apply it.

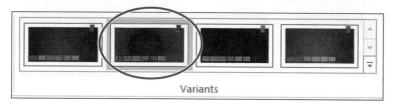

Variants

7. Save the presentation and leave it open for the next exercise.

Creating a Basic Presentation

Video Library   http://labyrinthelab.com/videos   Video Number: PP13-V0107

There is more to creating a presentation than placing one slide after another. Choosing the appropriate slide layout, just like choosing the appropriate design, will influence how well your audience understands your message. Use the following guidelines when choosing your slide design and layout:

■ **Know your audience:** Will you be speaking to accountants or artists?

■ **Know your purpose:** Are you introducing a product or giving a report?

■ **Know your expectations:** When the last word of this presentation has been given, how do you want your audience to respond to your facts? Are you looking for approval for a project or customers for a product?

Adding Slides

You can add slides to a presentation from the Ribbon or by right-clicking with the mouse. PowerPoint always places the new slide after the currently selected slide.

The Slides panel displays thumbnails of your presentation while you work in the Normal view. The Slide Sorter view, like the Slides panel, also displays thumbnails of your slides. This view can be useful when there are more slides than can fit in the Slides panel display.

QUICK REFERENCE	ADDING SLIDES
Task	**Procedure**
Add a slide with the Ribbon	■ Choose Home→Slides→New Slide ![icon].
Add a slide with the mouse	■ Right-click a slide on the Slides panel. ■ Choose New Slide from the pop-up (context) menu.

PowerPoint 2013

Add a New Slide

In this exercise, you will add a new slide to the presentation and then enter content.

1. Save your file as **PP01-D07-iJams-[FirstInitialLastName]**.

2. Follow these steps to add a new slide:

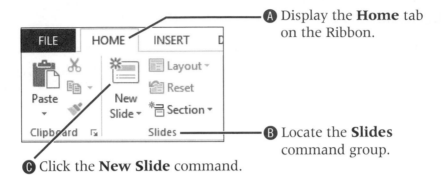

Ⓐ Display the **Home** tab on the Ribbon.

Ⓑ Locate the **Slides** command group.

Ⓒ Click the **New Slide** command.

PowerPoint adds a new slide to the presentation immediately after the title slide.

3. Click once in the title placeholder and then type **Our Services** as the title.

4. Click once on the **Click to Add Text** placeholder and then type the following list. Tap the Enter key after each list item except the last one.

   ■ **CD duplication on demand** Enter
   ■ **Jewel-case-insert printing** Enter
   ■ **Full-service online sales** Enter
   ■ **Downloadable MP3 distribution**

   PowerPoint adds a bullet in front of each line.

5. Save the presentation and leave it open for the next exercise.

Duplicating a Slide

Sometimes it is more efficient to duplicate a slide and then edit it rather than begin a new slide from scratch. Slides can be duplicated via the Slides panel.

QUICK REFERENCE	DUPLICATING A SLIDE
Task	**Procedure**
Duplicate a single slide	■ Right-click the slide you wish to duplicate in the Slides panel.
	■ Choose Duplicate Slide. The new slide is inserted below the original.
Duplicate multiple slides	■ Use Ctrl+click or Shift+click to select the desired slides in the Slides panel.
	■ Right-click any of the selected slides and choose Duplicate Slide. The new slides are inserted below the selected slides.

Indenting Bulleted Lists

Video Library   http://labyrinthelab.com/videos   Video Number: PP13-V0108

When using PowerPoint, you can effortlessly create bulleted lists to outline the thrust of your presentation. The bulleted list layout is an outline of nine levels. A different indentation is used for each level. The following illustration shows the Packaging Options slide you will create in the next exercise.

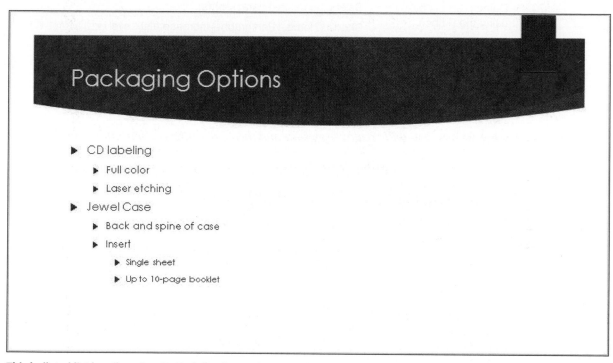

This bulleted list has three levels. Each level uses the same-shape character, but the text and bullet get smaller with each indentation.

Working with Bulleted Lists

When you use a document theme, each paragraph is automatically formatted as a bulleted list. The format includes a bullet style, indentation level, font type, and font size for each bulleted paragraph. This outline for the bulleted list is held within a placeholder or text box.

Working with List Levels

Indenting a bullet is referred to as demoting a bullet, or increasing the list level. Typically, a main bullet point has one or more sub-bullets. These sub-bullets, which are smaller than the main bullet, are created by increasing the list level. When a list level is increased, the bullets are indented toward the right. Conversely, decreasing a bullet's indent by moving it more toward the left and increasing the bullet size is referred to as promoting a bullet, or decreasing the list level. PowerPoint supports a main bullet and up to eight sub-bullets.

QUICK REFERENCE	WORKING WITH BULLETED LISTS
Task	**Procedure**
Turn bullets on and off	■ Select the desired paragraph(s). ■ Choose Home→Paragraph→Bullets ▤.
Promote bullets by using the Ribbon	■ Select the desired paragraph(s). ■ Choose Home→Paragraph→Decrease List Level ▤ or use Shift + Tab .
Demote bullets by using the Ribbon	■ Select the desired paragraph(s). ■ Choose Home→Paragraph→Increase List Level ▤ or tap Tab .

DEVELOP YOUR SKILLS PP01-D08

Create a Bulleted List

In this exercise, you will create a new slide and then enter information into a multilevel bulleted list.

1. Save your file as **PP01-D08-iJams-[FirstInitialLastName]**.

2. Choose **Home→Slides→New Slide** ▤.

   PowerPoint creates a new slide after the current slide.

3. Click in the title placeholder and type **Packaging Options**.

4. Click once in the text placeholder.

5. Type **CD labeling** and then tap Enter .

   PowerPoint formats the new blank paragraph with the same large bullet. Paragraph formats are carried to new paragraphs when you tap the Enter key.

6. Tap Tab .

   PowerPoint indents the paragraph. It also introduces a new, slightly smaller style for the level-2 paragraph.

7. Type **Full color**.

   PowerPoint formats the paragraph in a smaller font too.

8. Tap Enter .

   PowerPoint maintains the same level-2 formatting for the next paragraph.

9. Type **Laser etching** and then tap Enter .

10. While holding down Shift , tap Tab once.

    PowerPoint promotes the new paragraph back to the level-1 style, which is the level of the first paragraph on the slide.

Manipulate Heading Levels
You can also adjust the level after you have typed a paragraph.

11. Type these lines:

- **Jewel case**
- **Back and spine of case**

12. Follow these steps to indent the last bullet:

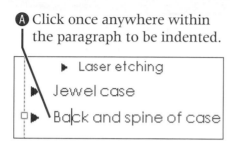

Ⓐ Click once anywhere within the paragraph to be indented.

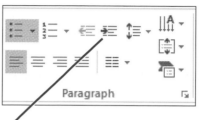

Ⓑ Choose **Home→ Paragraph→ Increase List Level**.

PowerPoint indents the paragraph and changes the bullet style. Demoting a paragraph makes it subordinate to the preceding paragraph.

13. Click the **Increase List Level** button three more times.

The bullet and font sizes change with each level increase. These formats are determined by the Ion Boardroom theme, on which the presentation is based.

14. Click **Home→Paragraph→Decrease List Level** three times until the bullet reaches the second indentation.

With each promotion, the bullet style changes.

Indent Multiple Bullets

15. Click once at the end of the last paragraph and then tap Enter.

16. Type these new lines:

- **Insert**
- **Single sheet**
- **Up to 10-page booklet**

17. Follow these steps to select the last two paragraphs for your next command:

Ⓐ Point at the beginning of *Single sheet*, taking care that a four-pointed arrow is not visible.

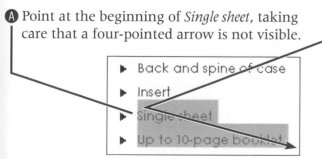

Ⓑ Drag down and right to select (highlight) to the end of the last paragraph; release the mouse button.

Ⓒ Ignore a Mini toolbar that appears. Take care not to click anywhere else on the slide before you perform the next step.

18. Choose **Home→Paragraph→Increase List Level**.

PowerPoint indents the two selected paragraphs.

19. Click anywhere outside the border to deselect the text. Your slide should match the following illustration.

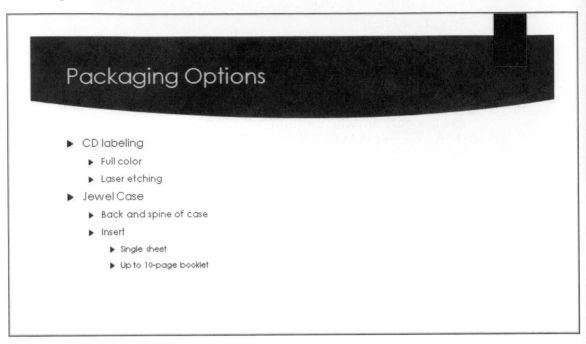

20. Save the presentation and leave it open for the next exercise.

Choosing the Slide Layout

Video Library   http://labyrinthelab.com/videos   Video Number: PP13-V0109

Slide layouts are named for the type of data they will contain. For example, the Title layout needs only a title and subtitle. The Content layout will hold other information on the slide, so it has a title and a bulleted list for points. Likewise, the Content with Caption layout is divided into three sections: title, text to one side, and an area for clip art or additional text. The slide layout organizes the information you put into the presentation by giving it a place on the slide. The new layout is applied to all selected slides. There are nine standard layouts, but many themes offer additional layouts.

FROM THE RIBBON
Home→Slides→
Layout ▼ menu

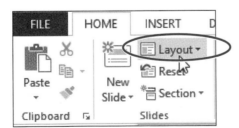

Clicking the Layout button in the Slides group on the Home tab allows you to apply a new layout to the selected slide(s).

Change the Slide Layout

In this exercise, you will add a new slide and then change its layout.

1. Save your file as **PP01-D09-iJams-[FirstInitialLastName]**.

2. If necessary, select the **Packaging Options** slide from the Slides panel on the left side of your screen.

3. Choose **Home→Slides→New Slide** 🖼️.

   PowerPoint adds another slide to the end of the presentation. Like the previous two slides, this one is set up to display a bulleted list.

4. Follow these steps to choose a new layout for the slide:

   Ⓐ Choose **Home→Slides→Layout menu button.**▼

   Ⓑ Choose the **Section Header** slide layout.

   PowerPoint applies the new layout. Now there are two placeholders, for a title and subtext.

5. Enter the following text:
   - Title: **Questions?**
   - Text: **End of our brief presentation**

   Your slide should resemble the following illustration.

6. Save the presentation and leave it open for the next exercise.

Delivering the Slide Show

Video Library   http://labyrinthelab.com/videos   Video Number: PP13-V0110

The slides are created, and the presentation is complete. The first phase of the presentation development is over. The next phase, delivering the presentation, is just beginning. Before you stand before an audience, familiarize yourself with the following tips.

Delivery Tips

It is not only what you say, but how you say it that makes the difference between an engaging presentation and an unsuccessful one. Lead your audience. Help them to focus on the message of your presentation, not on you as the presenter. Use the following *PEER* guidelines to deliver an effective presentation:

- **Pace:** Maintain a moderate pace. Speaking too fast will exhaust your audience, and speaking too slowly may put them to sleep. Carry your audience with you as you talk.
- **Emphasis:** Pause for emphasis. As you present, use a brief pause to emphasize your point. This pause will give the audience time to absorb your message.

- **Eye contact:** Address your audience. Always face your audience while speaking. A common mistake is to speak while walking or facing the projection screen. Don't waste all of the work you have done in the presentation by losing the interest of your audience now. If you are speaking from a lectern or desk, resist the temptation to lean on it. Stand tall, make eye contact, and look directly at your audience.
- **Relax:** You are enthusiastic and want to convey that tone to the audience. However, when you speak, avoid fast movement, pacing, and rushed talking. Your audience will be drawn to your movements and miss the point. Remember that the audience...lly... this material may be old hat to you, but it's new to them. So sp... pace, and stay calm.

Navigating Through a Slide Show

FROM THE KEYBOARD
Spacebar or → to advance a slide

Backspace or ← to back up a slide

You can use the mouse and/or simple keyboard commands to move through a slide show. These are the easiest ways to navigate from one slide to the next.

The Slide Show Toolbar

The Slide Show toolbar is your navigator during the slide show. It is hidden when a slide show starts, but becomes visible when you move your mouse around or point to the lower-left area of the screen. The Slide Show toolbar can be used to navigate a slide show or to draw attention to a specific area on a slide. However, use of this toolbar is unnecessary when you present a simple slide show like this one.

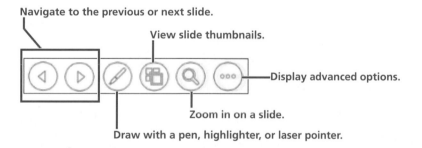

Navigate to the previous or next slide.

View slide thumbnails.

Display advanced options.

Zoom in on a slide.

Draw with a pen, highlighter, or laser pointer.

QUICK REFERENCE	USING BASIC SLIDE SHOW NAVIGATION
Task	**Procedure**
Advance a slide	■ Click once with the mouse, or tap Spacebar, →, Page Down, or Enter.
Back up a slide	■ Tap Backspace, Page Up, or ←.
Display the Slide Show toolbar	■ Move the mouse around on the screen for a moment.

PowerPoint 2013

Run the Slide Show

In this exercise, you will navigate through your slide show.

1. Follow these steps to start the slide show:

   Ⓐ Click the title slide in the Slides panel to select it.

   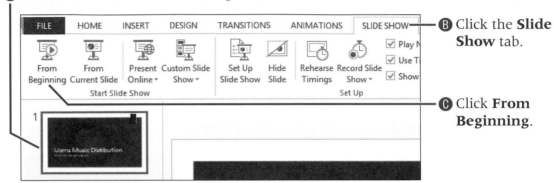

   Ⓑ Click the **Slide Show** tab.

   Ⓒ Click **From Beginning**.

2. Move the **mouse pointer** around the screen for a moment.
   Notice the Slide Show ⟨⟨⟩⟩⟨⟩ toolbar that appears near the bottom-left corner of the screen when the slides are in full-screen view.

3. Click the **mouse pointer** anywhere on the screen to move to the next slide.

4. Tap [Page Down] twice and then tap [Page Up] twice by using the keys near the main keyboard (not the keys on the numeric keypad).
   PowerPoint displays the next or previous slide each time you tap these keys.

5. Follow these steps to use the Slide Show toolbar:

   Ⓐ Point to the lower-left area of the slide to display the Slide Show toolbar.

   Ⓑ Click **Show all Slides** to display thumbnails of all slides.

6. Click the **Packaging Options** slide.
   As you can see, there are many ways to navigate slides in an electronic slide show.

End the Slide Show

7. Continue to click anywhere on the screen until the last slide appears (the Questions slide).

8. Click once on the last slide.
   The screen turns to a black background, with a small note at the top.

9. Click anywhere on the black screen to exit the slide show and return to the main PowerPoint window.

10. Feel free to practice running your slide show again.

11. Choose **File→Close** to close the presentation.

Getting Help

Video Library   http://labyrinthelab.com/videos   Video Number: PP13-V0111

PowerPoint, like many other software programs, has so many features that it is unlikely you will learn and remember everything about it at once. That is where PowerPoint Help comes in. You can use the help system to learn to perform specific tasks or browse general information about a variety of categories.

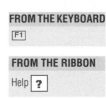

FROM THE KEYBOARD
F1

FROM THE RIBBON
Help ?

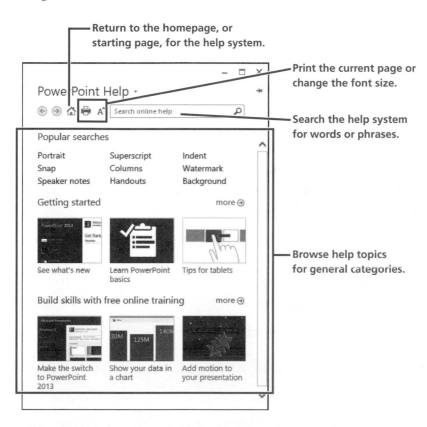

Using Online and Offline Help

If you are connected to the Internet when you open the PowerPoint Help window, PowerPoint connects to the Microsoft website and displays the most up-to-date help content. If you are not connected to the Internet, you can search for help topics in the offline help system that was installed on your computer when PowerPoint was installed.

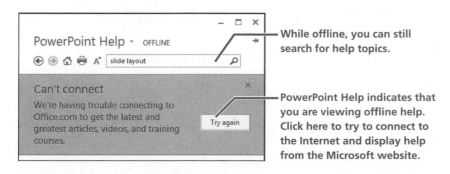

Use PowerPoint Help

In this exercise, you will use the PowerPoint Help system.

1. Click the **Help** ? button on the right side of the Ribbon.

2. Follow these steps to search for help on a specific topic:

Ⓐ Click in the search box, type **slide layout**, and tap Enter.

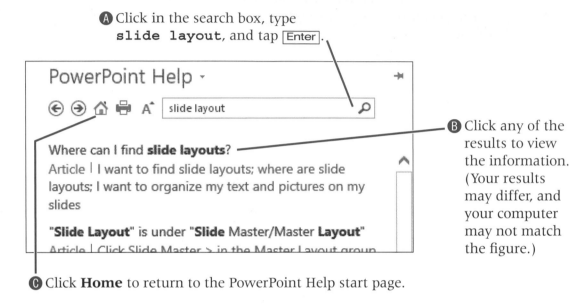

Ⓑ Click any of the results to view the information. (Your results may differ, and your computer may not match the figure.)

Ⓒ Click **Home** to return to the PowerPoint Help start page.

3. **Close** × the PowerPoint Help window.

4. Choose **File→Exit** to close PowerPoint.

Concepts Review

To check your knowledge of the key concepts introduced in this lesson, complete the Concepts Review quiz by choosing the appropriate access option below.

If you are...	Then access the quiz by...
Using the Labyrinth Video Library	Going to http://labyrinthelab.com/videos
Using eLab	Logging in, choosing Content, and navigating to the Concepts Review quiz for this lesson
Not using the Labyrinth Video Library or eLab	Going to the student resource center for this book

Reinforce Your Skills

Create a Presentation

In this exercise, you will begin to create a presentation for the Kids for Change organization—a community-based organization that helps socially aware youth plan and organize events that benefit their community. The presentation will be used to recruit new members and will be shown in high schools across the country.

Present PowerPoint

1. Start the **PowerPoint** program.

2. Click the **Blank Presentation** choice.
   A new presentation with a single slide is created.

3. **Save** 🖫 the file as **PP01-R01-Kids-[FirstInitialLastName]** in the **PP2013 Lesson 01** folder.

4. Click the **Design** tab and familiarize yourself with the various commands there.

5. Click the **Home** tab and familiarize yourself with the various commands there.

Apply a Document Theme

6. Choose **Design→Themes** and then choose the **Facet** theme.
   PowerPoint applies the theme to your presentation.

7. Locate **Design→Variants** and then choose the second (the blue) variation.
   PowerPoint applies the color variation to your presentation.

8. Click in the **Title** placeholder and type the title **Kids for Change**.

9. Click in the **Subtitle** placeholder and type the subtitle **I can make a difference**.
   As you type, the text is automatically colored because that is a design element of this particular document theme.

10. Save and then close the presentation. Submit your final file based on the guidelines provided by your instructor. Exit **PowerPoint**.
    To view examples of how your file or files should look at the end of this exercise, go to the student resource center.

Add Slides and Deliver a Presentation

In this exercise, you will complete the Kids for Change presentation by adding slides and text. Finally, you will deliver the presentation and learn how to find help in PowerPoint.

Create a Basic Presentation

1. Start **PowerPoint**; open **PP01-R02-Kids** from the **PP2013 Lesson 01** folder and save it as `PP01-R02-Kids-[FirstInitialLastName]`.

2. Choose **Home→Slides→New Slide** 📋.

   A single-column, bulleted list slide is added to the presentation. Notice that the Facet document theme is applied to the new slide.

3. Choose **Home→Slides→**📋 Layout ▾**→Two Content**.

   A new, two-column layout is applied to the slide.

4. Click in the **Title** placeholder and type the title `Events`.

5. Add the following text to the bulleted list on the left:

   - `iRecycling Day`
   - `Toy Collection`
   - `Shave and a Haircut`
   - `Diversity Festival`

6. Add the following text to the bulleted list on the right:

   - `Build-a-House`
   - `Bully No More`
   - `Adopt a Street`
   - `Tutoring`

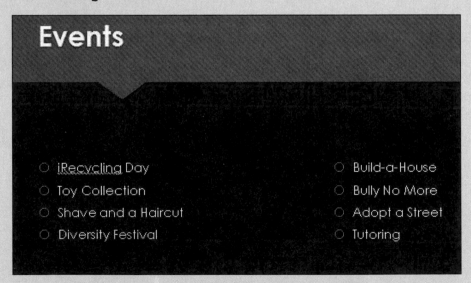

7. **Save** 💾 your presentation.

Create the Remaining Slides

8. Choose **Home→Slides→New Slide** 📋.

   A third slide is added to the presentation. The new slide has the same Two Content layout as the previous slide.

9. In the **Title** placeholder, enter the phrase **Program Benefits**.

10. In the first bullet of the left bulleted list, type **Personal** and tap ⌷Enter⌷.

11. Choose **Home→Paragraph→Increase List Level** 📊.

    The bullet is indented, and a new smaller bullet character is applied by the design template.

12. Add the following text to the bulleted list on the left:
    - **College application**
    - **Leadership skills**
    - **Sense of accomplishment**

13. In the first bullet of the bulleted list on the right, type **Community** and tap ⌷Enter⌷.

14. Choose **Home→Paragraph→Increase List Level** 📊.

    The bullet is indented, and a new smaller bullet character is applied by the design template.

15. Add the following text to the bulleted list on the right:
    - **Crime reduction**
    - **Increased literacy**
    - **Improved health**

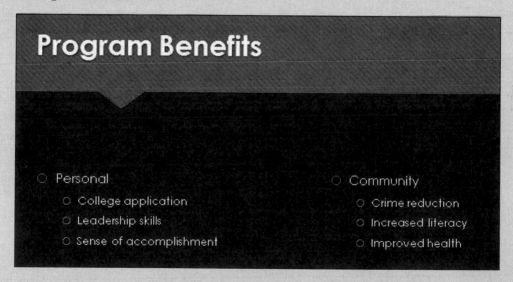

16. Choose **Home→Slides→New Slide** 📋.

17. Choose **Home→Slides→** 📋 Layout ▾ **→Title and Content**.

18. Type the title **Requirements**.

19. Type the following bullet points in the text box:
    - **You need**
    - **Positive attitude**
    - **Strong work ethic**
    - **Time commitment**
    - **One monthly event**
    - **One annual meeting**

20. Select the *Positive attitude* and *Strong work ethic* paragraphs and increase their list level.

21. Select the *One monthly event* and *One annual meeting* paragraphs and increase their list level.

22. Choose **Home→Slides→New Slide**.

23. Type **Regional Contact** for the title.

24. Type the following in the text box:
    - **Angelica Escobedo**
    - **(800) 555-1212**

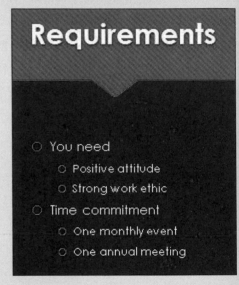

25. Click the **dashed border** around the text box so it turns solid, and then choose **Home→Paragraph→Bullets** to remove the bullets. *The bullets are removed from all paragraphs in the text box.*

26. Choose **Home→Paragraph→Center** to center the text on the slide.

Deliver a Slide Show

27. Select the first slide from the **Slides** panel on the left side of your screen.

28. Choose **Slide Show→Start Slide Show→From Beginning**. *The title slide will occupy your whole screen as the slide show starts.*

29. Walk through the presentation by clicking each slide until the presentation is ended.

30. Click once more to return to the PowerPoint program window.

31. Choose **Slide Show→Start Slide Show→From Beginning** 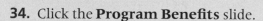 to start the slide show again.

32. After the slide show begins, position the mouse pointer at the bottom-left corner of the screen to display the **Slide Show** toolbar.

33. Click the **Show all Slides** button on the Slide Show toolbar.

    You will see thumbnails of each slide.

34. Click the **Program Benefits** slide.

35. Position the mouse pointer at the bottom-left corner of the screen to display the Slide Show toolbar.

36. Click the **More** button on the Slide Show toolbar.

    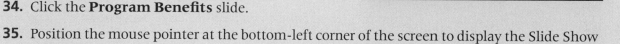

37. Click **End Show** on the pop-up menu to end the slide show.

38. Save the presentation.

Find Help in PowerPoint

39. Click the **Help** button at the top-right of the Ribbon.

40. Type `customize theme` in the search box and then tap `Enter`.

41. Click the first result shown in the Help window and then read the help topic.

42. Close the **Help window** and exit **PowerPoint**.

43. Submit your final file based on the guidelines provided by your instructor. Exit **PowerPoint**.

    To view examples of how your file or files should look at the end of this exercise, go to the student resource center.

Create and Deliver a Presentation

In this exercise, you will create a presentation for Kids for Change that promotes their special event of the month.

Present PowerPoint

1. Start the **PowerPoint** program.

2. Click the **Blank Presentation** choice.

    A new presentation with a single slide is created.

3. Save 🔲 your file as `PP01-R03-Kids-[FirstInitialLastName]` in the **PP2013 Lesson 01** folder.

Apply a Document Theme

4. Choose **Design→Themes→More** and then choose the **Slice** theme.
   PowerPoint applies the theme to your presentation.

5. Locate **Design→Variants** and then choose the fourth variation.
   PowerPoint applies the variation to your presentation.

6. Click in the **Title** placeholder and type the title `Kids for Change`.

7. Click in the **Subtitle** placeholder and type the subtitle `June Event`.
   As you type, the text is automatically colored because that is a design element of this particular document theme.

8. Save 🖫 your presentation.

Create a Basic Presentation

9. Choose **Home→Slides→New Slide** 📰.

10. Click in the **Title** placeholder and type the title `Shave and a Haircut`.

11. Add the following text to the bulleted list:
    - `Free haircuts`
    - `Free shaves`
    - `Free mustache and beard trimming`

12. Save your presentation.

Create the Remaining Slides

13. Choose **Home→Slides→New Slide** 📰.

14. Choose **Home→Slides→** 📰 Layout ▾ **→Two Content**.
    A new two-column layout is applied to the slide.

15. In the **Title** placeholder, type `Participating Locations`.

16. In the first bullet of the left bulleted list, type `Barbers` and tap [Enter].

17. Choose **Home→Paragraph→Increase List Level** 📑.

18. Add the following text to the bulleted list on the left:
    - `Sam the Barber`
    - `Hats Off`
    - `Clean Cuts`

19. In the first bullet of the bulleted list on the right, type `Shelters` and tap [Enter].

20. Choose **Home→Paragraph→Increase List Level** 📑.
    The bullet is indented, and a new smaller bullet character is applied by the design theme.

21. Add the following text to the bulleted list on the right:
    - `Shelter on Main`
    - `Helping Hand`
    - `Safe Night`

22. Choose **Home→Slides→New Slide** .

23. Choose **Home→Slides→ Layout ▾→Title and Content**.

24. Enter the title **Dates and Availability**.

25. Type the following bullet points in the text box:
    - **All Locations**
    - **Every Saturday in June**
    - **8:00am – 8:00pm**
    - **Availability**
    - **Free service to help our community's homeless**

26. Select the two paragraphs under **All Locations** and increase their list level.

27. Select the last paragraph and increase its list level.

28. Choose **Home→Slides→New Slide** to add the final slide to the presentation.

29. Type **Sponsored By** for the title.

30. Type the following in the text box:
    - **Kids for Change**

31. Click the dashed border around the text box so it turns solid, and then choose **Home→Paragraph→Bullets** to remove the bullets.

    The bullets are removed from all paragraphs in the text box.

32. Choose **Home→Paragraph→Center** ▤ from the Ribbon to center the text on the slide.

Deliver a Slide Show

33. Select the first slide from the **Slides** panel on the left side of your screen.

34. Choose **Slide Show→Start Slide Show→From Beginning** 📭 from the Ribbon.

    The Title slide will occupy your whole screen as the slide show starts.

35. Walk through the presentation by clicking each slide until the presentation is ended.

36. Click once more to return to the PowerPoint program window.

37. Choose **Slide Show→Start Slide Show→From Beginning** 📭 from the Ribbon to start the slide show again.

38. After the slide show begins, position the mouse pointer at the bottom-left corner of the screen to display the **Slide Show** toolbar.

39. Click the **Show all Slides** button on the **Slide Show toolbar**.

40. Click the **Participating Locations** slide.

41. Position the mouse pointer at the bottom-left corner of the screen to display the **Slide Show toolbar**.

42. Click the **More** button on the Slide Show toolbar.

43. Click **End Show** on the pop-up menu to end the slide show.

44. Save the presentation.

Find Help in PowerPoint

45. Click the **Help** button at the top-right of the Ribbon.

46. Type `save movie` in the search box and then tap Enter.

47. Click the first result shown in the Help window and then read the help topic.

48. Close the **Help window** and exit **PowerPoint**.

49. Submit your final file based on the guidelines provided by your instructor.

Apply Your Skills

Create a Presentation

In this exercise, you will begin to create a presentation for Universal Corporate Events, a meeting and event planning service that handles event planning for businesses.

Start PowerPoint and Apply a Theme to a New Presentation

1. Start **PowerPoint**; create a new, blank presentation named **PP01-A01-Events-[FirstInitialLastName]** in the **PP2013 Lesson 01** folder.

2. Apply the **Facet** design document theme.

3. Apply the fourth variation, as shown in the illustration at the end of the exercise.

4. Add the following text to the title slide:
   - Title: **Universal Corporate Events**
   - Subtitle: **Events made easy**

5. Save your presentation. Exit **PowerPoint**.

6. Submit your final file based on the guidelines provided by your instructor.
   To view examples of how your file or files should look at the end of this exercise, go to the student resource center.

Add Slides and Deliver a Slide Show

In this exercise, you will complete the Universal Corporate Events presentation and deliver a slide show. Finally, you will have an opportunity to find help in PowerPoint.

Add Slides to a Presentation

1. Start **PowerPoint**; open **PP01-A02-Events** from the **PP2013 Lesson 01** folder and save it as **PP01-A02-Events-[FirstInitialLastName]**.

2. Add a second slide with the following text:

Title	Event Types
Bulleted paragraphs	■ Celebrations
	■ Team building
	■ Tradeshows
	■ Ceremonies

3. Add a third slide with the following text:

Title	Services
Bulleted paragraphs	■ `Venue scouting`
	■ `Catering`
	■ `Invitations`
	■ `Stage and sound equipment`

4. Add a fourth slide and change its layout to a **Two Content** layout. Add the following text:

Title	Benefits
Left bulleted paragraphs	■ `Our jobs`
	■ `Deal with paperwork`
	■ `Guarantee safety`
	■ `Scheduling`
Right bulleted paragraphs	■ `Your jobs`
	■ `Relax`
	■ `Enjoy your event`

5. Select all but the first bullet in the left text box and increase the list level.

6. Select all but the first bullet in the right text box and increase the list level.

7. Add a final slide to the presentation and apply the **Section Header** layout.
   - ■ Title: `Universal Corporate Events`
   - ■ Text: `Events made easy`

Deliver a Slide Show

8. Select the first slide from the **Slides** panel on the left side of your screen.

9. Start the slide show from the beginning.

10. Advance to the second slide.

11. Use the Slide Show toolbar to display all the slides and then jump to the **Benefits** slide.

12. Continue navigating the slides until the slide show ends and you are returned to the main PowerPoint window.

13. Save the presentation.

Get Help in PowerPoint

14. Start **Help** and search for `clear text formatting`.

15. Read the first help topic and then close the Help window.

16. Exit **PowerPoint**.

17. Submit your final file based on the guidelines provided by your instructor.

To view examples of how your file or files should look at the end of this exercise, go to the student resource center.

Create and Deliver a Presentation

In this exercise, you will create a new presentation for Universal Corporate Events that outlines each of their services.

1. Start **PowerPoint**.

2. Click **Blank Presentation**.
   A new presentation with a single slide is created.

3. Save your file as `PP01-A03-Events-[FirstInitialLastName]` in the **PP2013 Lesson 01** folder.

Apply a Document Theme

4. Apply the **Retrospect** theme.
   PowerPoint applies the theme to your presentation.

5. Locate **Design→Variants** and then choose the third variation.

6. Click in the **Title** placeholder and type the title `Universal Corporate Events`.

7. Click in the **Subtitle** placeholder and type the subtitle `Services`.

8. Save your presentation.

Add Slides to a Presentation

9. Add a second slide with the following text:

Title	Venue Scouting
Bulleted paragraphs	■ Locate three potential venues ■ Provide digital tour ■ Provide transportation for up to four

10. Add a third slide with the following text:

Title	Catering
Bulleted paragraphs	■ Vegetarian and vegan options ■ Kosher options ■ Never frozen

11. Add a fourth slide and change its layout to a **Two Content** layout. Add the following text:

Title	Invitations
Left bulleted paragraphs	■ Creative ■ Graphic design ■ Matching envelopes
Right bulleted paragraphs	■ Business ■ Create mailing labels ■ Mail first class

12. Select all but the first bullet in the left text box and increase the list level.

13. Select all but the first bullet in the right text box and increase the list level.

14. Add a final slide to the presentation. Apply the **Title and Content** layout and add the following text:

Title	Stage and Sound Equipment
Bulleted paragraphs	■ Speaker podium and PA ■ 1200 watt sound system for bands ■ Portable dance floor

Deliver a Slide Show

15. Select the first slide from the **Slides** panel on the left side of your screen.

16. Start the slide show from the beginning.

17. Advance to the second slide.

18. Use the Slide Show toolbar to display all the slides and then jump to the **Catering** slide.

19. Continue navigating the slides until the slide show ends and you are returned to the main PowerPoint window.

20. Save the presentation.

Get Help in PowerPoint

21. Start **Help** and search for insert YouTube video.

22. Read the first help topic and then close the Help window.

23. Exit **PowerPoint**.

24. Submit your final file based on the guidelines provided by your instructor.

Extend Your Skills

In the course of working through the Extend Your Skills exercises, you will think critically as you use the skills taught in the lesson to complete the assigned projects. To evaluate your mastery and completion of the exercises, your instructor may use a rubric, with which more points are allotted according to performance characteristics. (The more you do, the more you earn!) Ask your instructor how your work will be evaluated.

PP01-E01 That's the Way I See It

You are creating a presentation for a charity that you feel strongly about in order to educate others about it. First, decide on a known charity you support or agree with. If you don't know of any charities, think of a few ideas for charities (such as saving animals or the environment, ensuring human rights, curing disease, etc.). Then, use the Internet to find a reputable charity that deals with one of those topics.

Create a new, blank presentation and save it as `PP01-E01-Charity-[FirstInitialLastName]` in the **PP2013 Lesson 01** folder. Apply the design theme and variation of your choice. Type the charity name as the slide title and type a short, descriptive phrase for the subtitle. Add a Title and Content slide that lists at least four actions the charity takes toward bettering their cause. Add a Two Content slide. On the left, list a few facts about the charity. On the right, list ways to donate to the charity. Create a final slide with the Section Header layout that duplicates the content shown on the title slide. View the presentation as a slide show and make a mental note of anything you want to change. When the slide show ends, make your changes and then save your presentation.

You will be evaluated based on the inclusion of all elements specified, your ability to follow directions, your ability to apply newly learned skills to a real-world situation, your creativity, and the relevance of your topic and/or data choice(s). Submit your final file based on the guidelines provided by your instructor.

PP01-E02 Be Your Own Boss

Your landscaping business, Blue Jean Landscaping, saves its customers money by having them share in the physical labor. In this exercise, you will create multiple slides with varying layouts and bulleted text to advertise your unique business to potential investors. To begin, create a new, blank presentation named `PP01-E02-BlueJean-[FirstInitialLastName]` and saved to the **PP2013 Lesson 01** folder.

Apply the desired design theme and variation. Use the company name as the slide title and create a catchy phrase for the subtitle. Add a Title and Content slide that lists four services your company provides. Add a Two Content slide that lists the mutual benefits to the company and the customer: the left column uses **Us** as the first bullet, and the right column uses **You** as the first bullet. Then list at least three benefits for the company (left) and at least three for the customer (right). Increase the list level of all bullets except the first in each column.

Create a final slide with the Section Header layout that duplicates the content on the title slide. Run the slide show. Use the Slide Show toolbar to navigate the slide show and experiment with the other buttons on the toolbar. When the presentation ends, close PowerPoint. You will be evaluated based on the inclusion of all elements specified, your ability to follow directions, your ability to apply newly learned skills to a real-world situation, your creativity, and your demonstration of an entrepreneurial spirit. Submit your final file based on the guidelines provided by your instructor.

Transfer Your Skills

In the course of working through the Transfer Your Skills exercises, you will use critical-thinking and creativity skills to complete the assigned projects using skills taught in the lesson. To evaluate your mastery and completion of the exercises, your instructor may use a rubric, with which more points are allotted according to performance characteristics. (The more you do, the more you earn!) Ask your instructor how your work will be evaluated.

PP01-T01 Use the Web as a Learning Tool

Throughout this book, you will be provided with an opportunity to use the Internet as a learning tool by completing WebQuests. According to the original creators of WebQuests, as described on their website (WebQuest.org), a WebQuest is "an inquiry-oriented activity in which most or all of the information used by learners is drawn from the web." To complete the WebQuest projects in this book, navigate to the student resource center and choose the WebQuest for the lesson on which you are currently working. The subject of each WebQuest will be relevant to the material found in the lesson.

WebQuest Subject: Compare Presentation Graphics Software.

Submit your final file(s) based on the guidelines provided by your instructor.

PP01-T02 Demonstrate Proficiency

Stormy BBQ, a restaurant featuring fresh, locally grown vegetables and local, farm-raised pork/beef, is considering expanding to new locations. Create a PowerPoint presentation to show at a local town hall meeting to convince the local residents and community leaders that Stormy BBQ would be a great fit for their community.

Use an appropriate theme for the business and its commitment to the community. Perhaps search for additional themes from the PowerPoint Start screen. Create at least five slides, including the title slide, with a different layout for each slide. At least one slide should include bullet points with varying list levels.

Save the file as **PP01-T02-Stormy-[FirstInitialLastName]** to the **PP2013 Lesson 01** folder. Submit your final file based on the guidelines provided by your instructor.

POWERPOINT 2013

Designing the Presentation

LEARNING OBJECTIVES

After studying this lesson, you will be able to:

- Use Outline view to create, move, and delete slides and edit text
- Create a presentation from a Microsoft Word outline
- Format and align text and adjust character spacing and line spacing
- Use Slide Sorter view and Sections
- Print a presentation

In this lesson, you will build on the fundamental design of the iJams presentation. To add professional credibility and make your presentation easier for an audience to follow, you will establish a consistent style throughout the presentation and format and organize the text. You will add from the Outline panel and organize your completed presentation by using Slide Sorter view and Sections. To quickly create a basic presentation, you will import a Microsoft Word outline. Finally, working with the printing function of PowerPoint 2013, you will examine page setup, print preview, print setup, and the output format options.

Designing a Presentation

Now that the initial slides of the iJams presentation are complete, you need to make sure that the style is consistent throughout the presentation. A consistent style appears more organized, is easier for an audience to follow, and adds professional credibility. You must also ensure that the slides are in a logical sequence so the presentation is clear.

Products and Promotional Items

- Audio CDs
- Downloadable MP3s
- T-shirts
- Baseball caps
- Stickers

- Pencils
- Key chains
- Posters
- Mugs
- Mouse pads

Sample of slide formatted with a layout Microsoft calls Two Content

Working with Slides

Video Library http://labyrinthelab.com/videos   Video Number: PP13-V0201

As your presentation progresses and you insert additional slides, you may want to change the slide layout or order. For example, some slides may require two columns of bulleted text while others require only one. PowerPoint makes it easy to change the order of slides by using Slide Sorter view.

Copying Text and Objects

You can move and copy text and objects by using drag and drop or the Cut, Copy, and Paste commands. It is usually most efficient to use drag and drop if you are moving or copying text or objects within a slide. Drag and drop is also effective for rearranging slides. Cut, Copy, and Paste are most efficient when moving or copying to a location not visible on the current screen.

FROM THE RIBBON
Home→Clipboard→Cut
Home→Clipboard→Copy
Home→Clipboard→Paste

FROM THE KEYBOARD
Ctrl+X to cut
Ctrl+C to copy
Ctrl+V to paste

PowerPoint 2013

QUICK REFERENCE	MOVING AND COPYING TEXT AND OBJECTS
Task	**Procedure**
Drag and drop	■ Select the desired text or click an object (e.g., placeholder box).
	■ Drag the text/object to the desired location. Press Ctrl while dragging to copy.
Right-drag and drop	■ Select the desired text or click an object (e.g., placeholder box).
	■ Use the right mouse button to drag the text/object to the desired location.
	■ Release the mouse button at the desired location and choose Move, Copy, or Cancel.

DEVELOP YOUR SKILLS PP02-D01

Add a New Slide to a Presentation

In this exercise, you will add a new slide to a presentation, enter a bulleted list, and change the layout of the slide. You can always change the layout for a slide after the slide has been created.

1. Start **PowerPoint**. Open **PP02-D01-Design** from the **PP2013 Lesson 02** folder and save it as **PP02-D01-Design-[FirstInitialLastName]**.

   Replace the bracketed text with your first initial and last name. For example, if your name is Bethany Smith, your filename will look like this: PP02-D01-Design-BSmith.

2. Select the **Our Services** slide from the **Slides** panel on the left side of your screen.

   The Our Services slide appears. New slides are inserted after the selected slide.

3. Choose **Home→Slides→New Slide** .

4. Click in the **Title placeholder** and type **Products and Promotional Items**.

5. Click in the **bulleted list placeholder** and type this list:

- Audio CDs
- Downloadable MP3s
- T-shirts
- Baseball caps
- Stickers
- Pencils
- Key chains
- Posters
- Mugs
- Mouse pads

When you begin typing Mugs, PowerPoint reformats the bullets with a smaller font size so they all fit in the box. As you type the last bullet point, the font gets even smaller. A long list of bullets can be overwhelming, so strive for no more than six bullets. If there is more information, consider breaking the list into two columns. You will use this technique next by choosing a different layout for the slide.

6. Follow these steps to change the slide layout:

Ⓐ Display the **Home** tab.

Ⓑ Click the **Layout** menu ▼.

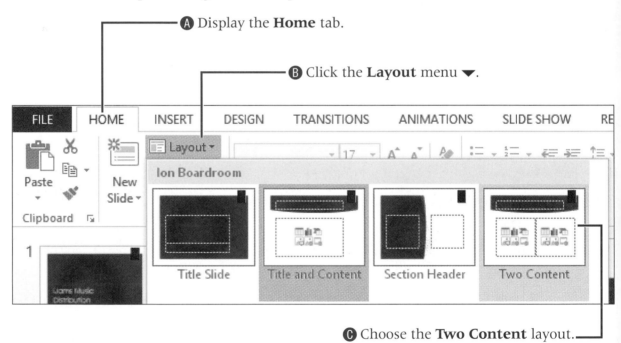

Ⓒ Choose the **Two Content** layout.

PowerPoint applies the Two Content layout to the current slide.

7. Follow these steps to move the last five bullets to the second box:

Ⓐ Select the last five bulleted paragraphs.

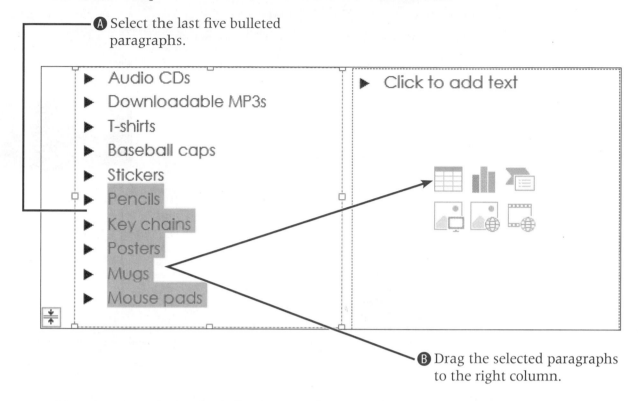

Ⓑ Drag the selected paragraphs to the right column.

This action moves the last five bulleted paragraphs into the right-side content area.

8. **Save** 🖫 the changes to your presentation.

Working with Outlines

Video Library   http://labyrinthelab.com/videos   Video Number: PP13-V0202

Although you have been working primarily in the slide to add or format text, the Outline panel is an alternative way to add, remove, and move text. The Outline panel is a useful interface to organize and structure your presentation.

Using the Outline Panel

The Outline panel helps you edit and reorganize slides. It's available on the left side of the screen in Outline view. You can type directly in the Outline panel to add or edit text on a slide. You can also select text from the Outline panel and format it with the standard Ribbon formatting commands. Any changes made in the Outline panel are immediately reflected in the actual slide.

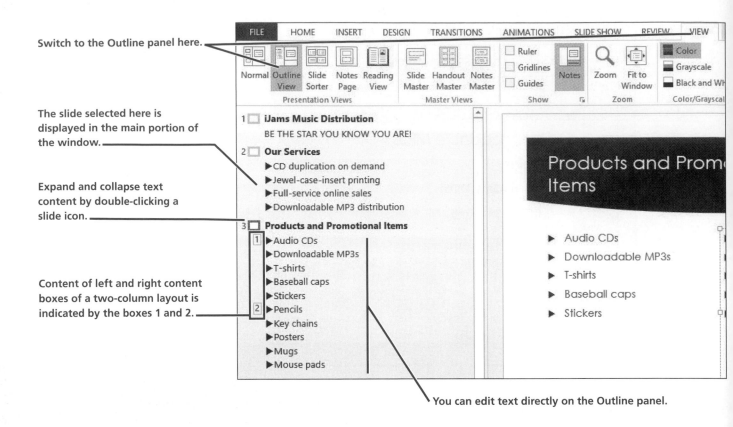

Switch to the Outline panel here.

The slide selected here is displayed in the main portion of the window.

Expand and collapse text content by double-clicking a slide icon.

Content of left and right content boxes of a two-column layout is indicated by the boxes 1 and 2.

You can edit text directly on the Outline panel.

QUICK REFERENCE	WORKING WITH OUTLINES
Task	**Procedure**
Select text in an outline	Drag over the desired text in the Outline panel.
Select an entire slide	Click the slide icon in the Outline panel.
Expand or collapse a slide	Double-click the slide icon in the Outline panel. Right-click the slide text in the Outline panel and choose Collapse (All) or Expand (All).
Add a new slide	Place the mouse pointer in the last group of bulleted paragraphs on a slide and press Ctrl + Enter.
Delete a slide	Right-click any text within a slide in the Outline panel and choose Delete Slide.

Add a Slide in the Outline Panel

In this exercise, you will work with the Outline panel to add text.

1. Save your file as **PP02-D02-Design-[FirstInitialLastName]**.

2. Follow these steps to select a slide while in the Outline panel:

A Click the **View** tab. ——————

B Click **Outline View**.

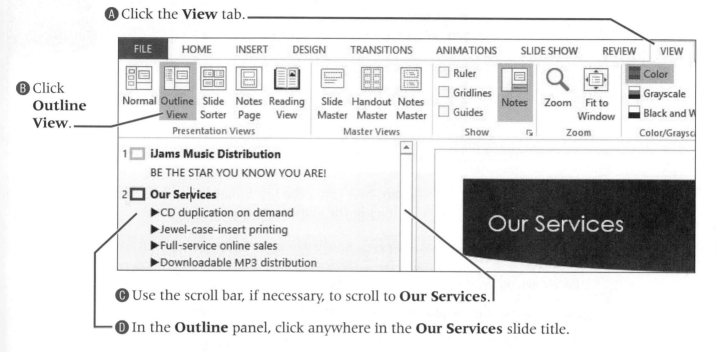

C Use the scroll bar, if necessary, to scroll to **Our Services**.

D In the **Outline** panel, click anywhere in the **Our Services** slide title.

3. Press Ctrl + Enter.

The insertion point moves to the first bulleted paragraph in the slide.

4. Press Ctrl + Enter again.

PowerPoint creates a new slide below the selected slide.

5. Follow these steps to add text to the new slide while in the Outline panel:

Ⓐ Type **Current Artists** here. Notice that the text also appears in the main portion of your window.

Ⓑ Press Ctrl + Enter to move to the first bulleted paragraph.

Ⓒ Type these bulleted paragraphs, tapping Enter after each.

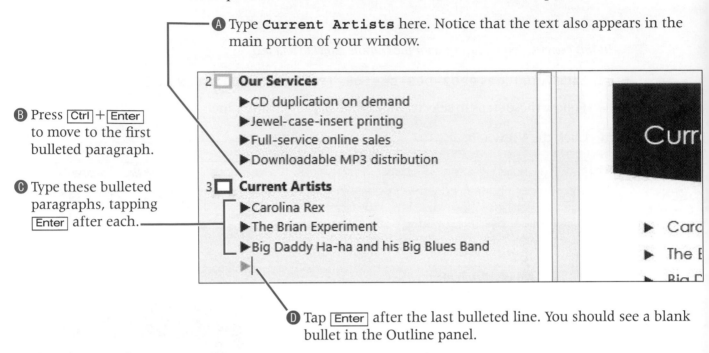

Ⓓ Tap Enter after the last bulleted line. You should see a blank bullet in the Outline panel.

PowerPoint adds a new slide to the presentation whenever the insertion point is positioned within the last box on a slide and the Ctrl + Enter keystroke combination is issued. At this point, you should have a new, bulleted paragraph visible in the outline below the Big Daddy Ha-ha *paragraph.*

6. Follow these steps to promote a paragraph to make a new slide:

Ⓐ Ensure that the insertion point is on the blank bulleted paragraph in the outline.

Ⓑ Choose **Home→Paragraph→ Decrease List Level**

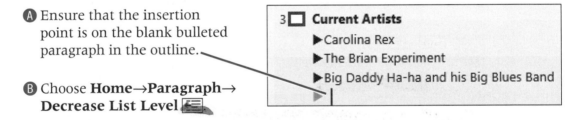

PowerPoint promotes the bulleted paragraph to create a new slide.

7. Type **New Artist Specials** and tap Enter.

Tapping Enter created a new slide. You must use Ctrl + Enter to add a bulleted paragraph after a slide's title. However, you will fix this by demoting the new slide in the next step.

8. Choose **Home→Paragraph→Increase List Level** .

The new slide created when you tapped Enter in step 7 has been converted to a bullet under the New Artist Specials title.

9. Complete the new slide in the outline as shown, tapping Enter after each paragraph (including the last one).

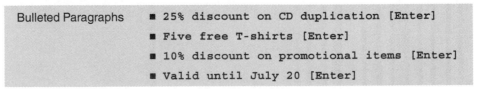

Bulleted Paragraphs
- `25% discount on CD duplication [Enter]`
- `Five free T-shirts [Enter]`
- `10% discount on promotional items [Enter]`
- `Valid until July 20 [Enter]`

10. Choose **Home→Paragraph→Decrease List Level** 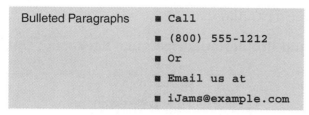 to promote the new paragraph that follows the *Valid until July 20* paragraph and convert it into a new slide.

11. Type `Contact Us` and then use Ctrl + Enter to create a bullet below the title.

12. Taking care not to tap Enter after the last bullet in this slide, complete the new slide as shown.

Bulleted Paragraphs	■ `Call`
	■ `(800) 555-1212`
	■ `Or`
	■ `Email us at`
	■ `iJams@example.com`

13. Save your presentation.

Collapsing and Expanding Slides

Video Library   http://labyrinthelab.com/videos   Video Number: PP13-V0203

As the Outline panel grows, it can be difficult to manage your slides when all the bulleted text is showing. PowerPoint lets you collapse slides so that only the title is visible. This makes it easier to manage your slides because more slides will be visible in the Outline panel.

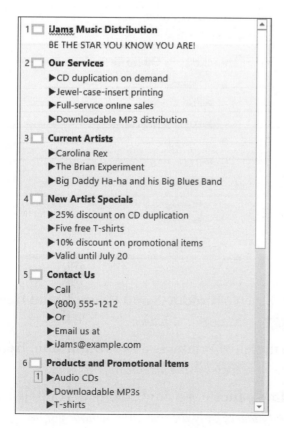

The same presentation in Outline view with all slides expanded and all slides collapsed

Use the Context Menu on the Outline Panel

In this exercise, you will use the context menu from the Outline panel.

1. Save your file as **PP02-D03-Design-[FirstInitialLastName]**.

2. Follow these steps to explore the Outline panel:

Ⓐ Scroll until **Products and Promotional Items** and **Packaging Options** are visible.

Ⓑ Each slide is represented by an icon. Slides with multiple bulleted lists use numbers for identification.

Ⓒ Click any bullet to select the bulleted text.

Ⓓ Click this slide icon to select all text on the slide.

Ⓔ Click to the right of the **Packaging Options** title text (outside the highlighted area) to deselect the slide.

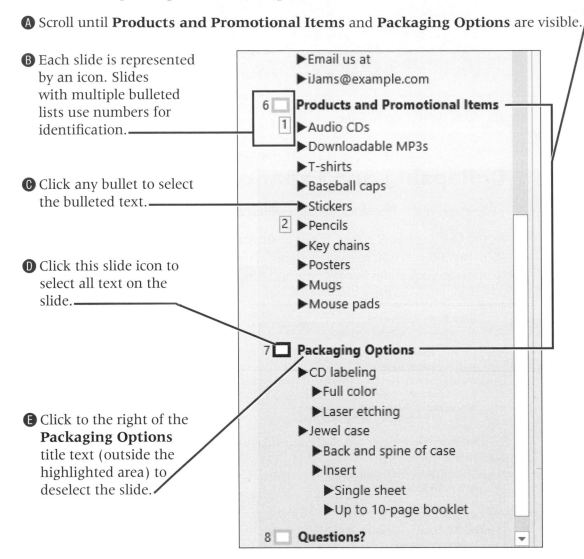

> ▶Email us at
> ▶iJams@example.com
> 6 ☐ **Products and Promotional Items**
>   1 ▶Audio CDs
>   ▶Downloadable MP3s
>   ▶T-shirts
>   ▶Baseball caps
>   ▶Stickers
>   2 ▶Pencils
>   ▶Key chains
>   ▶Posters
>   ▶Mugs
>   ▶Mouse pads
>
> 7 ☐ **Packaging Options**
>   ▶CD labeling
>   ▶Full color
>   ▶Laser etching
>   ▶Jewel case
>   ▶Back and spine of case
>   ▶Insert
>   ▶Single sheet
>   ▶Up to 10-page booklet
> 8 ☐ **Questions?**

3. Double-click the **slide icon** ☐ to the left of **Products and Promotional Items**.
   The bulleted paragraphs beneath the title are collapsed and hidden.

4. Double-click the **slide icon** ☐ to the left of **Products and Promotional Items** again.
   The bulleted paragraphs beneath the title are expanded and are once again visible.

5. Right-click anywhere in the **Outline panel** and choose **Collapse→Collapse All**.
   All bulleted paragraphs are collapsed and hidden. Only the slide titles remain visible.

6. Right-click anywhere in the **Outline panel** and choose **Expand→Expand All**.
   All bulleted paragraphs are expanded and are once again visible.

Move a Slide

The easiest way to move a slide in an outline is to first collapse all slides. Then you can click the desired slide title and drag it to its new position.

7. Right-click anywhere in the **Outline panel** and choose **Collapse→Collapse All**.

8. If necessary, scroll up until all slide icons and titles are visible in the **Outline panel**.

9. Follow these steps to move a slide:

Ⓐ Click the **slide icon** to select the entire **New Artist Specials** slide.

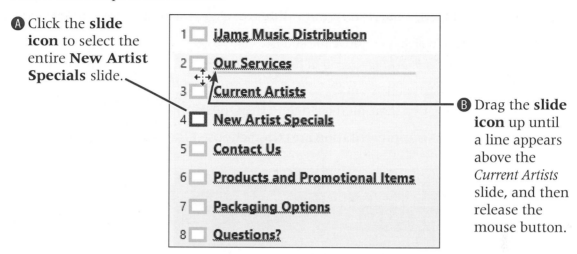

Ⓑ Drag the **slide icon** up until a line appears above the *Current Artists* slide, and then release the mouse button.

The New Artists Specials slide appears above the Current Artists slide.

10. Using this same method, move the **Packaging Options** slide to the second position, just below the title slide.

11. Save your presentation.

Deleting Slides

Video Library   http://labyrinthelab.com/videos   Video Number: PP13-V0204

You can delete a slide from a presentation by clicking the slide icon in the Outline panel to select the entire slide and then tapping the ⬚Delete⬚ key. Likewise, slides can be deleted in Normal and Slide Sorter views by choosing the desired slide(s) and tapping ⬚Delete⬚. If you inadvertently delete a slide, you can use the Undo button on the Quick Access toolbar to undo the latest action and restore the deleted slide. If you later decide that you want to keep the change, click the Redo button on the Quick Access toolbar to go back to the previous action.

FROM THE KEYBOARD
⬚Delete⬚ to remove a slide

PowerPoint 2013

Delete a Slide from the Outline

In this exercise, you will delete slides using the Outline panel.

1. Save your file as `PP02-D04-Design-[FirstInitialLastName]`.

2. Right-click anywhere in the **Outline panel** and choose **Expand→Expand All**.

3. Click the **Current Artists slide icon** [ ] (not the title text) to select the entire slide.

4. Tap `Delete` to remove the slide.

    A faded bullet may appear at the end of the previous slide. This is PowerPoint readying itself for additional text. The ghost bullet will not display on the slide itself.

5. Using this same method, delete the **Questions** slide.

6. Save your presentation and then choose **File→Close** to close it.

Working with Word Integration

Video Library   http://labyrinthelab.com/videos   Video Number: PP13-V0205

Microsoft Word is an excellent word processing program that integrates with PowerPoint. Outlines created in Word can easily be converted to a PowerPoint presentation. You may need to create a presentation based on an outline someone else created in Word, or you may find it easier to plan a presentation using a Word outline rather than starting PowerPoint first and wondering what slides you will create.

Creating a Presentation Outline in Word

Word's powerful outlining tool makes setting up and modifying outlines easy. You can create an outline in Word and import it to PowerPoint. To use Word outlines in PowerPoint, you must apply the appropriate styles to the paragraphs in the Word document prior to importing the outline. PowerPoint converts the Word outline by using these rules:

■ All level-1 paragraphs translate to Titles in a PowerPoint slide.

■ All level-2 paragraphs translate to level-1 body bullets in a PowerPoint slide.

■ All level-3 paragraphs translate to level-2 body bullets in a PowerPoint slide.

Once a Word outline is imported into PowerPoint, you can promote or demote the bullets, apply layouts and a design theme, and make other enhancements.

⊕ iJams Music Distribution
　　⊖ A Year of Success
⊕ Online Downloads
　　⊖ MP3 sales exceed $1M
　　⊖ 350 thousand new user accounts
⊕ Promotional Items
　　⊖ T-shirt sales exceed $500k
　　⊖ Total promotional item sales exceed $1.5M
⊕ New Hires
　　⊖ Jamal Lawrence – Web Master
　　⊖ Malika Fayza – Search Engine Specialist
　　⊖ Jin Chen – Marketing Analyst
⊕ Thank You!
　　⊖ Our Success Is Your Success

1 ☐ **IJAMS MUSIC DISTRIBUTION**
　　A Year of Success
2 ☐ **ONLINE DOWNLOADS**
　　MP3 sales exceed $1M
　　350 thousand new user accounts
3 ☐ **PROMOTIONAL ITEMS**
　　T-shirt sales exceed $500k
　　Total promotional item sales exceed $1.5M
4 ☐ **NEW HIRES**
　　Jamal Lawrence – Web Master
　　Malika Fayza – Search Engine Specialist
　　Jin Chen – Marketing Analyst
5 ☐ **THANK YOU!**
　　Our Success Is Your Success

SLIDE 1 OF 5

PowerPoint 2013

DEVELOP YOUR SKILLS PP02-D05

Create a Presentation and Import a Word Outline

In this exercise, you will create an outline in Word, use it to generate slides for a new presentation, and then modify the presentation.

1. Start **Word** and create a new, blank document.

2. Save your file as **PP02-D05-WordOutline-[FirstInitialLastName]** to the **PP2013 Lesson 02** folder.

   In the next few steps, you will type and apply Word styles to paragraphs.

3. With the blank document open, choose **View→Views→Outline**.

4. Type **iJams Music Distribution** and tap Enter.

5. Tap Tab. Then type **A Year of Success** and tap Enter.

   Tapping Tab increases the list level and creates a level-2 style.

6. Press Shift + Tab. Then type **Online Downloads** and tap Enter.

   Pressing Shift + Tab decreases the list level and returns the text to a level-1 style.

   Next, you will create two level-2-styled paragraphs that will eventually be converted to text bullets in a PowerPoint slide.

7. Tap Tab. Then type **MP3 sales exceed $1M** and tap Enter.

8. Type **350 thousand new user accounts** and tap Enter.

9. Now press Shift + Tab to return the indentation level to a level-1 style.

   You are now ready to continue typing the rest of the outline.

10. Complete the rest of the outline as shown, using [Enter] to create new paragraphs and [Tab] and [Shift] + [Tab] to adjust indent levels.

⊕ iJams Music Distribution
⊖ A Year of Success
⊕ Online Downloads
⊖ MP3 sales exceed $1M
⊖ 350 thousand new user accounts
⊕ Promotional Items
⊖ T-shirt sales exceed $500k
⊖ Total promotional item sales exceed $1.5M
⊕ New Hires
⊖ Jamal Lawrence – Web Master
⊖ Malika Fayza – Search Engine Specialist
⊖ Jin Chen – Marketing Analyst
⊕ Thank You!
⊖ Our Success Is Your Success

11. Save the file. Then close the outline and Word.

Word closes, and PowerPoint is visible.

Import the Outline

12. If necessary, restore **PowerPoint** from the **taskbar** (or start it, if necessary).

13. Choose **File→New** and click the **Blank Presentation** icon.

14. Save your file as **PP02-D05-WordOutline-[FirstInitialLastName]** to the **PP2013 Lesson 02** folder.

    You can use the same filename as the Word document because the Word and PowerPoint files have different file extensions.

15. Choose **Design→Themes→More** ⊡**→Ion** to apply a document theme.

16. Locate the **Design→Variants** group on the Ribbon and click the **third variation** (the purple one) to apply it to all slides.

17. Choose **Home→Slides→New Slide menu ▾→Slides From Outline**.

18. Use the **Insert Outline** dialog box to navigate to the **PP2013 Lesson 02** folder.

19. Choose **PP02-D05-WordOutline-[FirstInitialLastName]** and click **Insert**.

    PowerPoint will take a moment to import the outline. Note that the first slide is blank because PowerPoint inserted the slides from the outline after the existing blank title slide.

20. Choose **View→Presentation Views→Outline View** and examine the PowerPoint outline.

Each level-1 paragraph from the outline has become a slide title, and each level-2 paragraph has become a bulleted paragraph under the appropriate title.

21. Choose **View→Presentation Views→Normal** to view the slide thumbnails.

22. Choose the first slide (the blank one) and tap Delete.
The blank slide is deleted, and the iJams Music Distribution slide becomes selected.

Change a Layout

23. Choose **Home→Slides→Layout menu ▼→Title Slide**.
The layout of the selected slide changes.

24. Select the final slide, **Thank You**, and choose **Home→Slides→ Layout menu ▼→ Section Header**.

25. Choose the first slide, **iJams Music Distribution**.
Each slide is formatted with blue text because Word formatted the heading styles as blue.

Reset the Slide Formatting

26. With the first slide selected, choose **Home→Slides→Reset**.
The text formatting is removed and returns to the default setting for the current document theme. The slide subtitle is converted to uppercase because that is the formatting of the Ion theme.

27. Select the second slide, press Shift, select the last slide, and release Shift.
Slides 2–5 become selected.

28. Choose **Home→Slides→Reset** to reformat the text on the selected slides with the document theme formatting.

29. Save your presentation.

Formatting Your Presentation

Video Library   http://labyrinthelab.com/videos   Video Number: PP13-V0206

PowerPoint 2013 makes it so easy to create a presentation that the slides you create may not need any additional formatting. After all, the placeholders arrange the text, the bullets are automatic, and the color scheme is preformatted. However, in most cases, you will want to fine-tune your presentation. Formatting your presentation will make a good presentation even better.

Formatting Text

Formatting text is a common step in presentation development. For instance, when reviewing a slide, you might decide that the text could be emphasized by changing the font color. If you had the time, you could change the font color of each piece of text on the slide individually by using the Font group on the Home tab of the Ribbon. However, a more efficient way to change the font color is to first select the placeholder and then apply the color change. By selecting the placeholder, all text within the placeholder is changed in one swoop. The following illustration describes the buttons on the Home tab's Font group that assist you in formatting text.

FROM THE RIBBON
Home→Font→Bold
Home→Font→Underline
Home→Font→Italic

FROM THE KEYBOARD
Ctrl+B for bold
Ctrl+U for underline
Ctrl+I for italic

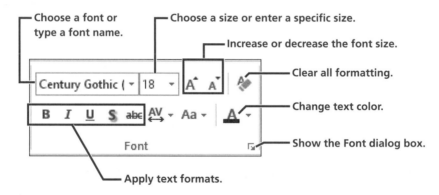

Setting Character Spacing

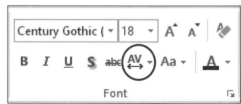

Character spacing refers to the horizontal space between characters. PowerPoint lets you adjust this spacing to give your text some breathing room. If none of the preset options fit your needs, you can enter a numerical value to specify the exact amount of spacing. In the professional world of print, this is referred to as *tracking* or *kerning*. You must first select characters before applying character spacing, or select the placeholder to apply spacing to all the text.

- ➡ MP3 sales exceed $1M
- ➡ 350 thousand new user accounts

- ➡ M P 3   s a l e s   e x c e e d $ 1 M
- ➡ 3 5 0   t h o u s a n d   n e w   u s e r   a c c o u n t s

The same slide with no character spacing (left) and a large amount of character spacing applied (right)

Setting the Text Case

A quick way to populate your slides with text is to copy text from an existing source, such as from an email message or Word document. However, the original text may not be formatted in the case appropriate for your slide. You can easily change the case of text, saving you from having to retype it.

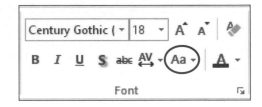

The following table illustrates the options available with the Change Case button.

TEXT CASE OPTIONS	
Menu Option	**How It Affects Text**
Sentence Case	Your text will look like this.
Lowercase	your text will look like this.
Uppercase	YOUR TEXT WILL LOOK LIKE THIS.
Capitalize Each Word	Your Text Will Look Like This.
Toggle Case	Wherever you typed an uppercase letter, it will become lowercase. Wherever you typed a lowercase letter, it will become uppercase.
	Example: If you type `Your Text Will Look Like This`, Toggle Case will change it to `yOUR tEXT wILL lOOK lIKE tHIS.`

DEVELOP YOUR SKILLS PP02-D06

Format Text

In this exercise, you will change the formatting of the fonts in the Title and Subtitle.

1. Save your file as **PP02-D06-WordOutline-[FirstInitialLastName]**.

2. Choose **View→Presentation Views→Normal** to return to Normal view, if necessary.

3. Display the **Home** tab so you can see the font settings as you work.

4. Click the title slide (the first one) to select it.

5. Follow these steps to select the subtitle placeholder box:

Ⓐ Click anywhere on the text to position the insertion point inside the handles for this text box. The dashed line indicates the text box border.

Ⓑ Click any edge of the dashed border to change it to a solid border (shown here).

The solid line indicates that the text box is selected. Any formatting change you make now will affect all text within the box. Notice also that the Font Size box on the Ribbon is currently set to 20. The Ion theme applied this font size to the subtitle.

6. Choose **Home→Font→Increase Font Size** [A] to increase the font size to **24**.

7. Choose **Home→Font→Bold** B.

   PowerPoint makes the text bold.

8. Choose **Home→Font→Shadow** S.

   The text stands out from the page a bit more because there is now a slight drop-shadow effect.

Format the Title

9. Click on the text of the title, **iJams Music Distribution**, and then click once on the dashed-line border to select the Title text box.

10. Choose **Home→Font→Font Size** ▼ and point to several different font sizes.

    Notice how Live Preview displays the slide title size changes as you point to different settings on the Font Size menu.

11. Set the **font size** to **96**.

    The text is not large enough. There is still some room to enlarge it so that the company name dominates the slide.

12. Click **96** in the **Home→Font→Font Size** menu.

13. Type **115** and tap Enter.

    PowerPoint increases the size of the text to 115. You can select a font size from the menu or type in your own value.

14. Save the presentation.

Setting Line Spacing

Video Library   http://labyrinthelab.com/videos   Video Number: PP13-V0207

Sometimes, instead of changing the font size or adding many hard returns, you need to only increase or decrease the spacing between lines to have the proper effect. Line spacing determines the amount of space between lines of text.

This setting is useful if text appears cramped and you wish to open up some breathing room between lines.

The same slide before and after applying Line Spacing

Adjust the Line Spacing

In this exercise, you will adjust the line spacing to increase the amount of space between bullets.

1. Save your file as **PP02-D07-WordOutline-[FirstInitialLastName]**.

2. Display the **New Hires** slide.

3. Click any of the names to display a dashed border.

4. Click the dashed border to select the entire text box.

5. Choose **Home→Paragraph→Line Spacing**▯→**2.0** to increase the spacing.

   PowerPoint redistributes the bulleted text vertically on the slide with more spacing between items.

6. Save and close your presentation.

Setting Paragraph Alignment

Video Library   http://labyrinthelab.com/videos   Video Number: PP13-V0208

In time, you will be able to "eye" a presentation and notice if the paragraph alignment is not balanced. You can select one or more paragraphs and then click an alignment button on the Ribbon to make the change. Use the following buttons from the Home→Paragraph group on the Ribbon to realign paragraphs.

PARAGRAPH ALIGNMENT BUTTONS		
Purpose	**Button**	**Example**
Left-align	▤	This text has been left aligned. Notice how the left edge is in a straight line, but the right edge appears jagged.
Center-align	▤	This text has been center aligned. Notice how the text is balanced and centered.
Right-align	▤	This text has been right aligned. Notice how the right edge is in a straight line.
Justify	▤	This text has been justify aligned. Notice how the text is spaced to maintain straight lines on the left and right.

It is often easiest to read left-aligned text because the eye can more easily find the starting point of subsequent lines.

PowerPoint 2013

Format the Contact Us Slide

In this exercise, you will reformat the Contact Us slide.

1. Open **PP02-D08-Contact** from your **PP2013 Lesson 02** folder and save it as **PP02-D08-Contact-[FirstInitialLastName]**.

2. If necessary, scroll down; select **slide 5, Contact Us**.

3. Click in the bulleted list and then click a border of the text box.

4. Choose **Home→Paragraph→Bullets** ▤ to remove the bullets.

5. Choose **Home→Paragraph→Center** ▤.

6. Select the entire telephone number.

   A faded formatting box appears. Pointing your mouse at it will cause it to become more visible. You may format the selected text from this formatting box, but we will use the Ribbon as in the next steps.

7. Choose **Home→Font→Font Size** ▼ and increase the size to **32**.

8. Using the same method, increase the size of the last line (the email address) to **32**.

9. Save your presentation.

Using the Format Painter

Video Library   http://labyrinthelab.com/videos   Video Number: PP13-V0209

Common to all Office programs, the Format Painter is a great tool that simplifies the formatting process. The Format Painter copies all text formats including the typeface, size, color, and attributes such as bold, italic, and underline. It also copies formatting applied to shapes or clip art. The Format Painter helps you easily maintain a standardized, uniform look in your presentation.

Loading the Format Painter

The key to using the Format Painter successfully is understanding when it is loaded. After formatting has been copied to the Format Painter, its Ribbon icon appears pressed in. This pressed-in icon indicates that the Format Painter is loaded and ready to use.

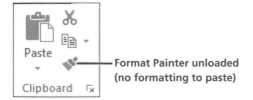 Format Painter unloaded (no formatting to paste)

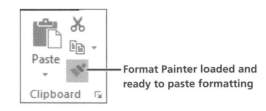 Format Painter loaded and ready to paste formatting

QUICK REFERENCE	COPYING FORMATS WITH THE FORMAT PAINTER
Task	**Procedure**
Copy formats with the Format Painter	■ Select the object (text, picture, drawn line, etc.) with the format you wish to copy. ■ Choose Home→Clipboard→Format Painter 🖌. ■ Select the object at the new location to which you wish to copy formatting.
Use the Format Painter repeatedly	■ Select the object with formatting to be copied. ■ Double-click Home→Clipboard→Format Painter 🖌. ■ Click with the Format Painter on all objects to which you wish the formatting copied. (The Format Painter will remain active until you switch it off.) ■ Click once on the Format Painter to switch it off again, or tap Esc.

When the Format Painter is loaded, the mouse pointer changes from an arrow ⤴ to a brush 🖌.

Copy Formatting with the Format Painter

In this exercise, you will copy and paste text formatting with the Format Painter.

1. Save your file as **PP02-D09-Contact-[FirstInitialLastName]**.

2. Select the fourth slide, **New Artist Specials**.

3. Double-click *free* in the second bullet to select it.

4. Choose **Home→Font→Font Size→32**.

5. Choose **Home→Font→Text Shadow S**.

6. Follow these steps to choose a font color:

   Ⓐ Choose **Home→Font→Font Color menu ▼**.   Ⓑ Locate the **Theme Colors**.

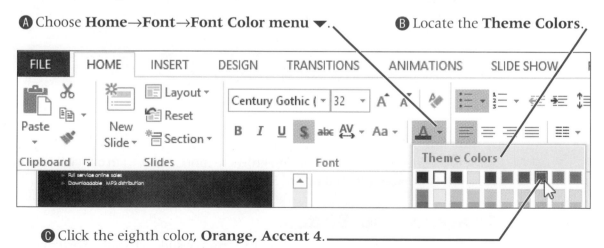

   Ⓒ Click the eighth color, **Orange, Accent 4**.

7. Choose **Home→Clipboard→Format Painter 🖌**.

   The Format Painter icon is pressed in and is now loaded.

8. Click once on *July* in the last bullet.

   The formatting is copied to the word July, and the Format Painter icon on the Ribbon becomes unloaded.

9. Choose **Home→Clipboard→Format Painter** 🖌️.

   The Format Painter has been reloaded with the formatting from the word July because that is where the insertion point is.

10. Click once on *20* in the last bullet.

    The formatting is copied to 20, and the Format Painter on the Ribbon becomes unloaded.

Use the Format Painter Repeatedly

11. Select the third slide, **Our Services**.

12. Drag across *on demand* in the first bullet to select it.

13. Choose **Home→Font→Bold** B.

14. Choose **Home→Font→Italic** *I*.

15. Choose **Home→Font→Font Color** ▼**→Theme Colors→Red Accent 2**.

16. Double-click **Home→Clipboard→Format Painter** 🖌️.

    Double-clicking the Format Painter will keep it loaded until you turn it off.

17. Click the word *online* in the third bullet.

    The formatting is copied to online, and the Format Painter remains loaded.

18. Click the word *sales* in the third bullet.

19. Click the words *MP3* and *distribution* in the last bullet.

20. Choose **Home→Clipboard→Format Painter** 🖌️.

    The Format Painter has been unloaded.

21. Save your presentation.

Using the Slide Sorter

Video Library   http://labyrinthelab.com/videos   Video Number: PP13-V0210

Up until now, you've been working in Normal view, which is good for manipulating a handful of slides. However, as your presentation grows to more slides than are visible in Normal view, you will want to explore the function of Slide Sorter view.

Rearranging Slides

PowerPoint's Slide Sorter view is used to rearrange slides. In Slide Sorter view, each slide is a thumbnail image so the entire presentation is visible at a glance. As your presentation grows, often the order of the slides needs to be changed to create a logical concept flow. Using the Drag and Drop method in Slide Sorter view, you can quickly reorganize your slides by moving them to the correct spot.

Use the Slide Sorter View

In this exercise, you will practice using Slide Sorter view.

1. Save your file as **PP02-D10-Contact-[FirstInitialLastName]**.

2. Choose **View→Presentation Views→Slide Sorter** ⊞.

3. Follow these steps to move a slide:

Ⓐ If necessary, drag the **Zoom** slider to change the zoom percentage until all six slides are shown. (Your slides may display differently.)

Ⓑ Drag the **Our Services** slide to the left of **Packaging Options**. (Your slides may display differently.)

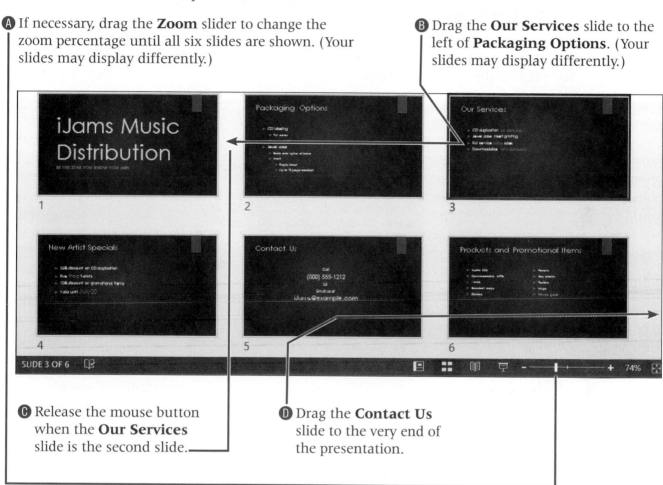

Ⓒ Release the mouse button when the **Our Services** slide is the second slide.

Ⓓ Drag the **Contact Us** slide to the very end of the presentation.

4. Choose **Views→Presentation Views→Normal** ⊞.

5. Save and close the presentation.

Organizing with Sections

Video Library http://labyrinthelab.com/videos   Video Number: PP13-V0211

Using the Slide Sorter with individual slides works well for small presentations. For presentations containing many slides, PowerPoint 2013's Sections feature helps you keep them organized.

Creating Sections

Sections are always created before the selected slide and include all following slides. This often results in a section containing more slides than intended. The fix is to simply create another section after the intended last slide.

QUICK REFERENCE	USING SECTIONS
Task	**Procedure**
Create a section	■ Select the first slide from the Slides panel for the section. ■ Choose Home→Slides→Section→Add Section. ■ Select the slide after the last in the section and choose Home→Slides→Section→Add Section.
Name a section	■ Right-click the section's title bar and choose Rename Section. ■ Type the new name for the section and click Rename.
Move a section	■ Drag a section's title bar above/below another section title bar.
Collapse or expand a section	■ Double-click the section's title bar.
Remove a section	■ Right-click the section's title bar and choose Remove Section (delete section and leave slides); choose Remove Section & Slides (delete section and its slides).

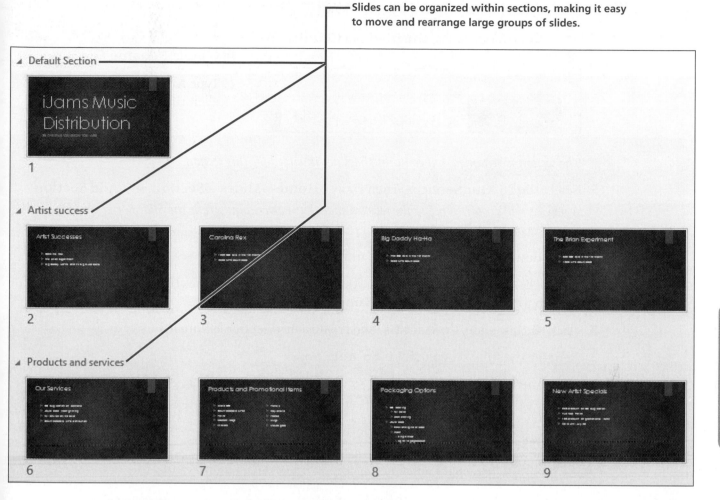

Slides can be organized within sections, making it easy to move and rearrange large groups of slides.

Create Sections

In this exercise, you will create sections.

1. Open **PP02-D11-Sections** from your **PP2013 Lesson 02** folder and save it as `PP02-D11-Sections-[FirstInitialLastName]`.

   With so many slides, it may be easier to work in Slide Sorter view.

2. Choose **View→Presentation Views→Slide Sorter**.

3. Select slide 2, **Artist Successes**. Then choose **Home→Slides→Section ▼→Add Section**.

   A new section named Untitled Section is created before the selected slide. Every slide below it is included in the section.

PowerPoint 2013

4. Follow these steps to rename the section:

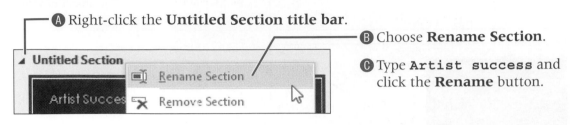

Ⓐ Right-click the **Untitled Section title bar**.

Ⓑ Choose **Rename Section**.

Ⓒ Type **Artist success** and click the **Rename** button.

The section is renamed, but contains slides not intended for this section.

5. Select slide 6, **Our Services**. Then choose **Home→Slides→Section ▼→Add Section**.
   A new section is started before the selected slide, but PowerPoint scrolls the Slide Sorter window to the top of the presentation.

6. Scroll down until you see the new, untitled section.

7. Right-click the **Untitled Section** title bar, choose **Rename Section**, and rename the section to **Products and services**.

8. Click the last slide, **Contact Us**, and create a new section before it.

9. Rename the final section **Call to action**.

10. Save your presentation.

Managing Sections

Video Library   http://labyrinthelab.com/videos   Video Number: PP13-V0212

Once sections have been created, they can be dragged and rearranged in either the Slides panel or Slide Sorter view. Individual slides can even be dragged from one section to another. Additionally, sections can be collapsed, similar to slide titles in Outline view. Collapsed sections hide the slides, making it easy to drag and reorder the sections. However, the collapsed sections hide slides only when editing. The collapsed slides will display as normal when running the slide show.

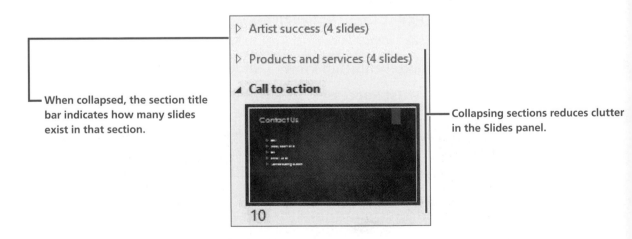

When collapsed, the section title bar indicates how many slides exist in that section.

Collapsing sections reduces clutter in the Slides panel.

Manage Sections

In this exercise, you will rearrange slides by using sections.

1. Save your presentation as **PP02-D12-Sections-[FirstInitialLastName]**.

2. With the presentation still displaying Slide Sorter view, scroll until you can see the **Artist success** section title bar, if necessary.

3. Double-click the **Artist success** section title bar to collapse it.

4. Double-click the **Products and services** section title bar.

5. Choose **View→Presentation Views→Normal**.
    The sections do not remain collapsed when you change views.

6. Follow these steps to rearrange the sections:

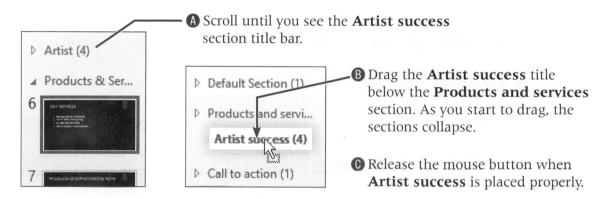

Ⓐ Scroll until you see the **Artist success** section title bar.

Ⓑ Drag the **Artist success** title below the **Products and services** section. As you start to drag, the sections collapse.

Ⓒ Release the mouse button when **Artist success** is placed properly.

7. Choose **View→Presentation Views→Slide Sorter**.

8. Click anywhere in the gray area outside the slide thumbnails to deselect any slides.

9. Scroll down, if necessary, until you see the entire **Call to Action** section with the **Contact Us** slide.

10. Use the **Zoom slider**, if necessary, to make the view smaller.
    You should see all slides in both the Products and Services and Call to Action sections.

11. Drag the last slide of the **Products and Services** section (New Artist Specials) to the left of the **Contact Us** slide to move it to the Call to Action section.

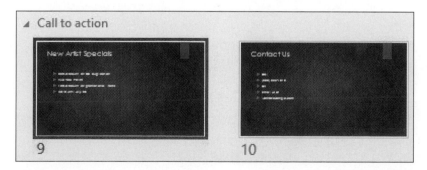

12. Save your presentation.

Printing Your Presentation

Video Library   http://labyrinthelab.com/videos   Video Number: PP13-V0213

Ninety percent of the time, you will be viewing or projecting the presentations you create from a PC or notebook computer. However, there may be times when a hard copy of the presentation is needed. In this lesson, you will simply explore the options of printing a presentation.

Knowing What You Can Print

PowerPoint can create the following types of printouts:

- **Slides:** Prints each slide of a presentation on a separate page
- **Handouts:** Prints one or more slides per page, leaving room for attendees to jot notes during the presentation
- **Speaker Notes:** Prints each slide on a separate page, with any speaker notes you created for the slide below
- **Outline:** Prints a text outline of each slide, similar to what is seen in the Outline panel

Previewing a Printout

The Print window, found in Backstage view, lets you see how each slide will be printed. You can then refine the appearance before printing.

FROM THE RIBBON
File→Print to display the Print tab in Backstage view

Using the Print Shortcut

If you have customized your Quick Access toolbar to display the Quick Print icon, you may find it tempting to just click it. However, before this becomes a habit, know that a click of this button sends the entire presentation to the current printer, whether or not you want to make adjustments. If you are working with a document theme that has a colored background, the printing process will not only be painstakingly slow, but may also waste your toner or ink!

FROM THE KEYBOARD
Ctrl+P to display the Print tab in Backstage view

The Quick Print button on the Quick Access toolbar sends your presentation directly to the printer.

Preview a Printout

In this exercise, you will use Backstage view to preview a printout.

1. Choose **File→Print**.
2. Follow these steps to examine the print options:

A Use the **left arrow** or scroll bar to return to the first slide.

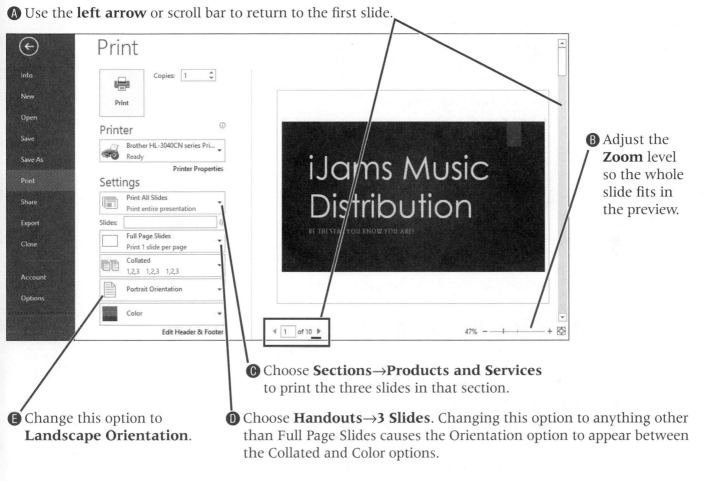

B Adjust the **Zoom** level so the whole slide fits in the preview.

C Choose **Sections→Products and Services** to print the three slides in that section.

E Change this option to **Landscape Orientation**.

D Choose **Handouts→3 Slides**. Changing this option to anything other than Full Page Slides causes the Orientation option to appear between the Collated and Color options.

3. Click the **Back** ⊕ button at the top of Backstage view to return to the main PowerPoint screen without printing. Close **PowerPoint**.

Concepts Review

To check your knowledge of the key concepts introduced in this lesson, complete the Concepts Review quiz by choosing the appropriate access option below.

If you are...	Then access the quiz by...
Using the Labyrinth Video Library	Going to http://labyrinthelab.com/videos
Using eLab	Logging in, choosing Content, and navigating to the Concepts Review quiz for this lesson
Not using the Labyrinth Video Library or eLab	Going to the student resource center for this book

Reinforce Your Skills

Work with Outlines and Formatting

In this exercise, you will format some slides in the Kids for Change presentation.

Work with Slides

1. Start **PowerPoint**. Open **PP02-R01-Design** from the **PP2013 Lesson 02** folder and save it as `PP02-R01-Design-[FirstInitialLastName]`.

2. Select the second slide, **Events**.

3. Choose **Home→Slides→Layout→Two Content** to change the slide layout to a two-column layout.

4. Select the last four paragraphs in the left column and drag them to the right column.

Work with Outlines

5. Choose **View→Presentation Views→Outline View**.

6. Locate the **Program Benefits** slide in the Outline panel.

7. Click to the right of the word *health* in the last paragraph of the **Program Benefits** slide in the Outline panel.

8. Tap [Ctrl]+[Enter] to create a slide.

9. Type `Requirements` in the Outline panel as the slide title.

10. Tap [Enter] and then tap [Tab] to create a new, bulleted paragraph.

11. Type `You need` in the Outline panel.

12. Tap [Enter] and then tap [Tab] to create a new, bulleted paragraph.

13. Type `Positive attitude`, tap [Enter], and type `Strong work ethic` to create another indented paragraph.

14. Tap [Enter] and then tap [Shift]+[Tab] to create and demote the next bullet.

15. Type `Time commitment`.

16. Tap [Enter] and then tap [Tab].

17. Type `One monthly event`, tap [Enter], and type `One annual meeting` to create the final two paragraphs.

18. Choose **Home→Slides→Layout→Title and Content**.

Format a Presentation

19. Choose **View→Presentation Views→Normal** and select the title slide from the **Slides** panel.

20. Click the **Title** box, and then click again on the edge of the box to select it.

21. Choose **Home→Font→Increase Font Size** once to increase the font size to **60**.

22. Choose **Home→Font→Bold**.

23. Display the **Requirements** slide on the Slides panel.

24. Choose **Home→Slides→New Slide**.

25. Type `Remember` as the title.

26. Type the following as bulleted paragraphs:
    - `Think globally, act locally.`
    - `Or think locally, act globally.`
    - `Just...`
    - `Think and act!`

27. Select the bulleted text box by clicking the border.

28. Choose **Home→Paragraph→Bullets** to remove the bullets from all paragraphs.

29. Choose **Home→Paragraph→Center** to center the text on the slide.

30. Choose **Home→Paragraph→Line Spacing→2.0** to increase the vertical spacing between bullets.

31. Select the text *think and act!*

32. Choose **Home→Font→Increase Font Size** four times to increase the size to 32.

Use Format Painter

33. With the *think and act!* text still selected, double-click the **Home→Clipboard→Format Painter** button to load it for multiple uses.

34. Click the words *Think* and *act* in the first line, and then click the words *think* and *act* in the second line to duplicate the formatting.

35. Choose **Home→Clipboard→Format Painter** to turn off the Format Painter.

36. Save the presentation; submit your final file based on the guidelines provided by your instructor. Exit **PowerPoint**.

    To view examples of how your file or files should look at the end of this exercise, go to the student resource center.

Import from Word; Organize and Print a Presentation

In this exercise, you will import an outline from Word, create sections, rearrange sections and slides, and print a slide.

Integrate with Word

1. Start **Microsoft Word**. Open **PP02-R02-Outline** from the **PP2013 Lesson 02** folder.

2. Choose **View→Views→Outline**.

3. Read over the outline. Then close **Word**.

4. Start **PowerPoint** and click **Blank Presentation**.

5. Save your file as `PP02-R02-Outline-[FirstInitialLastName]` in the **PP2013 Lesson 02** folder.

6. Choose **Design→Themes→Ion** to apply a design theme.

7. Choose **Home→Slides→New Slide ▼→Slides from Outline** to begin importing the Word outline.

8. Navigate to your **PP2013 Lesson 02** folder and double-click the **PP02-R02-Outline** Word document to import the outline and create the slides.

9. Select **slide 1** in the Slides panel and tap ⎡Delete⎤ to delete the blank slide.

10. Click **slide 1** in the Slides panel to ensure it is selected, scroll to the bottom of the Slides panel, and ⎡Shift⎤+click the final slide, **slide 7**, so all slides are selected.

11. Choose **Home→Slides→Reset** to reset the formatting of all slides.

Organize with Sections

12. Click slide 2, **College Application**, in the Slides panel to select it and deselect the others.

13. Choose **Home→Slides→Section→Add Section** to add a new section starting with the **College Application** slide.

14. Choose **Home→Slides→Section→Rename Section**.

15. Type `Personal Benefits` and then click **Rename**.

16. Click slide 4, **Crime Reduction**, in the Slides panel to select it and deselect the others.

17. Choose **Home→Slides→Section→Add Section** to add a new section starting with the **College Application** slide.

18. Choose **Home→Slides→Section→Rename Section**.

19. Type `Community Benefits` and then click **Rename**.

Use the Slide Sorter

20. Choose **View→Presentation Views→Slide Sorter**.

21. Drag the **Zoom** slider in the lower-right area of the PowerPoint window until all seven slides are visible.

22. Drag the **Leadership Skills** slide so it is between the College Application and Sense of Accomplishment slides.

23. Drag the **Community Benefits** section header up so that it is before the Personal Benefits section.

24. Save the presentation.

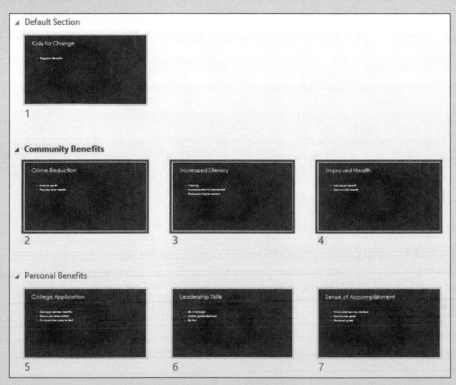

Print Your Presentation

25. Choose **File→Print** to display the Print tab in Backstage view.

26. Use the scroll bar at the right of the PowerPoint window to navigate the slides until slide 3, **Increased Literacy**, displays.

27. Choose your printer from the **Printer** option. Your instructor may prefer you to choose the PDF option.

28. Opt to print only the current slide; opt to print full-page slides, one slide per page.

29. Set the color option to **Grayscale**; print one copy.

30. Submit your final file based on guidelines provided by your instructor. Exit **PowerPoint**.
To view examples of how your file or files should look at the end of this exercise, go to the student resource center.

PowerPoint 2013

Create a Presentation from a Word Outline

In this exercise, you will import a Word outline to create the initial slides. You will then reset the formatting of the slides and arrange the slides into sections. Finally, you will print a slide.

Import an Outline and Reset Formatting

1. Start **PowerPoint** and click **Blank Presentation**.

2. Save your file as **PP02-R03-Outline-[FirstInitialLastName]** in the **PP2013 Lesson 02** folder.

3. Choose **Design→Themes→Retrospect** to apply a design theme.

4. Choose **Home→Slides→New Slide ▾→Slides from Outline** to begin importing a Word outline.

5. Navigate to your **PP2013 Lesson 02** folder and double-click the **PPT02-R03-Outline** Word document to import the outline and create the slides.

6. Select **slide 1** in the Slides panel and tap ⌨Delete to delete the blank slide.

7. Click **slide 1** in the Slides panel to ensure it is selected, scroll to the bottom of the Slides panel, and ⌨Shift +click the final slide, **slide 6**, so that all slides are selected.

8. Choose **Home→Slides→Reset** to reset the formatting of all slides.

Create Additional Slides

9. Choose **Views→Presentation Views→Outline View**.

10. Locate the **Bully No More** slide in the Outline panel.

11. Click to the right of the word *programs* in the last paragraph of the Bully No More slide in the Outline panel.

12. Tap ⌨Ctrl + ⌨Enter to create a slide.

13. Type **Kids for Change** in the Outline panel as the slide title, tap ⌨Enter, and then tap ⌨Tab to create a new, bulleted paragraph.

14. Type **Part of the Solution** in the Outline panel.

15. Choose **Home→Slides→Layout→Section Header**.

16. Scroll to the top of the Outline panel and click anywhere in the text of the first slide to select the slide.

17. Choose **Home→Slides→Layout→Title Slide**.

Copy Formatting

18. Choose **Views→Presentation Views→Normal**.

19. Display slide 4, **Toy Collection**.

20. Select the text *foster homes*.

21. Choose **Home→Font→Bold**.

22. Double-click the **Home→Clipboard→Format Painter** button to load the Format Painter for multiple uses.

23. Click each of the words *emergency, responders, Child,* and *Services* to copy the bold formatting.

24. Choose **Home→Clipboard→Format Painter** to unload the Format Painter.

Organize with Sections

25. Choose **View→Presentation Views→Slide Sorter**.

26. Slide the **Zoom** slider at the bottom-right of the PowerPoint window until all seven slides are visible.

27. Click the **iRecycling Day** slide to select it.

28. Choose **Home→Slides→Section→Add Section** to create a new section.

29. Right-click the untitled section heading and choose **Rename Section**.

30. Type `Community` and then click **Rename**.

31. Click the **Bully No More** slide.

32. Choose **Home→Slides→Section→Add Section**.

33. Right-click the untitled section heading and choose **Rename Section**.

34. Type `School` and then click **Rename**.

35. Drag the **Tutoring** slide to the right of the **Bully No More** slide to move it to the **School** section.

36. Save the presentation.

Print Slides

37. Choose **File→Print** to display the Print tab in Backstage view.

38. Use the scroll bar at the right of the PowerPoint window to navigate the slides until **slide 1** displays.

39. Choose your printer from the **Printer** option. Use the PDF option if specified by your instructor.

40. Specify to print a **Custom Range** of **slides 1–3**; specify **3 slides per page**.

41. Set the color option to **Black and White**; print one copy.

42. Submit your final file based on guidelines provided by your instructor. Exit **PowerPoint**.

Apply Your Skills

Reformat a Presentation

In this exercise, you will create a presentation for Universal Corporate Events based on a Microsoft Word outline. You will then add a slide and format text.

Create a Word Outline

1. Start **Word** and click **Blank Document**.

2. Save the file as **PP02-A01-Outline-[FirstInitialLastName]** in your **PP2013 Lesson 02** folder.

3. Choose **View→Views→Outline**.

4. Type the following text, using `Enter`, `Tab`, and `Shift` + `Tab` as needed to create an outline in Word.

   ⊕ Universal Corporate Events
      ⊖ Events made easy
   ⊕ Event Types
      ⊖ Celebrations
      ⊖ Ceremonies
      ⊖ Team building
      ⊖ Trade shows
   ⊕ Services
      ⊖ Catering
      ⊖ Invitations
      ⊖ Stage and sound equipment
      ⊖ Venue scouting
   ⊕ Benefits
      ⊕ Our Jobs
         ⊖ Deal with paperwork
         ⊖ Guarantee safety
         ⊖ Scheduling
      ⊕ Your Jobs
         ⊖ Relax
         ⊖ Enjoy your event
   ⊕ Universal Corporate Events
      ⊖ Events made easy
   —

5. Save and then close your file. Exit **Word**.

Import a Word Outline

6. Start **PowerPoint** and click **Blank Presentation**.

7. Save your file as `PP02-A01-Outline-[FirstInitialLastName]` to your **PP2013 Lesson 02** folder.

8. Choose **Home→Slides→New Slide→Slides from Outline**.

9. Browse to the **PP2013 Lesson 02** folder and double-click the **PP02-A01-Outline-[FirstInitialLastName]** Word outline.

10. Delete the blank first slide.

Work with an Outline

11. Display the presentation in **Outline View**.

12. Click at the end of the last paragraph of the **Benefits** slide in the Outline panel.

13. Press Ctrl + Enter to create a new slide.

14. Type `Specialties`, tap Enter, and then tap Tab.

15. Type the following paragraphs, tapping Enter after each except the last one.

    `Custom catering`
    `Individual transportation`
    `Group transportation`
    `Line dancing`
    `Graphic design`
    `Radio promotion`
    `Emergency medical`
    `Large-item printing`

Formatting a Presentation

16. Apply the **Facet** design document theme.

17. Display the presentation in **Normal** view.

18. Ensure that the Specialties slide is displayed and then apply the **Two Content** layout.

19. Select the last four paragraphs on the **Specialties** slide and move them to the new right-column placeholder.

20. Click **slide 1** in the Slides panel and then choose **Home→Slides→Layout→Title Slide**.

21. Click **slide 1** in the Slides panel and then Shift + click **slide 6** to select all slides.

22. Choose **Home→Slides→Reset**.

23. Display slide 4, **Benefits**.

24. Select the **Our Jobs** paragraph; bold the text.

25. Choose **Home→Font→Character Spacing→Loose** to spread the text out horizontally.

Using the Format Painter

26. Load the **Format Painter** with the formatting.

27. Drag across the *Your Jobs* paragraph to copy the formatting to the paragraph.

28. Save your presentation. Submit your final file based on the guidelines provided by your instructor. Exit **PowerPoint**.

    To view examples of how your file or files should look at the end of this exercise, go to the student resource center.

APPLY YOUR SKILLS PP02-A02

Organize and Print a Presentation

In this exercise, you will use Slide Sorter view to create sections and organize the slides within a presentation. You will then print a portion of the presentation.

Using the Slide Sorter

1. Start **PowerPoint**. Open **PP02-A02-Outline** from the **PP2013 Lesson 02** folder and save it as `PP02-A02-Outline-[FirstInitialLastName]`.

2. Display the presentation in **Slide Sorter** view.

3. Drag the **Zoom** slider in the lower-right area of the PowerPoint window until you can see all six slides.

Rearranging Slides

4. Drag the **Benefits** slide so that it is after the **Specialties** slide.

5. Drag the **Services** slide so that it is before the **Event Types** slide.

Sections

6. Click the **Services** slide and then add a section.

7. Rename the new section `Services`.

8. Click the **Benefits** slide and then add a section.

9. Rename the new section `Closing`.

10. Save the presentation.

Print a Presentation

11. Choose **File→Print**.

12. Select the **Specialties** slide.

13. Using the **Grayscale** option, print the single slide. Print the slide as a PDF file if directed to do so by your instructor.

14. Close the presentation and exit **PowerPoint**.

15. Submit your final file based on the guidelines provided by your instructor.

    To view examples of how your file or files should look at the end of this exercise, go to the student resource center.

Create, Format, and Organize a Presentation

In this exercise, you will create and import an outline from Word and then design and format a presentation.

Outline in Word

1. Start **Word** and use **Outline View** to create an outline that will produce the following slides:

SLIDES	
Title	**Bullets**
Universal Corporate Events	Specialized
Specialties	■ Custom catering ■ Individual transportation ■ Group transportation ■ Line dancing ■ Graphic design ■ Radio promotion ■ Emergency medical ■ Large-item printing
Catering	■ Vegan dishes ■ Kosher dishes ■ Meat-lovers dishes ■ Desserts
Transportation	■ Individual limos ■ Group buses for 6–50
Line Dancing	■ Experienced dance leaders ■ Country, pop, and hip-hop
Graphic Design	■ Invitation graphics ■ Signs ■ Banners
Radio Promotion	■ Script writing ■ Voice talent ■ High-definition recording
Emergency Medical	■ CPR-certified staff ■ Onsite portable defibrillators
Large-Item Printing	■ Canvas, polyester, or vinyl ■ Up to 64 square feet

2. Save the outline to your **PP2013 Lesson 02** folder as **PP02-A03-Outline-[FirstInitialLastName]** and close Word.

3. Start **PowerPoint** and create a new, blank presentation in the **PP2013 Lesson 02** folder named **PP02-A03-Outline-[FirstInitialLastName]**.

4. Import the **PP02-A03-Outline-[FirstInitialLastName]** Word outline.

5. Delete the blank first slide.

Work with Slides and Formatting

6. Select all slides in the Slides panel and use the **Reset** command to reset the formatting.

7. Apply the **Ion Boardroom** theme with the **orange variation**.

8. Change the layout of the first slide to **Title Slide**.

9. Change the layout of the second slide to **Two Content**.

10. Move the last four paragraphs of the second slide into the new right-column placeholder.

11. Increase the line spacing of both columns on **slide 2** to **2.0**.

Work with an Outline

12. Display the presentation in **Outline View**.

13. Collapse all the slides on the Outline panel.

14. Select the **Specialties** slide in the Outline panel and then expand only that one slide.

15. In the Outline panel, move the *Large-item printing* paragraph below the *Graphic design* paragraph.

16. In the Outline panel, move the *Large-Item Printing* slide below the **Graphic Design** slide.

17. Display the presentation in **Normal** view.

Formatting a Presentation

18. Display the **Catering** slide.

19. Make the word *Vegan* bold and italic and then use the **Format Painter** to copy the formatting to the words *Kosher* and *Meat-lovers*.

20. Change the case of all eight paragraphs on the **Specialties** slide to **Capitalize Each Word**.

Using the Slide Sorter

21. Display the presentation in **Slide Sorter** view.

22. Create a new section starting with **slide 1** named `Intro`.

23. Create a new section starting with the **Catering** slide named `Food and Entertainment`.

24. Create a new section starting with the **Transportation** slide named `Logistics and Emergency`.

25. Create a new section starting with the **Graphic Design** slide named `Promotion`.

26. Move the **Line Dancing** slide to the end of the **Food and Entertainment** section.

27. Move the **Emergency Medical** slide to the end of the **Logistics and Emergency** section.

28. Move the entire **Promotion** section so that it is before the **Logistics and Emergency** section.

29. Save the presentation.

Print a Presentation

30. Print the slides in the **Promotion** section in the **Handouts (3 slides per page)** format so that only a single page prints. Print in **Grayscale** to save on color ink. (Or print to PDF if instructed to by your instructor.)

31. Submit your final file based on the instructions provided by your instructor. Exit **PowerPoint**.

Ppo2 - Eol - Recipe - آلو ٹکی پکوڑے

آلو
مصالح

Computer Class Information

Fall 2015 Term **8/31/15 to** **11/6/15** 	The last day of FALL 2015 term will be Friday, November 6, 2015
WINTER 2015 Term **11/16/15 to** **2/12/16**	WINTER catalogs will be mailed out to Santa Clara residents on October 16, 2015 Registration for **WINTER** term will begin Monday, October 19, 2015 **WINTER** term will begin **Monday, November 16, 2015**
WINTER Holidays	November 23 to Nov 27, Thanksgiving Holiday December 21 to January 4, 2016, Christmas Holiday Martin Luther King, Jr. Birthday – January 17, 2016

Extend Your Skills

In the course of working through the Extend Your Skills exercises, you will think critically as you use the skills taught in the lesson to complete the assigned projects. To evaluate your mastery and completion of the exercises, your instructor may use a rubric, with which more points are allotted according to performance characteristics. (The more you do, the more you earn!) Ask your instructor how your work will be evaluated.

PP02-E01   **That's the Way I See It**

You're teaching a cooking class and need a presentation to show others how to make your signature dish. Choose a recipe that you know well, or find one online. When you're ready, create a new presentation named **PP02-E01-Recipe-[FirstInitialLastName]** in your **PP2013 Lesson 02** folder.

Apply the design theme and variation of your choice. If you can't find a design theme you like, use PowerPoint's Start screen to search for others. Type the recipe name as the slide title and create an engaging subtitle. Add a Title and Content slide that lists the ingredients. Create at least three more slides, each of which describes a few fun facts about one of the ingredients (look it up or make it up).

Add a slide that lists a brief description of each step. Each paragraph should contain no more than four words. Create an additional slide for each step, using the brief description as the slide title and bulleted paragraphs to further explain the step. Copy the brief descriptions one by one and paste them onto the additional slides. Create an **Ingredients** section that contains all the ingredient slides and a **Steps** section that includes all the step slides.

Run the slide show and make note of anything you want to change. When the slide show ends, make the necessary changes and then save your presentation. You will be evaluated based on the inclusion of all elements specified, your ability to follow directions, your ability to apply newly learned skills to a real-world situation, your creativity, and the relevance of your topic and/or data choice(s). Submit your final file based on the guidelines provided by your instructor.

PP02-E02   **Be Your Own Boss**

Open **PP02-E02-BlueJean** from the **PP2013 Lesson 02** folder and save it as **PP02-E02-BlueJean-[FirstInitialLastName]**. View the presentation as a slide show and ask yourself if the slides are easy to read and in the best order. Based on your evaluation, use the skills taught in this lesson to make the necessary changes, ensuring that you cover these edits.

- Change the document theme.
- Adjust the text layout.
- Rearrange the order of slides.
- Edit text.

Be sure the design and formatting are consistent from slide to slide. Use the Format Painter to quickly duplicate formatting changes. Add at least three more slides, such as those to describe Blue Jean Landscaping products, a brief company history, or a price list. Rearrange the slides and create at least two sections to group slides in a logical order.

You will be evaluated based on the inclusion of all elements specified, your ability to follow directions, your ability to apply newly learned skills to a real-world situation, your creativity, and your demonstration of an entrepreneurial spirit. Submit your final file based on the guidelines provided by your instructor.

Transfer Your Skills

In the course of working through the Transfer Your Skills exercises, you will use critical-thinking and creativity skills to complete the assigned projects using skills taught in the lesson. To evaluate your mastery and completion of the exercises, your instructor may use a rubric, with which more points are allotted according to performance characteristics. (The more you do, the more you earn!) Ask your instructor how your work will be evaluated.

PP02-T01 Use the Web as a Learning Tool

Throughout this book, you will be provided with an opportunity to use the Internet as a learning tool by completing WebQuests. According to the original creators of WebQuests, as described on their website (WebQuest.org), a WebQuest is "an inquiry-oriented activity in which most or all of the information used by learners is drawn from the web." To complete the WebQuest projects in this book, navigate to the student resource center and choose the WebQuest for the lesson on which you are currently working. The subject of each WebQuest will be relevant to the material found in the lesson.

WebQuest Subject: Designing an Effective Presentation

Submit your final file(s) based on the guidelines provided by your instructor.

PP02-T02 Demonstrate Proficiency

Stormy BBQ is sponsoring a Father's Day picnic. Create a PowerPoint presentation to display on the widescreen monitors at Stormy's to play during business hours that gives details about the event.

Create an outline in Microsoft Word that will produce at least five slides when imported into PowerPoint. The slides should describe the picnic and various events and entertainment. Save the Word outline as **PP02-T02-FathersDay-[FirstInitialLastName]** to your **PP2013 Lesson 02** folder.

Import the outline into PowerPoint to create the initial slides. Use an appropriate theme and change the slide layouts as necessary. Format the text so important words stand out, but be careful not to overdo it! Experiment with character and line spacing, paragraph alignment, and other formatting. Use the Format Painter to quickly reuse preferred formatting. Create sections for different parts of the event, such as for food, games, and other activities.

Save your presentation as **PP02-T02-FathersDay-[FirstInitialLastName]** in your **PP2013 Lesson 02** folder.

Submit your final file based on the guidelines provided by your instructor.

Adding Graphics, Animation, and Sound

LEARNING OBJECTIVES

After studying this lesson, you will be able to:

- Add clip art, photos, screenshots, and shapes to a presentation
- Remove backgrounds and apply artistic effects to slide images
- Add transition effects to a slide show
- Add animation to objects on a slide
- Add sound effects to transitions and animations

In this lesson, you will enhance a presentation that currently includes only text. You will use online clip art to add interest to the presentation, a drawing object to add spark, and slide transitions and animation to "bring the presentation to life."

Adding Eye Candy

The iJams presentation is evolving nicely. However, you know you will have to add some pizzazz to it if iJams is to contend with competitors. Although you have created an error-free, technically perfect presentation, you can see that something is definitely missing! You decide that if used sparingly, clip art and animation will enhance the presentation.

The iJams presentation with stock clip art added

Working with Online Pictures

Video Library   http://labyrinthelab.com/videos   Video Number: PP13-V0301

You can search for and insert clip art from the Internet directly from within PowerPoint. Adding clip art will help you emphasize key points and add polish to the presentation as a whole. The Microsoft Office website has a clip art collection of more than 130,000 pieces of art—and it grows daily. There is clip art available for any occasion.

While the term *clip art* is an industry-standard term referring to predrawn artwork that is added to computer documents, Microsoft uses the terms *clip art* and *online pictures* inconsistently to refer to the same thing. For example, PowerPoint's Online Pictures button opens the Insert Pictures dialog box, which allows you to search the Office.com website for clip art.

Using Text and Object Layouts

PowerPoint creates slides with different layouts, such as slides with titles only and slides with titles and text. These slide layouts allow you to easily create slides with a standardized title and bulleted text. Many of PowerPoint's layouts, including the Title and Content layout and the Two Content layout, provide placeholders for titles, text, and various types of content including tables, charts, clip art from the Internet, pictures from your computer, organizational charts, and movies.

PowerPoint 2013

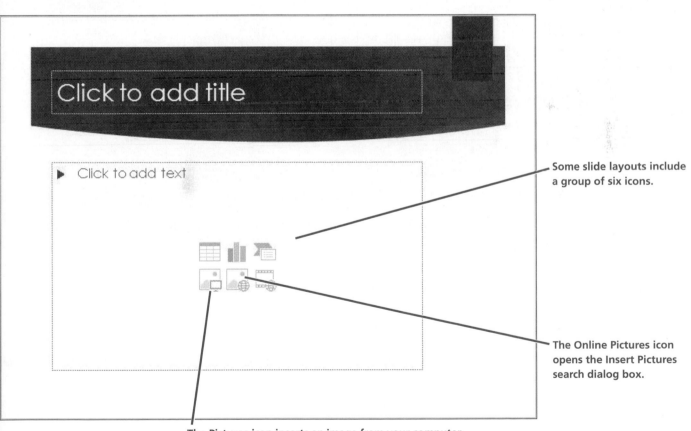

Some slide layouts include a group of six icons.

The Online Pictures icon opens the Insert Pictures search dialog box.

The Pictures icon inserts an image from your computer.

Slide Insert Shortcuts				
Icon	**What It Does**		**Icon**	**What It Does**
▦	Inserts a table		▤	Inserts an image
⏍	Inserts a chart or graph		▨	Inserts a SmartArt graphic
▥	Opens the Online Pictures dialog box to insert clip art		▨	Inserts a video clip

Deleting Placeholder Text

Sometimes you may decide to replace all text on a slide with a graphic. Deleting all text inside a placeholder results in the slide displaying its six default insert icons, making it easy to insert clip art or other objects.

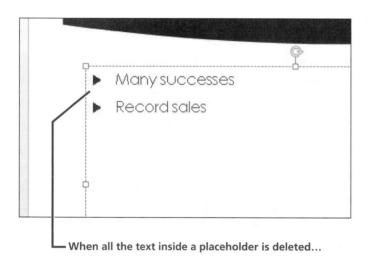

When all the text inside a placeholder is deleted…

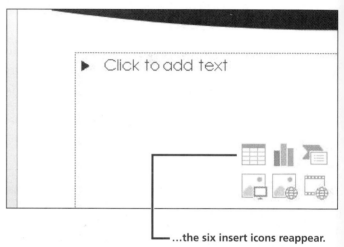

…the six insert icons reappear.

Get a Slide Ready for Clip Art

In this exercise, you will get a slide ready to accept clip art.

1. Start **PowerPoint**. Open **PP03-D01-Animation** from the **PP2013 Lesson 03** folder, and save it as **PP03-D01-Animation-[FirstInitialLastName]**.

   Replace the bracketed text with your first initial and last name. For example, if your name is Bethany Smith, your filename would look like this: PP03-D01-Animation-BSmith.

2. Select the **Our Services** slide from the **Slides panel**.

3. Choose **Home→Slides→New Slide** ▧.

   A new slide is inserted below Our Services. The new slide uses the same layout as the Our Services slide.

Choose a Layout and Format Text

4. Follow these steps to apply a slide layout suitable for clip art:

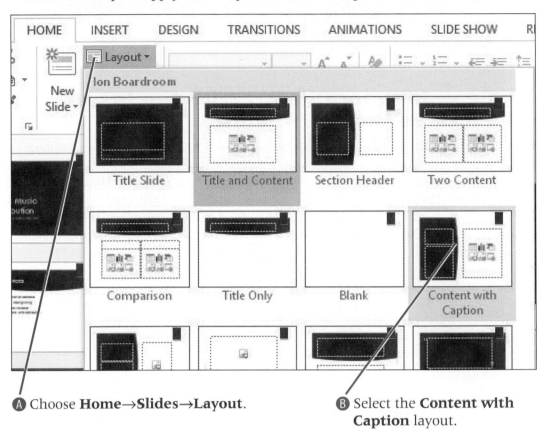

A Choose **Home→Slides→Layout**.

B Select the **Content with Caption** layout.

5. In the Title placeholder, type **Our Recent Success**.

6. In the text box beneath the title, type:

Top of the Rock [Enter] **Excellence in Service to Musicians** [Enter] **League of Electronic Music Distributors.**

7. Select the text *Top of the Rock;* choose **Home→Font→Font Size menu** ▼ and then choose **24**.

8. Choose **Home→Font→Bold**.

9. Select the text *League of Electronic Music Distributors.*

10. Choose **Home→Font→Italic**.

Your slide is ready for clip art.

11. Click in the large text placeholder at the right and type:

Many successes [Enter]

Record-breaking sales

You decide instead to replace the bulleted text with clip art. You will delete all the text in the placeholder so the slide displays the six insert icons again.

12. Click inside the text box, if necessary, to display its dashed border.

13. Click the dashed border to select the text box.

14. Tap Delete.

The text is deleted, and the six insert icons reappear.

15. Save your presentation.

Searching for Clip Art with the Insert Pictures Search Window

Video Library   http://labyrinthelab.com/videos   Video Number: PP13-V0302

The Insert Pictures search window replaces the Clip Art panel that existed in previous versions of PowerPoint. This new window lets you search for clip art on the Office.com Clip Art website or from the Bing™ search engine. Each piece of clip art is associated with keywords that describe its characteristics. The first illustration that follows describes the Insert Pictures search window. The second illustration shows the images that can be located by using the keyword *awards* or *prizes*.

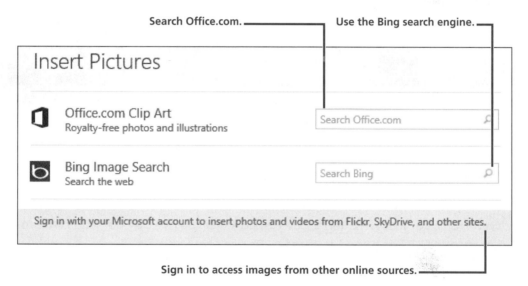

Search Office.com. ———————————   Use the Bing search engine. ———

Sign in to access images from other online sources. ————

Begin a new search from a different search engine.　　　　　　　View a larger version of the image.

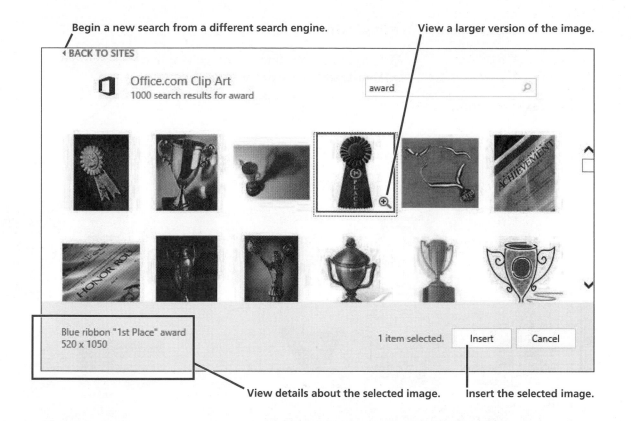

Office.com Clip Art
1000 search results for award

award 🔍

Blue ribbon "1st Place" award
520 x 1050

1 item selected. | Insert | Cancel

View details about the selected image.　　　Insert the selected image.

DEVELOP YOUR SKILLS PP03-D02

Insert Clip Art

In this exercise, you will insert clip art to add visual interest to a slide.

1. Save your file as **PP03-D02-Animation-[FirstInitialLastName]**.

2. On the **Our Recent Success** slide, click the **Online Pictures** 🖼 icon to open the Insert Pictures search window.

3. Type **award** in the Office.com search box and then tap Enter.

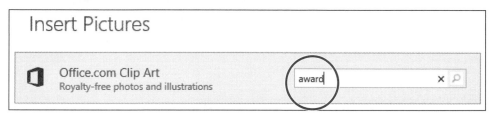

4. Follow these steps to insert a picture on the slide:

Ⓐ Scroll until you find an image you like. Your results may differ from the figure.

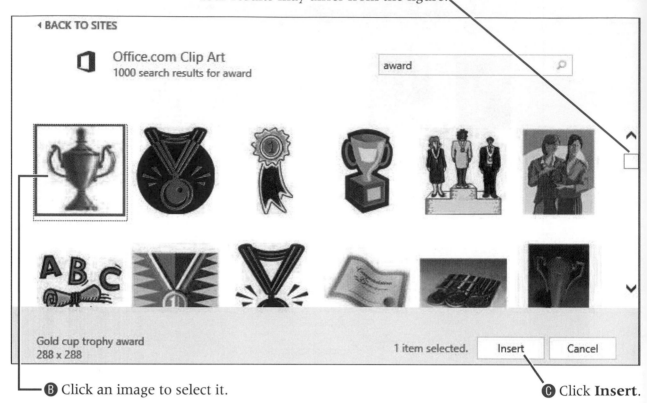

Ⓑ Click an image to select it.

Ⓒ Click **Insert**.

The clip art image is inserted on the slide and replaces the large text box.

5. Save the presentation.

Moving, Sizing, and Rotating Objects

Video Library   http://labyrinthelab.com/videos   Video Number: PP13-V0303

When you click an object (such as a clip art image), sizing handles and a rotate handle appear. You can easily move, size, and rotate the selected object.

Adjust the width/height by dragging the top, side, or bottom handle.

The circular rotate handle rotates the object.

Adjust the width and height proportionately by dragging a corner handle.

Point to an object to display the Move pointer, which allows you to drag the object.

Stacking Objects

Sometimes when you insert a picture, it overlaps text or some other object. You can change the stacking order of objects, such as pictures and shapes, by moving them forward or backward.

If an object is covering text...

...send it behind the text.

PowerPoint 2013

STACKING OBJECTS	
Task	**Procedure**
Move an object back one object at a time	Select the object and then choose Picture Tools→Format→Arrange→Send Backward.
Move an object up one object at a time	Select the object and then choose Picture Tools→Format→Arrange→Bring Forward.
Move an object to the very back of a slide	Select the object and then choose Picture Tools→Format→Arrange→Send Backward ▼→Send to Back.
Move an object to the very front of a slide	Select the object and then choose Picture Tools→Format→Arrange→Bring Forward ▼→Bring to Front.

DEVELOP YOUR SKILLS PP03-D03
Move and Size Clip Art

In this exercise, you will manipulate clip art, sizing and moving it to place it on the slide.

1. Save your file as **PP03-D03-Animation-[FirstInitialLastName]**.

2. Follow these steps to rotate the clip art image:

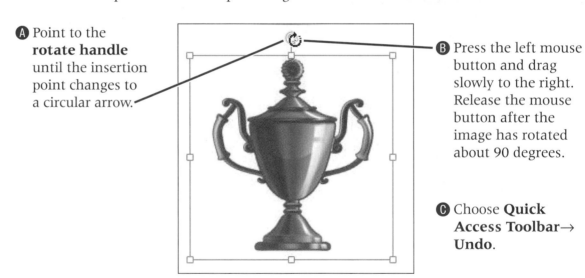

Ⓐ Point to the **rotate handle** until the insertion point changes to a circular arrow.

Ⓑ Press the left mouse button and drag slowly to the right. Release the mouse button after the image has rotated about 90 degrees.

Ⓒ Choose **Quick Access Toolbar→ Undo**.

3. Follow these steps to resize the clip art image:

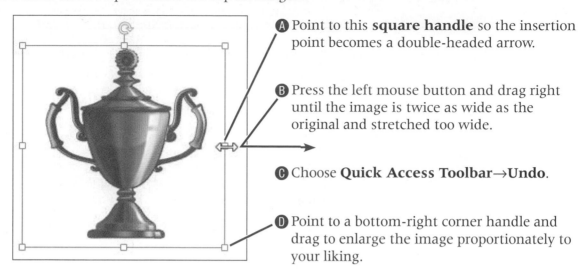

A Point to this **square handle** so the insertion point becomes a double-headed arrow.

B Press the left mouse button and drag right until the image is twice as wide as the original and stretched too wide.

C Choose **Quick Access Toolbar→Undo**.

D Point to a bottom-right corner handle and drag to enlarge the image proportionately to your liking.

4. Point to the image itself (not the border or a resize handle) until the pointer becomes a four-headed arrow. Drag so the image is centered next to the bar of text.

Compare your slide to the following illustration.

5. Save your presentation.

Formatting Clip Art

Video Library   http://labyrinthelab.com/videos   Video Number: PP13-V0304

After your image is on the slide, use the various groups on the contextual Format tab to add effects or align your image. You can add borders, drop-shadows, or bevels, or rotate your image in 3-D from the Picture Styles group on the Format tab. Other groups on this tab allow you to align, flip, crop, or perform basic image-editing tasks.

QUICK REFERENCE	PERFORMING CLIP ART TASKS
Task	**Procedure**
Insert a clip art image from an online source	■ Click the Online Pictures shortcut 🖼️ or choose Insert→Images→Online Pictures. ■ Enter a search term and tap Enter. ■ Click the desired thumbnail and then click Insert.
Insert an image from your computer	■ Click the Pictures shortcut 🖼️ or choose Insert→Images→Pictures. ■ Browse your computer's location for an image. ■ Click the desired image and then click Insert.
Resize a clip art image	■ Click the clip art image to display its border. ■ Drag any square handle along the top, bottom, or sides of the clip art's border to resize the image wider or taller. ■ Drag any handle in the clip art's corners to resize the image proportionately.
Move a clip art image	■ Point to the image until the mouse pointer becomes a four-headed arrow. ■ Drag the image to the desired location.
Rotate a clip art image	■ Click the clip art image to display its border. ■ Point to the rotate handle above the clip art's top border until the mouse pointer becomes a circular arrow. ■ Drag left or right to rotate the image.
Format a clip art image	■ Click the clip art image to display its border. ■ Choose Format→Picture Styles and then choose a command.

DEVELOP YOUR SKILLS PP03-D04
Insert and Format Clip Art

In this exercise, you will work with the Ribbon to insert and format an image on your slide.

1. Save your file as **PP03-D04-Animation-[FirstInitialLastName]**.

2. Display the **title slide**.

3. Choose **Insert→Images→Online Pictures** 🖼️.

4. Follow these steps to insert clip art on the title slide:

A Type **cd** in the Office.com search box and then tap Enter.

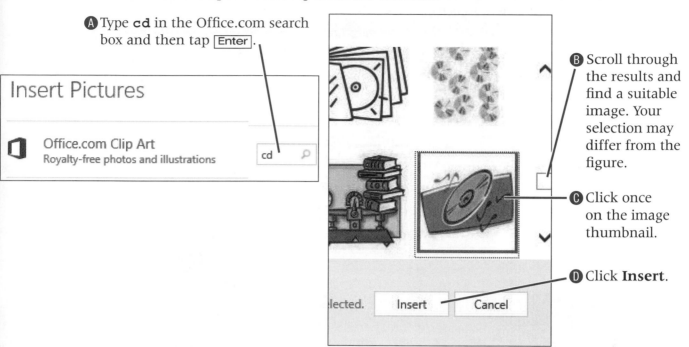

Insert Pictures

Office.com Clip Art
Royalty-free photos and illustrations

cd

B Scroll through the results and find a suitable image. Your selection may differ from the figure.

C Click once on the image thumbnail.

D Click **Insert**.

...ected.   Insert   Cancel

Size and Position the Image

Next, you will use the Format contextual tab to experiment with effect options.

5. Drag the image to the top of the slide so it no longer overlaps the text. Then drag the top-right corner handle toward the top-right corner of your slide to enlarge the image proportionately.

Be careful not to size it too large; the image should still fit on the slide.

iJams Music
Distribution

6. Choose **Format→Arrange→Align→Align Center**.

Selecting an image object forces the display of the contextual Format tab.

7. Make sure the image displays handles to indicate it is selected and then choose **Format→Picture Styles→Picture Effects**.

8. Roll your insertion point over several of the items in the **Picture Effects** gallery to view a Live Preview of each effect.

As you have seen with other commands, Live Preview makes it easy to anticipate the effect of a command without the need to undo it if you don't like the effect.

9. Choose **Format→Picture Styles→Picture Effects→Glow→Gold, 18 pt glow, Accent color 3**.

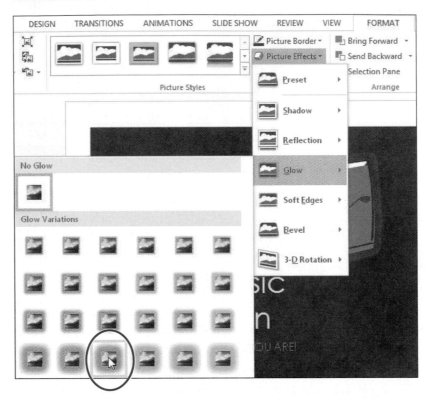

PowerPoint applies a glowing effect to the edge of the image.

10. If necessary, resize and move your image so it doesn't overlap the text.

11. Save your presentation.

Adding Other Graphics

Video Library   http://labyrinthelab.com/videos   Video Number: PP13-V0305

Sometimes you just can't find that perfect image through clip art. Often you can incorporate more-unique and personal imagery if you take your own pictures or download professional photographs from a commercial website. PowerPoint 2013 includes tools and features to make the most of your images, including the ability to remove a background and add artistic effects.

Removing a Background

Many times a photograph contains more than what you need. In the past, it was necessary to use a graphics-editing program to remove the background or other unwanted elements. PowerPoint 2013 includes a feature that allows you to remove backgrounds with just a few clicks. When removing a background, the original picture is not harmed, because PowerPoint works on a copy of the picture embedded in the slide. Additionally, nothing is actually removed from the picture. PowerPoint just hides areas of the picture that you mark to be removed. The hidden areas can always be made visible again. You can adjust the settings of the removal tool at any time after the background's initial removal, so there is no need to worry about getting it perfect on your first try.

The Background Removal tool overlays in purple the areas to be removed.

With just a few clicks, the background can be removed.

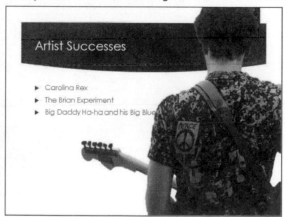

DEVELOP YOUR SKILLS PP03-D05
Remove a Background

In this exercise, you will insert a picture and remove the background.

1. Save your file as **PP03-D05-Animation-[FirstInitialLastName]**.

2. Scroll down the Slides pane, if necessary, and select the **Artist Successes** slide.

3. Choose **Insert→Images→Pictures**.

4. Navigate to your **PP2013 Lesson 03** folder, select the **PP03-D05-Guitarist** picture, and click **Insert**.

   The picture is inserted on the slide, but contains more imagery than we need.

Remove the Background

5. Drag the picture up so its top snaps to the top of the slide.

6. Drag the bottom handle down until the bottom of the picture snaps to the bottom of the slide.

   The picture now covers the whole slide.

7. Choose **Picture Tools→Format→Adjust→Remove Background**.

   PowerPoint places a rectangular border inside the picture and does its best to guess what you want to remove. A purple overlay indicates the content that will be removed. You will adjust this.

8. Drag the top-right handle of the rectangular box inside the picture so it snaps to the top-right corner of the picture.

9. Drag the bottom-left handle of the rectangular box down and right so the entire guitar is inside the box.

   Your slide should resemble the following figure, but it will not be exact.

   When you resize the box inside the picture, PowerPoint adjusts the purple overlay. The overlay still needs to be adjusted so you can see the whole guitarist.

10. Choose **Background Removal→Refine→Mark Areas to Keep**.

11. Follow these steps to adjust the overlay:

Ⓐ Point to the top of the left shoulder and drag down to the bottom of the elbow to tell PowerPoint not to remove this area.

Ⓑ Point to the left edge of the guitar and drag right to keep this area.

Ⓒ Drag over any other purple on the guitarist or the guitar.

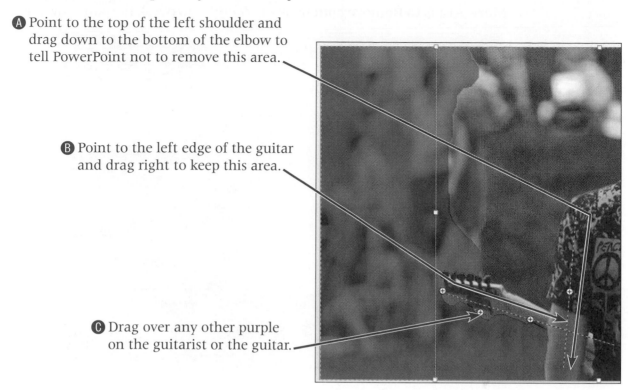

12. Choose **Background Removal→Refine→Mark Areas to Remove**.

13. Follow these steps to define areas to be removed:

Ⓐ Drag over the background to tell PowerPoint to remove this area.

Ⓑ Drag over this section to remove it as well.

14. You will probably have to go back and forth with the **Mark Areas to Keep** and **Mark Areas to Remove** buttons as you continue to tweak the purple overlay.

15. Choose **Background Removal→Close→Keep Changes**.

16. Drag the image to the right so all three bulleted paragraphs are visible. If your slide doesn't resemble the following figure, choose **Picture Tools→Format→Adjust→Remove Background** to adjust the overlay.

Part of the image extends to the right beyond the slide. While it may look strange in Normal view, it will look fine as a slide show. The areas outside the slide will not display.

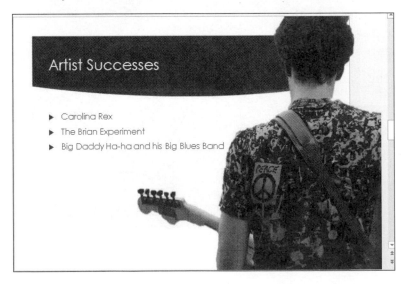

17. Save your presentation.

Applying Artistic Effects

Video Library http://labyrinthelab.com/videos Video Number: PP13-V0306

PowerPoint 2013 includes artistic effects that can be applied to pictures, making photographs look like pencil sketches, cement, or pastels. Additionally, pictures can be recolored to create a color cast that blends with your theme.

The picture before any effect has been applied

The picture after the Pencil Sketch and Recolor effects have been applied

QUICK REFERENCE	MODIFYING PICTURES
Task	**Procedure**
Remove a background	■ Select the picture and choose Picture Tools→Format→Adjust→Remove Background.
	■ Adjust the marquee to include the portion of the picture you want to keep.
	■ Choose Background Removal→Refine→Mark Areas to Keep and drag over additional areas to include.
	■ Choose Background Removal→Refine→Mark Areas to Remove and drag over additional areas to exclude.
	■ Choose Background Removal→Refine→Keep Changes.
	■ Choose Picture Tools→Format→Adjust→Remove Background to adjust the background removal at any time.
Apply artistic effects	■ Select the picture and choose Picture Tools→Format→Adjust→Artistic Effects.
	■ Choose an effect to apply the default settings, or choose Artistic Effects Options to customize the settings.
	■ If you choose to customize, choose an effect from the drop-down menu, adjust the settings, and click Close.

Apply Artistic Effects

In this exercise, you will apply artistic effects to a picture to enhance its visual appeal.

1. Save your file as **PP03-D06-Animation-[FirstInitialLastName]**.

2. If necessary, select the picture on the sixth slide, **Artistic Successes**.

3. Choose **Picture Tools→Format→Adjust→Artistic Effects**.

4. Point to several effects to see how they change the picture on the slide. Notice that a ToolTip appears when you point to an effect, indicating its name.

5. Select the **Pencil Grayscale** effect.

6. Choose **Picture Tools→Format→Adjust→Color**.

7. Point to several color adjustments to see how they change the picture on the slide. *Notice the ToolTip that appears.*

8. Select the **Teal, Accent Color 5 Light** adjustment.

9. Save your presentation.

Inserting a Screenshot

Video Library   http://labyrinthelab.com/videos   Video Number: PP13-V0307

Sometimes you may want to include a picture of something on your computer screen, such as a program window or web page, in a presentation. PowerPoint's Screenshot tool lets you insert a picture of any open window or program or drag on your screen to define an area to insert.

The Screenshot command is available on the Insert tab.

You can insert any open window as a picture.

You can drag on the screen to define an area to capture.

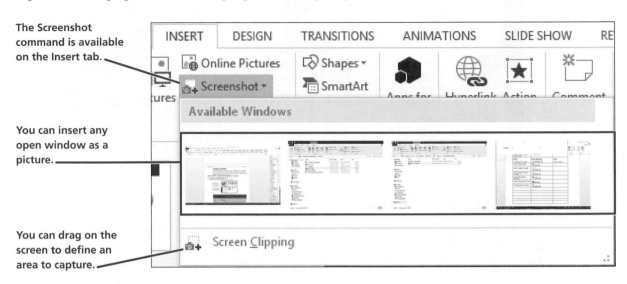

QUICK REFERENCE	INSERTING A SCREENSHOT
Task	**Procedure**
Insert a picture of an entire program window	■ Start the program or open the window you want to capture.
	■ Return to PowerPoint and choose the desired slide.
	■ Choose Insert→Images→Screenshot menu ▼→desired screenshot.
Insert a picture of a portion of the screen	■ Display the program or window you wish to insert.
	■ Return to PowerPoint and choose the desired slide.
	■ Choose Insert→Images→Screenshot menu ▼→Screen Clipping.
	■ Drag to define the area you wish to insert, or tap Esc to leave the Screen Clipping tool.

Working with Shapes

Video Library   http://labyrinthelab.com/videos   Video Number: PP13-V0308

PowerPoint offers more than 150 shapes that you can add to your slides. You can use these shapes to build your own custom flowcharts, mathematical equations, speech and thought bubbles, or other design. Shapes can even include text.

PowerPoint 2013

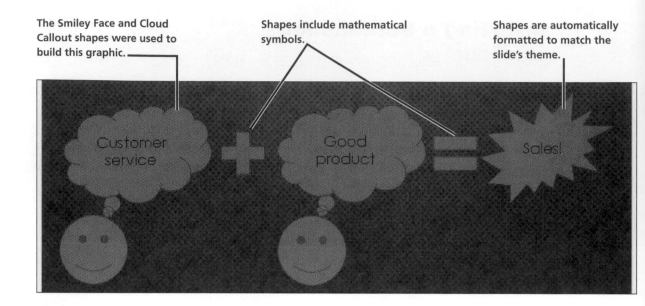

The Smiley Face and Cloud Callout shapes were used to build this graphic.

Shapes include mathematical symbols.

Shapes are automatically formatted to match the slide's theme.

Adding a Shape

When adding a shape to a slide, you can stretch it to make it wider/narrower or taller/shorter. All shapes are preformatted with a specific ratio of width to height, so stretching a shape can sometimes make it appear unbalanced. You can use the Shift key to maintain the original width-to-height ratio.

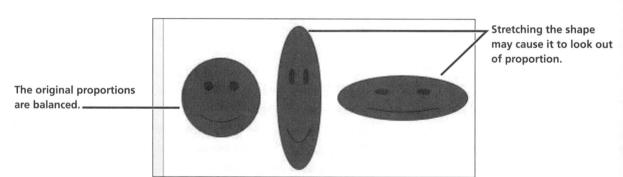

The original proportions are balanced.

Stretching the shape may cause it to look out of proportion.

Adding Text to a Shape

You can easily add text to a shape, but the text does not automatically resize itself to fit nicely. Text will, however, automatically wrap to the next line so there is no need to tap Enter as you type.

Text will automatically wrap to the next line but will not automatically get smaller to fit inside the shape.

You may need to adjust the text size to get it to fit.

Task	Procedure
Add a shape	■ Choose Insert→Illustrations→Shapes ▼. ■ Select the desired shape and then drag on the slide to draw the shape. ■ Hold [Shift] as you drag the shape to maintain the original proportions.
Add text to a shape	■ Add a shape to a slide. ■ With the shape selected and displaying a solid border, start typing.

Resizing a Shape

Shapes can be resized and rotated just like clip art. Additionally, some shapes include a yellow square that you can use to change the shape's properties. For example, you can change the Smiley Face shape to a frown or you can change the head and body of an arrow shape.

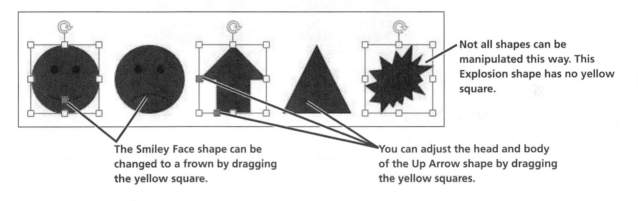

Not all shapes can be manipulated this way. This Explosion shape has no yellow square.

The Smiley Face shape can be changed to a frown by dragging the yellow square.

You can adjust the head and body of the Up Arrow shape by dragging the yellow squares.

Merging Shapes

New in PowerPoint is the ability to merge shapes. This feature allows you to create your own custom shape by combining existing shapes into a single one. The benefit of this is that your new custom shape has a single outline and truly looks like a single shape rather than several overlapped shapes.

PowerPoint 2013

The Merge Shapes command is available from the Drawing Tools→Format tab.

DRAWING TOOLS

NSERT DESIGN TRANSITIONS ANIMATIONS SLIDE SHOW REVIEW VIEW FORMAT

Abc Abc Abc

Shape Fill ▾
Shape Outline ▾
Shape Effects ▾

A A A

Bring Fo
Send Bac
Selection

Union
Combine
Fragment
Intersect
Subtract

Shape Styles

WordArt Styles

Non-merged shapes look like they are overlapped.

Merged shapes have a single outline.

Formatting Shapes and Shape Text

While shapes and the text they contain are automatically formatted to match the slide's theme, you may want a more exciting look such as a drop-shadow or three-dimensional effect. Adding a Shape Style or WordArt Style can make your shape graphics really pop.

This is the original shape and text.

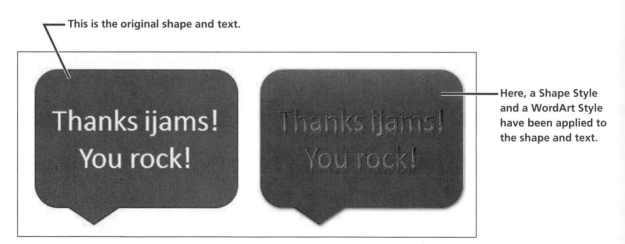

Thanks ijams! You rock!

Thanks ijams! You rock!

Here, a Shape Style and a WordArt Style have been applied to the shape and text.

QUICK REFERENCE	FORMATTING A SHAPE AND SHAPE TEXT
Task	**Procedure**
Format a shape	▪ Select the desired shape.
	▪ Choose a command from Drawing Tools→Format→Shape Styles.
Format shape text	▪ Select the desired shape.
	▪ Choose a command from Drawing Tools→Format→WordArt Styles.

DEVELOP YOUR SKILLS PP03-D07

Add and Format a Shape with Text

In this exercise, you will add and format a shape with text.

1. Save your file as **PP03-D07-Animation-[FirstInitialLastName]**.

2. Display the seventh slide, **Carolina Rex**.

3. Choose **Insert→Illustrations→Shapes ▼→Stars and Banners→5-Point Star**.

4. Hold Shift as you drag on the slide to create a star shape.

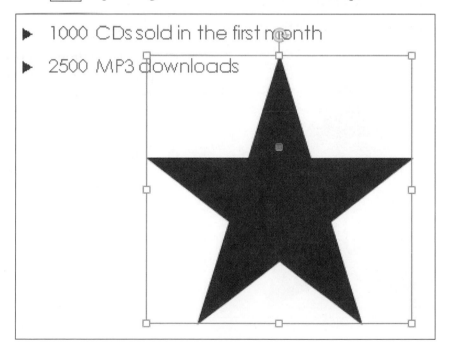

5. Type the following: `Top Seller!`

Your star shape should resemble this figure, though your text may fit on a single line.

6. Click the dashed border of the shape so it turns solid.

When the shape is selected, you can format its text.

7. Choose **Home→Font→Font Size ▼→44**.

The font size increases, but the text no longer fits nicely inside the shape. You will fix this in the next few steps.

Customize the Shape

8. Follow these steps to change the shape of the star and make the text fit nicely:

A Drag the **yellow square** up a little bit to change the shape of the star.

B Try to match your star shape to the figure. You may have to drag the yellow diamond up or down.

Format the Shape and Text

9. Choose **Drawing Tools→Format→Shape Styles→More→Intense Effect – Purple, Accent 6**.

    The shape changes color and appears three-dimensional. However, the text remains the same.

10. Choose **Drawing Tools→Format→WordArt Styles→More→Fill – White, Outline – Accent 1, Shadow**.

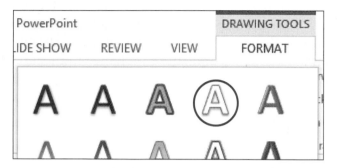

The text within the shape changes.

11. If necessary, change the size of the star shape so the text fits on two lines.

12. Save your presentation.

Working with Slide Transitions

Video Library http://labyrinthelab.com/videos   Video Number: PP13-V0309

A slide transition is the animation between slides. Used properly, these transitions can add zest and excitement to your presentation and provide a distinct breaking point between slides. PowerPoint 2013 includes many transitions that are often used in video production, such as 3-D rotations and other animated effects.

The Vortex transition occurring between two slides

PowerPoint 2013

Consistency within a presentation helps keep the audience focused. Avoid using different transitions within a single presentation.

Creating Transitions in Slide Sorter View

Most of the time, you will want to apply the same transition to the entire presentation. Maintaining a consistent transition style looks more professional (less haphazard) and is less distracting for the audience. Using the Slide Sorter view is a quick and easy way to accomplish this task. You can apply transitions to a single slide, multiple slides, or all slides in a presentation. When you apply a transition, it animates the change from one slide to another, not individual elements of the slide.

Selecting Slides for Transitions

To easily select all slides in a presentation from Slide Sorter view, click to select any slide and then press Ctrl + A. All slides will be selected. Then, choose Transitions→Transitions to This Slide and select a transition effect. The transition will be applied to all selected slides. You can also use this method from the Normal view's Slides panel to select all slides in a presentation.

To apply a transition to a single slide, select a single slide in either Normal or Slide Sorter view and then choose a slide transition. The transition will be applied to the selected slide.

The Transitions Tab

The Transitions tab contains the Transitions to This Slide group, which you use to implement your slide transitions. The Transitions tab contains commands to apply transitions, sound, and other transition options.

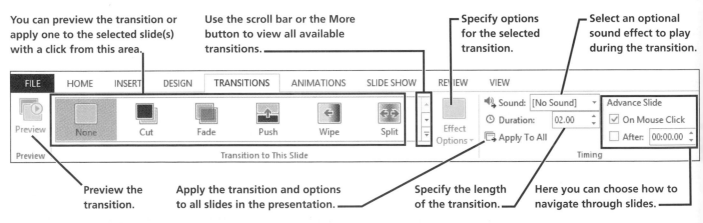

QUICK REFERENCE | ADDING TRANSITIONS TO A PRESENTATION

Task	Procedure
Add transitions to an entire presentation	■ From Slide Sorter view, press Ctrl + A. ■ Choose Transitions→Transition to This Slide and select the desired transition.
Set a transition for individual slides	■ Select the desired slide(s). (Remember that transitions are seen when navigating to a slide when a slide loads.) ■ Choose Transitions→Transition to This Slide and select the desired transition.

Apply Transition Effects

In this exercise, you will apply a transition to all slides except the title slide to make the slide show more interesting.

Choose Transition Effects

1. Save your file as **PP03-D08-Animation-[FirstInitialLastName]**.

2. Choose **View→Presentation Views→Slide Sorter** ▦.

3. Choose the **Transitions** tab.

4. Click the **Our Services** slide to select it.

5. Use Shift+click on the **Contact Us** slide.
   Slides 2–11 are selected.

6. Follow these steps to apply a transition effect to the selected slides:

Ⓑ Choose **Vortex**. A preview of the transition appears on each slide.

Ⓐ Click the **More** button and locate the Exciting category.

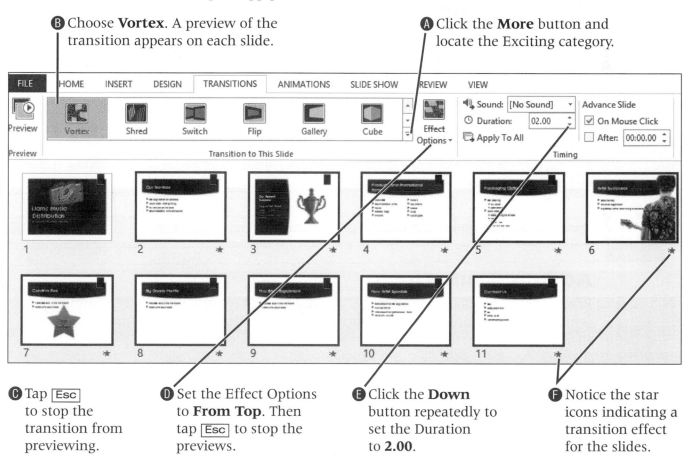

Ⓒ Tap Esc to stop the transition from previewing.

Ⓓ Set the Effect Options to **From Top**. Then tap Esc to stop the previews.

Ⓔ Click the **Down** button repeatedly to set the Duration to **2.00**.

Ⓕ Notice the star icons indicating a transition effect for the slides.

The title slide does not have the star icon because there is no transition applied to it.

Run the Presentation

7. Choose **Slide Show→Start Slide Show→From Beginning** .

   The title slide appears without a transition. The title slide would have opened with the Vortex transition if you had applied the transition to it.

8. Click the mouse button to advance to the next slide.

   The Vortex transition effect displays as the slides advance.

9. Continue to click the mouse button until you reach the end of the presentation and the Slide Sorter window reappears.

10. Save your presentation.

Using Slide Animation

Video Library http://labyrinthelab.com/videos   Video Number: PP13-V0310

Whereas transitions are applied to slides as a whole, animations are applied to individual objects *within* a slide. Animations begin only after any transition effect is completed. Some examples of animation include the following:

- A clip art image that moves across the slide to its final location
- A slide that starts out empty, and then has a title and other elements that fade into view with a mouse click
- Bulleted paragraphs that fly in from the bottom of the slide, one by one, each time the presenter clicks with the mouse

Less is more. Animation can distract an audience, so use it sparingly.

Adding Animations

PowerPoint offers more than 40 animations you can add to objects on a slide by using a single command. For example, the Fade animation tells PowerPoint to gradually make objects on a slide fade into view after any transition effect is completed.

None removes an animation from an object.

Point to an animation to preview it. Click an animation to apply it.

Animations not represented by icons within the gallery can be accessed here.

Commonly used animations are available from the Animations tab on the Ribbon.

Additional animations may be previewed by scrolling down.

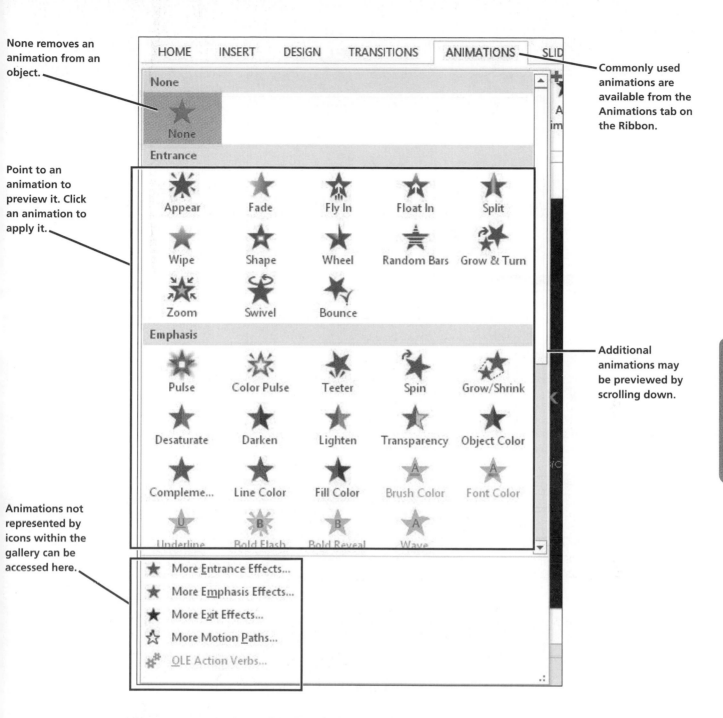

Setting Animation Options

After applying an animation to an object, you will likely want to set the animation options to control exactly how the animation effect works. The available options differ based on whether the animation was applied to text or an image. The options also differ based on the animation itself. Additionally, you can set timing options to control the speed of the animation.

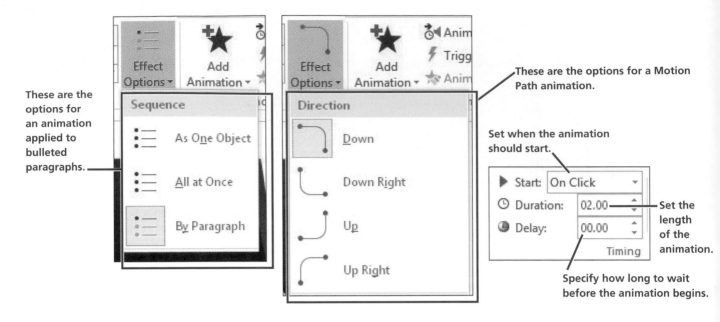

These are the options for an animation applied to bulleted paragraphs.

These are the options for a Motion Path animation.

Set when the animation should start.

Set the length of the animation.

Specify how long to wait before the animation begins.

QUICK REFERENCE	ADDING ANIMATION TO SLIDES
Task	**Procedure**
Apply a common animation to an object on a slide	■ Display the slide containing the object(s) to be animated. ■ Select the object (text object, picture, etc.) on the slide you wish to animate. ■ Choose Animations→Animation; choose the desired animation.
Set animation options	■ Select the object containing the animation. ■ Choose Animation→Animation→Effect Options menu ▼ and then choose the desired option. ■ Set the options in the Animation→Timing group if desired.
Remove an animation	■ Select the object containing the animation. ■ Choose Animation→Animation→None.

DEVELOP YOUR SKILLS PP03-D09
Apply Animation to Bulleted Paragraphs

In this exercise, you will apply an animation to text objects on a slide to draw attention to them.

1. Save your file as **PP03-D09-Animation-[FirstInitialLastName]**.

2. Choose **View→Presentation Views→Normal** ▣.

3. Display the **Our Services** slide.

4. Click once in the **bulleted text** so a dashed border appears around the text box.

5. Choose **Animations→Animation→More→Entrance→Float In**.

   The animation previews, and you see each first-level paragraph animate across the slide.

6. Choose **Animations→Animation→Effect Option→Float Down** to have the paragraphs animate from the top of the slide down.

   The numbers next to each bulleted paragraph indicate the order in which the animation is applied. By default, each paragraph will animate after a mouse click.

7. Choose **Slide Show→Start Slide Show→From Beginning** to start the slide show.

8. Click anywhere with the mouse to advance to the second slide.

   The transition effect animates, but no bulleted paragraph appears yet.

9. Click anywhere with the mouse.

   The first bulleted paragraph animates into view.

10. Continue clicking until all four bulleted paragraphs are visible and the slide show advances to the third slide, Our Recent Success.

11. Tap Esc to end the slide show and return to Normal view.

12. Save your presentation.

Using the Animation Pane

Video Library   http://labyrinthelab.com/videos   Video Number: PP13-V0311

By using the Animation pane, you have many more choices for effects than you have in the animation menu you used previously. You can also individually set the animation for each element on a slide. When using the Animation pane, you can control the visual effects, timing, and sequencing of the animation process. For example, rather than having to click each time to display the next animated bulleted paragraph, you can set it so that the animation starts automatically after the slide transition and continues until all objects on the slide have been animated.

Budgeting Your Time

Using the Animation pane to customize each animation is a time-consuming process. Be prepared to spend a significant amount of time selecting each animated object individually and then setting its options. The following figure describes the options on the Animation pane.

PowerPoint 2013

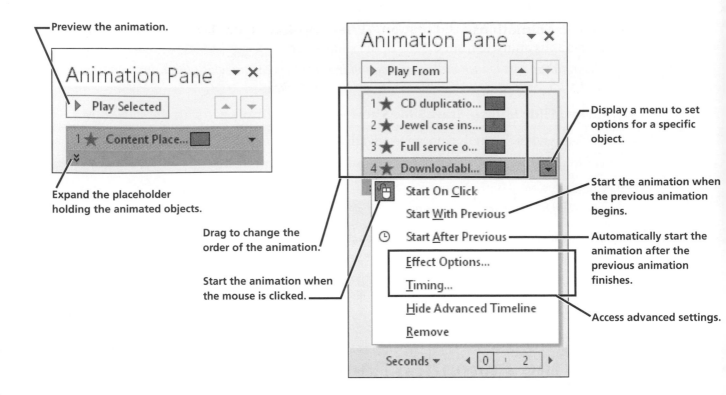

Preview the animation.

Expand the placeholder holding the animated objects.

Drag to change the order of the animation.

Start the animation when the mouse is clicked.

Display a menu to set options for a specific object.

Start the animation when the previous animation begins.

Automatically start the animation after the previous animation finishes.

Access advanced settings.

Use the Animation Pane

In this exercise, you will use the Animation pane to configure the bulleted paragraphs to animate automatically after the slide transition completes. This reduces the need for you to click constantly during a slide show.

1. Save your file as **PP03-D10-Animation-[FirstInitialLastName]**.

2. Display the second slide, **Our Services**.

3. Click once in the bulleted text so a dashed border appears around the text box.

4. Choose **Animations→Advanced Animation→Animation Pane**.
   The Animation pane displays on the right side of the screen.

5. Follow these steps to begin to configure the advanced animation settings:

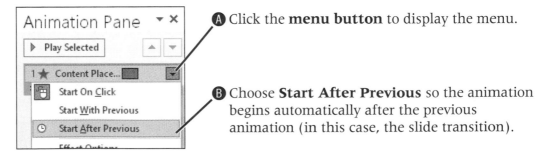

A Click the **menu button** to display the menu.

B Choose **Start After Previous** so the animation begins automatically after the previous animation (in this case, the slide transition).

Notice that the numbers next to each bulleted paragraph in the Animation panel have changed to zeros, indicating their animations all happen at the same time, automatically, after the slide transition.

6. Click the **Click to Expand Contents** bar to show each individual paragraph.

7. Follow these steps to customize the animation for the last paragraph:

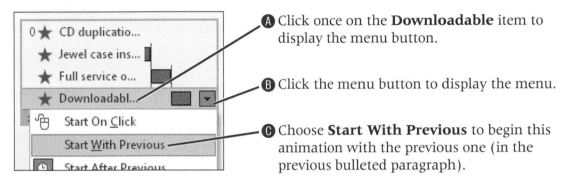

Ⓐ Click once on the **Downloadable** item to display the menu button.

Ⓑ Click the menu button to display the menu.

Ⓒ Choose **Start With Previous** to begin this animation with the previous one (in the previous bulleted paragraph).

8. Choose **Slide Show→Start Slide Show→From Beginning**.

9. Click anywhere with the mouse to advance to the second slide.

   The bulleted paragraphs animate automatically after the slide transition ends. Each animation happens sequentially, except for the last bulleted paragraph, which animates with the previous item.

10. Tap ⌈Esc⌉ to end the slide show and return to Normal view.

11. Save your presentation.

Adding Sound Effects

Video Library http://labyrinthelab.com/videos Video Number: PP13-V0312

PowerPoint 2013 provides audio clips and sound effects to accompany or accentuate your slide elements. For example, you may attach sound effects to slide transitions or animations. You can use the Transitions tab to add a sound to a slide transition or the Animation pane to add a sound to an animation.

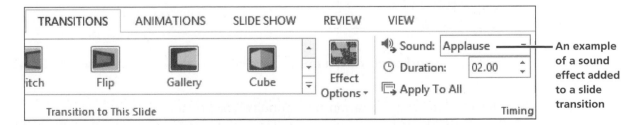

An example of a sound effect added to a slide transition

Adding a Sound Effect to an Animation

Sometimes you don't want a sound effect to play during a slide transition, but rather when an animation causes an object to move across the slide. The following table describes the steps used to apply sound effects to animations.

QUICK REFERENCE	ADDING SOUND TO SLIDES
Task	**Procedure**
Add sound to an animation	■ Display the slide with the animation to which you wish to add sound (or add an animation to the slide object).
	■ Choose Animations→Advanced Animation→Animation Pane.
	■ Click the menu button for the object to receive sound and choose Effect Options.
	■ In the Enhancements section of the dialog box, choose the sound you wish to apply; click OK.
Add sound to a transition	■ Select a slide from the Slides panel or Slide Sorter view.
	■ Choose Transitions→Timing→Sound menu and then select a sound effect. The sound will play as the selected slide loads.

DEVELOP YOUR SKILLS PP03-D11

Apply Sound Effects

In this exercise, you will apply two sounds to the presentation to enhance an animation.

1. Save your file as **PP03-D11-Animation-[FirstInitialLastName]**.

2. Choose the **Our Recent Success** slide and then select the clip art object.

3. Choose **Animations→Animation→More→Entrance→Bounce**.

4. Click the drop-down menu for the clip art animation in the Animation pane and choose **Effect Options**.

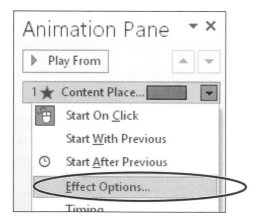

5. Click the **Sound drop-down menu** in the Effect tab and choose the **Applause** sound effect.

6. Click **OK**, and the animation and sound will be previewed.

Apply a Transition Sound Effect

7. Display the **Our Services** slide.

8. Follow these steps to add a transition sound effect:

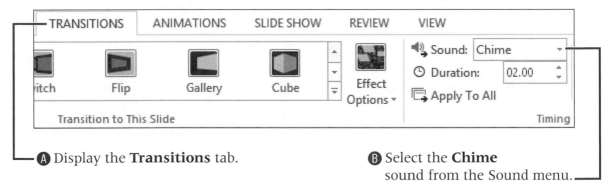

Ⓐ Display the **Transitions** tab.

Ⓑ Select the **Chime** sound from the Sound menu.

PowerPoint applies the Chime sound to the transition effect for this slide.

9. Choose **Slide Show→Start Slide Show→From Beginning** 🔁.

10. Navigate through the presentation until you hear the applause and see the Bounce animation on the Our Recent Success slide.

You may not be able to hear the sound effect if your computer does not have speakers.

11. Press the ⌷Esc⌷ key to end the slide show early and return to Normal view.

12. Close the **Animation pane**.

13. Save your presentation and exit **PowerPoint**.

Concepts Review

To check your knowledge of the key concepts introduced in this lesson, complete the Concepts Review quiz by choosing the appropriate access option below.

If you are...	Then access the quiz by...
Using the Labyrinth Video Library	Going to http://labyrinthelab.com/videos
Using eLab	Logging in, choosing Content, and navigating to the Concepts Review quiz for this lesson
Not using the Labyrinth Video Library or eLab	Going to the student resource center for this book

Reinforce Your Skills

Work with Images

In this exercise, you will add clip art to the Kids for Change animation presentation to add visual interest.

Prepare a Slide for ClipArt

1. Start **PowerPoint**. Open **PP03-R01-KidsClipArt** from the **PP2013 Lesson 03** folder and save it as `PP03-R01-KidsClipArt-[FirstInitialLastName]`.

2. Choose the **Events** slide (the second slide).

3. Choose **Home→Slides→Layout→Two Content**.

Insert ClipArt

4. Click the **Online Pictures** ![icon] icon on the slide to display the Insert Pictures search window.

5. Type `calendar` in the Office.com search box and tap [Enter].

6. Scroll through the results until you find an appropriate image.

7. Choose a clip art image that appeals to you and click **Insert**.

Move and Size Clip Art

8. Drag any of the image's corner handles to resize it so it fills the right half of the slide.

9. Drag from the center of the image to move and position it so it does not overlap any text.

10. Drag the rotate handle above the top edge of the image to rotate it slightly for visual interest.

Format Clip Art

11. Locate the **Picture Tools→Format→Picture Styles** group of commands.

12. Point to several of the thumbnail samples in the **Picture Styles gallery** to preview them and then click one to apply it. Choose a style that works well with your image. The following figure shows the **Reflected Rounded Rectangle** style applied.

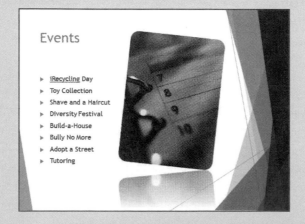

Remove a Background

13. Display the **Contact Us** slide.

14. Choose **Insert→Images→Pictures**.

15. Browse to your **PP2013 Lesson 03** folder and insert the **PP03-R01-Phone** image.

16. With the phone image selected on the slide, choose **Picture Tools→Format→ Adjust→Remove Background**.

17. Drag the handles of the Background Removal border so the phone and wire are inside the border and then choose **Background Removal→Close→Keep Changes**.

Apply Artistic Effects

18. With the phone image selected on the slide, choose **Picture Tools→Format→Adjust→ Artistic Effects→Pencil Sketch**.

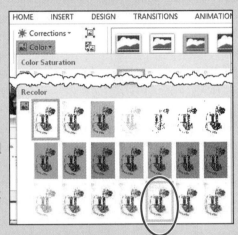

19. Choose **Picture Tools→Format→Adjust→Color →Recolor→Dark Green, Accent Color 4 Light**.

20. Move the phone, if necessary, so it is roughly centered below the phone number.

21. Save the changes and then exit **PowerPoint**. Submit your final file based on the guidelines provided by your instructor.

    To view examples of how your file or files should look at the end of this exercise, go to the student resource center.

REINFORCE YOUR SKILLS PP03-R02

Add Shapes and Animations

In this exercise, you will create a custom shape of a house and incorporate animation to add visual appeal to the presentation.

Add and Resize a Shape

1. Start **PowerPoint**. Open **PP03-R02-KidsAnimated** from the **PP2013 Lesson 03** folder and save it as **PP03-R02-KidsAnimated-[FirstInitialLastName]**.

2. Display the second slide, **This Month**.

3. Choose **Insert→Illustrations→Shapes→Rectangles→Rectangle**.

4. Drag on the slide to draw a rectangle. Resize and move it so it roughly matches this figure.

5. Choose **Insert→Illustrations→Shapes→Basic Shapes→Isosceles Triangle**.

6. Drag on the slide to draw a triangle to act as the roof of the house. Resize and move it so it roughly matches the figure in step 8.

7. Choose **Insert→Illustrations→Shapes→Rectangles→Rectangle**.

8. Drag on the slide to draw a small rectangle to act as a chimney. Resize and move it so it roughly matches this figure.

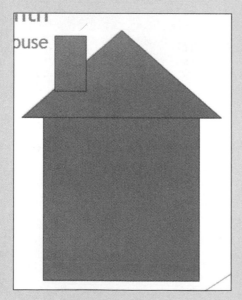

Merge Shapes

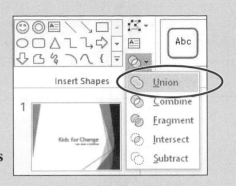

9. Click the large rectangle on the slide to select it, Shift+click the triangular roof, and Shift+click the small chimney so that all three shapes are selected.

10. Choose **Drawing Tools→Format→Insert Shapes→Merge Shapes→Union**.

11. Choose **Insert→Illustrations→Shapes→Rectangles →Rectangle**.

12. Drag on the slide to draw a rectangle to act as the door. Resize and move it so it roughly matches this figure.

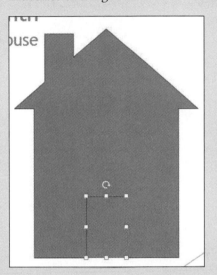

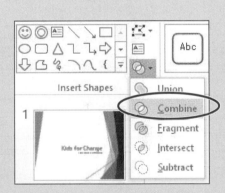

13. Click the door shape to select it, if necessary, and then Shift+click the house so both shapes are selected.

14. Choose **Drawing Tools→Format→Insert Shapes→Merge Shapes→Combine**.

Format and Add Text to a Shape

15. Click the dashed border of the shape to select it.

16. Type **Home** Enter **Sweet** Enter **Home** Enter.

17. Click the dashed border of the shape to select it.

18. Choose **Home→Font→Font Size→36**. If your text no longer fits in the shape, choose a smaller font size or adjust the size of the house shape.

19. Choose **Drawing Tools→Format→Shape Styles→More→Intense Effect – Blue, Accent 2** (the bottom thumbnail in the third column).

20. Resize and move the shape so it fits in the upper-right area of the slide. You may have to adjust the font size.

Apply Transition Effects

21. Select slide 2, **This Month**, in the Slides panel.

22. ⌈Shift⌉+click the last slide in the Slides panel so all but the title slide are selected.

23. Choose **Transitions→Transition to This Slide→More→Random Bars**.

Add Animation

24. Display the second slide, **This Month**, if necessary.

25. Click the house shape to select it.

26. Choose **Animations→Animation→More→Entrance→Bounce**.

27. Choose **Animations→Timing→Start→After Previous**.

28. Click the up arrow on the **Animations→Timing→Delay** box four times to set the delay to 1 second.

29. Display the third slide, **Event Benefits**.

30. Click in any text in the left column so a dashed border appears around the text box.

31. Choose **Animations→Animation→More→Entrance→Float In**.

32. Click in any of the text in the right column so a dashed border appears around the text box.

33. Choose **Animations→Animation→More→Entrance→Float In**.

34. Choose **Animations→Advanced Animation→Animation Pane**.

35. Click the arrows to expand the top group of content in the Animation pane.

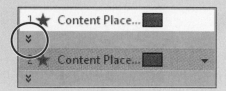

36. Click the second item, **Homeless families**, to display its menu button.

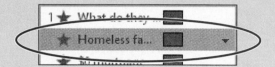

37. Click the item's menu button and then choose **Start After Previous**.

38. Click the third item, **$0 mortgage**, to display its menu button.

39. Click the item's menu button and then choose **Start After Previous**.

40. Click the fourth item, **A fresh start**, to display its menu button.

41. Click the item's menu button and then choose **Start After Previous**.

42. Expand the contents of the second group of content and set each item in the second group to **Start After Previous**.

Add a Sound Effect to an Animation

43. Display the second slide, **This Month**.

44. Click the house shape to select it.

45. Click the single item in the Animation pane, click its menu button, and choose **Effect Options** to view the effect's options.

46. Set the **Sound** menu to **Whoosh** and then click **OK**.

47. Close the **Animation pane**.

48. Choose **Slide Show→Start Slide Show→From Beginning** and click each slide until the slide show ends and you return to Normal view.

49. Save the changes and then exit **PowerPoint**. Submit your final file based on the guidelines provided by your instructor.

To view examples of how your file or files should look at the end of this exercise, go to the student resource center.

Add Visual Interest

In this exercise, you will add images and animation to a presentation.

Prepare a Slide for ClipArt

1. Start **PowerPoint**. Open **PP03-R03-KidsVisual** from the **PP2013 Lesson 03** folder and save it as **PP03-R03-KidsVisual-[FirstInitialLastName]**.

2. Display the third slide.

3. Choose **Home→Slides→Layout→Two Content**.

Insert ClipArt

4. Click the **Pictures** icon on the slide to insert a picture from your computer.

5. Browse to your **PP2013 Lesson 03** folder and insert the **PP03-R03-Girl** picture.

6. Drag the picture to roughly fill the right side of the slide.

7. Display the fourth slide.

8. Choose **Home→Slides→Layout→Two Content**.

9. Click the **Pictures** icon on the slide to insert a picture from your computer.

10. Browse to your **PP2013 Lesson 03** folder and insert the **PP03-R03-Truck** picture.

11. Drag the truck picture to roughly center it on the slide.

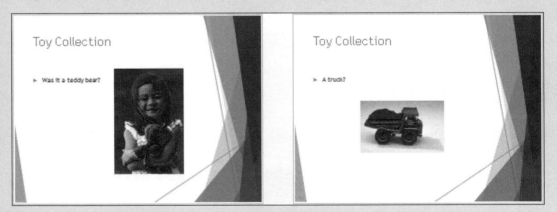

12. Display the fifth slide.

13. Choose **Insert→Images→Online Pictures**.

14. Type **toy** in the Office.com search box and tap Enter.

15. Scroll through the results until you find a toy you like, and then click the toy to select it.

16. Continue to scroll and look for more toys. Ctrl + click additional toys to add them to your selection. After you have selected a total of six toys, click **Insert**.

Move, Size, and Rotate ClipArt

17. Click an empty area of the slide to deselect the inserted pictures.

18. Click one of the toys on the slide to select it.

19. Drag a corner handle on the picture's border to make the picture smaller.

20. Drag the rotate handle above the top edge of the picture to slightly rotate it.

21. Drag the picture to move it to a position of your liking.

22. Resize, rotate, and move the remaining toys so your slide roughly matches the following figure. *Do not be concerned if the picture backgrounds overlap each other at this point.*

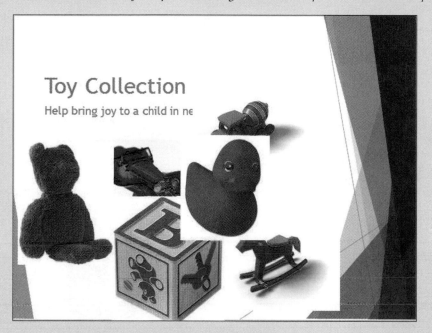

Format Clip Art

23. Display the third slide and click the picture of the girl and her teddy bear.

24. Choose **Picture Tools→Format→Picture Styles→More→Rotated, White**.

25. Drag the picture to reposition it, if necessary.

Remove a Background

26. Display slide 4 and click the truck picture.

27. Choose **Picture Tools→Format→Adjust→Remove Background**.

28. Drag the handles of the background removal border until the truck fits inside it.

29. Choose **Background Removal→Refine→Mark Areas to Remove**.

30. Drag on the light colored areas on the ground near the tires to remove them.

31. Choose **Background Removal→Close→Keep Changes**.

32. Drag a corner handle of the truck's border to resize it and then drag the truck into position so it roughly matches the following figure.

33. Display slide 5 and remove the background of the pictures so they can be overlapped.

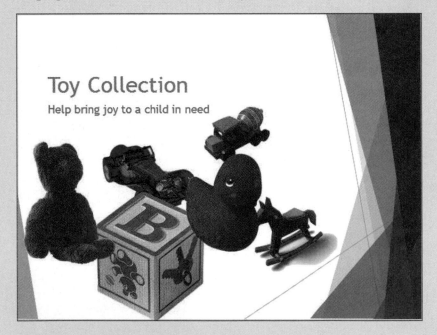

Apply Artistic Effects

34. Display slide 3 and click the picture of the girl.

35. Choose **Picture Tools→Format→Adjust→Artistic Effects→Glow, Diffused**.

Add and Format a Shape with Text

36. Choose **Insert→Illustrations→Shapes→Stars and Banners→Up Ribbon**.

37. [Shift]+drag to create a proportional ribbon that fills the left side of the slide under the text.

38. Type **My 1st toy**.

39. Click the blue ribbon shape to select it.

40. Tap [Ctrl]+[C] to copy the shape.

41. Display the fourth slide with the truck.

42. Tap [Ctrl]+[V] to paste the shape.

43. Drag the truck picture so the blue ribbon doesn't overlap it.

44. Click the blue ribbon shape to select it.

45. Choose **Drawing Tools→Format→Shape Styles→Shape Effects→Reflection→Reflection Variations→Half Reflection, Touching**.

46. Choose **Home→Clipboard→Format Painter** to copy the formatting.

47. Display the third slide and click the blue ribbon to duplicate the shape's effect.

Apply Transition Effects

48. Choose **View→Presentation Views→Slide Sorter**.

49. Click slide 2 and then [Shift]+click slide 5 so that all but the title slide are selected.

50. Choose **Transitions→Transition to This Slide→More→Exciting→Vortex**.

51. Choose **Transitions→Transition to This Slide→Effect Options→From Top**.

52. Click the down arrow of the **Transitions→Timing→Duration** box until the Duration is set to **02.00**.

Apply Animation

53. Double-click slide 5 to display it in **Normal** view.

54. Click one of the toys on the slide to select it.

55. Choose **Animations→Animation→More→Entrance→Grow & Turn**.

56. Click a second toy on the slide to select it.

57. Choose **Animations→Animation→More→Entrance→Grow & Turn**.

58. One at a time, click each remaining toy and apply the **Grow & Turn** animation.

Use the Animation Pane

59. Choose **Animations→Advanced Animation→Animation Pane**.

60. Click the first animated item in the Animation pane to display its menu button.

61. Click the menu button and choose **Start After Previous**.

62. One at a time, click each remaining item and set them to **Start After Previous**.

Add a Sound Effect to an Animation

63. Click the last item in the Animation pane, click its menu button, and choose **Effect Options**.

64. Set the sound effect to **Applause** and then click **OK**.

65. Close the **Animation** pane.

66. Choose **Slide Show→Start Slide Show→From Beginning** and click each slide to view the presentation, returning to **Normal** view when you are finished.

67. Save the changes and then exit **PowerPoint**. Submit your final file based on the guidelines provided by your instructor.

Apply Your Skills

Work with Images

In this exercise, you will add pictures and remove the backgrounds for the Universal Corporate Events presentation. You will also format the pictures to enhance the visual appeal of the slides.

Prepare a Slide for and Insert Clip Art

1. Start **PowerPoint**. Open **PP03-A01-UniversalClipArt** from the **PP2013 Lesson 03** folder and save it as `PP03-A01-UniversalClipArt-[FirstInitialLastName]`.

2. Choose the **Catering** slide (the third slide).

3. Apply the **Two Content** layout.

4. Apply the **Two Content** layout to slides 4–9.

5. Display slide 3.

6. Click the **Online Pictures** icon on the slide to display the Insert Pictures search window.

7. Search for and insert a photo appropriate for a catering slide.

8. Search for and insert an appropriate photograph on slides 4–9. The photograph should represent the slide's text content.

Move, Size, and Rotate Objects

9. Resize and reposition the photographs on each slide so they fill the right half of the slide.

Format Clip Art

10. Add a **Picture Style** or **Picture Effect** to each photograph. Use a maximum of two styles of effects.

Remove a Background and Apply Artistic Effects

11. Remove the backgrounds of each photo. You may want to resize or move the photos after removing the background.

12. Display slide 5, **Graphic Design**, and apply an **Artistic Effect** to the photo.

13. Save the changes and then exit **PowerPoint**. Submit your final file based on the guidelines provided by your instructor.

    To view examples of how your file or files should look at the end of this exercise, go to the student resource center.

Add Shapes and Animations

In this exercise, you will add shapes and animation to a presentation.

Add and Resize a Shape with Text

1. Start **PowerPoint**. Open **PP03-A02-UniversalAnimated** from the **PP2013 Lesson 03** folder and save it as **PP03-A02-UniversalAnimated-[FirstInitialLastName]**.

2. Display the third slide, **Vegan**.

3. Insert the **Explosion 1** shape.

4. Type **Certified Vegan!**

5. Resize and reposition the shape so it fills the area below the text.

6. Enlarge the font size of the shape's text to be as large as possible while remaining inside the shape.

7. Add the **Explosion 2** shape to slide 4 with the text **Certified Kosher!**

8. Resize and reposition the **shape** so it fills the area below the text.

9. Enlarge the font size of the shape's text to be as large as possible while remaining inside the shape.

10. Add the **Up Ribbon** shape to slide 5 with the text **Certified Organic!**

11. Resize and reposition the shape so it fills the area below the text.

12. Enlarge the font size of the shape's text to be as large as possible while remaining inside the shape.

Merge and Format Shapes

13. Display the last slide.

14. Insert a **Rectangle** shape and resize it so it is tall and thin.

15. Insert a **Teardrop** shape and adjust the size and shape so it looks like a candle flame. Position it on top of the thin rectangle.

16. Merge the **Rectangle** and **Teardrop** shapes into a single candle shape.

17. Copy the new candle shape and paste three copies on the slide, arranging them similarly to the following figure.

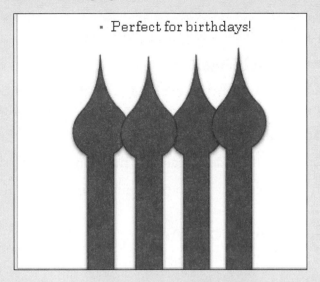

18. Apply the **Intense Effect – Blue-Gray, Accent 2** Shape Style to the shapes on slides 3–6.

Apply Transition Effects and Animations

19. Select all slides but the title slide.

20. Apply the **Checkerboard** transition and set the **Effect Options** to **From Top**.

21. Display the second slide, **Catering**.

22. Apply the **Fade** animation to the bulleted paragraphs.

23. Use the Animation pane to select the Kosher Dishes item and set it to **Start With Previous**.

24. Set *Meat-lovers dishes* and *Desserts* to **Start With Previous** so that all four paragraphs will fade in at the same time after a click.

Add a Sound Effect to an Animation

25. Select the *Vegan dishes* item in the Animation pane and apply the **Applause** sound effect.

26. Close the **Animation pane**.

27. Choose **Slide Show→Start Slide Show→From Beginning** and click each slide until the slide show ends and you return to Normal view.

28. Save the changes and then exit **PowerPoint**. Submit your final file based on the guidelines provided by your instructor.

    To view examples of how your file or files should look at the end of this exercise, go to the student resource center.

Add Visual Interest

In this exercise, you will add images and animation to a presentation.

Prepare a Slide for and Insert Clip Art

1. Start **PowerPoint**. Open **PP03-A03-UniversalVisual** from the **PP2013 Lesson 03** folder and save it as `PP03-A03-UniversalVisual-[FirstInitialLastName]`.

2. Display the second slide and change its layout to **Two Content**.

3. Use the **Online Pictures** icon on the slide to search **Office.com** and insert a photo of a bus.

4. Use the **Ribbon** to search **Office.com** for a photo of a limousine and another photo of a ferry boat, and then insert them.

Move, Size, Rotate, and Format Clip Art

5. Resize and position the three images on the slide to your liking.

6. Apply a **Picture Style** to each of the pictures. Use the same style on all three pictures to maintain consistency.

Remove a Background and Apply Artistic Effects

7. Display the title slide.

8. Insert the **PPT03-A03-Hand** picture from the **PP2013 Lesson 03** folder.

9. Use the **Background Removal** tool to remove the white background of the picture.

10. Move the picture to the lower-right corner of the slide.

11. Apply the **Photocopy** artistic effect to the picture.

12. Adjust the **Color** of the picture to a **Color Tone** of **Temperature: 7200k**.

Add, Merge, and Format Shapes

13. On the third slide, draw a wide **Rounded Rectangle**, a small **Rounded Rectangle**, and two **Circles** and then arrange them into the shape of a bus.

14. Merge the shapes into a single bus shape.

15. On the fourth slide, use the **Rectangle**, **Oval**, **Right Triangle**, and **Manual Operation** shapes to create a limousine. (The Manual Operation shape is in the Flowchart category.)

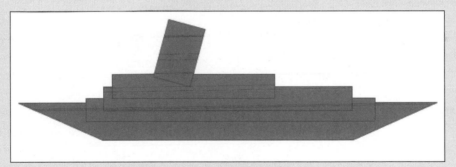

16. Merge the shapes into a single shape.

17. On the fifth slide, use the **Rectangle** and **Manual Operation** shapes to create a ferry boat.

18. Merge the shapes into a single shape.

19. Apply the **Intense Effect – Olive Green, Accent 3** Shape Style to each of the shapes on slides 3–5.

20. Resize and position the shapes so they fill the maximum area of their slides without overlapping the text.

Apply Transition Effects and Add Animation

21. Apply the **Reveal** transition to all but the title slide.

22. Set the **Effect Option** on all slides to **Through Black from Right**.

23. Set the **Duration** on all slides to **3 seconds**.

24. Apply the **Fly In** animation to the hand picture on the title slide.

25. Set the **Effect Option** to **From Right**.

Use the Animation Pane to Add Sound

26. Use the **Animation Pane** to add the **Whoosh** sound effect to the hand's animation.

27. Close the **Animation** pane.

28. Choose **Slide Show→Start Slide Show→From Beginning** and click each slide to view the presentation, returning to **Normal** view when you are finished.

29. Save the changes and then exit **PowerPoint**. Submit your final file based on the guidelines provided by your instructor.

Extend Your Skills

In the course of working through the Extend Your Skills exercises, you will think critically as you use the skills taught in the lesson to complete the assigned projects. To evaluate your mastery and completion of the exercises, your instructor may use a rubric, with which more points are allotted according to performance characteristics. (The more you do, the more you earn!) Ask your instructor how your work will be evaluated.

PP03-E01 That's the Way I See It

New PowerPoint users often overuse transitions, animation, and sound effects. In this exercise, you will see how sometimes less is more. Create a presentation with at least six slides. Every slide except the title slide should include a title, text, and an image. Apply any design theme and variation. Make sure the presentation focuses on a single idea (for example, a classic car collection, your favorite movies, or inspirational people). Apply a different transition to each slide. Apply a different animation to each text block and each image. Add a different sound effect to each slide. In other words—overdo it! Save your file as **PP03-E01-AnimationOverkill-[FirstInitialLastName]** in the **PP2013 Lesson 03** folder. View the presentation as a slide show.

Save a copy of the presentation as **PP03-E01-AnimationAppropriate-[FirstInitialLastName]**. Edit the presentation so that each slide uses the same subtle transition. Remove the animation from each image, and standardize the animation on the text blocks. Choose a subtle Entrance animation. Remove all sound effects. Save your changes. View the revised presentation as a slide show and compare it to your "overkill" version.

You will be evaluated based on the inclusion of all elements specified, your ability to follow directions, your ability to apply newly learned skills to a real-world situation, your creativity, and the relevance of your topic and/or data choice(s). Submit your final files based on the guidelines provided by your instructor.

PP03-E02 Be Your Own Boss

In this exercise, you will edit the animation on the Blue Jean Landscaping presentation. Open **PP03-E02-BlueJeanAnimated** from the **PP2013 Lesson 03** folder and save it as **PP03-E02-BlueJeanAnimated-[FirstInitialLastName]**. View the presentation as a slide show and notice where the animations occur. Edit the presentation so the animations occur when a slide is clicked rather than automatically. Also, make sure the bulleted text animates one line at a time. Add a final slide using the Section Header layout. Use the title **Get Outside More** and the subtitle **It'll do you good!**. Insert **PPT03-E02-Flowers** from the **PP2013 Lesson 03** folder. Make these changes:

- Remove the photo background.
- Move the image to appear behind the text.
- Apply an adjustment to make it less distracting.
- Apply the same slide transition used by the other slides.
- Add a sound effect that you feel is appropriate.

You will be evaluated based on the inclusion of all elements specified, your ability to follow directions, your ability to apply newly learned skills to a real-world situation, your creativity, and your demonstration of an entrepreneurial spirit. Submit your final file based on the guidelines provided by your instructor.

Transfer Your Skills

In the course of working through the Transfer Your Skills exercises, you will use critical-thinking and creativity skills to complete the assigned projects using skills taught in the lesson. To evaluate your mastery and completion of the exercises, your instructor may use a rubric, with which more points are allotted according to performance characteristics. (The more you do, the more you earn!) Ask your instructor how your work will be evaluated.

PP03-T01 Use the Web as a Learning Tool

Throughout this book, you will be provided with an opportunity to use the Internet as a learning tool by completing WebQuests. According to the original creators of WebQuests, as described on their website (WebQuest.org), a WebQuest is "an inquiry-oriented activity in which most or all of the information used by learners is drawn from the web." To complete the WebQuest projects in this book, navigate to the student resource center and choose the WebQuest for the lesson on which you are currently working. The subject of each WebQuest will be relevant to the material found in the lesson.

WebQuest Subject: Licensing Media Usage

Submit your final file(s) based on the guidelines provided by your instructor.

PP03-T02 Demonstrate Proficiency

Stormy BBQ needs a slideshow to play on television screens throughout their seating area. It should feature images of mouth-watering barbeque. Create a PowerPoint presentation with at least five slides. Each slide should display a single photo of delicious barbeque. Remove the backgrounds from the images you use, as necessary. Use slide transitions to fade one slide into the next. Include an animated title on each slide that names the dish.

Choose one slide on which to add a shape. Add a shape from the Stars and Banners category with the text **Blue Ribbon Winner**. Format the shape and its text to add visual interest while keeping the text easy to read.

Save the presentation as **PP03-T02-BBQSlideShow-[FirstInitialLastName]** in your **PP2013 Lesson 03** folder.

Submit your final file based on the guidelines provided by your instructor.

Inserting Charts

LESSON OUTLINE

Inserting Charts

Working with External Excel Documents

Creating SmartArt Diagrams

Concepts Review

Reinforce Your Skills

Apply Your Skills

Extend Your Skills

Transfer Your Skills

LEARNING OBJECTIVES

After studying this lesson, you will be able to:

- Insert charts to display numerical data
- Link to and use data in an Excel spreadsheet to create a chart
- Format charts and change chart types
- Repair broken links to external documents
- Create SmartArt diagrams

A cornerstone of the Microsoft Office suite of programs is the seamless way programs join, or integrate with each other. For example, in this lesson, you will learn how to place an Excel workbook into a PowerPoint presentation to harness the strength of Excel features in PowerPoint. You will also take advantage of the Microsoft Graph charting program to create dynamic and precise charts in your presentation. Finally, you will use SmartArt to add a beautifully arranged organization chart that is clear, concise, and stylish.

Adding Charts to Presentations

You continue to develop PowerPoint presentations for iJams, deciding it is time to expand iJams by opening a recording studio that local musicians can rent to record their original music. You schedule a meeting with the loan committee at Twilight Hollow Bank. You are concerned that you will have to re-create your best Excel workbook of financial projections until you remember that you can simply link the Excel file to the PowerPoint presentation.

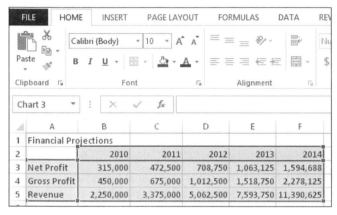

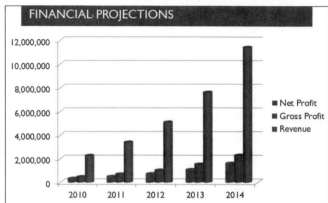

Inserting Charts

Video Library   http://labyrinthelab.com/videos   Video Number: PP13-V0401

PowerPoint is an intensely visual application. Although it is often the case that you will be creating presentations that represent concepts or goals, you may also present financial statistics or numerical data. PowerPoint allows you to create charts based on numerical data in a spreadsheet. If Microsoft Excel is installed, PowerPoint and Excel will work together to provide you with advanced options to design the chart layout and edit chart data. Without Excel installed, PowerPoint will use Microsoft Graph to create a new chart. Excel offers the more intuitive Ribbon interface, provides more formatting options, and creates more visually appealing charts than Microsoft Graph. Therefore, it is recommended that you use Excel to create charts for your PowerPoint presentations. In fact, if Excel is installed, PowerPoint launches it automatically whenever you insert a new chart.

Creating Embedded Charts

PowerPoint has four layouts (Title and Content, Two Content, Comparison, and Content with Caption) that make inserting new charts simple. Each of these common layouts includes an Insert Chart icon that you can click to insert a new chart. What if your slide doesn't use one of these layouts? You can always insert a chart manually from the Ribbon, no matter what layout your slide uses.

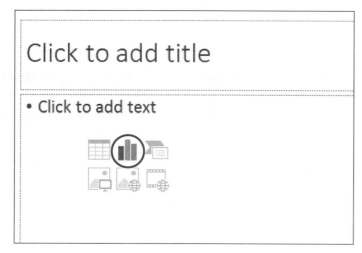

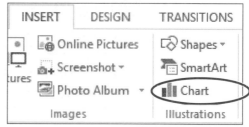

You can insert a chart via the Insert Chart slide icon or from the Ribbon.

Microsoft Graph

If Excel is not installed, PowerPoint launches a Microsoft Graph datasheet when you insert a new chart. (Microsoft Graph is a small program installed with many Office applications.) Charts created in Microsoft Graph lack the Chart Tools contextual Ribbon tabs and commands that are available with an Excel-generated chart for advanced formatting and easy editing (these tabs are discussed later in this lesson). A Microsoft Graph chart can be converted to Office 2013 format, which results in the contextual Ribbon tabs being made available and chart data editing handled by Excel. However, without Excel installed, a converted chart is not editable. The rest of this lesson assumes that you have Excel installed.

To convert a Microsoft Graph chart to Office 2013 format, double-click the chart on the slide and choose Convert. However, remember that Excel must be installed to edit numeric data in a converted chart.

Microsoft Graph datasheet

		A	B	C	D	E
		1st Qtr	2nd Qtr	3rd Qtr	4th Qtr	
1	East	20.4	27.4	90	20.4	
2	West	30.6	38.6	34.6	31.6	
3	North	45.9	46.9	45	43.9	
4						

Presentation1 - Datasheet

Excel spreadsheet

	A	B	C	D
1		Series 1	Series 2	Series 3
2	Category 1	4.3	2.4	2
3	Category 2	2.5	4.4	2
4	Category 3	3.5	1.8	3
5	Category 4	4.5	2.8	5

When you insert a new chart, PowerPoint starts you out with generic data labels and numbers that you replace with your own.

Choosing a Chart Type

Certain chart types are best suited to display specific types of data. Some of the most commonly used chart types are described in the following table.

Chart Type	Icon	Best Used to...
Column	Column	Show one-time (nonadjacent) results, such as those of a survey, depicted as vertical bars
Bar	Bar	Show the same type of results as a column chart, but with horizontal bars
Line	Line	Show continual change over time, such as profit / loss over several months
Pie	Pie	Compare a portion or portions to a whole, such as hours spent on various tasks in a single day

Editing Chart Data

When you create a new chart, PowerPoint launches a minimal version of Excel called Chart. A button at the top of the Chart window opens the full version of Excel. This way, you can edit data in a simple interface (Chart), or edit the data directly in Excel and take advantage of Excel's powerful tools for working with numeric data. Don't be confused when you insert a new chart and see data already entered in the spreadsheet window. This is sample data that PowerPoint inserts to get you started; simply replace it with your headings and numbers.

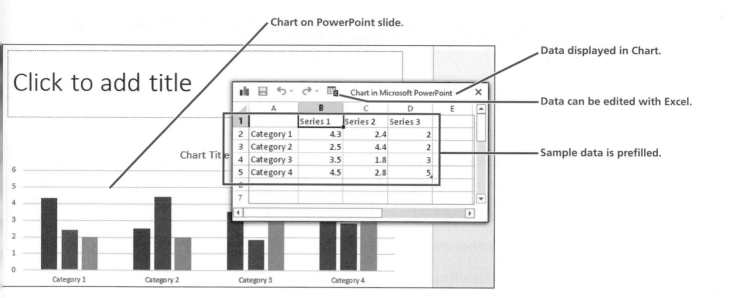

Chart on PowerPoint slide.

Data displayed in Chart.

Data can be edited with Excel.

Sample data is prefilled.

Formatting Charts

After a chart has been inserted, simply click the chart to select it. PowerPoint's Chart tools are displayed in the Ribbon as the Design and Format contextual tabs. You can use these tabs to create, modify, and format your chart without leaving the PowerPoint window.

DEVELOP YOUR SKILLS PP04-D01

Insert a Chart

In this exercise, you will create a chart inside your PowerPoint presentation and revise the default datasheet with your own custom data.

The instructions for this and other charting exercises assume that Excel 2013 is installed on your computer.

1. Start **PowerPoint**. Open **PP04-D01-Chart** from the **PP2013 Lesson 04** folder and save it as `PP04-D01-Chart-[FirstInitialLastName]`.

   Replace the bracketed text with your first initial and last name. For example, if your name is Bethany Smith, your filename would look like this: PP04-D01-Chart-BSmith.

2. Display slide 3, **Our Expansion Plan**.

   In the next few steps, you will add a new slide after Our Expansion Plan.

3. Choose **Home→Slides→New Slide** 🖼️.

4. Choose **Home→Slides→** 🔲 Layout ▾ **→Two Content**.

   PowerPoint will apply the new layout, which includes a placeholder box on the left that you will use for your text, and a placeholder box on the right that you will use for your chart.

5. Type `Year-To-Date Results` as the title.

   The title is automatically formatted with all capitals because that is defined by the theme.

6. Click in the placeholder box on the left side and add the following bulleted text items, pressing ⏎Enter after each one except the last:

- **25% growth rate** ⏎Enter
- **Positive cash flow** ⏎Enter
- **Margins increasing**

Set Up the Chart

7. Click the **Insert Chart** 📊 icon in the middle of the placeholder box on the right side.

   The Insert Chart dialog box appears. Knowing the type of data you are charting will make it easier to select the appropriate type of chart. You are charting one-time results, so a column or bar graph is appropriate.

8. Follow these steps to insert a chart from the Insert Chart dialog box:

Ⓐ Choose the **Column** category.

Ⓑ Choose the **3-D Clustered Column** chart type.

Ⓒ Click **OK**.

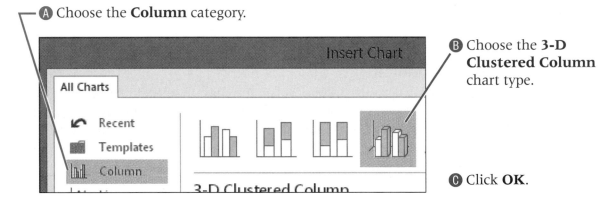

The chart opens with sample data. You will replace the sample data with your own headings and numbers.

9. Follow these steps to set up the chart datasheet:

Ⓐ Click the cell with the text **Category 1**, type **Q1**, and tap ⏎Enter.

Ⓑ Enter the **remaining data** shown here. Click a cell, type the cell data, and then click another cell.

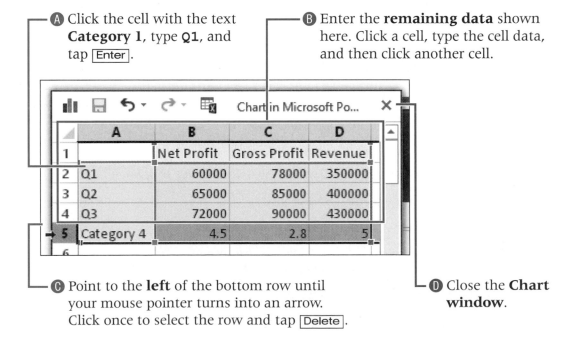

Ⓒ Point to the **left** of the bottom row until your mouse pointer turns into an arrow. Click once to select the row and tap ⏎Delete.

Ⓓ Close the **Chart window**.

Your slide should now resemble the following illustration. Notice how tightly squeezed the chart appears. In the next topic, you will learn how to modify a chart to aid readability and make it visually attractive.

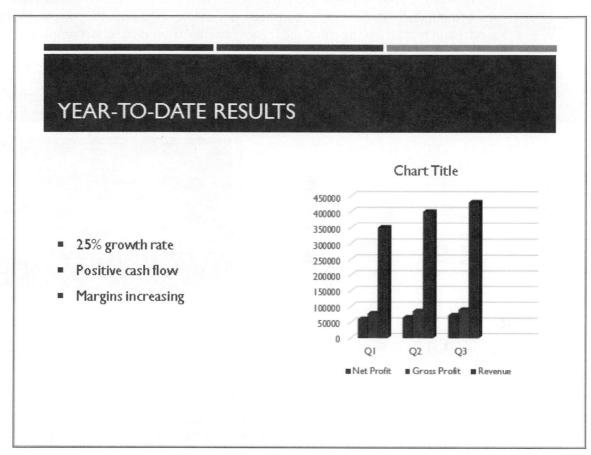

10. Save your presentation.

Modifying Charts

Video Library   http://labyrinthelab.com/videos   Video Number: PP13-V0402

After you insert a chart, you can make changes to it as necessary. For example, you can edit the chart data, change the color scheme, and even change to a different chart type. As you would expect, the two Chart Tools contextual tabs on the Ribbon give access to these modification commands.

If you don't see the Chart Tools contextual tabs, make sure that the chart is selected (displays sizing handles).

Changing the Chart Size and Layout

You can size the chart by dragging the sizing handles, and you can position the chart by dragging it to a different location. These handles work just as they do on clip art and other figures on slides. You can also choose a different layout for the chart from the Design tab under Chart Tools.

Changing the Chart Type

Sometimes you may want to change the chart type to better display the data. For example, you might want to switch from a normal bar chart to a 3-D-style bar chart. Or you may want to use a stacked bar chart style if space is limited on the slide. Additionally, you can change the chart's layout and reposition the chart's text components around the chart graphic.

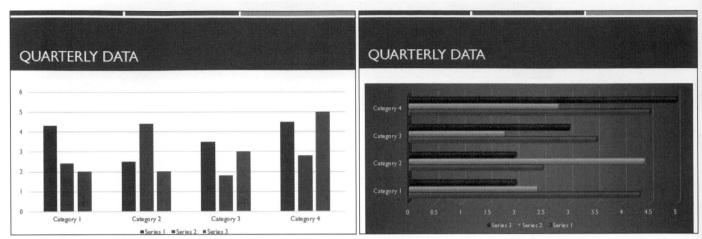

The same chart data first displayed as a Clustered Column, then as a 3-D Clustered Bar

QUICK REFERENCE	CHARTING IN POWERPOINT
Task	Procedure
Insert a chart	Click the Insert Chart icon on the slide or choose Insert→Illustrations→Chart.
Change the size of a chart	Point to a sizing handle around the chart's border. When the double-headed arrow appears, click and then drag the border.
Change the chart type	Select the chart and then choose Chart Tools→Design→Type→Change Chart Type.
Modify chart data	Select the chart and then choose Chart Tools→Design→Data→Edit Data.
Change the chart layout	Select the chart and then choose a layout from the Chart Tools→Design→Quick Layout gallery.

Modify a Chart

In this exercise, you will modify the chart slide by adjusting its size and editing the chart data.

1. Save your file as **PP04-D02-Chart-[FirstInitialLastName]**.

2. Follow these steps to resize the chart:

Ⓐ If necessary, click anywhere in the chart to display its border.

Ⓑ Point to the center of the left border until your mouse pointer becomes a double-arrow. Then, drag the border left until its left edge is just to the left of the letter *R* in *Results*.

Ⓒ Use the same method to drag the right border until it snaps to the right edge of the slide.

Ⓓ Use the same method to drag the bottom border until it snaps to the bottom edge of the slide.

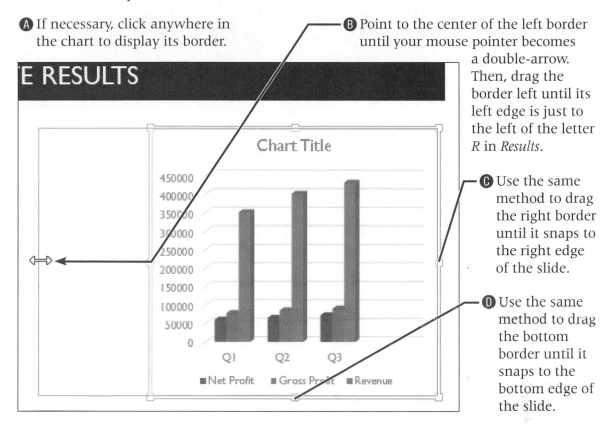

You have resized the chart but have maintained some breathing room (white space) between the left border of the chart and the bulleted text. You have also maintained some white space between the right edge of the chart and the slide's right edge.

3. Make sure the chart is still selected and the Chart Tools contextual tabs are visible.

4. Choose **Chart Tools→Design→Data→Edit Data** ⊞.

This is an embedded chart. You can always edit the data in an embedded chart by selecting this command.

5. Follow these steps to edit the chart:

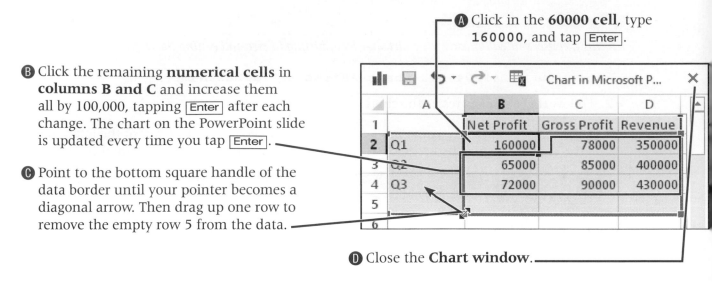

Ⓐ Click in the **60000 cell**, type `160000`, and tap `Enter`.

Ⓑ Click the remaining **numerical cells** in **columns B and C** and increase them all by 100,000, tapping `Enter` after each change. The chart on the PowerPoint slide is updated every time you tap `Enter`.

Ⓒ Point to the bottom square handle of the data border until your pointer becomes a diagonal arrow. Then drag up one row to remove the empty row 5 from the data.

Ⓓ Close the **Chart window**.

Now let's change the chart type to a more visually interesting style.

6. Follow these steps to change the chart type:

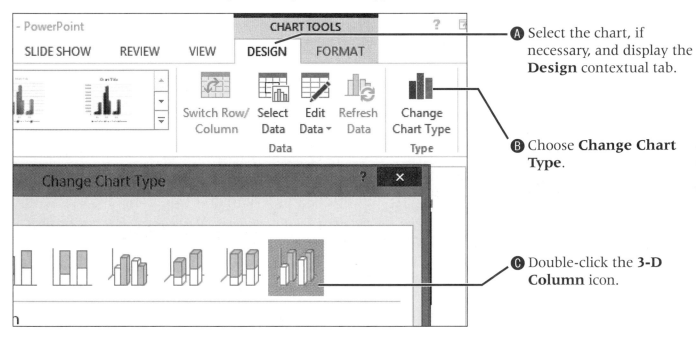

Ⓐ Select the chart, if necessary, and display the **Design** contextual tab.

Ⓑ Choose **Change Chart Type**.

Ⓒ Double-click the **3-D Column** icon.

The chart type changes. However, the bars in the graph are too congested, and the text is difficult to read.

7. Choose **Chart Tools→Design→Chart Layouts→ Quick Layout→Layout 3**.
PowerPoint rearranges the slide layout to remove the text on the right side of the chart. The slide itself has a title, so we will delete the additional title inside the chart.

8. Click once on the **Chart Title** so it displays handles and then tap ⌊Delete⌋.

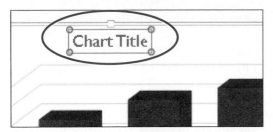

The chart title disappears. Your slide should resemble the following illustration.

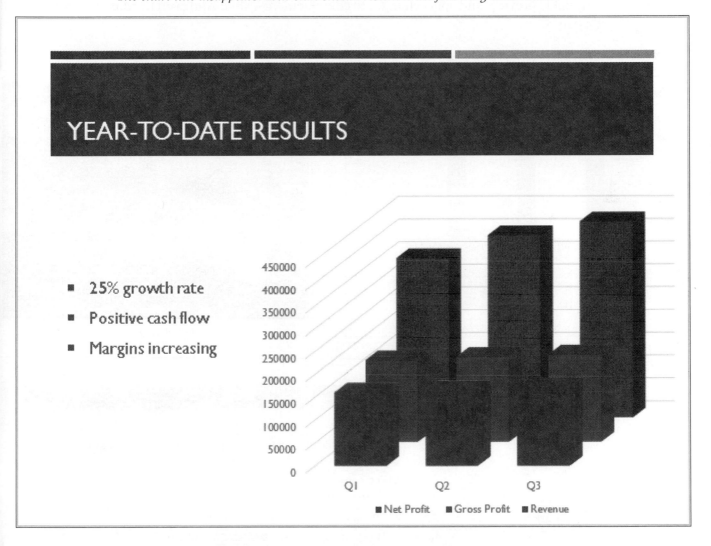

9. Save your presentation.

Changing Chart Style and Color Scheme

Video Library http://labyrinthelab.com/videos Video Number: PP13-V0403

You can format your charts with predesigned styles that alter several characteristics of the charts, including text used as labels, chart color fills, and effects. Additionally, you can change the colors used in a chart to make it stand out from the rest of the slide, or just make it easier to see from a distance.

While these changes can be made from the Ribbon, PowerPoint 2013 includes new chart buttons, which are also available in Excel, allowing easier access to style and color changes. PowerPoint charts now display three small buttons to the right of a selected chart, allowing you to quickly preview and apply changes to chart elements, style, and even the data being displayed.

Styles and colors can be changed here.

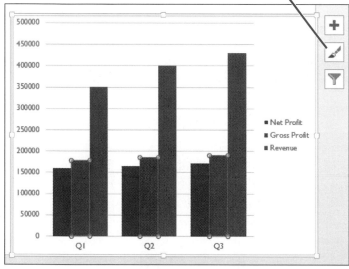

The default chart.

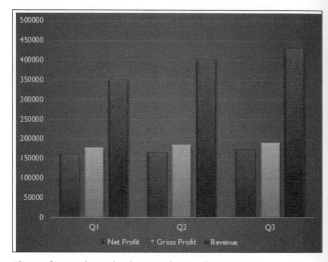

Chart after style and color are changed.

CHART BUTTONS		
Button Name	**Icon**	**What It Does**
Chart Elements	+	■ Show or hide chart title, axis labels, gridlines, and other chart elements. ■ The same options are available from Chart Tools→Design→Chart Layouts→Add Chart Element.
Chart Styles	✎	■ Change a chart style or color scheme. ■ The same options are available from Chart Tools→Design→Chart Styles.
Chart Filter	▼	■ Filter chart data to display only desired data.

Style and Color a Chart

In this exercise, you will modify the chart elements, style, and color scheme by using the new chart buttons.

1. Save your file as **PP04-D03-Chart-[FirstInitialLastName]**.

2. Follow these steps to change the chart's style:

Ⓐ Select the chart, if necessary, to display the **chart buttons**. Ⓑ Click the **Chart Styles** button.

Ⓒ Click **Style**.

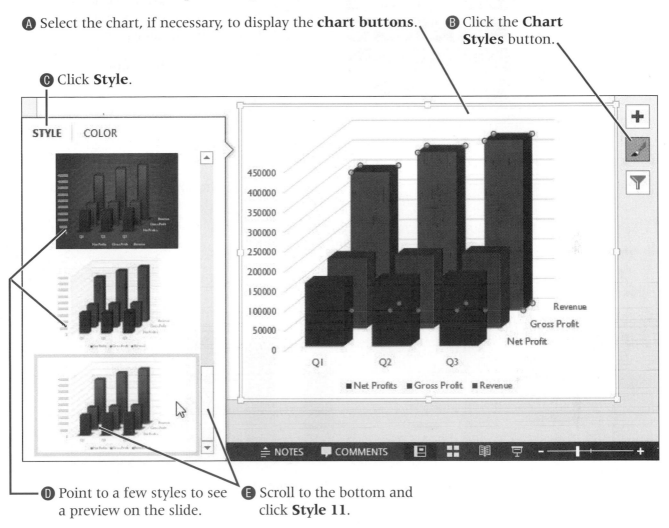

Ⓓ Point to a few styles to see a preview on the slide. Ⓔ Scroll to the bottom and click **Style 11**.

The new style added back text to the right of the chart. You will delete it later in this exercise.

3. Follow these steps to change the chart's color scheme:

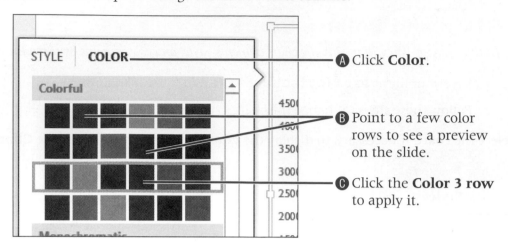

Ⓐ Click **Color**.

Ⓑ Point to a few color rows to see a preview on the slide.

Ⓒ Click the **Color 3 row** to apply it.

4. Follow these steps to change the chart's elements:

Ⓐ Click the **Chart Elements** button.

Ⓑ Point to each unchecked item to see a preview of the item on the chart. Do not click!

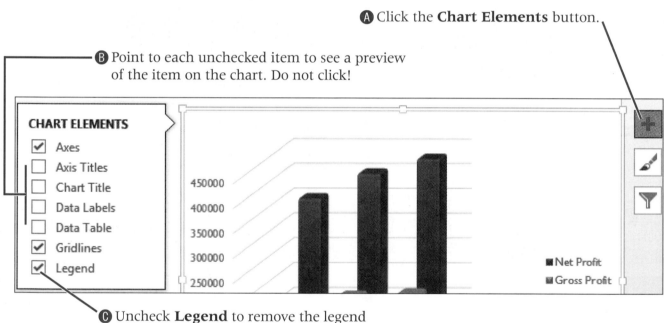

Ⓒ Uncheck **Legend** to remove the legend from the right side of the chart.

5. Click on the slide, but off the chart, to deselect it.

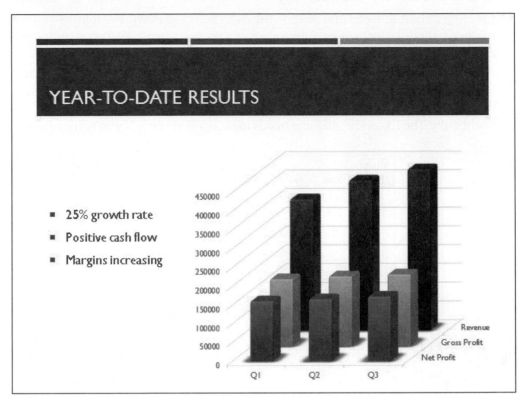

6. Save your presentation.

Working with External Excel Documents

Video Library   http://labyrinthelab.com/videos   Video Number: PP13-V0404

Office 2013 provides a variety of tools and techniques to let you exchange data between applications. Object Linking and Embedding (OLE) allows you to create links between source documents and destination documents. For example, you may want a chart in an existing Excel document to appear in a PowerPoint presentation. This makes it possible for another individual or department to maintain the Excel spreadsheet and its numerical data while you simply link to it and display an attractive chart based on its contents.

Benefits of Linking

Creating a chart in Excel and linking the chart object to PowerPoint gives you the opportunity to maintain modularity over presentation components. The Excel data remains in the Excel spreadsheet, which can be maintained by the financial wizards, while the PowerPoint presentation remains totally under your control as a separate document. Any changes made to the Excel document can be reflected in the chart displayed on the PowerPoint slide. Don't be worried if, during your actual presentation, the Excel spreadsheet is not available. The chart will still display beautifully. The Excel spreadsheet needs to be available only if you want to edit the chart data.

Changes to the Excel spreadsheet data here…

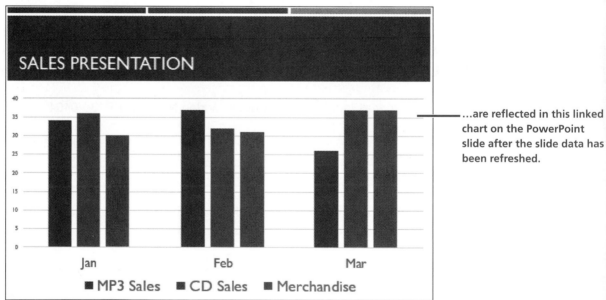

…are reflected in this linked chart on the PowerPoint slide after the slide data has been refreshed.

Changes to a linked Excel document *do not* result in automatic updating of the PowerPoint chart; you must manually refresh the PowerPoint chart's data to see the updated content.

Only Data Is Linked

A linked chart on a PowerPoint slide is linked to the Excel *data*, not to the Excel chart. The chart on the Excel spreadsheet simply establishes the initial link to its data. So, deleting or changing the format of the Excel chart has no effect on the PowerPoint chart. In the preceding illustration, notice that the formatting on the Excel chart is quite different from that on the PowerPoint slide. This independence allows PowerPoint to format the chart so it is consistent with the presentation theme's colors and fonts.

Linking Excel Charts

Your first step in linking to an Excel spreadsheet is to create the Excel spreadsheet that contains numerical data and an Excel chart. You simply copy and paste the chart (not the spreadsheet cells containing numerical data) from the Excel spreadsheet into your slide. The chart on the PowerPoint slide will be linked to the Excel spreadsheet's numerical data by default.

QUICK REFERENCE	LINKING CHARTS ON SLIDES
Task	**Procedure**
Link a chart	■ Select the Excel chart and choose Home→Clipboard→Copy.
	■ Select the desired PowerPoint slide and choose Home→Clipboard→Paste.
Edit linked data	■ Select the PowerPoint chart and choose Chart Tools→Design→Data→Edit Data.
	■ If available, the linked document will open. Edit the data in the Excel spreadsheet (not on the Excel chart), and save your changes.
Refresh chart data linked to an external file	■ Select the PowerPoint chart and choose Chart Tools→Design→Data→Refresh Data.
Repair a broken link	■ Select the chart, choose File→Info, and click the Edit Links to Files link.
	■ Click the Change Source button.
	■ Navigate to the source file, select it, and click Open.
	■ Click Close.

Paste Options

After you paste a chart from Excel, PowerPoint displays a set of three Paste Options buttons that allow you to control formatting of the pasted chart. The following table shows the function of each button.

PASTE OPTIONS		
Option	**Icon**	**What It Does**
Use Destination Theme & Embed Workbook	📋	■ Changes the formatting of the chart to match the slide theme. ■ This is the default setting.
Keep Source Formatting & Embed Workbook	📋	■ Keeps the formatting of the Excel chart.
Picture	📋	■ Pastes the chart as a picture. The data is no longer editable.

DEVELOP YOUR SKILLS PP04-D04

Link to an Excel Chart

In this exercise, you will link to an existing Excel chart. You will then edit the Excel data to update the chart in PowerPoint.

1. Start **Microsoft Office Excel 2013**.

   The Excel program loads, and the Excel window appears.

2. Choose **Open Other Workbooks** from the bottom of the left column of Excel's Start screen.

3. Click **Computer→Browse**, navigate to the **PP2013 Lesson 04** folder, and open **PP04-D04-FinancialProjections**.

4. Click anywhere on the **Excel** chart to select it.

   A border appears around the chart to indicate that it has been selected.

5. Choose **Home→Clipboard→Copy**.

6. Close **Excel**.

   Excel closes, and you are returned to the PowerPoint window.

Link the Chart to PowerPoint

7. Save your PowerPoint presentation as `PP04-D04-Chart-[FirstInitialLastName]`.

8. Choose the **Year-To-Date Results** slide.

9. Choose **Home→Slides→New Slide** 🖼.

10. Choose **Home→Slides→** 🔲 Layout ▾ **→Title Only**.

    The new slide's layout is converted to the Title Only layout.

11. Click the title box of the new slide, type **Financial Projections**, and click below the title in a blank area of the slide.

The title box becomes deselected.

12. Choose **Home→Clipboard→Paste** 📋.

PowerPoint pastes the chart into the slide.

13. Tap [Esc] twice to dismiss the Paste Options buttons and accept the default setting.

Resize and Format the Chart

14. Follow these steps to resize the chart:

Ⓐ Point to the **bottom-left** sizing handle on the chart border until your mouse pointer becomes a white double-arrow, and then drag the border to the bottom-left corner of the slide.

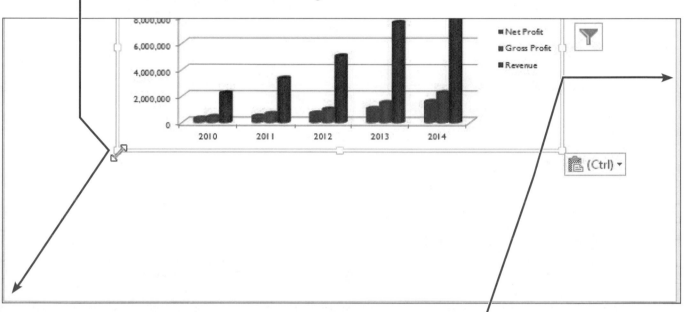

Ⓑ Using this same method, drag the **right edge** of the chart border until it snaps to the right edge of the slide.

The chart's text is too small to read comfortably. You will fix that in the next step.

15. Make sure the chart is selected and its border is displayed. Then choose **Home→ Font→Font Size menu** ▼**→20**.

All text on the chart is enlarged to size 20 and is easier to read. Your slide should resemble the following illustration.

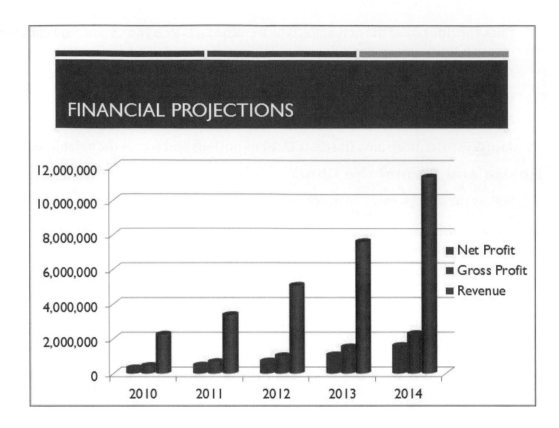

16. Save your presentation.

Effects of Linking

Video Library http://labyrinthelab.com/videos   Video Number: PP13-V0405

When working with a linked chart, any changes made to the Excel spreadsheet are reflected in the PowerPoint chart, but not necessarily immediately. If the data is edited from within PowerPoint, the slide's chart is updated automatically. However, if the data is edited by opening Excel outside PowerPoint, the chart data must be refreshed in PowerPoint before the changes are visible on the slide. If you choose to paste unlinked, changes to the Excel spreadsheet will have no effect on the chart in the PowerPoint slide. If you attempt to edit linked chart data from within PowerPoint, a Linked Data window will open and present the linked spreadsheet, ready for editing. The Linked Data window will also give you the option to open the spreadsheet in Excel. If the linked spreadsheet cannot be found, you will not be able to edit the chart data until the link is repaired.

Edit Data in a Linked Spreadsheet

In this exercise, you will edit the data in a linked Excel spreadsheet.

1. Save your file as **PP04-D05-Chart-[FirstInitialLastName]**.

2. Select the **Financial Projections** slide. If necessary, click the chart to select it; choose **Chart Tools→Design→Data→Edit Data**.

   The Linked Data window opens the data source for the chart.

3. Follow these steps to edit the chart data:

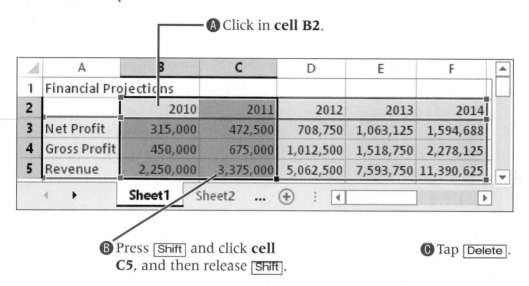

Ⓐ Click in **cell B2**.

Ⓑ Press ⎣Shift⎦ and click **cell C5**, and then release ⎣Shift⎦.

Ⓒ Tap ⎣Delete⎦.

   The selected data is deleted, and the change shows immediately on the slide, but there is a large gap on the chart where the data used to display. You will fix this in the next step.

4. Follow these steps to remove the empty cells:

Ⓐ Point to the **square handle** in the bottom-right corner of **cell A1** until your pointer is a **diagonal double-arrow**.

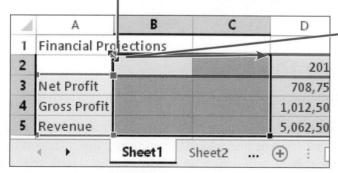

Ⓑ Drag the **handle** to the right, to the **bottom-right corner** of **cell C2**.

Ⓒ Close the **Linked Data** window and click **Save** when prompted to save changes to the Excel spreadsheet.

   The blank cells are removed from the chart on the slide.

5. Save the presentation.

Editing the Source (Linked) Document

Video Library   http://labyrinthelab.com/videos   Video Number: PP13-V0406

If you make a change to the source document outside PowerPoint, you must manually refresh the data to see the changes on the slide. Refreshing data is possible only if you have healthy links (PowerPoint can locate the source document).

DEVELOP YOUR SKILLS PP04-D06
Edit and Refresh the Data Source

In this exercise, you will edit and refresh the data source.

1. Start **Microsoft Office Excel 2013**.

2. Choose **Open Other Workbooks** from the bottom of the left column of Excel's Start screen.

3. Click **Computer→Browse**, navigate to the **PP2013 Lesson 04** folder, and open **PP04-D04-FinancialProjections**.

4. Click in **cell A5** and type **Big Money**.

   Excel replaces the word Revenue *with* Big Money.

5. Save the worksheet and exit **Excel**.

Refresh the Data Source

6. In **PowerPoint**, display the last slide, **Financial Projections**, if necessary.

   Notice that the chart legend to the right of the chart still shows the word Revenue. *It must be refreshed to reflect the changes in the data source.*

7. Save your presentation as **PP04-D06-Chart-[FirstInitialLastName]**.

8. Select the chart so the **Chart Tools** contextual tabs appear.

9. Choose **Chart Tools→Design→Data→Refresh Data**.

   PowerPoint refreshes the chart legend and now shows the phrase Big Money.

10. Save your presentation.

Maintaining Healthy Links

Video Library   http://labyrinthelab.com/videos   Video Number: PP13-V0407

Linked objects can reflect changes in the source document only if the link is maintained. Moving files to other locations on your file system or renaming files can lead to broken links, and your linked objects (like charts) will no longer reflect changes made to the source document.

If you try to edit chart data in PowerPoint and the Excel spreadsheet fails to open, you probably have a broken link.

Example

If you copied a chart from an Excel spreadsheet named Chart Data that was stored in a folder named My Excel Documents, PowerPoint would be looking for a file with that name in that location. If you moved the Excel file (or the containing folder) to another folder or changed its name, PowerPoint would no longer be able to find it; therefore, any changes made to the spreadsheet would have no effect on the chart in PowerPoint. And if you tried to edit the data from within PowerPoint, PowerPoint would not be able to find the Excel spreadsheet and thus would not be able to edit the data.

The following figure illustrates the prompt that PowerPoint displays if you break a link to an external file—for example, if you move or rename the data source file, and then try to edit a chart from PowerPoint.

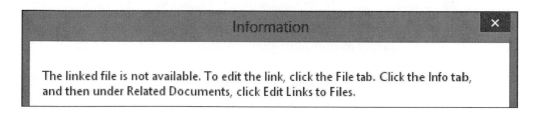

Information   ×

The linked file is not available. To edit the link, click the File tab. Click the Info tab, and then under Related Documents, click Edit Links to Files.

Break and Repair a Link

In this exercise, you will break a link by renaming the linked data file, and then you will repair the link from within PowerPoint.

1. Save your file as **PP04-D07-Chart-[FirstInitialLastName]**.

2. **Minimize** ⎯ the PowerPoint window to the taskbar.

3. Follow the instructions for your version of Windows to open a window for your file storage location:

   ■ **Windows 7:** Use **Start→Computer** and open your file storage location.

   ■ **Windows 8:** Use the **File Explorer icon** on the **taskbar** to open a folder window and then open your file storage location.

4. Open the **PP2013 Lesson 04** folder.

In the next step, you will rename a file. Most windows systems hide the ends of filenames (called extensions). If they are visible, take care not to change them.

5. Follow these steps to rename the Excel worksheet file:

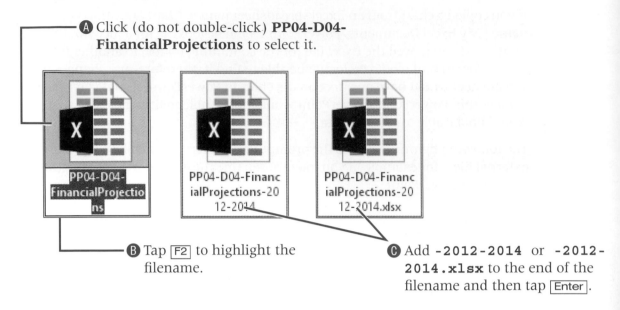

Ⓐ Click (do not double-click) **PP04-D04-FinancialProjections** to select it.

Ⓑ Tap F2 to highlight the filename.

Ⓒ Add **-2012-2014** or **-2012-2014.xlsx** to the end of the filename and then tap Enter.

If the filename displayed the .xlsx file extension, be sure your new filename looks like PP04-D04-FinancialProjections-2012-2014.xlsx. Otherwise, your filename should simply be PP04-D04-FinancialProjections-2012-2014. By renaming the source document, you have broken its link to PowerPoint.

6. Close the folder window and then click the **PowerPoint** button on the Windows taskbar to restore PowerPoint to the screen.

7. Click the chart to select it, if necessary.

8. Choose **Chart Tools→Design→Data→Edit Data** .

You receive an error. PowerPoint is looking for a source document named PP04-D04-FinancialProjections, but you changed the name of the file.

9. Click **OK** in the error box.

Fix the Broken Link

10. Choose **File→Info** and then click **Edit Links to Files** at the bottom-right of the right column.

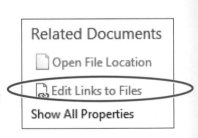

The Links dialog box appears, listing all links to external files from the presentation. In this case, there is just one linked item, the Excel spreadsheet.

11. Click **Change Source**.

12. In the **Change Source** dialog box, navigate to the **PP2013 Lesson 04** folder, select **PP04-D04-FinancialProjections-2012-2014**, and click **Open**.

PowerPoint updates the link. There may not be enough space in the dialog box to make the new name visible.

13. Click [Close] to close the **Links** dialog box.

You have reestablished the link between the PowerPoint chart and the Excel source document.

Test the Repaired Link

14. Click **Back** ← to close Backstage view; click the chart to select it, if necessary.

    The chart must be selected in order to display the Chart Tools contextual tabs.

15. Choose **Chart Tools→Design→Data→Edit Data** 📝.

    The source document opens, ready to edit.

16. Click in **cell A5**. Then type **Revenue** and tap ⏎ Enter.

    Excel replaces Big Money *with the new word, and the change is immediately visible on the slide.*

17. Close the **Linked Data** window and click **Save** when prompted.

18. Save your presentation.

Creating SmartArt Diagrams

Video Library   http://labyrinthelab.com/videos   Video Number: PP13-V0408

SmartArt graphics are diagrams that automatically resize to accommodate the text within and allow the average user to enhance slides with visually appealing figures without having to learn advanced graphics software. With SmartArt, you simply select the type of diagram you'd like to create and type your text. The SmartArt diagram automatically sizes and flows your text. It also inherits colors and 3-D effects from your document theme. The resulting diagrams can help crystallize concepts in your presentation so that the audience will clearly understand your ideas. Using SmartArt, you can add graphics to your presentations, such as the following:

- Organization charts
- Flowcharts
- Colorful lists
- And many other sophisticated graphics

Inserting and Formatting SmartArt Graphics

Most slide layouts include an Insert SmartArt Graphic icon. Alternatively, SmartArt can be inserted at any time via the Ribbon. When you click the Insert SmartArt Graphic icon, the Choose a SmartArt Graphic dialog box appears. You can choose a diagram type from the gallery and then construct the diagram directly on the slide. PowerPoint displays examples and descriptions of the various SmartArt graphics as you select them in the gallery.

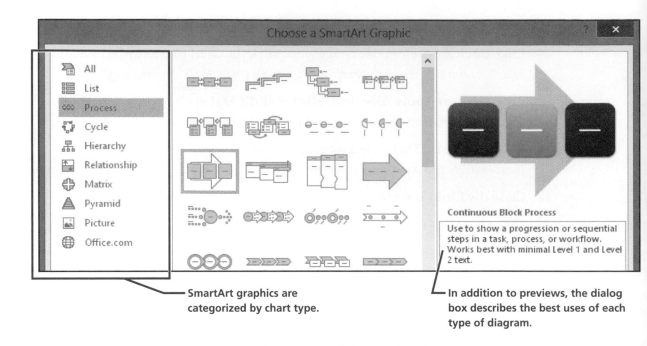

SmartArt graphics are categorized by chart type.

In addition to previews, the dialog box describes the best uses of each type of diagram.

SMARTART GRAPHIC CHART TYPES	
Graphic Category	**Usage**
List	Show nonsequential or grouped blocks of information
Process	Show a progression or sequential flow of data
Cycle	Show a continuing sequence of stages
Hierarchy	Show hierarchal relationships
Relationship	Show ideas, show interlocking or overlapping information, or show relationships to a central idea
Matrix	Show the relationships of components to a whole
Pyramid	Show proportional, interconnected, hierarchical, or containment relationships
Picture	Show a variety of information by using a central picture or several accent pictures
Office.com	Includes graphics from a variety of categories that can be downloaded from the Office.com website

Example

As you create your presentation, you need to include an organization chart that features the key players in your project or the leadership team of your organization. You give the command to insert a SmartArt graphic, browse through the Hierarchy list, and then choose an organization chart. You type the various organizational units in the SmartArt's text box. Three minutes later, you're finished!

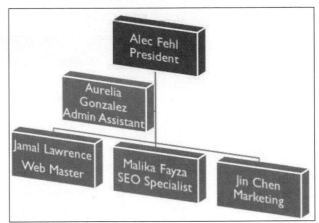

SmartArt organization charts automatically create and align boxes and lines as you type the names of the persons and departments.

QUICK REFERENCE	INSERTING SMARTART
Task	**Procedure**
Insert a new SmartArt graphic	■ Click the Insert SmartArt Graphic ▨ icon in the center of a slide, or choose Insert→Illustrations→SmartArt. ■ In the Choose a SmartArt Graphic dialog box, select a category of graphics to view the thumbnails and samples. ■ Select a thumbnail and click OK.
Edit and format SmartArt	■ Select the SmartArt graphic (or any shape that is part of the graphic). ■ Drag the handles on the shape's border to resize the shape. ■ Make changes to the graphic's color, effects, or layout by choosing the commands from SmartArt Tools→Design or SmartArt Tools→Format. ■ Reset a SmartArt graphic to its default settings by choosing SmartArt Tools→Design→Reset→Reset Graphic.
Add a new element to a SmartArt graphic	■ Select one of the shapes in the SmartArt graphic. ■ Choose SmartArt Tools→Design→Create Graphic→Add Shape menu ▼ and select where you want the new shape to appear relative to the selected shape.

DEVELOP YOUR SKILLS PP04-D08
Set Up an Organization Chart

In this exercise, you will create an organization chart in PowerPoint, adding text to the various levels of the chart.

1. Save your file as **PP04-D08-Chart-[FirstInitialLastName]**.

2. Select the **Financial Projections** slide and choose **Home→Slides→New Slide**.

3. Choose **Home→Slides→** ▤ Layout ▾ **→Title and Content**.

4. Type **Our Management Team** in the Title placeholder.

5. Click the **Insert SmartArt Graphic** ▨ icon in the middle of the slide.
   The Choose a SmartArt Graphic dialog box appears.

6. Follow these steps to insert an organization chart:

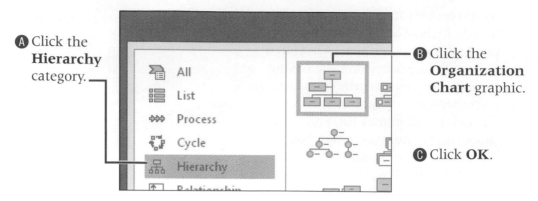

Ⓐ Click the **Hierarchy** category.

Ⓑ Click the **Organization Chart** graphic.

Ⓒ Click **OK**.

A sample organization chart is inserted. The contextual SmartArt Tools tabs appear on the right side of the Ribbon, including Design and Format.

Add Text

7. Follow these steps to add text to the organization chart:

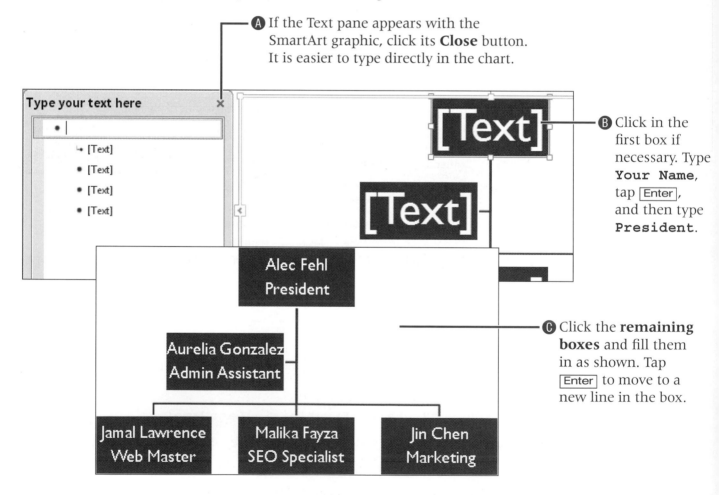

Ⓐ If the Text pane appears with the SmartArt graphic, click its **Close** button. It is easier to type directly in the chart.

Ⓑ Click in the first box if necessary. Type **Your Name**, tap Enter, and then type **President**.

Ⓒ Click the **remaining boxes** and fill them in as shown. Tap Enter to move to a new line in the box.

8. Save your presentation.

Formatting SmartArt

Video Library http://labyrinthelab.com/videos Video Number: PP-13-V0409

After a SmartArt graphic has been added to a slide, you can format its colors and other effects. For example, you can customize the graphic's text formatting, color scheme, and other features. Many SmartArt graphics have 3-D schemes and other cool effects that you can experiment with to add visual impact to a slide.

Adding Elements to SmartArt

You can also add elements to an original SmartArt graphic. For example, an organization chart might need a new branch for adding a department or lateral relationship. You may insert additional shapes above, below, or next to an existing shape. The SmartArt graphic will automatically resize itself and scale its text to accommodate the extra shapes.

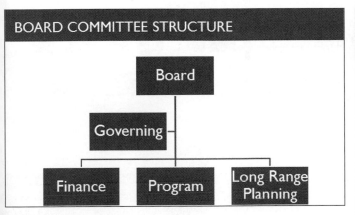

When a shape was inserted next to the Long Range Planning box, PowerPoint automatically resized the SmartArt to make room for the new, blank shape.

PowerPoint 2013

DEVELOP YOUR SKILLS PP04-D09

Add Shapes and Format SmartArt

In this exercise, you will add a new position in the organization chart and enhance its appearance with a different formatting effect.

1. Save your file as **PP04-D09-Chart-[FirstInitialLastName]**.

2. Click in the **Malika Fayza** box in the organization chart.

   This selects the appropriate box so you can add another shape beside it.

3. Choose **SmartArt Tools→Design→Create Graphic→Add Shape menu ▼→Add Shape After**.

   A new box is added to the right of the Malika Fayza box and is ready to accept text.

4. Type **Brett Schneider** in the new box, tap Enter to move to a second line in the box, and type **Fulfillment**.

Format the Chart

5. Follow these steps to format the chart:

Ⓐ Choose **SmartArt Tools→Design→ SmartArt Styles→More.**

Ⓑ Select the **3D→Polished** style.

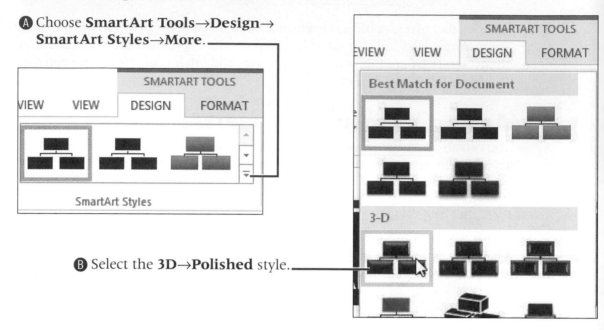

The Polished style is applied to every box in the chart.

6. Follow these steps to change the chart's colors:

Ⓐ Choose **SmartArt Tools→Design→ SmartArt Styles→Change Colors.**

Ⓑ Select the **Colorful→Colorful – Accent Colors** style.

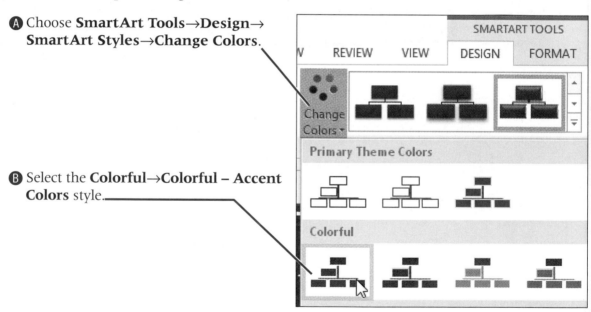

The organization chart should resemble the following illustration.

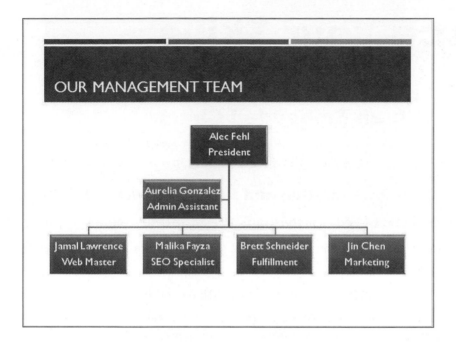

7. Save the presentation and then exit **PowerPoint**.

Concepts Review

To check your knowledge of the key concepts introduced in this lesson, complete the Concepts Review quiz by choosing the appropriate access option below.

If you are...	Then access the quiz by...
Using the Labyrinth Video Library	Going to http://labyrinthelab.com/videos
Using eLab	Logging in, choosing Content, and navigating to the Concepts Review quiz for this lesson
Not using the Labyrinth Video Library or eLab	Going to the student resource center for this book

Reinforce Your Skills

Work with an Embedded Chart

In this exercise, you will create a new presentation for Kids for Change and add a chart slide to the presentation. You will change the chart type to a pie chart to better display the data.

Begin a New Presentation and Insert a Chart

1. Start **PowerPoint** and click the **Blank Presentation** icon.

2. Save your file as `PP04-R01-Members-[FirstInitialLastName]` in the **PP2013 Lesson 04** folder.

3. Choose **Design→Themes** and select the **Slice** theme.

   Remember, the default themes are listed in alphabetical order. Point to a theme thumbnail and pause for a moment to view the theme name in a pop-up ToolTip.

4. In the **Title** box, type `Kids for Change`.

5. Click in the **Subtitle** box and type `New Members`.

6. Choose **Home→Slides→New Slide** and type `2013 New Members` in the title box.

7. Click the **Insert Chart** icon in the content placeholder box.

Modify a Chart

8. Choose the **3-D Clustered Bar** chart type and click **OK**.

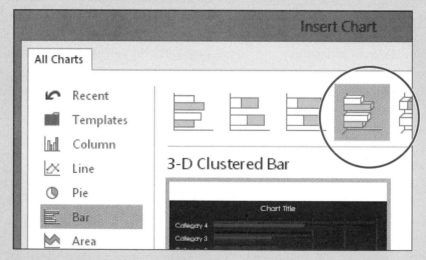

You will now enter the chart data.

9. Enter the data in **columns A and B** as shown and then delete the data in **columns C and D**. (The column headings will default to Column 1 and Column 2.)

◢	A	B	C	D
1		2013	Column1	Column2
2	9 and under	21		
3	10 to 12	36		
4	13 to 15	36		
5	16 to 17	47		
6				

10. Drag the bottom-right handle of cell D5 to the bottom-right corner of **cell B5** to remove the empty columns from the chart.

◢	A	B	C	D
1		2013	Column1	Column2
2	9 and under	21		
3	10 to 12	36		
4	13 to 15	36		
5	16 to 17	47		
6				

11. Close the **Chart** window.

In the next steps, you will edit the chart data.

12. Click the chart on the slide to select it, if necessary, and choose **Chart Tools→Design→ Data→Edit Data**.

13. Click in **cell B4**, type **34**, and tap ⌈Enter⌉ to change the value.

14. Click the chart to display its border, and then click the chart border.

15. Close the **Chart** window.

The chart bars are updated, and the 13 to 15 bar is now shorter than the 10 to 12 bar.

Because the chart shows pieces of a whole (total new members broken down by age), a pie chart is a better choice, so you will change the chart type.

16. Choose **Chart Tools→Design→Type→Change Chart Type**.

17. Choose **3-D Pie** as the chart type and click **OK**.

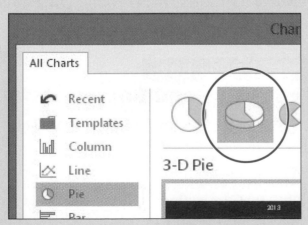

Change Chart Layout and Size

18. Choose **Chart Tools→Design→Chart Layouts→Quick Layout→Layout 1**.

The chart layout is changed, and percentages now display on each pie slice.

Change Chart Style

19. Choose **Chart Tools→Design→Chart Styles→Style 2**.

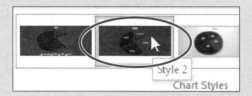

Change Chart Size

20. Drag the **bottom-right handle** of the chart's border to the **bottom-right corner** of the slide.

21. Drag the **left-center handle** of the chart's border to the right until the chart no longer overlaps the slide title.

22. Click the chart's title, **2013**, and tap ⌐Delete⌐.

23. Choose **Home→Font→Font Size menu ▼→20**.

24. Save the changes and then exit **PowerPoint**. Submit your final file based on the guidelines provided by your instructor.

To view examples of how your file or files should look at the end of this exercise, go to the student resource center.

REINFORCE YOUR SKILLS PP04-R02

Work with a Linked Chart and SmartArt

In this exercise, you will link to an external data source, repair a broken link to a linked chart, and add SmartArt to display member and participant numbers.

Link to and Format an Excel Chart

1. Start **PowerPoint**. Open **PP04-R02-Projections** from the **PP2013 Lesson 04** folder and save it as `PP04-R02-Projections-[FirstInitialLastName]`.

2. Display slide 2 and choose **Home→Slides→New Slide**.

3. Type **Participant Projections** as the slide title.

4. Start **Excel**. Open **PP04-R02-Projections** from the **PP2013 Lesson 04** folder.

5. Click the chart on the Excel spreadsheet to select it.

6. Choose **Home→Clipboard→Copy**.

7. Exit **Excel**.

8. Click the **PowerPoint slide** so that the slide title is deselected.

9. Choose **Home→Clipboard→Paste**.

10. Drag the **top-left handle** of the chart's border to the **top-left corner** of the slide.

11. Drag the **center-right handle** of the chart's border toward the right until the chart is as wide as possible but the chart buttons are still visible.

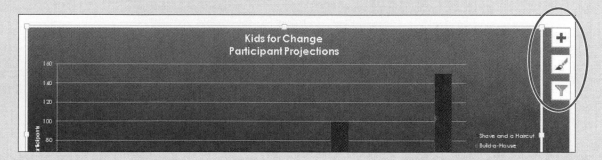

12. Click the **Chart Elements** button to the right of the chart.

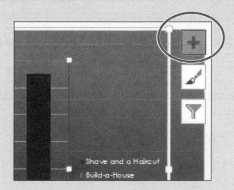

13. Choose to not display the **Chart Title** and remove the checkmark from **Primary Horizontal**.

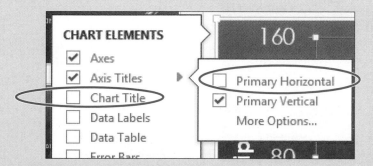

14. Tap ⎡Esc⎤ to close the **Chart Elements** menu.

15. Click the chart to display its border, and then click the chart border.

16. Choose **Home→Font→Font Size menu ▼→28**.

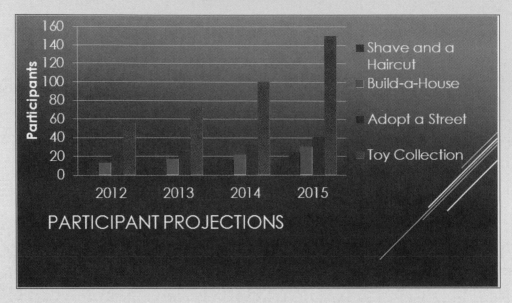

Edit a Linked Data Source and Repair a Broken Link

17. Display slide 2, **2013 New Members**.

18. Click the chart to select it.

19. Choose **Chart Tools→Design→Data→Edit Data**.

A message appears, informing you that PowerPoint cannot find the linked Excel spreadsheet.

20. Click **OK** to close the Information box.

21. Choose **File→Info** and then click the **Edit Links to Files** link at the bottom of the right column.

You will now perform the steps necessary to repair the link.

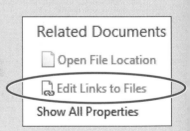

22. Click the entry that ends with **2013members.xlsx** and then click **Change Source**.

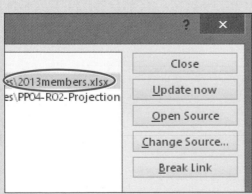

23. Browse to the **PP2013 Lesson 04** folder, if necessary. Select the **PP04-R02-Members** file and click **Open**.

24. Click **Close** to close the **Links** dialog box.

25. Click **Back** 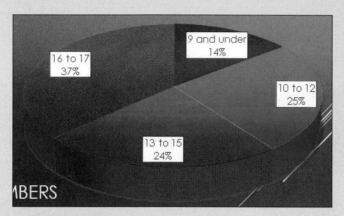 to exit Backstage view.

    Now that the link is fixed, you will edit the data.

26. Choose **Chart Tools→Design→Data→Edit Data**.

27. Click **cell B5**, type **53**, and tap Enter.

    The chart on the slide is immediately updated.

28. Close the **Linked Data** window and click **Save** when prompted.

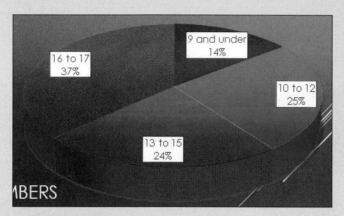

Insert SmartArt

29. Display slide 3, **Participant Projections**.

30. Choose **Home→Slides→New Slide**.

31. Choose **Home→Slides→Layout→Title and Content**.

32. Type **Current Members** as the slide title.

33. Click the **SmartArt** icon on the slide.

34. Click the **Process** category, choose **Step Up Process**, and then click **OK**.

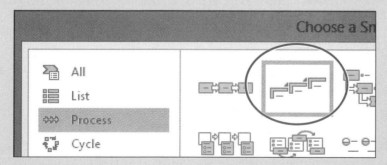

Although the Process category is typically used to show sequential steps, you will use this graphic to show age groups of members, from least members to the most members.

PowerPoint 2013

35. If the text box appears next to the SmartArt graphic, close it.

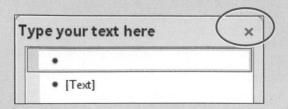

36. Type the text in each section of the SmartArt graphic as shown:

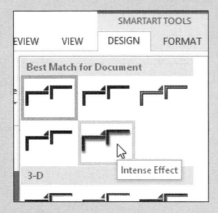

Format and Add Elements to SmartArt

37. With the SmartArt graphic selected, choose **SmartArt Tools→Design→SmartArt Styles→More→Best Match for Document→Intense Effect**.

38. Click the text **Teens** to select that SmartArt text box.

39. Chose **SmartArt Tools→Design→Create Graphic→Add Shape menu ▼→Add Shape Before**.

40. Type **Under 10** in the new text box.

41. Save the changes and then exit **PowerPoint**. Submit your final file based on the guidelines provided by your instructor.

To view examples of how your file or files should look at the end of this exercise, go to the student resource center.

Work with Charts and SmartArt

In this exercise, you will use charts and SmartArt to compare Kids for Change events from several communities.

Begin a New Presentation and Create an Embedded Chart

1. Start **PowerPoint** and click the **Blank Presentation** icon.

2. Save your file as **PP04-R03-Events-[FirstInitialLastName]** in your **PP2013 Lesson 04** folder.

3. Choose **Design→Themes** and select the **Integral** theme.

4. In the **Title** box, type **Kids for Change**.

5. Click in the **Subtitle** box and type **2013 Events**.

6. Choose **Home→Slides→New Slide**.

7. Type **Event Totals** as the title.

8. Click the **Insert Chart** icon on the slide.

Modify a Chart Type

9. Click the **Bar** category, click the **Clustered Bar** chart type, and click **OK**.

10. Type the following data in rows 1 and 2 of the Chart spreadsheet:

	A	B	C	D	E	F
1		Westville	North Haven	Sunny Downs	Goodview	Echo Falls
2	2013	8	12	2	6	8

11. Drag the **bottom-right handle of cell F5** up to the **bottom-right corner of cell F2** to exclude rows 3 through 5.

12. Close the **Chart** window.

    You will now work to format the chart.

13. Choose **Chart Tools→Design→Chart Styles→More→Style 4**.

14. Choose **Chart Tools→Design→Quick Layout→Layout 2**.

15. Click the **Chart Elements** button to the right of the chart.

16. Uncheck **Axes** and then tap Esc to close the **Chart Elements** menu.

17. Click the **chart title** and type **2013 Events**.

18. Drag the right edge of the chart until it snaps to the right edge of the slide to widen it.

19. Choose **Home→Font→Font Size menu ▼→28**.

Edit Chart Data and Change a Chart Type

20. Choose **Chart Tools→Design→Data→Edit Data** 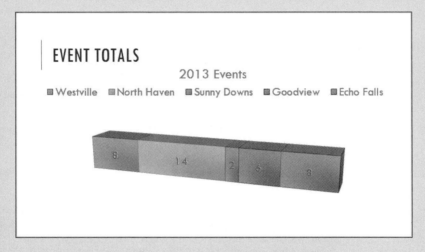.

21. Click **cell C2**, type **14**, and tap [Enter].

22. Close the **Chart** window.

23. Choose **Chart Tools→Design→Type→Change Chart Type**.

24. Choose the last chart type in the **Bar** category, **3-D 100% Stacked Bar**, and click **OK**.

25. Drag the **bottom-left handle** of the chart's border to the **bottom-left corner** of the slide.

26. Drag the **top-middle handle** of the chart's border up until the **top edge** of the chart touches the bottom of the slide's title text.

Change Chart Colors

27. Choose **Chart Tools→Design→Chart Styles→Change Colors→Color 2**.

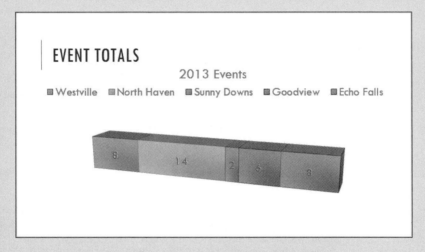

Link to an Excel Chart

28. Start **Excel** and choose **Open Other Workbooks**.

29. Browse to your **PP2013 Lesson 04** folder and double-click the **PP04-R03-Events** workbook file.

30. Click the **chart** to select it and then choose **Home→Clipboard→Copy**.

31. Exit **Excel**.

32. In PowerPoint, choose **Home→Slides→New Slide**.

33. Type **Event Popularity** as the slide title.

34. Choose **Home→Slides→Layout→Title Only**.

35. Choose **Home→Clipboard→Paste**.

36. Drag the **bottom-left handle** of the chart's border to the **bottom-left corner** of the slide.

37. Drag the **top-right handle** of the chart's border up and to the right, until the top edge of the chart touches the bottom of the title text and the chart is as wide as possible while keeping the chart buttons visible, as in the following figure.

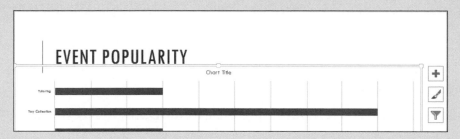

38. Click the **chart title** and tap ⌊Delete⌋.

39. Choose **Home→Font→Font Size menu ▼→24**.

Break a Link

40. Minimize **PowerPoint**.

41. Use **Computer** or **File Explorer** to navigate to the **PP2013 Lesson 04** folder and locate the **PP04-R03-Events** workbook.

42. Click the **PP04-R03-Events** workbook to select it and tap ⌊F2⌋ to highlight the filename.

43. Type `PP04-R03-Events2013` and tap ⌊Enter⌋ to rename the file.

Fix a Broken Link and Edit a Linked Data Source

44. Click the **PowerPoint** button on the **Windows taskbar** to restore PowerPoint.

45. Click the chart to select it, if necessary.

46. Choose **Chart Tools→Design→Data→Edit Data**.

47. Click **OK** to dismiss the **Information** dialog box.

48. Choose **File→Info→Edit Links to Files**.

49. Click **Change Source**, navigate to the **PP2013 Lesson 04** folder, and double-click the **PP04-R03-Events2013** workbook.

50. Click the **Close** button.

51. Click the **Back** button at the top of the left column to exit Backstage view.

At the time of this writing, a bug in PowerPoint causes the chart to no longer display even though the data is still linked. It may be necessary to delete and copy/paste the chart again if Microsoft hasn't released an update yet.

52. Choose **Chart Tools→Design→Data→Edit Data**.

53. Click **cell E2** and type 0.

54. Click **cell E3** and type 1.

55. Click **cell E5** and type 1.

56. Close the **Linked Data** window and click **Save** when prompted.

Edit and Refresh External Data

57. Start **Excel** and choose **Open Other Workbooks**.

58. Browse to your **PP2013 Lesson 04** folder and double-click **PP04-R03-Events2013**.

59. Click **cell C9** and type **0**, and then click **cell C8** and type **4**.

60. Click **cell E9** and type **0**, and then click **cell E8** and type **3**.

61. Save the **Excel** workbook and exit **Excel**.

62. In **PowerPoint**, choose **Chart Tools→Design→Data→Refresh Data**.

Insert SmartArt

63. Choose **Home→Slides→New Slide**.

64. Choose **Home→Slides→Layout→Title and Content**.

65. Type **Most Popular** as the **slide title**.

66. Click the **Insert SmartArt** icon on the slide.

67. Choose the **Pyramid** category, the **Basic Pyramid** graphic, and then click **OK**.

68. Click the **bottom text box** of the pyramid and type **Bully No More**.

69. Click the **middle text box** of the pyramid and type **Adopt a Street**.

70. Click the **top text box** of the pyramid and type **Toy Collection**.

Format SmartArt

71. Choose **SmartArt Tools→Design→SmartArt Styles→More→3-D→Brick Scene**.

72. Choose **SmartArt Tools→Design→SmartArt Styles→Change Colors→Colorful→Colorful – Accent Colors**.

73. Drag the **top-center handle** of the SmartArt border to the **top** of the slide.

74. Drag the **bottom-right handle** of the SmartArt border to the **bottom-right corner** of the slide.

Add Elements to SmartArt

75. Click in the **bottom text box** of the pyramid.

76. Choose **SmartArt Tools→Design→Create Graphic→Add Shape menu ▼→Add Shape After**.

77. Type **Diversity Festival** in the bottom text box.

78. Save the changes and then exit **PowerPoint**. Submit your final file based on the guidelines provided by your instructor.

Apply Your Skills

Insert and Format an Embedded Chart

In this exercise, you will create a new presentation for Universal Corporate Events and add a nicely formatted, embedded chart to the presentation.

Begin a New Presentation and Create an Embedded Chart

1. Start **PowerPoint** and create a new, blank presentation.

2. Save the file as **PP04-A01-Review-[FirstInitialLastName]** in your **PP2013 Lesson 04** folder.

3. Apply the **Retrospect** theme.

4. Type the title **Universal Corporate Events** and the subtitle **Quarterly Review**.

5. Add a new slide with the title **Quarterly Breakdown**.

6. Insert a **Clustered Column** chart.

7. Enter this data:

◢	A	B	C	D	E
1		Jan-Mar	Apr-Jun	Jul-Sep	Oct-Dec
2	Total Events	22	72	34	115

8. Drag the data's border so that only **rows 1 and 2** are included and then close the **Chart window**.

Edit Chart Data and Change Chart Type, Layout, and Style

9. Edit the chart's data so that **cell B2** has a value of **18** and **cell E2** has a value of **132**.

10. Change the chart type to **3-D Clustered Column**.

11. Change the chart layout to **Layout 2**.

12. Change the chart style to **Style 11**.

Select Chart Elements and Change Chart Size and Text

13. Remove the chart's **Title, Gridlines, and Primary Vertical Axis label**.

14. Resize the chart so it fills the maximum area of the slide without overlapping the slide title.

15. Set the font size of the chart to **24**.

16. Click the number **18** above the first bar, locate the **Chart Tools→Format→Shape Styles gallery**, and choose the first style, **Colored Outline – Black, Dark 1**.

17. Apply the same **Shape Style** to the numbers on top of the remaining bars.

18. Save the changes and then exit **PowerPoint**. Submit your final file based on the guidelines provided by your instructor.

To view examples of how your file or files should look at the end of this exercise, go to the student resource center.

APPLY YOUR SKILLS PP04-A02

Work with Linked Charts and SmartArt

In this exercise, you will add a chart linked to an external data source. You will also add and format SmartArt.

Link and Format a Chart

1. Start **PowerPoint**. Open **PP04-A02-Projections** from the **PP2013 Lesson 04** folder and save it as `PP04-A02-Projections-[FirstInitialLastName]`.

2. Add a new third slide with the title `Event Projections`.

3. Start **Excel**. Open **PP04-A02-Projections** from the **PP2013 Lesson 04** folder.

4. Copy the chart from the **Excel spreadsheet** and paste it onto the **Event Projections PowerPoint slide**. Then exit **Excel**.

5. Resize the chart so it fills the maximum area of the slide without overlapping the slide title.

6. Use the **Chart Elements** button to display **Data Labels**.

7. Set the font size of the chart to **28**.

8. Change the colors of the chart to **Color 2**.

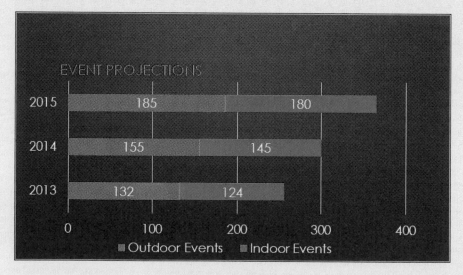

Fix a Broken Link and Edit a Linked Data Source

9. Select the chart on **slide 2** and attempt to edit the data.

   You must repair the broken link before you can edit the data.

10. Edit the link to the chart so that instead of pointing to the **Events2013.xlsx** workbook, the chart points to **PP04-A02-Events**.

11. Edit the chart data so that **cell B2** (Award Ceremonies value) is **67** instead of 7.

Insert and Modify SmartArt

12. Add a new fourth slide with the **Title and Content** layout.

13. Use `Growth` as the slide title.

14. Add the **Process→Upward Arrow** SmartArt graphic to the slide.

15. Type `Improved Catering` in the **left text box**, `Economic Transportation` in the **middle text box**, and `Building Ownership` in the **right text box**.

16. Add a shape **after** the right-most text box with the text `Growth in 2014`.

17. Use the **SmartArt Tools→Design** tab to apply the **Colorful→Colorful Range – Accent Colors 3-4** colors to the SmartArt.

18. Use the **SmartArt Tools→Design** tab to apply the **3-D→Polished** SmartArt Style.

19. Select each text box in the SmartArt graphic and use the Font Color menu on the **Home** tab to change all the SmartArt text colors to **Green, Accent 3**.

20. Enlarge the graphic and make the text **bold**.

21. Save the changes and then exit **PowerPoint**. Submit your final file based on the guidelines provided by your instructor.

    To view examples of how your file or files should look at the end of this exercise, go to the student resource center.

APPLY YOUR SKILLS PP04-A03

Work with Charts and SmartArt

In this exercise, you will add and format charts and SmartArt to the Universal Corporate Events presentation.

Begin a New Presentation and Create an Embedded Chart

1. Start **PowerPoint**. Create a new, blank presentation and save it to your **PP2013 Lesson 04** folder as `PP04-A03-Supplies-[FirstInitialLastName]`.

2. Apply the **Ion** theme with the **fourth (orange) variant**.

3. Give the slide a title of `Universal Corporate Events` and a subtitle of `Supplies`.

4. Change the font size of the slide title to **40**.

5. Add a second slide with the title `Projected Catering Supplies for 2014` and use the icon on the slide to insert a **Clustered Column** chart.

6. Type the following data in the spreadsheet and remove **row 5** from the chart data.

⬆	A	B	C	D
1		2012	2013	2014
2	Bamboo Skewers	1250	1300	1500
3	Foil Pans	251	372	475
4	Foil Trays	175	310	400
5	Category 4	4.5	2.8	5

Format a Chart and Edit Chart Data

7. Resize the chart so it fills the maximum area of the slide without overlapping the slide title.

8. Delete the **chart title**.

9. Apply **Chart Style 6**.

10. Use the **Chart Elements** button to display the **Data Labels** and hide the **Gridlines** and **Primary Vertical axis**.

11. Apply the **Color 3** colors to the chart and increase the **font size** to **24**.

12. Edit the chart data to include the following data in **row 5**. Be sure to extend the data's border so row 5 is included in the chart.

3	Foil Pans	251	372	475
4	Foil Trays	175	310	400
5	Sterno Cans	200	250	290

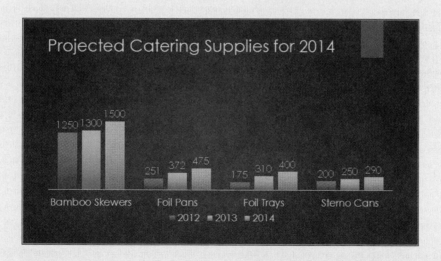

Link a Chart and Change and Format a Linked Chart

13. Create a new third slide with the title **Popular Dishes** and set the slide layout to **Title Only**.

14. Start **Excel**. Open **PP04-A03-Favorites** from the **PP2013 Lesson 04** folder.

15. Copy the chart from the **Excel spreadsheet** and paste it onto the **Popular Dishes PowerPoint slide**. Exit **Excel**.

16. Resize the chart so it fills the maximum area of the slide without overlapping the slide title.

17. Change the chart type to **3-D Pie**.

18. Apply a **Chart Style** of **Style 1** to the chart.

19. Change the layout of the chart to **Layout 1**.

20. Use the **Chart Elements button** next to the chart to hide the **Chart Title** and show **Data Labels→Data Callout**.

21. Set the font size of the chart to **24**.

Break and Fix a Link and Edit a Linked Data Source

22. Minimize **PowerPoint** and use **Computer** or **File Explorer** to navigate to the **PP2013 Lesson 04** folder and locate the **PP04-A03-Favorites** workbook.

23. Rename the file `PP04-A03-Favorites2013`.

24. Restore **PowerPoint**, click the chart, and attempt to edit the data.

25. Dismiss the **Information** dialog box.

26. Edit the link to the spreadsheet so PowerPoint can find the newly named **PP04-A03-Favorites2013** file.

   At the time of this writing, a bug in PowerPoint causes the chart to no longer display even though the data is still linked. It may be necessary to delete and copy/paste the chart again if Microsoft hasn't released an update yet.

27. Edit the chart data to show **1938** servings of **Grilled Shrimp**.

28. Save the presentation and exit **PowerPoint**.

Edit and Refresh External Data

29. Start **Excel** and open **PP04-A03-Favorites2013**.

30. Change the **Lasagna** servings to **1164** and the **Eggplant** servings to **1223**.

31. Save the **Excel** workbook and exit **Excel**.

32. Start **PowerPoint** and open **PP04-A03-Supplies-[FirstInitialLastName]**.

33. Refresh the data on **slide 3**.

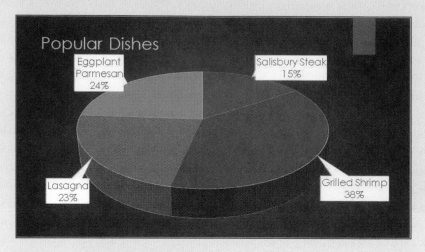

Insert and Format SmartArt

34. Create a **new fourth slide** with the **Title and Content** layout and a **slide title** of `Catering Goals`.

35. Insert a **Relationship→Radial Cycle** graphic.

36. In the **top circle**, type `Flavorful`. In the **right circle**, type `Healthy`. In the **left circle**, type `Economical`. In the **inner circle**, type `Respected and Desired`.

37. Click in the **bottom circle**, click the **text box's border**, and tap `Delete`.

38. Apply the **3-D→Polished** SmartArt Style to the graphic.

39. Apply the **Primary Theme Colors→Dark 2 Fill** color.

40. Resize the SmartArt so it fills the maximum area of the slide without overlapping the slide title.

41. **Bold** the text and add a **text shadow**.

42. Save the changes and then exit **PowerPoint**. Submit your final file based on the guidelines provided by your instructor.

Extend Your Skills

In the course of working through the Extend Your Skills exercises, you will think critically as you use the skills taught in the lesson to complete the assigned projects. To evaluate your mastery and completion of the exercises, your instructor may use a rubric, with which more points are allotted according to performance characteristics. (The more you do, the more you earn!) Ask your instructor how your work will be evaluated.

PP04-E01 That's the Way I See It

Charts are often used in advertising to exaggerate results. Interview ten people and ask them to choose their favorite item from a list of three things (such as ice-cream flavors, cell-phone brands, or musical genres). Create a new presentation with an appropriate title and subtitle on the first slide. Apply an appropriate design theme. On a second slide, add a title and insert a pie chart that displays your survey results. Label each pie slice with a percentage to exaggerate the results. (Showing 60 percent prefer chocolate is more impressive than showing only six people!) Use the Chart Elements button to experiment with showing/hiding chart elements. Ensure that all information displays without looking too busy, and that the chart and labels are large enough for an audience to see when the slide show is presented. Add a third slide that displays the survey results as a visually appealing SmartArt graphic. Save the file as **PP04-E01-Survey-[FirstInitialLastName]** in the **PP2013 Lesson 04** folder.

You will be evaluated based on the inclusion of all elements specified, your ability to follow directions, your ability to apply newly learned skills to a real-world situation, your creativity, and the relevance of your topic and/or data choice(s). Submit your final file based on the guidelines provided by your instructor.

PP04-E02 Be Your Own Boss

In this exercise, you will create a presentation to show the flowers planted by your company, Blue Jean Landscaping, as well as a graphic to explain the basics of garden health for your clients. Create a new, blank presentation named **PP04-E02-BlueJeanChart-[FirstInitialLastName]** in the **PP2013 Lesson 04** folder. Apply the Wisp theme, the title **Blue Jean Landscaping**, and the subtitle **Flowers Planted**. Create a second slide with the Title Only layout and the title **Flowers Planted**. In Excel, create a new, blank spreadsheet that lists flowers down column A and numbers down column B. The spreadsheet should show **Roses – 972, Daisies – 473, Tulips – 554, Sunflowers – 576**, and **Asters – 327**. Select the cells containing data and insert a chart on the Excel spreadsheet. Save the spreadsheet as **PP04-E02-FlowerData-[FirstInitialLastName]**. Copy the chart and paste it onto the PowerPoint slide. Change the chart type in PowerPoint to best display the data. Apply chart elements, chart style, chart layout, and color to maintain a high level of readability.

Create a third slide with the title **Garden Health** and insert a SmartArt graphic appropriate for displaying these sequential steps: **Repel Bugs, Replenish Soil, Eliminate Weeds, Provide Water, Check Daily**. Format the SmartArt so it is attractive and easy to read.

You will be evaluated based on the inclusion of all elements specified, your ability to follow directions, your ability to apply newly learned skills to a real-world situation, your creativity, and your demonstration of an entrepreneurial spirit. Submit your final file based on the guidelines provided by your instructor.

Transfer Your Skills

In the course of working through the Transfer Your Skills exercises, you will use critical-thinking and creativity skills to complete the assigned projects using skills taught in the lesson. To evaluate your mastery and completion of the exercises, your instructor may use a rubric, with which more points are allotted according to performance characteristics. (The more you do, the more you earn!) Ask your instructor how your work will be evaluated.

PP04-T01 Use the Web as a Learning Tool

Throughout this book, you will be provided with an opportunity to use the Internet as a learning tool by completing WebQuests. According to the original creators of WebQuests, as described on their website (WebQuest.org), a WebQuest is "an inquiry-oriented activity in which most or all of the information used by learners is drawn from the web." To complete the WebQuest projects in this book, navigate to the student resource center and choose the WebQuest for the lesson on which you are currently working. The subject of each WebQuest will be relevant to the material found in the lesson.

WebQuest Subject: Using Different Chart Types

Submit your final file(s) based on the guidelines provided by your instructor.

PP04-T02 Demonstrate Proficiency

Stormy BBQ is displaying the results of a customer survey on their in-house television screens. New surveys have come in, and the data must be updated. Additionally, many customers report that the current survey results are hard to read.

Open **PP04-T02-BBQ** from the **PP2013 Lesson 04** folder and save it as **PP04-T02-BBQ-[FirstInitialLastName]**. Edit the chart data, after repairing the link, to indicate that 2 kids like the prices, 3 kids like the service, 115 kids like the ribs, 110 adults like the ribs, and 80 adults like the prices.

Apply an appropriate design theme to the presentation. Enlarge and format the chart, hiding/showing chart elements as necessary. Ensure that the chart is attractive and easy to read. On a third slide, create a SmartArt graphic that displays the top three reasons why people love Stormy's.

Submit your final file based on the guidelines provided by your instructor.

Preparing a Presentation

LEARNING OBJECTIVES

After studying this lesson, you will be able to:

- Edit document properties
- Create and print speaker notes and handouts
- Use proofing tools such as Spell Check, Find, and Replace
- Create agenda and hyperlinked summary slides
- Draw on slides during a slide show

PowerPoint 2013 supplies you with robust tools for both the development and delivery of your presentation. In this lesson, you will focus on the automatic editing features of PowerPoint 2013 as well as the slide show delivery options. All of these tools work together to refine and polish the presentation so that it is visually pleasing, grammatically correct, and effortlessly delivered.

Preparing the Presentation

Green Clean is a janitorial product supplier and cleaning service contractor to small businesses, shopping plazas, and office buildings. Several presentations that promote the business already exist. With the style, graphics, and animation in place, you use PowerPoint's editing tools to check that the spelling is correct. You also use the enhanced Slide Show toolbar to work on the delivery of the presentation. Knowing that most people in the audience will not remember everything in the presentation, you decide to create a summary slide and use the Laser Pointer tool to remind them of key points. You also realize that creating handouts will help the audience remember the services of Green Clean.

A summary slide with links to each presentation slide

Preparing a Presentation

Video Library http://labyrinthelab.com/videos   Video Number: PP13-V0501

PowerPoint 2013 has printing and editing features that can help you prepare for a presentation and give attendees a printed copy of:

- **Speaker notes:** You can draft and print notes about what you will say as each slide is displayed.
- **Editing tools:** You can use Spell Check, Find and Replace, and smart tag features to polish the presentation.
- **Printed handouts:** You can select from a variety of formats to print the presentation on paper for distribution.

Creating Speaker Notes

It's a known fact: Speaking before a group can be intimidating. Even an experienced presenter feels a flurry of anxiety before a presentation. The best way to thwart that anxiety is to be fully prepared. Consider using speaker notes to help with your delivery. Speaker notes are printable comments that you add to slides. They are not visible to the audience. Speaker notes can help you stay on track because if you suddenly freeze, you will be able to scan the notes you carefully prepared to keep your delivery style smooth. Using speaker notes can help you deliver an enthusiastic, informative presentation with confidence. In Normal view, speaker notes are shown below the slide in a small scrolling box. In Notes view, they are shown below the slide in a large box.

The Notes view lets you draft notes to be printed with a miniature image of each slide.

PowerPoint 2013

DEVELOP YOUR SKILLS PP05-D01
Add Speaker Notes

In this exercise, you will add speaker notes to a few slides of the Green Clean Notes presentation.

1. Open **PP05-D01-Notes** from the **PP2013 Lesson 05** folder and save it as **PP05-D01-Notes-[FirstInitialLastName]**.

   Replace the bracketed text with your first initial and last name. For example, if your name is Bethany Smith, your filename would look like this: PP05-D01-Notes-BSmith.

2. Choose **View→Presentation Views→Notes Page**.

   PowerPoint displays a full-screen view that includes the current slide and the notes area. However, notice that the phrase Click to add text *in the notes area is difficult to read.*

3. Adjust the zoom control percentage on the **Zoom slider** in the bottom-right corner of the PowerPoint window to **100%**.

4. If necessary, scroll until the phrase *Click to add text* is visible in the notes section on the title slide.

5. Click on the phrase *Click to add text* and type this replacement phrase: **Don't forget to thank the following people:**

6. Tap Enter to move the insertion point to the next line, and then type these three lines, tapping Enter after each line except the last:

   Talos Bouras - Sales Manager Enter
   Michael Chowdery - Purchasing Manager Enter
   Ahn Tran - Office Manager

   You can apply formatting to the content of speaker notes by using the same techniques used on slides.

7. Select (highlight) the last three lines you just typed and choose
Home→Paragraph→Bullets.

PowerPoint applies bullets to the three selected lines, making the note easier to read. Your notes section should resemble this figure.

Don't forget to thank the following people:
- Talos Bouras – Sales Manager
- Michael Chowdery – Purchasing Manager
- Ahn Tran – Office Manager

8. Scroll through the presentation until you reach the **Our Services** slide and add this text in the notes section: `Mention the 2012 Green USA magazine article ranking us as the most eco-friendly janitorial service.`

9. Scroll to the **Products Sold** slide and add this text to the notes section: `Once again, mention Green USA magazine article.`

10. Scroll to the **Administrative Staff** slide and add these notes: `Over 30 employees` Enter `Growing rapidly.`

11. Select the two lines you just typed and choose **Home→Paragraph→Bullets**.

At this point, four slides in your presentation should contain speaker notes.

View the Notes

12. Choose **View→Presentation Views→Normal**.

13. Choose **File→Print**.

14. Follow these steps to choose and preview the notes pages:

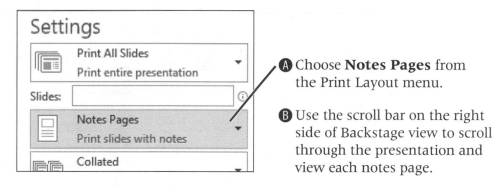

Ⓐ Choose **Notes Pages** from the Print Layout menu.

Ⓑ Use the scroll bar on the right side of Backstage view to scroll through the presentation and view each notes page.

15. Click the **Back** button to close Backstage view without printing.

16. Save your presentation.

Editing Document Properties

Video Library   http://labyrinthelab.com/videos   Video Number: PP13-V0502

Before making your presentations public, it is a good idea to identify the author, title, subject, and other details about the presentation. This information, called the Document Properties, is stored within the presentation file but is not visible on any slide or during a slide show. Specifying the Document Properties can be helpful when, several months after a presentation has been given, you need to determine who created the presentation or for what it was used. You can view and edit the Document Properties via the Document panel.

The Document panel can be turned on from the Info tab of Backstage view.

ⓘ Document Properties ▼ Location:	E:\Green Clean\Pitch.pptx	✱ Required field ✕

Author:	Title:	Subject:
Alec Fehl	Prospective Client Presentatiс	
Keywords:	Category:	Status:
		Complete

Comments:
2013 sales pitch

A variety of fields allow you to specify details about the presentation.

DOCUMENT PROPERTY FIELDS

Field	Possible Usage
Author	Indicate the person or people who created the presentation.
Title	Show the title of the presentation.
Subject	Give the main idea of the presentation, similar to the subject line of an email.
Keywords	List words or short phrases that identify the main idea of the presentation. For example: *services offered, products sold, new client incentives.*
Category	Indicate the broad category of the presentation. For example: *sales* or *prospective client presentation.*
Status	Name the current status of the presentation. For example: *complete, draft,* or *obsolete.*
Comments	Add notes, messages, or instructions you may wish to include for other people who may be working on the presentation or for people who are viewing the presentation on their own.

DEVELOP YOUR SKILLS PP05-D02

Edit Document Properties

In this exercise, you will edit the Document Properties of a presentation.

1. Save the presentation as **PP05-D02-Notes-[FirstInitialLastName]**.

2. Click the **File** tab to display Backstage view.

3. Follow these steps to display the Document panel:

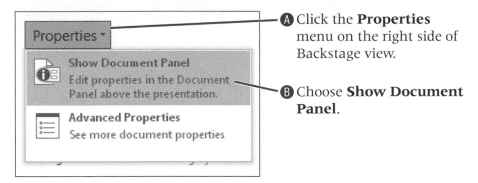

Ⓐ Click the **Properties** menu on the right side of Backstage view.

Ⓑ Choose **Show Document Panel**.

4. Follow these steps to edit the document properties:

Ⓐ Fill in the **Author, Title**, **Status**, and **Comments** fields as indicated, using your actual name as the Author.

Ⓑ Close the Document panel.

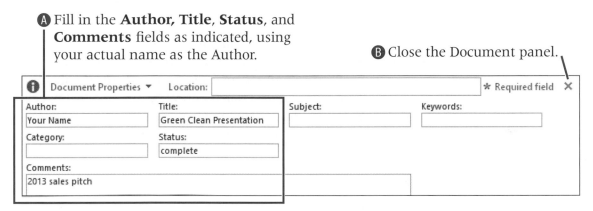

5. Save your presentation.

Editing Your Presentation

Video Library   http://labyrinthelab.com/videos   Video Number: PP13-V0503

To assist you in editing your presentation, PowerPoint 2013 provides a powerful set of editing tools. They include Spell Check, Find, and Replace.

Using Spell Check Features

PowerPoint's Spell Check features work both automatically and manually to help you look for spelling errors in a presentation. By default, apparent spelling errors are flagged as you type, allowing you to easily identify possible errors and fix them manually. PowerPoint's AutoCorrect feature automatically corrects spelling errors as you type, without flagging them. You can also perform a manual review of all content in a presentation.

Checking Spelling as You Type

If you are familiar with Microsoft Office, you probably have used the Spell Check command. PowerPoint's Spell Check feature automatically checks the entire presentation for misspelled words. To indicate a misspelled word, PowerPoint places a wavy red line under the word. You can right-click the misspelled word to display a shortcut menu with suggested replacements for the word. Choosing a replacement from this menu corrects the error as you work.

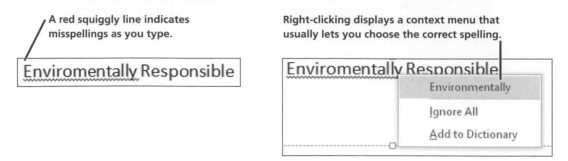

A red squiggly line indicates misspellings as you type.

Right-clicking displays a context menu that usually lets you choose the correct spelling.

The Spell Check Dictionary

PowerPoint installs with a dictionary of standard words. You can add new words to PowerPoint's Spell Check dictionary (which is also shared with the other Office Suite applications). For example, your industry may use special words not included in the standard dictionary. Adding such words to the dictionary prevents their being flagged as misspelled in the future. You can also tell the Spell Check feature to ignore a single instance of a word, or all instances of a word in a particular presentation, without actually adding it to the dictionary.

AutoCorrect

The AutoCorrect feature automatically corrects spelling errors as you type, with no user intervention. PowerPoint keeps a list of common spelling errors mapped to the correct spelling. For example, *abbout* is mapped to *about*. Therefore, if *abbout* were typed on a slide, it would automatically be corrected to *about*. AutoCorrect is also configured by default to correct words with two initial capitals, to capitalize the first letter of sentences, and to capitalize names of days.

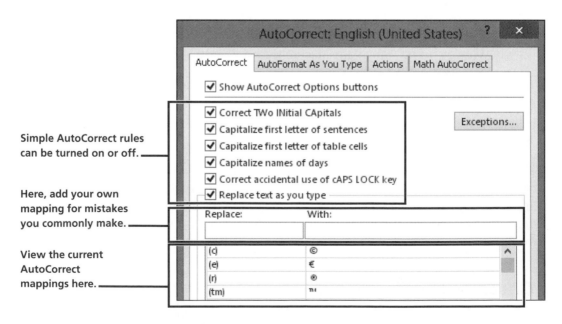

Simple AutoCorrect rules can be turned on or off.

Here, add your own mapping for mistakes you commonly make.

View the current AutoCorrect mappings here.

QUICK REFERENCE	WORKING WITH AUTOCORRECT
Task	**Procedure**
Access the AutoCorrect dialog box	■ Choose File→Options. ■ Select the Proofing category then click AutoCorrect Options.
Create a custom mapping	■ Display the AutoCorrect dialog box. ■ Type the mistake you commonly make in the Replace text box. For example: *lodical*. ■ Type the correct spelling in the With text box. For example: *logical*. ■ Click Add.
Remove a custom mapping	■ Display the AutoCorrect dialog box. ■ Select the desired mapping and click Delete.

DEVELOP YOUR SKILLS PP05-D03

Use AutoCorrect

In this exercise, you will explore the features of AutoCorrect.

This exercise assumes that the spelling dictionary and AutoCorrect options are in their default states. If other students have used the computer before you to complete this exercise, it's likely the spelling dictionary and AutoCorrect options have already been configured. Check with your instructor to see whether your computer utilizes software such as Faronics Deep Freeze to reset any changes made to the system.

1. Save the presentation as `PP05-D03-Notes-[FirstInitialLastName]`.

2. Choose the **title slide** of the presentation.

3. Choose **View→Presentation Views→Notes Page**.

4. In the **Speaker Notes** section, click after the last line and tap Enter.

5. Type this text (be sure to misspell *customer* as indicated):

   `Amy Wyatt - Cutsomer`

   The word customer *is misspelled, but AutoCorrect hasn't fixed it yet. You must indicate that you are through with a word by tapping* Enter *or* Spacebar.

6. Tap Spacebar.

   The word is automatically corrected because PowerPoint is preconfigured to replace cutsomer *with* customer.

7. Continue typing `Service Rep` Enter so the full line reads *Amy Wyatt - Customer Service Rep* and an empty bullet appears in a new line.

8. Type `Isaac Carter - intranet snd Website` (be sure to misspell *and* as *snd*).

   AutoCorrect did not correct the misspelling because replacing snd *with* and *is not a default mapping in PowerPoint. You can create custom mappings for words you mistype often.*

9. Tap ⌨Backspace⌨ until the words *snd Website* are deleted. The mouse pointer should be positioned just after the word *intranet*.

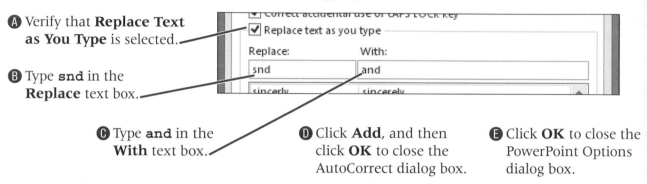

10. Choose **File→Options**.

11. Select the **Proofing** category and then click the **AutoCorrect Options** button.

12. Follow these steps to create a custom mapping:

Ⓐ Verify that **Replace Text as You Type** is selected.

Ⓑ Type **snd** in the **Replace** text box.

Ⓒ Type **and** in the **With** text box.

Ⓓ Click **Add**, and then click **OK** to close the AutoCorrect dialog box.

Ⓔ Click **OK** to close the PowerPoint Options dialog box.

13. Tap ⌨Spacebar⌨ and type **snd Website**. Be sure to misspell *snd* again.
    The word is corrected automatically now that a custom mapping exists.

14. Save your presentation.

Using the Spelling Panel

Video Library   http://labyrinthelab.com/videos   Video Number: PP13-V0504

FROM THE RIBBON
Review→Proofing→ Spelling

FROM THE KEYBOARD
F7 to open the Spelling panel

You can also systematically review all spelling in the presentation with PowerPoint's Spelling panel. This panel reviews not only the slides but also the speaker notes for any incorrectly spelled words. The Spelling panel also offers additional choices not available in the shortcut spelling menu displayed when you right-click.

- **Ignore/Ignore All:** Use the Ignore button to ignore the current instance of the word. Use Ignore All to ignore every occurrence of the word in a presentation.

- **Change/Change All:** Use the Change button to change the current instance of the word to that chosen in the Change To box, or use Change All to change all occurrences of the word in the entire presentation.

- **Add:** Inserts the word in the dictionary.

- **AutoCorrect:** Automatically changes the word on the slide to the suggested word in the Change To box. An AutoCorrect mapping is also added in the AutoCorrect options.

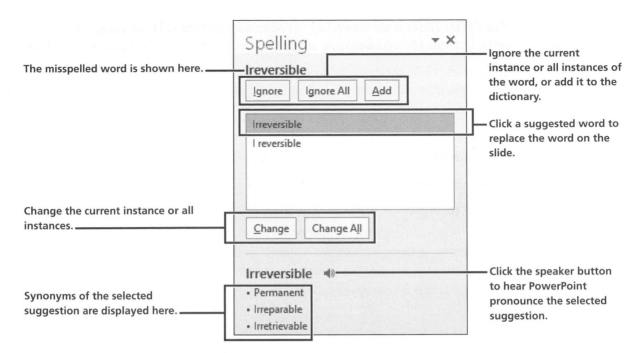

The misspelled word is shown here. → **Spelling**

Ignore the current instance or all instances of the word, or add it to the dictionary.

Click a suggested word to replace the word on the slide.

Change the current instance or all instances.

Synonyms of the selected suggestion are displayed here.

Click the speaker button to hear PowerPoint pronounce the selected suggestion.

TIP

Spell Check is not infallible. Incorrect spellings of standard words won't always be caught—for example, *It's there problem now* will not be corrected with *their*.

QUICK REFERENCE	INVOKING SPELL CHECK
Task	**Procedure**
Check the spelling of a single word	■ Right-click the word you wish to check. ■ Select a replacement word in the context menu or choose Spelling for more options.
Check the spelling of the entire presentation	■ Choose Review→Proofing→Spelling.

DEVELOP YOUR SKILLS PP05-D04
Use Spell Check

In this exercise, you will explore the features of Spell Check.

NOTE

This exercise assumes that the spelling dictionary and AutoCorrect options are in their default state. If other students have used the computer before you to complete this exercise, it's likely the spelling dictionary and AutoCorrect options have already been configured.

1. Save the presentation as **PP05-D04-Notes-[FirstInitialLastName]**.

2. Choose **View→Presentation Views→Normal**, and then select the sixth slide, **Welcome Aboard Specials**.

3. Click after the last sentence, tap `Enter`, and type this text, making sure to misspell as indicated: `15% discount on EcoGreen brand cleaing supplies`

EcoGreen is a brand name, so even though it is flagged as misspelled with a wavy red underline, you will ignore it for the moment. Cleaing is misspelled and is flagged with a wavy red underline. It will have to be corrected.

4. Right-click *cleaing* and choose *cleaning* from the shortcut menu.

The spelling is corrected, and the wavy red underline disappears.

Use the Spelling Command

5. Choose **Review→Proofing→Spelling**.

The Spelling panel appears, and the name Talos, used in a speaker note on the title slide, is flagged as a misspelling. Although it's spelled correctly, Spell Check reports it as an error because the name isn't in the dictionary. Because this is a name you may use in other presentations, you will add it to the dictionary so it is never flagged as misspelled. Keep in mind that a different word may appear if you have spelling errors in your presentation that occur prior to the name Talos.

6. Click **Add** to add the word *Talos* to the dictionary.

Talos' last name, Bouras, is flagged as a misspelling.

7. Click **Add** to add the word *Bouras* to the dictionary.

Michael Chowdery's last name is flagged as a misspelling. As this name is close to the word chowder, you will ignore it rather than add it to the dictionary.

8. Click **Ignore All** to ignore all instances of the word throughout all slides.

The word is not added to the dictionary, so it will be flagged as a misspelling if it is used in other presentations. However, clicking Ignore All results in it no longer being flagged as misspelled in this presentation.

9. When the words **Ahn**, **Riso**, **Hazell**, and **D'Andre** are found, click **Ignore All**.

The word EcoGreen is finally displayed. Because this is a brand name, it is not a misspelling but rather an unrecognized spelling.

10. Click **Add** to add the word *EcoGreen* to the dictionary.

No other misspelled words are found, and a message appears informing you that the spell check is complete.

11. Click **OK** to close the Spell Check Complete message box.

12. Save your presentation.

Using the Custom Dictionary and AutoCorrect

Video Library   http://labyrinthelab.com/videos   Video Number: PP13-V0505

Adding a word to the dictionary during a spell check permanently alters the dictionary that PowerPoint uses. This has an effect on future uses of PowerPoint because the added word will no longer be flagged as a misspelled word. On your home computer, that's fine. But in a school computer lab, it is nice to remove your custom words so other computer users can have the benefit of using PowerPoint in its default state.

QUICK REFERENCE	REMOVING CUSTOM WORDS FROM THE SPELLING DICTIONARY
Task	**Procedure**
Remove a custom word from the spelling dictionary	■ Choose File→Options and then choose the Proofing category. ■ Click the Custom Dictionaries button. ■ Click the Edit Word List button to open the CUSTOM.DIC dialog box. ■ Scroll through the word list and select the word to remove. ■ Click Delete to remove the selected word (or Delete All to remove all custom words). Click OK.

DEVELOP YOUR SKILLS PP05-D05
Clean Up the Custom Dictionary and AutoCorrect

In this exercise, you will remove all the custom words from the dictionary and remove custom AutoCorrect mappings so other computer users can use PowerPoint in its default state.

1. Choose **File→Options**.

2. Choose **Proofing** from the left side of the PowerPoint Options dialog box.

3. Click the **Custom Dictionaries** button in the middle of the dialog box.
   The Custom Dictionaries dialog box opens.

4. Click the **Edit Word List** button in the top-right corner of the Custom Dictionaries dialog box.

5. Click **Delete All** to remove all the custom words.

6. Click **OK** to confirm the deletion.

7. Click **OK** to close the dialog box.

8. Click **OK** to close the Custom Dictionaries dialog box.

Reset the AutoCorrect Custom Mappings

9. Click the **AutoCorrect Options** button at the top of the PowerPoint Options dialog box.

10. Type **snd** in the **Replace** box to quickly find the *snd* mapping you created earlier.
    The AutoCorrect mapping snd *to* and *is highlighted.*

11. Click **Delete**. Then click **OK** to close the AutoCorrect dialog box.

12. Click **OK** to close the PowerPoint Options dialog box.

Using Find and Replace

Video Library   http://labyrinthelab.com/videos   Video Number: PP13-V0506

FROM THE KEYBOARD

Ctrl+F for Find

Ctrl+H for Replace

FROM THE RIBBON

Home→Editing→ Find

Home→Editing→ Replace

As you edit the presentation, you may decide to replace one term with a new one. Use the Find feature to find a word or phrase in the presentation. What you do after you find it is up to you. You might make a correction, change the phrasing, or add or remove content from the slide. Using the Find and Replace feature, you can quickly search throughout the presentation for one term and replace it with another simultaneously. The Find and Replace dialog boxes are very similar. In fact, the Replace dialog is simply an extension of the Find dialog. Both allow you to type a word or phrase or select from previously entered terms. The Find and Replace commands, like the Spelling command, search for text on both slides and speaker notes.

Three Useful Options

The Find and Replace dialog boxes have useful options to enhance searches:

- **Match Case:** You can make searches case sensitive, so that searching for *Dog* would not find *dog*.

- **Find Whole Words Only:** You can search for whole words only. For example, if you searched for *cat*, then *catalyst* and *scattered* would be found because they contain the characters *c-a-t*. With the Find Whole Words Only option enabled, a search for *cat* would find only the word *cat*.

- **Replace All:** The Replace All option, available from the Replace dialog box only, replaces all occurrences of the term with a single click throughout the entire presentation. This includes bulleted and non-bulleted text, slide titles, and speaker notes.

 The Find Whole Words Only option is not available if you enter more than one word in the Find What box.

This button changes the Find dialog box into a Replace dialog box.

Use these buttons to find and replace words manually.

Find

Find what:
techniques

☐ Match case
☐ Find whole words only

Find Next
Close
Replace...

Replace

Find what:
techniques

Replace with:
methods

☐ Match case
☐ Find whole words only

Find Next
Close
Replace...
Replace All

This button automatically replaces every instance of the word(s) throughout the presentation.

DEVELOP YOUR SKILLS PP05-D06
Use the Replace Command

In this exercise, you will switch text by using the Replace dialog box.

1. Save the presentation as **PP05-D06-Notes-[FirstInitialLastName]**.

2. Select the **Our Services** slide and note that the second bullet shows *Restroom*.

3. Select the **Products Sold** slide and note that the sixth bullet shows *Restroom*.

4. Select the **Welcome Aboard Specials** slide and note that the third bullet contains the word *Restroom*.

   You will change the word Restroom *to* Bathroom *on only two of the slides.*

5. Select the first slide in the presentation, the title slide.

6. Choose **Home→Editing→Replace**.

7. Type **Restroom** in the **Find What** box.

8. Type **Bathroom** in the **Replace With** box.

9. Remove any checkmarks from the Match Case or Find Whole Words Only options.

   You wish to find every instance of the word restroom, *regardless of whether it is capitalized.*

10. Click **Find Next**.

    The Our Services slide is displayed, and the word Restroom *is selected (highlighted).*

11. Click **Replace** to replace this instance of *Restroom* with *Bathroom*.

    The change is made, and the next occurrence is automatically found. The Products Sold slide is displayed, and the word Restroom *is selected.*

12. Click **Replace** to replace this instance of *Restroom* with *Bathroom*.

    The change is made, and the third occurrence is automatically found. The Welcome Aboard Specials slide is displayed, and the word Restroom *is selected.*

13. Click **Close** to close the Replace dialog box without replacing the word on the Welcome Aboard Specials slide.

PowerPoint 2013

14. Navigate to the **Our Services** and **Products Sold** slides and verify that *Restroom* has been replaced with *Bathroom*.

15. Navigate to the **Welcome Aboard Specials** slide and verify that *Restroom* was not replaced.

Replace All Terms in a Presentation

On second thought, you realize that Restroom *was a better word after all. You will use the Replace dialog to quickly revert all instances of* Bathroom *back to* Restroom.

16. Choose **Home→Editing→Replace**.

17. In the **Find What** box, type `Bathroom`. In the **Replace With** box, type `Restroom`. Be sure to type an initial capital letter in each entry.

18. Select the **Match Case** checkbox to ensure that only occurrences of *Bathroom*, and not *bathroom*, are found.

19. Click **Replace All**.

    PowerPoint makes all the replacements throughout the presentation and displays a summary dialog box informing you that two replacements were made.

20. Click **OK** to close the informational dialog box.

21. Close the **Replace** dialog box.

22. Navigate to the **Our Services** and **Products Sold** slides and verify that the term *Bathroom* has been replaced with *Restroom*.

23. Save your presentation.

Printing Handouts

Video Library   http://labyrinthelab.com/videos   Video Number: PP13-V0507

You can reinforce the main points of your presentation by providing your participants with handouts. Participants will be able to walk away from your presentation with more than a vague memory of your slide show; all of the facts you presented during the presentation will go with them as a reference. Handouts can be printed in a wide range of layouts, from two to nine slides per page. For example, printing three slides on a page places three small slides on the left side and multiple lines on the right for note taking.

Handout with three slides per page

Handout with six slides per page

Using Handout Masters

In any presentation, there is a single handout master that controls the format of the handout sheets. Any changes you make on the master apply instantly to all handout pages in the presentation. The master maintains a consistent look throughout your handout. This is helpful because you need to change only a single handout master, and the layout, look, and feel of multiple handouts will be affected. Options that you can set on the handout master, which affect all printed handout sheets, are summarized below.

FROM THE RIBBON
View→Master Views→
Handout Master

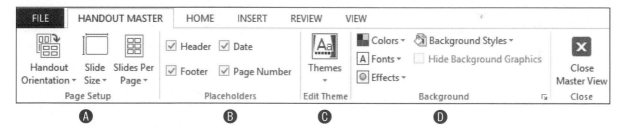

A	**Page Setup options**	■ **Handout Orientation:** This setting changes the orientation of the slides on the handouts without changing their orientation in the presentation.
		■ **Slide Size:** Use this setting to change between standard and wide-screen formats.
		■ **Slides Per Page:** Only the 3 Slides Per Page setting includes lines next to the slides for note taking. This can also be configured in the Print Preview and Print dialog boxes.
B	**Placeholders options**	■ **Header/Footer:** The header appears in the top-left corner of the handout; the footer appears in the bottom-left corner.
		■ **Date:** This displays in the top-right corner of the handout.
		■ **Page Number:** This displays in the bottom-right corner of the handout.
C	**Edit Theme options**	■ You can apply a theme to handouts and alter various theme options.
D	**Background options**	■ **Background Styles:** You can display a solid color, gradient, texture, or picture in the background of the handouts.

Using Handout Headers and Footers

You can set up a header and footer to print on all pages of a handout. These work just like headers and footers in a word processor document. Headers appear at the top, or head, of the document. Footers appear at the bottom, or foot, of a document. Headers and footers often include the presenter's name, occasion, date, and other information, which is helpful when attendees reference the handouts later, after the presentation.

Green Clean End of Year Review		Presented on 1/31/2013

These headers will print at the top of each handout page.

Printing Handouts

Printing handouts is similar to printing slides. Printing handouts is a simple matter of changing printing options on the Print tab of Backstage view.

QUICK REFERENCE	WORKING WITH HANDOUTS
Task	**Procedure**
Design a handout master	■ Choose View→Master Views→Handout Master.
	■ Use the Handout Master tab commands to format your handouts.
	■ Choose Handout Master→Close→Close Master View to return to your presentation.
Print handouts	■ Choose File→Print.
	■ From the Print Layout menu, select a handout layout.

DEVELOP YOUR SKILLS PP05-D07
Print Handouts with a Header and Footer

In this exercise, you will add the date and event to the header and footer of the handouts. The handouts will then be previewed in a special print layout.

1. Save the presentation as **PP05-D07-Notes-[FirstInitialLastName]**.

2. Choose **View→Master Views→Handout Master** to display the handout master for the current presentation.

3. Follow these steps to set up header sheets:

Ⓐ Verify that all four of the **Placeholders** checkboxes have a checkmark.

Ⓑ Scroll to the top of the handout, if necessary.

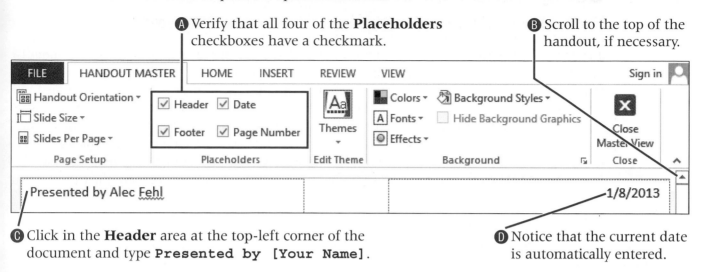

Ⓒ Click in the **Header** area at the top-left corner of the document and type `Presented by [Your Name]`.

Ⓓ Notice that the current date is automatically entered.

4. Scroll down to the bottom of the document, click in the bottom-left Footer placeholder, and type `Green Clean Janitorial Service`.

5. Choose **Handout Master→Close→Close Master View** to return to the presentation.

Use Print Preview

6. Choose **File→Print**.

7. Follow these steps to set the handout layout:

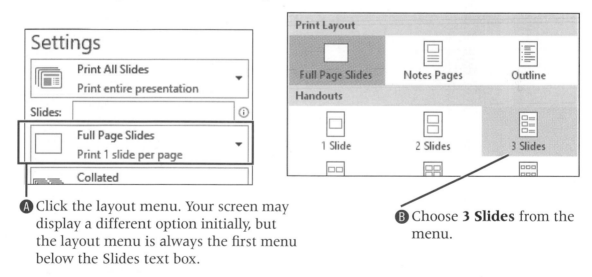

Ⓐ Click the layout menu. Your screen may display a different option initially, but the layout menu is always the first menu below the Slides text box.

Ⓑ Choose **3 Slides** from the menu.

8. Use the scroll bar on the right side of Backstage view to browse through the pages.

9. Choose a different handout format from the layout menu, such as the six slides per page format.

Notice that the three slides per page format is the only one that displays note lines.

10. Click the **Back** ⬅ button to exit Backstage view.

11. Save your presentation.

Using Slide Footers

Video Library   http://labyrinthelab.com/videos   Video Number: PP13-V0508

Just as you can place a header or footer on a handout, you can also place footers on the slides in your presentation. Slide footers often display the date, event name, slide number, or other text that you want visible through the presentation. Although the term *footer* implies being inserted along the bottom of a slide, this will change depending on the slide layout and document theme. For example, some slide footers display along the top of the title slide. The same is true for the other elements, such as the slide number and date. These elements will display in different locations on a slide depending on the slide layout and document theme. Additionally, you may opt to display footers on all slides in the presentation, all slides except the title slide, or selected slides only.

Slide footers and handout footers are completely separate settings.

Footer elements appear in different locations depending on the document theme and slide layout.

Dating Slide Footers

If you choose to include the date, you will need to decide whether you want it updated automatically so your presentation always displays the current date/time—or if you prefer to type in a static date/time that never changes unless you edit it manually. If you choose to update automatically, you may display the date in several formats, including numbers only, day or month spelled out, and the time.

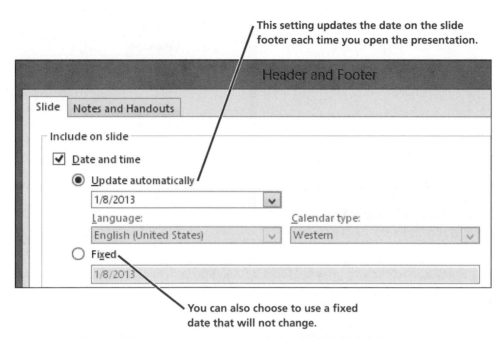

This setting updates the date on the slide footer each time you open the presentation.

You can also choose to use a fixed date that will not change.

QUICK REFERENCE	WORKING WITH SLIDE FOOTERS
Task	**Procedure**
Add slide headers and footers	■ Select the slides(s) to which you want the command applied (not necessary if you will apply the settings to all slides).
	■ Choose Insert→Text→Header & Footer.
	■ Make the desired settings and click Apply (or Apply to All).

DEVELOP YOUR SKILLS PP05-D08

Set Up a Slide Footer

In this exercise, you will create a slide footer and apply it to all slides in the presentation.

1. Save the presentation as **PP05-D08-Notes-[FirstInitialLastName]**.

2. Choose the **Monthly Events** slide (the fourth slide).

3. Choose **Insert→Text→Header & Footer**.

4. Follow these steps to configure your footer:

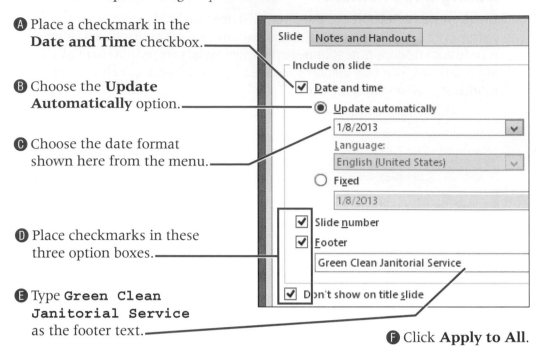

A Place a checkmark in the **Date and Time** checkbox.

B Choose the **Update Automatically** option.

C Choose the date format shown here from the menu.

D Place checkmarks in these three option boxes.

E Type **Green Clean Janitorial Service** as the footer text.

F Click **Apply to All**.

PowerPoint applies the settings to all slides in the presentation. You could have chosen to apply the footer to just the currently displayed slide. The footer should appear at the bottom of the Monthly Events slide.

5. Browse through the presentation and notice that the footer appears on every slide except the title slide.

6. Save your presentation.

Printing Transparencies

In addition to printing handouts and slides to share with your audience, you can also print transparencies to use with an overhead projector, which displays printouts on a large screen similar to a movie projector. While there is no Print Transparency option in PowerPoint, you can simply print your slides, handouts, or notes onto transparency film if your printer supports it. You will need to check the documentation for your printer to learn how to specify transparency film, as the steps vary from printer to printer.

Enhancing Presentation Navigation

Video Library   http://labyrinthelab.com/videos   Video Number: PP13-V0509

Audience members can become anxious before a presentation if they have no idea how long the presentation will run or what topics will be covered. An agenda slide can help alleviate that anxiety. Additionally, if attendees have questions at the end of a presentation, a summary slide offers a visual recap of topics covered and can include navigation that aids the presenter in displaying previous slides without fumbling around trying to locate the desired slide.

Creating Agenda and Summary Slides

Many presentations begin with an agenda slide that outlines the various topics to be covered in the presentation and end with a summary slide that offers a brief recap of what was covered. Savvy presentation designers often integrate hyperlinks in their summary slide to provide not only a review of the presentation, but a way to navigate to any slide quickly should attendees have questions about previous slides at the end of a presentation.

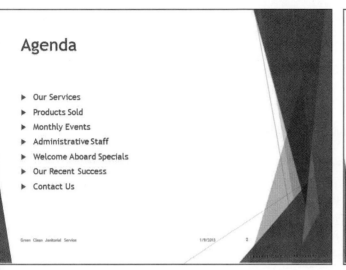

The agenda slide overview makes it easier for the audience to anticipate and follow the flow of your presentation.

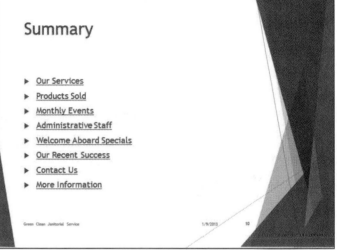

A summary slide allows the presenter to review what the presentation covered. Hyperlinks on the slide make it easy to jump back to specific parts of the presentation.

DEVELOP YOUR SKILLS PP05-D09

Create Agenda and Summary Slides

In this exercise, you will create an agenda slide and a summary slide.

1. Save the presentation as **PP05-D09-Notes-[FirstInitialLastName]**.

2. Select the title slide and choose **Home→Slides→New Slide**.

3. Type **Agenda** for the slide title. Then, type the following in the text box:

   ■ **Our Services** Enter
   ■ **Products Sold** Enter
   ■ **Monthly Events** Enter
   ■ **Administrative Staff** Enter
   ■ **Welcome Aboard Specials** Enter
   ■ **Our Recent Success** Enter
   ■ **Contact Us**

   Notice that the bulleted text you just typed matches the titles of the slides in the presentation. The agenda slide is complete.

Create a Summary Slide

4. Select the **Agenda** slide from the Slides panel on the left side of the PowerPoint window, and then choose **Home→Clipboard→Copy**.

   The entire slide is copied to the Clipboard.

5. Select the last slide, Contact Us, and choose **Home→Clipboard→Paste**.

   The Agenda slide is duplicated after the Contact Us slide, becoming the new last slide in the presentation.

6. Change the title of the last slide from *Agenda* to `Summary`.

7. Save your presentation.

Using Hyperlinks in Presentations

Video Library   http://labyrinthelab.com/videos   Video Number: PP13-V0510

If you've ever browsed a website, you have used hyperlinks. A hyperlink on a web page is text or an image that, when clicked, takes you to another web page. A hyperlink in PowerPoint functions the same as a hyperlink on a web page. You can create hyperlinks in PowerPoint that take you to another slide in the same presentation, open a file on your computer, or take you to a website (provided you are connected to the Internet).

Clicking the Products Sold hyperlink on the summary slide navigates the presenter to the Products Sold slide.

Inserting Hyperlinks

PowerPoint 2013 offers two ways to insert hyperlinks. Though there are slight differences between the two options, the method you choose depends largely on personal preference. This lesson focuses on the Hyperlink dialog box, but both options are described here.

■ **Hyperlink dialog box:** Create hyperlinks that, when clicked, open an existing web page, an existing file, another slide in the current presentation, or an email program with the recipient's email address prefilled.

■ **Action dialog box:** Create hyperlinks or buttons that do everything a regular hyperlink will do, but can also launch other programs, play sounds, and accomplish other complex tasks. Additionally, actions can be made to work when clicked or when the presenter simply points to a hyperlink/button.

Creating Hyperlinks for Slide Navigation

Navigating a presentation doesn't have to be linear. That is, you don't have to start with slide 1, go to slide 2, go to slide 3, and continue sequentially until the end. You can use the Slide Show toolbar to navigate to any slide, but this can break the flow of your presentation because the pop-up menu may clash with the color scheme or document theme. An alternative is to create a slide of hyperlinks that navigate to each slide in the presentation. Hyperlinks can be created in Normal or Outline view, but function only when clicked in Slide Show view.

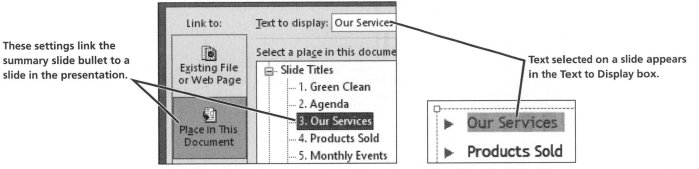

These settings link the summary slide bullet to a slide in the presentation.

Text selected on a slide appears in the Text to Display box.

Integrate hyperlinks into a summary slide to allow quick navigation to any slide should attendees have questions or want to revisit a specific slide.

QUICK REFERENCE	WORKING WITH HYPERLINKS
Task	**Procedure**
Insert a hyperlink	■ Select the text/object to turn into a hyperlink. ■ Choose Insert→Links→Hyperlink. ■ In the Link To section, select the hyperlink type (link to a file or web page, link to another slide in the presentation, or link to an email address). ■ Select the file, type the web page URL, select the slide, or type the email address. Click OK.
Edit a hyperlink	■ Select the text or object that contains the hyperlink. ■ Choose Insert→Links→Hyperlink. ■ Modify your selection in the Edit Hyperlink dialog box and click OK.
Remove a hyperlink	■ Select the text or object that contains the hyperlink. ■ Choose Insert→Links→Hyperlink. ■ Click the Remove Link button at the bottom-right area of the Edit Hyperlink dialog box.

DEVELOP YOUR SKILLS PP05-D10
Add Hyperlinks to a Presentation

In this exercise, you will create hyperlinks on the existing Summary slide.

1. Save the presentation as **PP05-D10-Notes-[FirstInitialLastName]**.
2. If necessary, select the **Summary** slide.
3. Click after the last line, *Contact Us*, and tap Enter to create a new, blank line.
4. Type **More Information**.
5. Select the text you just typed and choose **Insert→Links→Hyperlink** to open the Insert Hyperlink dialog box.

6. Follow these steps to create a link to a website:

Green Clean is a fictitious company, and you will create the hyperlink to point to a fictitious website for that company.

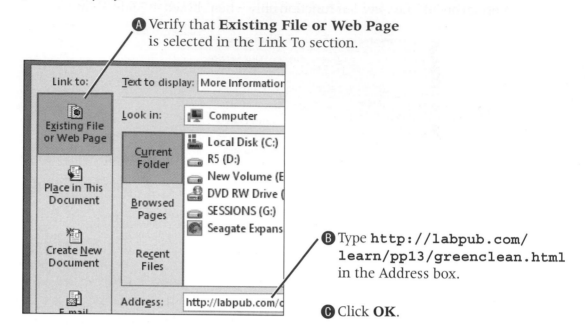

Ⓐ Verify that **Existing File or Web Page** is selected in the Link To section.

Ⓑ Type `http://labpub.com/ learn/pp13/greenclean.html` in the Address box.

Ⓒ Click **OK**.

The More Information text becomes underlined to indicate it is a hyperlink. It has also changed color to match the hyperlink color defined by the document theme.

Create Hyperlinks to Two Slides

7. Select the text *Our Services* on the Summary slide so it becomes highlighted.

8. Choose **Insert→Links→Hyperlink** to open the Insert Hyperlink dialog box.

9. Follow these steps to create a hyperlink to the Our Services slide:

Ⓐ Select the **Place in This Document** option.

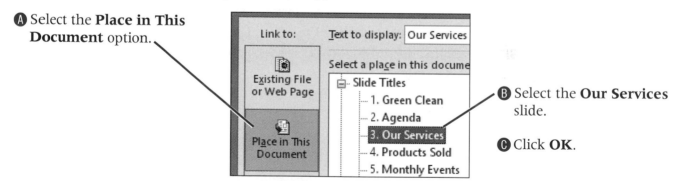

Ⓑ Select the **Our Services** slide.

Ⓒ Click **OK**.

The Our Services text becomes underlined to indicate it is a hyperlink. It has also changed color to match the hyperlink color defined by the document theme.

10. Select the *Products Sold* text, and then choose **Insert→Links→Hyperlink**.

Notice that Place in This Document is already selected from the left side of the dialog box as PowerPoint has remembered your previous selection.

11. Select the **Products Sold** slide and click **OK**.

The Products Sold text becomes underlined and has changed color.

Finish the Navigation Slide

Now you will finish creating a navigation scheme from the Summary slide.

12. Follow these steps to add a hyperlink to the Monthly Events slide:

   ■ Select *Monthly Events* on the Summary slide.

   ■ Choose **Insert→Links→Hyperlink**.

   ■ Choose the **Monthly Events** slide from the Slide Titles list and click **OK**.

13. Repeat step 12 for the remaining four bulleted items on the Summary slide, creating links to the appropriate slides.

   You will test the hyperlinks in the next exercise.

14. Save your presentation.

Repairing and Removing Hyperlinks

Video Library   http://labyrinthelab.com/videos   Video Number: PP13-V0511

Sometimes you may want to remove or edit a hyperlink on a slide. You can edit and remove hyperlinks in the Normal view by using the Hyperlink command. In most cases, the easiest way to edit a hyperlink is to choose a command from the shortcut menu after a right-click.

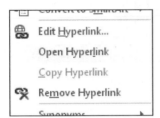

A right-click on a hyperlink displays useful editing commands.

The Necessity to Check Links

It is imperative that you check *every* hyperlink in a presentation. Your professional credibility is at risk if you lead a malfunctioning presentation. If you find during rehearsal that a hyperlink doesn't work, or that it isn't needed at all, you can easily repair or remove it.

Test and Repair Hyperlinks

In this exercise, you will test and explore how to repair hyperlinks.

1. Save the presentation as **PP05-D11-Notes-[FirstInitialLastName]**.

2. Choose **Slide Show→Start Slide Show→From Beginning**.

3. Click through the presentation until you reach the **Summary** slide.

4. Click the **Our Services** hyperlink to immediately navigate to the Our Services slide.

5. Point at the lower-left corner of the slide to display the Slide Show toolbar.

6. Follow these steps to return to the Summary slide:

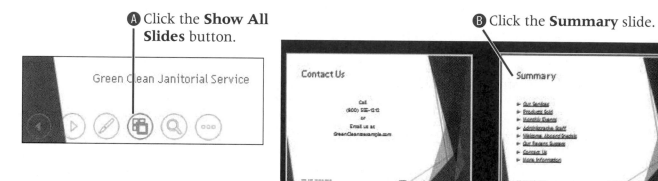

Ⓐ Click the **Show All Slides** button.

Ⓑ Click the **Summary** slide.

Notice that the Our Services hyperlink is now a different color. This indicates a visited link (a hyperlink that has been used).

7. Test the other hyperlinks to verify that they navigate to the correct slide (remember, the More Information link will open your web browser and attempt to connect to the Labyrinth website). Use the **Slide Show toolbar** to return to the Summary slide when needed.

8. Tap Esc to end the slide show and return to Normal view.

   If one of your hyperlinks navigated to the wrong slide, you will make the fix(es) next. If all of your hyperlinks worked, read through the next few steps to learn how to repair and remove hyperlinks should you have the need in the future.

Repair Hyperlinks

9. Click once in the text of your bad hyperlink. If all of your links worked, click inside the *Our Services* text.

   Note that the entire line does not have to be highlighted. Your cursor simply needs to be flashing in the text.

10. Choose **Insert→Links→Hyperlink**.

11. Follow these steps to repair or remove a hyperlink:

Ⓐ Select the correct slide to repair a bad link and click **OK**.

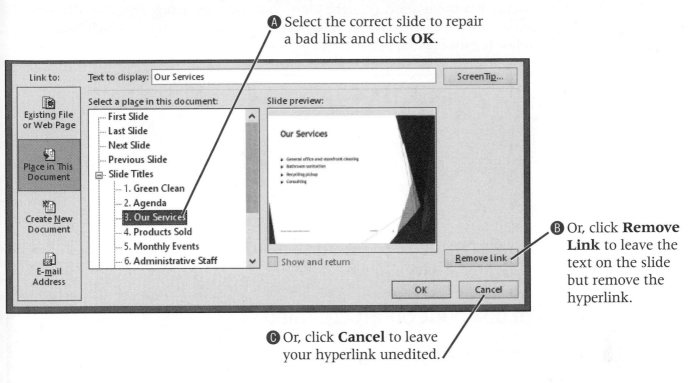

Ⓑ Or, click **Remove Link** to leave the text on the slide but remove the hyperlink.

Ⓒ Or, click **Cancel** to leave your hyperlink unedited.

12. Continue to repair any hyperlinks necessary, and then view the slide show to test your repairs.

13. Save your presentation.

Using the Slide Show Toolbar

Video Library   http://labyrinthelab.com/videos   Video Number: PP13-V0512

The Slide Show toolbar is enhanced in PowerPoint 2013. Normally when you begin a slide show, your mouse pointer is in the form of the Arrow tool, which is used to click slides or objects on a slide. The Pointer option is used to select other tools, such as various pens and a highlighter, which enable you to draw, write, and highlight elements of your slides as you deliver the presentation.

Annotating with Pen Tools

As you deliver your presentation, the audience may ask for more detail on a key issue. This is where PowerPoint's pen tools can help. With the Pointer options, you can immediately respond to the request by using the Pen or Highlighter to annotate slides, thus emphasizing important information. When the presentation ends, you will be asked whether you want to keep or discard any annotations. If you choose to keep them, they are saved with the presentation and will be there when you open it again and run the slide show. If you choose to discard the annotations, they disappear immediately and are

FROM THE KEYBOARD
Ctrl+P to activate the Pen

Ctrl+I to activate the Highlighter

Ctrl+L to activate the Laser Pointer

Ctrl+A to activate the Arrow

not saved with the presentation. Alternatively, you can use the Laser Pointer tool to focus your audience's attention without drawing on the slide. While you can change the color of the Pen and Highlighter tools, the Laser Pointer is always red. Examine the features of each Pointer tool in the table following the illustration.

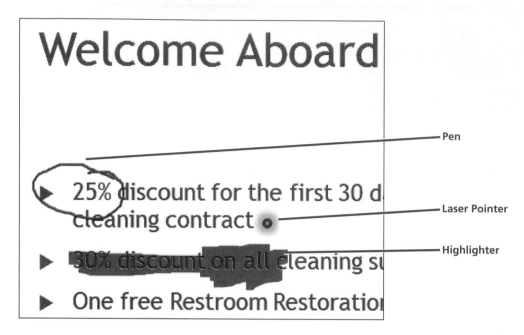

Summary of Pointer Tools

The following is a summary of what is available in the Pointer tools menu:

- **Laser Pointer:** Simulates a laser pointer that focuses attention without drawing on the slide.
- **Pen:** Draws and writes with different colors.
- **Highlighter:** Highlights the text or image with a wide stroke of color.
- **Eraser:** Removes lines or highlighting from the slides.
- **Ink Color:** You can choose from the full spectrum of colors available in PowerPoint to change ink color.

DEVELOP YOUR SKILLS PP05-D12
Use Pointer Options in a Slide Show

In this exercise, you will use each Pointer tool available in the Pointer menu.

1. In **Normal** view, select the title slide and then choose **Slide Show→Start Slide Show→From Beginning**.

2. Navigate to the **Monthly Events** slide.

3. Move the mouse around until the **Slide Show toolbar** appears in the lower-left corner of the screen.

4. Click the **Pointer** 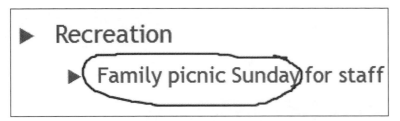 button on the toolbar and choose the **Pen**.

   The arrow turns into the point of a pen. You may need to move your mouse around a bit to see where the pointer is, because the pen tip is very small.

5. Click the **Pointer** again and then choose **Ink Color** and a shade of blue.

   Notice the wide range of colors available to you.

6. Drag with the **Pen** tool to draw an oval around the text *Family picnic Sunday*.

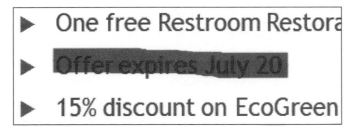

You might draw like this to emphasize this point during the presentation.

Use the Highlighter Tool

7. Tap Spacebar to move forward to the next slide. Continue tapping Spacebar until the **Welcome Aboard Specials** slide is displayed.

8. Click the **Pointer** button and choose the **Highlighter**.

9. Drag to highlight the *Offer expires* line.

> ► One free Restroom Restora
> ► Offer expires July 20
> ► 15% discount on EcoGreen

The Highlighter is actually a wide stroke of color. You may wish to move it back and forth more than once to cover the text completely. The Highlighter tool is another useful way to emphasize a point during a presentation.

Change the Color of the Highlighter Tool

10. Tap Spacebar until the **Contact Us** slide is displayed.

11. Click the **Pointer** button and then choose **Ink Color** and a shade of blue.

    Notice that the Pointer button icon now displays the highlighter, as that is the current tool.

12. Highlight the phone number and email address as shown in the following illustration. Remember, you may have to drag the mouse across the text several times to achieve the desired thickness of the highlight.

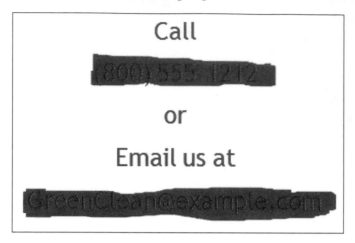

Erase the Pointer Tool Annotations

13. Click the **Pointer** ⟨✎⟩ tool and choose **Eraser**. Click once on the highlighted email address to erase its highlighting, but leave the highlighting on the phone number.

Notice that the highlighting is erased with one click.

Use the Laser Pointer

14. Click the **Pointer** ⟨◇⟩ tool and choose **Laser Pointer**.

The Laser Pointer does not draw on the slide.

15. Drag under the email address as if you were drawing with the Pen or Highlighter. Notice that the Laser Pointer does not draw on the slide.

16. Click anywhere on the slide and notice that the slide show does not advance to the next slide.

You must deselect the current tool to navigate the slide show by clicking.

Discard Annotations

17. Click the **Pointer** ⟨✎⟩ tool and choose **Laser Pointer** to deselect the current tool.

18. Click to the end of the slide show. Choose **Discard** when prompted to keep or discard the annotations.

Slide Zoom

Video Library   http://labyrinthelab.com/videos   Video Number: PP13-V0513

If items on a slide are too small to see from the back of the audience during a slide show, you can use the new Slide Zoom tool to zoom in. Unfortunately, you cannot control the zoom level. PowerPoint zooms in to a preset level.

QUICK REFERENCE	USING SLIDE ZOOM
Task	**Procedure**
Zoom in	■ Start a slide show and click the Slide Zoom button in the Slide Show toolbar.
	■ Click the area of the slide to enlarge.
Zoom out	■ Right-click the slide or tap [Esc].

DEVELOP YOUR SKILLS PP05-D13
Use Slide Zoom

In this exercise, you will use Slide Zoom to enlarge an area of a slide.

1. Choose **Slide Show→Start Slide Show→From Beginning** to begin the slide show presentation.

2. Navigate to the **Contact Us** slide.

3. Move the mouse around until the **Slide Show toolbar** appears in the lower-left corner of the screen.

4. Click the **Zoom** ⊙ button on the toolbar.

5. Click the phone number to zoom in.

6. Drag the slide up to move the email address to the center of the screen.

7. Right-click anywhere on the slide to zoom out.

8. Tap [Esc] to end the slide show.

Presenter View

Video Library   http://labyrinthelab.com/videos   Video Number: PP13-V0514

Presenter view is enhanced in PowerPoint 2013, and operates two ways depending on the number of monitors your computer is connected to. With dual monitors (or a computer screen and a projector), the slide show is shown on one screen for the audience while the presenter sees different information on the computer screen. The information seen only by the presenter includes:

■ A timer so the presenter knows how much time the current slide has been displayed

■ The current time

■ The current slide with easy access to an always-visible Slide Show toolbar

■ Slide navigation tools

■ Preview of the next slide

■ Speaker notes with font size controls

The audience sees the normal slide show.

The presenter's view offers more tools and information.

Presenter View with a Single Screen

If your computer has a single screen, you can still use Presenter view to practice your delivery of a presentation. If Presenter view is enabled, and you run a slide show on a single computer monitor, only the Presenter view (not the audience view) is shown. When you are finished rehearsing, disable Presenter view to run the presentation as a regular slide show.

FROM THE RIBBON

Slide Show→
Monitors→Use
Presenter View

DEVELOP YOUR SKILLS PP05-D14
Use Presenter View

In this exercise, you will view a slide show in Presenter view.

1. Place a checkmark in the **Slide Show→Monitors→Use Presenter View** box to enable Presenter view.

2. Choose **Slide Show→Start Slide Show→From Beginning**.

3. Take a moment to familiarize yourself with the information above the main slide.

The time spent on the current slide is shown here.
The current time is shown here.

4. Click the **Pointer** button on the toolbar and notice that you have access to all the pointer tools.

5. Click the **Pointer** button again to close the menu.

6. Click the **Show All Slides** button on the toolbar.

7. Click the **Agenda** slide to display it.

8. Click the **Slide Zoom** button on the toolbar.

9. Click the *Monthly Events* bullet to zoom in.

10. Right-click anywhere on the main slide to zoom out.

11. Click the **Black or Unblack Slide Show** button on the toolbar.

The main slide turns black. This is helpful to return the audience's focus to you as you speak or make a special point.

12. Click the **Black or Unblack Slide Show** button on the toolbar to unblack the slide.

13. Click the **More Slide Show Options** button on the toolbar.

14. Read the menu options and then click the **More Slide Show Options** button to close the menu.

15. Click the main slide to navigate to the next slide.
    The Our Services slide displays as the main slide. The right column indicates that the next slide will be Products Sold. Speaker notes for the current slide are also displayed in the right column.

16. Click the **Make the Text Larger** button at the bottom of the right column to increase the size of the speaker note's text.

17. Tap [Esc] to end the slide show.

18. Remove the checkmark from the **Slide Show→Monitors→Use Presenter View** box to disable Presenter view.

19. Exit **PowerPoint**.

Concepts Review

To check your knowledge of the key concepts introduced in this lesson, complete the Concepts Review quiz by choosing the appropriate access option below.

If you are...	Then access the quiz by...
Using the Labyrinth Video Library	Going to http://labyrinthelab.com/videos
Using eLab	Logging in, choosing Content, and navigating to the Concepts Review quiz for this lesson
Not using the Labyrinth Video Library or eLab	Going to the student resource center for this book

Reinforce Your Skills

Work with Speaker Notes and Proof a Presentation

In this exercise, you will add speaker notes by using the Notes Page view. You will also check the presentation for spelling errors and use Replace to quickly change text on multiple slides.

Add Speaker Notes

1. Start **PowerPoint** and maximize the program window.

2. Open **PP05-R01-Proofing** from the **PP2013 Lesson 05** folder and save it as **PP05-R01-Proofing-[FirstInitialLastName]**.

3. Choose **View→Presentation Views→Notes Page**.

4. Type **Welcome new members and thank the community organizer** in the Notes text box below the first slide.

5. Use the scroll bar on the right side of the screen to navigate to the **Events** slide and add this text to the speaker notes area:

   Reminder that events are spaced out across the year. Not all held in a single month.

Edit Document Properties

6. Choose **View→Presentation Views→Normal**.

7. Choose **File→Properties→Show Document Panel**.

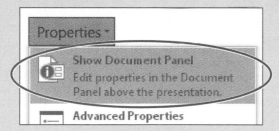

8. Type your name in the **Author** box.

9. Type **This presentation has been spell checked** in the **Comments** box.

10. Close the **Document panel**.

Use AutoCorrect

11. Display the **Program Benefits** slide.

12. Choose **Home→Slides→New Slide** and change the layout to **Title and Content**.

13. Type **Help Us Help You** as the title.

14. Type the following as the slide's only bullet, being sure to misspell as indicated: `Acheive great things for your community!`

    Note that Achieve *is autocorrected as you type.*

15. Click the dashed border around the bulleted text and then choose **Home→Paragraph→Bullets** to remove the bullets.

16. Choose **Home→Paragraph→Center**.

Use Spell Check

17. Choose **Review→Proofing→Spelling**.

18. Use **Ignore All** in the Spelling panel to ignore all instances of *Kidz*.

19. Use **Ignore** to ignore the single instance of *iRecycling*.

20. Select the suggested spelling *Personal* and then click **Change**.

21. Select the suggested spelling *accomplishment* and then click **Change**.

22. Click **OK** when prompted that the spell check is complete.

Use the Replace Command
You will replace all occurrences of Kidz *with* Kids *in the next few steps.*

23. Choose **Home→Editing→Replace**.

24. Type `Kidz` in the **Find What** box and type `Kids` in the **Replace With** box.

25. Click **Replace All**.

26. Click **OK** when prompted that the replacement is complete.

27. Close the **Replace dialog box**.

Print Handouts with a Header and Footer

28. Choose **View→Master Views→Handout Master**.

29. Locate the **Handout Master→Placeholders** group.

30. Clear the checkboxes for **Header** and **Footer** and ensure that the checkboxes for **Date** and **Page Number** are selected.

31. Choose **File→Print**.

32. Set the **Print Layout** option to print **6 Slides Horizontal**.

33. Set the color to **Pure Black and White**.

34. Print one copy and submit it to your instructor based on the guidelines provided.

35. Save and close the file. Exit **PowerPoint**.

36. Submit your final file based on the guidelines provided by your instructor.

    To view examples of how your file or files should look at the end of this exercise, go to the student resource center.

Work with Hyperlinks and Advanced Presentation Tools

In this exercise, you will add a slide footer and create agenda and summary slides. You will also create and test hyperlinks and work with annotation tools and Presenter view.

Set Up a Slide Footer

1. Start **PowerPoint**. Open **PP05-R02-Links** from the **PP2013 Lesson 05** folder and save it as **PP05-R02-Links-[FirstInitialLastName]**.

2. Choose **Insert→Text→Header & Footer**.

3. Check the **Date and Time** box, set the date to **Update Automatically**, and change the date format to display the month name, day, and year.

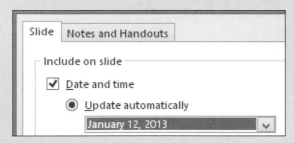

4. Select the **Slide Number** checkbox.

5. Select the **Footer** checkbox and type **Events and Benefits**.

6. Ensure that a checkmark is in the **Don't Show on Title Slide** box and click **Apply to All**.

   The footer displays along the right edge of the slides rather than across the bottom because that is part of the design theme.

Create Agenda and Summary Slides

7. Choose **Home→Slides→New Slide** and type **Agenda** as the title.

   Notice that the footer is automatically included on the new slide because you clicked Apply to All *when previously adding the footer.*

8. Choose **Home→Slides→Layout→Title and Content**.

9. Type the following for the bulleted text: **Events** [Enter] **Program Benefits** [Enter] **Contact Us.**

10. Click the **Agenda** slide in the **Slides panel** to select it.

11. Choose **Home→Clipboard→Copy**.

12. Choose **Home→Clipboard→Paste**.

13. Change the title of slide 3 from *Agenda* to **Summary** and drag the slide so it is after the Contact Us slide.

Add Hyperlinks to a Presentation

14. Select the text **Events** on the **Summary** slide.

15. Choose **Insert→Links→Hyperlink**.

16. Choose **Place in This Document**, select the **Events** slide, and click **OK**.

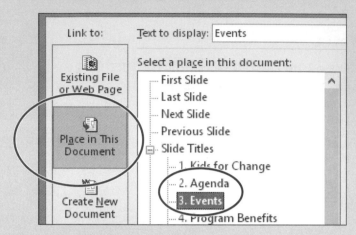

17. Select the text *Program Benefits* on the **Summary** slide.

18. Choose **Insert→Links→Hyperlink**.

19. Choose **Place in This Document**, select the **Program Benefits** slide, and click **OK**.

20. Select the text **Contact Us** on the **Summary** slide.

21. Choose **Insert→Links→Hyperlink**.

22. Choose **Place in This Document**, select the **Contact Us** slide, and click **OK**.

Test and Repair Hyperlinks

23. Choose **Slide Show→Start Slide Show→From Beginning**.

24. Click until the **Events** slide displays and then click the *Want to volunteer?* link.
The link takes you to the title slide instead of to the Contact Us slide. You will fix that in the next few steps.

25. Click until the **Summary** slide appears.

26. Click the *Events* link and note whether it takes you to the **Events slide**.

27. Return to the **Summary** slide and test the next two links, noting whether they take you to the correct slide.

28. Tap ⌨Esc to exit the slide show.

29. Display the **Events** slide, right-click the *Want to volunteer?* link, and choose **Edit Hyperlink**.

30. Choose the **Contact Us** slide and click **OK**.

31. If necessary, display the **Summary** slide. Edit any link that navigated to the wrong slide during the slide show.

Use Pointer Options in a Slide Show

32. Choose **Slide Show→Start Slide Show→From Beginning**.

33. Navigate to the **Events** slide.

34. Point to the lower-left corner of the slide until the **Slide Show toolbar** appears, and then click the **Pointer** button. Select the **Pen** tool.

35. Point to the lower-left corner of the slide until the **Slide Show toolbar** appears, and then click the **Pointer** button.

36. Choose the color **Purple** and draw an oval around *iRecycling Day*.

37. Point to the lower-left corner of the slide until the **Slide Show toolbar** appears, and then click the **Pointer** button. Select the **Highlighter** tool.

38. Point to the lower-left corner of the slide until the **Slide Show toolbar** appears, and then click the **Pointer** button.

39. Choose the color **Light Blue**.

40. Drag to highlight *Toy Collection*.

41. Point to the lower-left corner of the slide until the **Slide Show toolbar** appears, and then click the **Pointer** button.

42. Click **Highlighter** to deselect the Highlighter and return to the Arrow tool.

43. Navigate to the **Contact Us** slide.

Use Slide Zoom

44. Point to the lower-left corner of the slide until the **Slide Show toolbar** appears, and then click the **Slide Zoom** button.

45. Click the number **800** and then drag the slide to center the phone number on the screen.

46. Right-click the slide to zoom out.

47. Tap [Esc] to end the slide show. Click **Keep** when prompted to keep the ink annotations.

Use Presenter View

48. Select the **Slide Show→Monitors→Use Presenter View** checkbox.

49. Choose **Slide Show→Start Slide Show→From Beginning**.

50. Navigate through the slide show and experiment with the **Slide Show toolbar** buttons under the main slide.

51. Tap [Esc] to exit the slide show and **Discard** any ink annotations if prompted.

52. Remove the checkmark from the **Slide Show→Monitors→Use Presenter View** box.

53. Save and close the file. Exit **PowerPoint**.

54. Submit your final file based on the guidelines provided by your instructor.

To view examples of how your file or files should look at the end of this exercise, go to the student resource center.

REINFORCE YOUR SKILLS PP05-R03

Prepare a Presentation

In this exercise, you will prepare a presentation by adding speaker notes and entering document properties. You will proof the spelling and replace text. You will also create agenda and summary slides and practice the presentation by using advanced slide show tools.

Add Speaker Notes

1. Start **PowerPoint**. Open **PP05-R03-Prepare** from the **PP2013 Lesson 05** folder and save it as PP05-R03-Prepare-[FirstInitialLastName].

2. Display **slide 2** and choose **View→Presentation Views→Notes Page**.

3. In the speaker notes box, type Benefits of each.

4. Scroll to the **Goals** slide and add the speaker note 5 houses built last year.

5. Scroll to the **Sponsors** slide and type these speaker notes:
Builder Mart 20% discount for all volunteers [Enter]
Pinky's donating free use of all tools [Enter]
Lorenzo's donating all lumber

6. Select the three lines of speaker notes you just typed and choose **Home→Paragraph→Bullets**.

7. Choose **View→Presentation Views→Normal**.

Edit Document Properties

8. Choose **File→Properties→Show Document Panel**.

9. Type your name in the **Author** box and type Build-a-House Promo in the **Subject** box.

10. Delete any text in any of the other **Document Properties boxes**. Then close the **Document panel**.

Use AutoCorrect

11. Choose **File→Options**.

12. Select the **Proofing** category and then click the **AutoCorrect Options** button.

13. In the **Replace** box, type housw and in the **With** box, type house.

14. Click **OK** twice to close all dialog boxes and return to the slide.

15. Display the **Goals** slide and then click at the end of the last bullet and tap [Enter].

16. Type Finish first housw by end of March.
The misspelled housw *is automatically corrected.*

Use Spell Check

17. Choose **Review→Proofing→Spelling**.

18. Type `Mart` in the **Change To** box and click **Change**.

19. When *Greenview* is found, click **Ignore**.

20. When *communaty* is found, select the suggestion of *community* and click **Change**.

21. Click **OK** when prompted that the spell check is complete.

Clean Up the Custom Dictionary and AutoCorrect

22. Choose **File→Options**.

23. Select the **Proofing** category and then click the **AutoCorrect Options** button.

24. In the **Replace** box, type `housw`.

25. Click **Delete**.

26. Click **OK** twice to close all dialog boxes and return to the slide.

Use the Replace Command

27. Choose **Home→Editing→Replace**.

28. In the **Find What** box, type `The Home Sweet Home Project`. In the **Replace With** box, type `Build-a-House`.

29. Click **Replace All**.

30. Click **OK** when prompted that two replacements were made and then close the **Replace** dialog box.

31. Display the title slide and verify that the subtitle has been replaced with *Build-a-House*.

32. Display the **Purpose** slide and verify that the last bullet has been replaced with *Build-a-House*.

Print Handouts

33. Choose **File→Print**.

34. In the **Slides** box, type `1-3` to print only the first three slides.

35. Set the **Print Layout** option to print **3 Slides**.

36. Set the color to **Pure Black and White**.

37. Print one copy and submit it to your instructor based on the guidelines provided.

Set Up a Slide Footer

38. Choose **Insert→Text→Header & Footer**.

39. Select the **Date and Time** checkbox.

40. Select the **Fixed** option and accept the default format.

41. Select the **Slide Number** checkbox.

42. Select the **Footer** checkbox and type `Build-a-House 2013` in the Footer box.

43. Ensure that **Don't Show on Title Slide** is selected and then click **Apply to All**.

Create Agenda and Summary Slides

44. Display the title slide and choose **Home→Slides→New Slide**.

45. Type `Agenda` as the title.

46. Type the following bullets:

    `Purpose` [Enter]
    `Goals` [Enter]
    `Sponsors` [Enter]
    `Under Way`

47. Click the **Agenda** slide's thumbnail in the **Slides panel** and then choose **Home→Clipboard→Copy**.

48. Display the **Under Way** slide.

49. Choose **Home→Clipboard→Paste** and then change the title of the new slide from *Agenda* to `Summary`.

Add Hyperlinks to a Presentation

50. Select the text **Purpose** on the **Summary** slide.

51. Choose **Insert→Links→Hyperlink**.

52. Choose **Place in This Document**, select the **Purpose** slide, and click **OK**.

53. Link the remaining text on the **Summary** slide to their respective slides.

Test and Repair Hyperlinks

54. Choose **Slide Show→Start Slide Show→From Beginning**.

55. Click until the **Goals** slide displays and then click the *LEED Certification* link. *PowerPoint displays an error box because the link is broken.*

56. Click **OK** to dismiss the error box.

57. Click until the **Summary** slide appears.

58. Click the *Purpose* link and note whether it takes you to the **Purpose slide**.

59. Return to the **Summary** slide and test the remaining links, noting whether they take you to the correct slide.

60. Tap [Esc] to exit the slide show.

61. Display the **Goals** slide, right-click the *LEED Certification* link, and choose **Edit Hyperlink** from the context menu.

62. In the **Address** box, change the last part of the address from *.orb/* to `.org/` and click **OK**.

63. If necessary, display the **Summary** slide and repair any broken link so it navigates to its respective slide.

Use Pointer Options in a Slide Show

64. Choose **Slide Show→Start Slide Show→From Beginning**.

65. Navigate to the **Goals** slide.

66. Point to the lower-left corner of the slide until the **Slide Show toolbar** appears, and then click the **Pointer** button. Select the **Pen** tool.

67. Point to the lower-left corner of the slide until the **Slide Show toolbar** appears, and then click the **Pointer** button.

68. Choose the color **Yellow** and draw an oval around *LEED Certification*.

69. Point to the lower-left corner of the slide until the **Slide Show toolbar** appears, and then click the **Pointer** button. Select the **Highlighter** tool.

70. Point to the lower-left corner of the slide until the **Slide Show toolbar** appears, and then click the **Pointer** button.

71. Choose the color **Light Green** then drag to highlight the last bullet.

72. Point to the lower-left corner of the slide until the **Slide Show toolbar** appears, and then click the **Pointer** button.

73. Click **Highlighter** to deselect the Highlighter and return to the Arrow tool.

74. Navigate to the **Under Way** slide.

Use Slide Zoom

75. Point to the lower-left corner of the slide until the **Slide Show toolbar** appears, and then click the **Slide Zoom** button.

76. Click the number **17** in the first bullet and then drag the slide to center the address on the screen.

77. Right-click the slide to zoom out.

78. Tap Esc to end the slide show. Click **Keep** when prompted to keep the ink annotations.

Use Presenter View

79. Select the **Slide Show→Monitors→Use Presenter View** checkbox.

80. Choose **Slide Show→Start Slide Show→From Beginning**.

81. Navigate through the slide show and experiment with the **Slide Show toolbar** buttons under the main slide.

82. Tap Esc to exit the slide show and **Discard** any ink annotations if prompted.

83. Remove the checkmark from the **Slide Show→Monitors→Use Presenter View** box.

84. Save and close the file. Exit **PowerPoint**.

85. Submit your final file based on the guidelines provided by your instructor.

Apply Your Skills

Work with Speaker Notes and Proof a Presentation

In this exercise, you will add speaker notes by using the Notes Page view. You will also check the presentation for spelling errors and use the Replace command to quickly change text on multiple slides.

Add Speaker Notes and Edit Document Properties

1. Start **PowerPoint** and maximize the program window.

2. Open **PP05-A01-UniversalProofing** from the **PP2013 Lesson 05** folder and save it as `PP05-A01-UniversalProofing-[FirstInitialLastName]`.

3. Add this speaker note to the **Specialties** slide: `We have experts and specialists in all fields.`

4. Add this speaker note to the **Catering** slide: `Food allergies and special requests happily honored.`

5. Display the **Document panel** and add your name as the **Author**.

6. Type `Complete` in the **Status** box and clear the remaining boxes of any text.

7. Close the **Document panel**.

Use AutoCorrect, Spell Check, and the Replace Command

8. Display the **Emergency Medical** slide and add the text `Other equippment provided` as a new third bullet.

   PowerPoint automatically corrects the misspelled word.

9. Check the spelling of the presentation and correct each misspelled word.

10. Display each slide to verify that no text is flagged with a wavy red underline.

    You will replace all occurrences of meals *with* dishes *in the next few steps.*

11. Display the **Replace** dialog box and replace every occurrence of *meals* with *dishes*.

Print Handouts

12. Print one handout in **Pure Black and White** with **9** slides per page and submit it to your instructor based on the guidelines provided.

13. Save and close the file. Exit **PowerPoint**.

14. Submit your final file based on the guidelines provided by your instructor.

    To view examples of how your file or files should look at the end of this exercise, go to the student resource center.

Work with Hyperlinks and Advanced Presentation Tools

In this exercise, you will add a slide footer and create agenda and summary slides. You will also create and test hyperlinks and work with annotation tools and Presenter view.

Set Up a Slide Footer and Create Agenda and Summary Slides

1. Start **PowerPoint**. Open **PP05-A02-UniversalLinks** from the **PP2013 Lesson 05** folder and save it as `PP05-A02-UniversalLinks-[FirstInitialLastName]`.

2. Insert a slide footer on all but the title slide that includes an automatically updated date and time in the default format, slide number, and the footer text **Our Specialties**.

3. Resize or reposition the images on each slide so they do not overlap the footers.

4. Create a new slide before the **Catering** slide with the title **Agenda**.

5. Type the titles of **slides 3–7** as the Agenda slide's bulleted text.

6. Duplicate the **Agenda** slide, change the slide title to **Summary**, and move the **Summary** slide to the end of the presentation.

Add, Test, and Repair Hyperlinks

7. Create a hyperlink for each bullet on the **Summary** slide that links to the bullet's respective slide.

8. View the slide show and test each link on the **Summary** slide and, if necessary, repair any broken links.

Use Pointer Options in a Slide Show

9. View the slide show and use the **Pen** tool to draw a green oval around the text *CPR certified staff* on the **Emergency Medical** slide.

10. Use the **Highlighter** to highlight, in yellow, the text *Other equipment provided* on the **Emergency Medical** slide.

Use Slide Zoom and Presenter View

11. Zoom in on the links on the **Summary** slide. Then, zoom out and end the slide show, saving the annotations.

12. Enable **Presenter view** and view the slide show again, using the tools in Presenter view to draw additional annotations.

13. End the slide show and discard any annotations you created while in Presenter view. Disable **Presenter view**.

14. Save and close the file. Exit **PowerPoint**.

15. Submit your final file based on the guidelines provided by your instructor.
    To view examples of how your file or files should look at the end of this exercise, go to the student resource center.

Prepare a Presentation

In this exercise, you will prepare a presentation by adding speaker notes and entering document properties. You will proof the spelling and replace text. You will also create agenda and summary slides and practice the presentation by using advanced slide show tools.

Add Speaker Notes and Edit Document Properties

1. Start **PowerPoint**. Open **PP05-A03-UniversalPrepare** from the **PP2013 Lesson 05** folder and save it as **PP05-A03-UniversalPrepare-[FirstInitialLastName]**.

2. Add speaker notes to the title slide with this text, formatted as bullets:

   New vegan options
   Food allergy accommodations by request
   Only organic beef

3. Edit the document properties to include **[your name]** as the author and **Catering Entrees** as the subject.

Use AutoCorrect

4. Add a new custom AutoCorrect mapping that replace the text **VT** with **Vegetarian**.

5. On the Vegetarian slide, type this text, allowing PowerPoint to autocorrect as you type:

   VT Lasagna [Enter]
   VT Mushroom Burger [Enter]
   VT Schnitzel

Use Spell Check

6. Check the spelling throughout the presentation and use your best judgment when selecting the replacement suggestions.

7. Remove the custom *VT* to *Vegetarian* mapping in the AutoCorrect options.

Use the Replace Command and Print Handouts

8. Use the **Replace** dialog box to replace *Meat* with *Steak*. Replace only bulleted text, not titles or subtitles.

9. Print one handout in **Pure Black and White** with **6** slides per page and submit it to your instructor based on the guidelines provided.

Set Up a Slide Footer and Create Agenda and Summary Slides

10. Insert a slide footer on all but the title slide that includes only the slide number and the footer text **Specialty Entrees**.

11. Create a new slide after the title slide with the title **Agenda**.

12. Type the titles of **slides 3–6** as the Agenda slide's bulleted text.

13. Duplicate the **Agenda** slide, change the slide title to **Summary**, and move the Summary slide to the end of the presentation.

Add, Test, and Repair Hyperlinks

14. Create a hyperlink for each bullet on the Summary slide that links to the bullet's respective slide.

15. View the slide show and test each link on the **Summary** slide. If necessary, repair any broken links.

Use Pointer Options in a Slide Show

16. View the slide show and use the **Highlighter** to highlight, in light blue, the text *Lasagna, Mushroom Burger*, and *Schnitzel* on the **Vegetarian** slide.

17. Use the **Pen** tool to draw one large, orange oval around the text *three Vegans* in the bulleted text on the **Vegan** slide.

Use Slide Zoom and Presenter View

18. Zoom in on the image on the **Kosher** slide. Then zoom out and end the slide show, saving the annotations.

19. Enable **Presenter view** and view the slide show again, using the tools in Presenter view to draw additional annotations.

20. End the slide show and discard any annotations you created while in Presenter view. Disable **Presenter view**.

21. Save and close the file. Exit **PowerPoint**.

22. Submit your final file based on the guidelines provided by your instructor.

Extend Your Skills

In the course of working through the Extend Your Skills exercises, you will think critically as you use the skills taught in the lesson to complete the assigned projects. To evaluate your mastery and completion of the exercises, your instructor may use a rubric, with which more points are allotted according to performance characteristics. (The more you do, the more you earn!) Ask your instructor how your work will be evaluated.

PP05-E01 That's the Way I See It!

Should people learn to spell? Or is this skill no longer necessary because computers and smart phones integrate spelling and grammar checking? Create a presentation with three slides with the following titles: `Do You Need to Know How to Spell?`, `Computer Spellcheck – Good or Bad?`, and `What Do I Misspell?`. On the first two slides, answer the slide's title question in the first bullet and type at least two more bullets giving reasons to support your answer. On the *What Do I Misspell* slide, list three words you commonly misspell. Insert a title slide at the beginning of the presentation with a meaningful title and subtitle.

Create an agenda slide after the title slide that lists the three questions. Create a summary slide at the end of the presentation that lists the three questions and links to their respective slides. Add slide footers that include the date and slide number. Apply a design theme and adjust the font sizes as you like. Save your file in the **PP2013 Lesson 05** folder as `PP05-E01-Spelling-[FirstInitialLastName]`.

You will be evaluated based on the inclusion of all elements specified, your ability to follow directions, your ability to apply newly learned skills to a real-world situation, your creativity, and the relevance of your topic and/or data choice(s). Submit your final file based on the guidelines provided by your instructor.

PP05-E02 Be Your Own Boss

In this exercise, you will proof a presentation created by one of your employees at Blue Jean Landscaping and then practice giving the presentation by using Presenter view. Open **PP05-E02-BlueJean** from the **PP2013 Lesson 05** folder and save it as `PP05-E02-BlueJean-[FirstInitialLastName]`. Create agenda and summary slides and have the summary slide bullets link to their respective slides. Add speaker notes to the Services slide, reminding yourself that custom fencing is also available. Add a slide footer to all slides, including the title slide, that has an automatically updated date showing the day of the week. Show the slide number also. Check the spelling of the presentation, fixing misspelled words as necessary. View the slide show in Presenter view and highlight the large 40% on the Savings slide. End the slide show, save the annotations, and disable Presenter view.

You will be evaluated based on the inclusion of all elements specified, your ability to follow directions, your ability to apply newly learned skills to a real-world situation, your creativity, and your demonstration of an entrepreneurial spirit. Submit your final file based on the guidelines provided by your instructor.

Transfer Your Skills

In the course of working through the Transfer Your Skills exercises, you will use critical-thinking and creativity skills to complete the assigned projects using skills taught in the lesson. To evaluate your mastery and completion of the exercises, your instructor may use a rubric, with which more points are allotted according to performance characteristics. (The more you do, the more you earn!) Ask your instructor how your work will be evaluated.

PP05-T01 Use the Web as a Learning Tool

Throughout this book, you will be provided with an opportunity to use the Internet as a learning tool by completing WebQuests. According to the original creators of WebQuests, as described on their website (WebQuest.org), a WebQuest is "an inquiry-oriented activity in which most or all of the information used by learners is drawn from the web." To complete the WebQuest projects in this book, navigate to the student resource center and choose the WebQuest for the lesson on which you are currently working. The subject of each WebQuest will be relevant to the material found in the lesson.

WebQuest Subject: Paths

Submit your final file based on the guidelines provided by your instructor.

PP05-T02 Demonstrate Proficiency

Stormy BBQ is creating a recipe book and plans to promote it by displaying a few easy recipes as a slide show on the restaurant televisions. To begin, create a blank presentation and save it as **PP05-T02-Recipes-[FirstInitialLastName]** in the **PP2013 Lesson 05** folder.

Use the Internet or a cookbook to find three easy sauce recipes appropriate for barbeque, grilling, or a cookout. Create a title slide with an appropriate title and subtitle. The second slide should display the ingredients of the first recipe, while the third slide should display the recipe steps. The next two slides should display the ingredients and steps for the second recipe. The final two slides should display the ingredients and steps for the third recipe. Use speaker notes on the second, fourth, and sixth slides to indicate the source of your recipe (where did you find it?)

Create agenda and summary slides that list each recipe and link the bullets on the summary slide to the respective ingredients slide. Add slide footers to all but the title slide that include only the slide number. Print handouts, in black and white, with three slides per page and print only slides 2, 4, and 6. Practice the slide show by using Presenter view. Discard any annotations and disable Presenter view when you are finished.

Submit your final file based on the guidelines provided by your instructor.

Adding Multimedia to Presentations

LESSON OUTLINE

Working with Multimedia

Using Audio in Presentations

Creating Slide Show Timings

Using Video in Presentations

Concepts Review

Reinforce Your Skills

Apply Your Skills

Extend Your Skills

Transfer Your Skills

LEARNING OBJECTIVES

After studying this lesson, you will be able to:

- Acquire and add audio to a presentation
- Acquire and add video to a presentation
- Edit movies and add movie effects
- Use slide show timings
- Loop a presentation endlessly

Sound and movies can enhance a slide show to the point that a presentation is more than just information—it's entertaining. PowerPoint 2013 makes the development of "infotaining" presentations quick and easy. And if you don't have your own audio or video files, PowerPoint offers an extensive gallery of sounds and animated images you can use. In this lesson, you will work with PowerPoint's media features to enhance your presentations.

Adding Multimedia to the Presentation

Green Clean annually donates to a variety of charities, including animal rescue charities and young musician scholarships. You have been charged with creating a few new presentations that will play in a kiosk in the lobby at Green Clean's main office. They will showcase the animals and young musicians who have benefited from Green Clean's generosity. You want the presentations to be entertaining and engaging, but also need them to run by themselves with no human physically clicking through the slides. You decide to add audio and video to the presentations and to use slide timings so that each presentation will run unattended.

The full-motion video on the slide includes audio, allowing viewers to hear and see the effects of Green Clean's charitable donations.

Working with Multimedia

Video Library   http://labyrinthelab.com/videos   Video Number: PP13-V0601

Multimedia, also called rich media, includes video and audio that can enhance a presentation. A photographer delivering a presentation may play a soundtrack of classical music while the slides display a gallery of wedding photos. A presentation used to train employees may have a spoken narration playing throughout the slideshow to explain company policy. A summer camp director giving a presentation to prospective families may include videos of camp activities. Multimedia may be incorporated so simply as to play an audible *click* when navigating to subsequent slides during a presentation. Although multimedia can add excitement to your presentation, it can become overwhelming and distracting if used in excess.

Add multimedia sparingly and only when there is true value in doing so.

Types of Multimedia

PowerPoint lets you add a variety of multimedia types to your presentation, including the following:

- **Audio:** This includes short sound effects such as a click or creaking door as well as entire songs or narration soundtracks. Most users will be familiar with MP3 or WAV sound files.
- **Video:** This can include home movies from your camcorder or downloaded videos from the Internet. PowerPoint does not let you create the video itself. You will need to create your video file in advance.

Linked Media Files

Most multimedia files exist as separate files outside your presentation that are linked to it. However, linked multimedia files function differently than linked data files such as a spreadsheet. You may already know that if a linked data file (such as an Excel spreadsheet containing a chart) is moved or renamed, your presentation will not suffer. The chart will still display, and you will encounter problems only if you try to edit the chart data. When a linked multimedia file is moved or renamed, it will not play during the presentation. Therefore, it is recommended that you store the presentation and all linked media files in the same folder—and don't change the names of the multimedia files after they have been linked. Then you can easily copy all the files in the presentation folder to other media, such as a USB drive or CD, to share with people.

Organizing Media with Subfolders

Video Library   http://labyrinthelab.com/videos   Video Number: PP13-V0602 and PP13-V0603

If you have many linked multimedia files, you may decide to keep your files organized in subfolders rather than having all of your files at the same level within a single folder. This makes it easier to find and launch your presentation and find any multimedia files you may need to edit.

PowerPoint 2013

When all files are in the same folder, finding the one you need may be difficult (left). Organizing your files by type in subfolders makes it easy to find what you want when you want it (right).

Create Multimedia Folders (Windows 8)

Windows 7 Users: *Skip to the next exercise.*

In this exercise, you will create folders to store your various types of multimedia files.

1. If necessary, click the **Desktop tile** on the **Windows 8 Start screen**.

2. Click the **File Explorer** icon on the Windows taskbar and then maximize the **File Explorer** window.

3. Navigate to the **PP2013 Lesson 06** folder and choose **View→Layout→Medium Icons**.

4. Choose **Home→New→New Folder**.

5. Type **Audio** as the folder name and tap Enter.

6. Repeat steps 4–5 to create a second folder named **Video**.

7. Click the **PP06-A01-TransportationNarration** file to select it.

8. Hold down Ctrl as you click these files to add them to the selection:

   - PP06-A03-Invites
   - PP06-R01-Castle
   - PP06-R01-Library
   - PP06-R01-Lunch
   - PP06-D03-bach-bwv813
   - PP06-R01-Makeup
   - PP06-R03-AudioBenefits

9. Once all eight audio files are selected, release Ctrl.

10. Drag any one of the selected audio files onto the **Audio** folder to move all eight selected files into that folder.

11. Click the **PP06-A02-Band** file to select it.

12. Hold down Ctrl as you click these files to add them to the selection:

    - PP06-D07-Classical
    - PP06-R02-ZeroPower
    - PP06-R03-Video

13. Once all four video files are selected, release Ctrl.

14. Drag any one of the selected video files onto the **Video** folder to move all four selected files into that folder.

15. Close the folder window.

Your lesson folder is now organized with multimedia subfolders.

Create Multimedia Folders (Windows 7)

Windows 8 Users: *Skip to the next topic.*

In this exercise, you will create folders to store your various types of multimedia files.

1. Choose **Start→Computer** from the lower-left corner of your screen.

2. Navigate to the **PP2013 Lesson 06** folder.

3. Follow these steps to change the folder view:

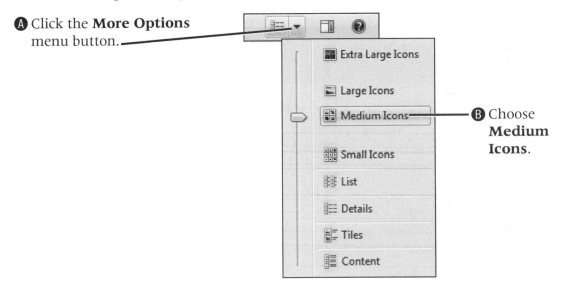

Ⓐ Click the **More Options** menu button.

Ⓑ Choose **Medium Icons**.

4. Choose **New Folder** from the **PP2013 Lesson 06** folder's command bar.

5. Type **Audio** as the folder name and tap Enter.

6. Repeat steps 4–5 to create a second folder named **Video**.

7. Click the **PP06-A01-TransportationNarration** file to select it.

8. Hold down Ctrl as you click these files:

- PP06-A03-Invites
- PP06-D03-bach-bwv813
- PP06-R01-Castle
- PP06-R01-Library
- PP06-R01-Lunch
- PP06-R01-Makeup
- PP06-R03-AudioBenefits

9. Once all eight audio files are selected, release Ctrl.

10. Drag any one of the selected audio files onto the **Audio** folder to move all eight selected files into that folder.

11. Click the **PP06-A02-Band** file to select it.

12. Hold down Ctrl as you click these files to add them to the selection:
    - PP06-D07-Classical
    - PP06-R02-ZeroPower
    - PP06-R03-Video

13. Once all four video files are selected, release Ctrl.

14. Drag any one of the selected video files onto the **Video** folder to move all four selected files into that folder.

    Your lesson folder is now organized with multimedia subfolders.

15. Close the folder window.

Using Audio in Presentations

Video Library http://labyrinthelab.com/videos   Video Number: PP13-V0604

You have many options for acquiring audio to use in a presentation. Popular sources include the following:

- Searching for audio with the Online Audio command on the PowerPoint Ribbon
- Ripping audio from a CD
- Downloading an audio file from the Internet
- Recording your own narration directly in PowerPoint or with your own software

Audio Snippets

PowerPoint comes with a library of sounds you can add to presentations. The Insert Audio dialog box is a great resource for finding short snippets of audio, such as a dog barking or a few bars of a musical composition. Searching for audio clips via the Insert Audio dialog box is similar to searching for clip art.

Audio File Types

An audio file only with a file type supported by PowerPoint may be added to a presentation. There are many types of audio formats, and PowerPoint supports the most popular ones. The following table lists the file types you can insert into a presentation.

SUPPORTED AUDIO FILE TYPES

File Type	Filename Extension	When to Use
AIFF audio file AU audio file	.aiff .au	■ Use as an alternative to WAV.
MIDI file	.mid, .midi	■ Use when computerized reproductions of instrumental music are desired. ■ Use when instrumental music is needed and small file size is important.
MP3 audio file Windows Media audio file	.mp3 .wma	■ Use for music ripped from a CD or recorded narration. *Example:* A song that plays across slides throughout the entire presentation.
Advanced Audio Coding—MPEG-4 audio file	.m4a, mp4	■ Use as an alternative to MP3.
Windows audio file	.wav	■ Use for small sound bites that are a few kilobytes in size. *Example:* A click sound or door slam effect.

Adding Audio to a Presentation

Video Library   http://labyrinthelab.com/videos   Video Number: PP13-V0605

Adding audio to a slide places a small speaker icon on the slide. This icon can be hidden from view during a slide show, or it can function as a start/stop button for the sound. When you insert audio onto a slide, you have the option to play the sound automatically after the slide loads, or when you click the audio icon on the slide.

A slide with a speaker icon, indicating audio has been added to the slide

QUICK REFERENCE	ADDING AUDIO TO A PRESENTATION
Task	**Procedure**
Add audio from an online source	■ Choose Insert→Media→Audio ▼→Online Audio. ■ Type your search term in the search box and tap `Enter`. ■ Click a clip's icon to preview it. Move your mouse pointer away from the icon to stop the preview. ■ Click the Insert button to place the selected clip on your slide. ■ Choose Audio Tools→Playback and configure how you want the audio to play.
Add audio from a file on your computer	■ Choose Insert→Media→Audio ▼→Audio on My PC. ■ Browse to a supported sound file, select it, and click Insert to *embed* the file, or click the arrow on the Insert button and then click Link to File to *link* to the audio file. ■ Choose Audio Tools→Playback and configure how you want the audio to play.
Record a narration	■ Choose Insert→Media→Audio ▼→Record Audio. ■ Click the Record button and speak into your computer's microphone. ■ Click the Stop button and then click OK.

Configuring Audio Options

When you add audio to a slide, you can choose to play the audio automatically or when clicked. If you choose to play the audio automatically, there is little reason to display the speaker icon on the slide because you no longer need to click it to play the audio. PowerPoint lets you hide the speaker icon in addition to setting a few more options, which are described in the following table.

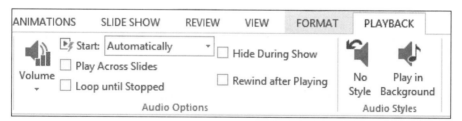

PowerPoint lets you set a variety of options for audio in presentations.

CONFIGURING AUDIO OPTIONS	
Option	**Description**
Volume	■ Choose an initial volume of Low, Medium, High, or Mute. The default is High.
Start	■ Automatically: Starts playing the audio automatically when the slide loads. ■ On Click: Starts playing the audio only when you click the speaker icon or the Play button.
Play Across Slides	■ If deselected, the audio stops when you navigate to the next slide. ■ If selected, the audio continues to play as you navigate from slide to slide.
Loop Until Stopped	■ If deselected, the sound stops after the audio file has played to the end. ■ If selected, the audio file starts over after it has played to the end.
Hide During Show	■ If deselected, the speaker icon displays on the slide during a slide show. ■ If selected, the speaker icon is hidden during a slide show.

The Rewind After Playing option is seldom used. In PowerPoint 2013, its behavior is buggy.

Configuring Audio Styles

Audio Styles are shortcut buttons that automatically set audio options. These buttons are simply time-savers.

CONFIGURING AUDIO STYLES	
Button	**Description**
No Style	■ When clicked, Start is set to On Click. Play Across Slides, Loop Until Stopped, and Hide During Show are all deselected.
Play in Background	■ When clicked, Start is set to Automatically. Play Across Slides, Loop Until Stopped, and Hide During Show are all selected.

Embedding Audio

Although you can link external audio files to a presentation like other multimedia content, it is also possible to embed such files into the presentation file itself. This topic explains why you may wish to use embedded audio.

Embedded Files

An embedded file is one that becomes absorbed into the presentation file itself rather than existing as a separate linked file. The obvious benefit of an embedded file is that you never have to worry about accidentally moving it or renaming it and not having it play in your presentation. The downside to using an embedded file is that it increases the file size of your presentation and is impossible to edit.

Embedded Audio Files

PowerPoint 2013 allows any type of audio file to be embedded. You can choose to embed (or link) an audio file from the Insert Audio dialog box. When you insert an audio file by using the Insert command, PowerPoint embeds the file.

DEVELOP YOUR SKILLS PP06-D02
Insert an Audio Clip

In this exercise, you will insert an audio clip from the Clip Art panel. You must have speakers connected to the computer with the volume turned up to hear the audio.

1. Start **PowerPoint** and make sure the PowerPoint window is **maximized**.

2. Open **PP06-D02-Beneficiaries** from the **PP2013 Lesson 06** folder and save it as `PP06-D02-Beneficiaries-[FirstInitialLastName]`.

   Replace the bracketed text with your first initial and last name. For example, if your name is Bethany Smith, your filename would look like this: PP06-D02-Beneficiaries-BSmith.

PowerPoint 2013

3. Choose **Insert→Media→Audio ▼→Online Audio**.

4. Type `classical` in the search box and tap Enter.

5. Click any one of the audio clip icons to preview the audio. Move your mouse away from the icon to stop the preview.

6. When you find an audio file you like, ensure it is selected and then click **Insert**.
   The Insert command embeds the audio file into the presentation.

7. Follow these steps to set how the audio starts:

Ⓐ Choose **Audio Tools→Playback**. If you do not see the Playback tab, click the speaker icon on the slide.

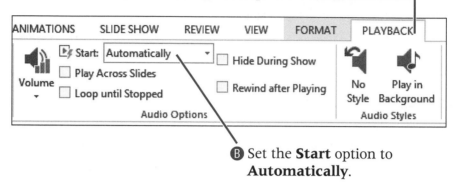

Ⓑ Set the **Start** option to **Automatically**.

8. Choose **Slide Show→Start Slide Show→From Beginning**.
   The sound starts to play immediately after the slide loads.

9. Move your mouse until the white mouse pointer arrow appears and then point at the speaker icon on the slide.
   A control bar appears indicating the progress. There is also a Pause button and volume control.

10. Click the **Pause** button to briefly stop the audio.

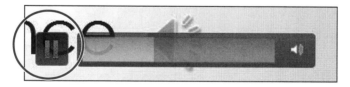

11. Move your mouse again until the white mouse pointer arrow appears and then point at the speaker icon.

12. Click the **Play** button to resume the audio.

13. Click anywhere on the slide to advance to the next slide.
    The audio stops when the presentation advances to the next slide.

14. Tap Esc to end the slide show and return to **Normal** view.

15. Save your presentation.

Acquiring More Audio

Video Library   http://labyrinthelab.com/videos   Video Number: PP13-V0606

Copying music from a CD into a digital music file on your computer is referred to as ripping and can be accomplished with software such as Windows Media Player or the free Audiograbber (http://www.audiograbber.org). Windows Media Player rips to the WMA format by default, but can rip to MP3 by installing a plug-in. Audiograbber is great in that it rips directly to MP3 with no additional configuration or plug-ins, so your ripped files are already in an appropriate format to use in a presentation—and a universal format to be played outside of your presentation. Be sure you are not violating any copyright laws if ripping sound from a CD.

Downloading Sound Effects

Many websites offer audio downloads in the form of sound effect clips, music background tracks, or promotional releases for bands. The web page for this book contains links to some free sound effects websites. Again, be aware of copyright law when downloading sound files.

Links to some popular audio websites are available on the web page for this book.

Recording a Narration

If your computer has a microphone, you can record your own narration directly from PowerPoint.

> **FROM THE RIBBON**
> Insert→Media→
> Audio ▼→
> Record Audio

Choosing an Audio File Format

Sounds from the Insert Audio dialog box are usually in WMA or WAV format, but what if you are creating your own audio file? Whether you decide to download, purchase, rip, or record audio, you'll need to decide on the file format. Should you use a WAV file? A WMA file? An MP3 file? A MIDI file? What about AIFF or AU? Because WAV and MP3 files are the most prevalent, and every modern PC can play these without additional software or codecs, you should stick to these two file types when ripping or recording your own narration.

MP3 Compared to WAV File Format

If the files are only a few kilobytes in size, it doesn't matter whether you use WAV or MP3. However, MP3 files are compressed, whereas WAV files are not. Although WAV files may sound a little better to the trained ear, an MP3 of the same sound will be about one-tenth of the file size. Most people can't tell any difference in quality between a WAV and MP3. The MP3 encoding process attempts to remove audio information that is outside the range of what humans can hear. In other words, the average person won't miss the audio that was removed from an MP3 file but will certainly notice the smaller file size.

 Dancing Queen
MID File
77.3 KB

 Dancing Queen
MP3 File
3.54 MB

 Dancing Queen
WAV File
39.0 MB

The same song saved as a 77.3 KB MIDI file, 3.54 MB MP3, and 39 MB WAV.

WMA File Format

The WMA format is an alternative to MP3 with comparable compression and quality, but not all music player software and hardware support the WMA format.

Because the MP3 format is more universally supported, it is recommended over the WMA format.

MIDI File Format

MIDI files also have their place and are probably the third type of sound file you are likely to use. MIDI files don't contain sound information like WAV or MP3 files. They simply provide instructions to the computer to reproduce the sounds of musical instruments. What you hear when you play a MIDI file depends on your computer's sound hardware. Your computer may really sound like a violin when you play that MIDI file of a Paganini violin concerto, whereas another computer will not sound like a true violin at all.

It is important to note that MIDI files cannot reproduce vocal tracks and should be used only when instrumental music is desired. (They are great for karaoke!)

DEVELOP YOUR SKILLS PP06-D03
Add Audio from an External File

In this exercise, you will add an audio file to a presentation and configure a playback option.

1. Save the presentation as **PP06-D03-Beneficiaries-[FirstInitialLastName]**.

2. Display the title slide.

3. Click once (do not double-click) to select the speaker icon on the title slide. Then tap Delete to remove the sound from the slide.

4. Choose **Slide Show→Start Slide Show→From Beginning** and preview the entire slide show. Return to the first slide in Normal view when you are finished.

   While the fading slide transitions certainly enhance the presentation, some nice music in the background would really set the mood.

5. Choose **Insert→Media→Audio ▾→Audio on My PC**.

6. Navigate to your **PP2013 Lesson 06\Audio** folder, select **PP06-D03-bach-bwv813**, and click **Insert**.

   Remember that your computer may be configured to hide the file extensions and the .mp3 portion of the filename may not be displayed. The Insert command embeds the audio file into the presentation.

7. Choose **Audio Tools→Playback** and set the **Start** option to **Automatically**.

   This option will start playing the audio automatically when the slide loads during the slide show.

8. Save your presentation.

Linking Audio

Video Library   http://labyrinthelab.com/videos   Video Number: PP13-V0607

Linking media files instead of embedding them keeps the file size of the presentation smaller, which is good if you need to email the presentation to someone. However, the linked media must remain in the same location (the same folder) relative to the PowerPoint file, or the presentation won't be able to find the media to play it during a slide show.

Whether you choose to embed or link media is largely personal preference. While linking maintains a smaller presentation, embedding is often less problematic.

DEVELOP YOUR SKILLS PP06-D04

Break and Repair a Link to a Media File

In this exercise, you will determine whether a sound is embedded or linked. You will then purposefully break the link to a linked file to see what happens when you attempt to play the presentation. Finally, you will repair the link and confirm that the media file plays.

1. Save the presentation as **PP06-D04-Beneficiaries-[FirstInitialLastName]**.

2. Choose **File→Info**.

3. Locate the **Related Documents** section at the bottom of the right column of Backstage view and note the absence of a link to Related Documents.

Related Documents Open File Location Show All Properties	Edit Links to Files is not displayed, indicating no linked files.

Related Documents
  Open File Location
  Edit Links to Files
Show All Properties
	If there were linked files, Edit Links to Files would be displayed as shown here.

4. Click **Back** ⬅ to exit Backstage view.

5. Click the speaker icon on the slide and tap Delete to delete the embedded audio file.

6. Choose **Insert→Media→Audio→Audio on My PC**.

7. Browse to your **PP2013 Lesson 06\Audio** folder.

PowerPoint 2013

8. Follow these steps to link to, rather than embed, the audio file:

Ⓐ Click once on **PP06-D03-bach-bwv813** to select it.

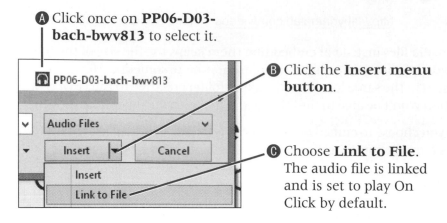

Ⓑ Click the **Insert menu button**.

Ⓒ Choose **Link to File**. The audio file is linked and is set to play On Click by default.

9. Choose **File→Info**.

10. Locate the **Related Documents** section at the bottom of the right column of Backstage view and notice that the Edit Links to Files link exists, indicating there are now linked files.

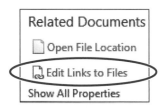

11. Click **Back** ⊙ to exit Backstage view.

12. Choose **Slide Show→Start Slide Show→From Beginning**.

13. Move your mouse until the mouse pointer white arrow appears.

14. Point at the speaker icon on the slide and then click the **Play** button on the control bar. *The audio file plays.*

15. Tap Esc to end the slide show and return to **Normal view**.

Break the Link

16. Minimize **PowerPoint**.

17. Navigate to your **PP2013 Lesson 06\Audio** folder and locate the **PP06-D03-bach-bwv813** file.

If your computer is configured to display file extensions, the filename will be displayed as PP06-D03-bach-bwv813.mp3. If your computer is configured to hide file extensions, the filename will be displayed as PP06-D03-bach-bwv813 without any file extension.

18. Right-click the **PP06-D03-bach-bwv813** file and choose **Rename**.

19. Follow the appropriate instruction to rename the file:
    - If the filename displays as PP06-D03-bach-bwv813 (no file extension), rename the file **PP06-D03-Bach**.
    - If the filename is displayed as PP06-D03-bach-bwv813.mp3, rename the file **PP06-D03-Bach.mp3**, taking care not to delete the .mp3 filename extension.

20. Maximize **PowerPoint** and choose **Slide Show→Start Slide Show→From Beginning**.

21. Move your mouse until the mouse pointer white arrow appears.

22. Point at the speaker icon on the slide and then click the **Play** button on the control bar.
    The audio file fails to play because the link to the file has been broken. The message Media Not Found *appears in the progress bar.*

23. Tap Esc to end the slide show and return to **Normal view**.

Repair the Link

24. Choose **File→Info** and click **Edit Links to Files**.

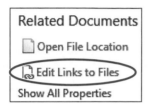

25. Click the link to **PP06-D03-bach-bwv813** and then click **Change Source**.

26. Navigate to your **PP2013 Lesson 06\Audio** folder, select **PP06-D03-Bach**, and click **Open**.

27. You just repaired the link. The Links dialog box displays the path to the source file you selected. Click **Close** to close the **Links** dialog box.

28. Choose **Slide Show→Start Slide Show→From Beginning**.

29. Move your mouse until the mouse pointer white arrow appears.

30. Point at the speaker icon on the slide and then click the **Play** button on the control bar.
    The sound plays because the link has been repaired.

31. Tap Esc to end the slide show and return to **Normal view**.

32. Save the presentation.

Creating Slide Show Timings

Video Library   http://labyrinthelab.com/videos   Video Number: PP13-V0608

When using background music or a narration, you often want the slide show timed to the audio so the soundtrack and slides end at the same time. Rather than guessing when to advance to the next slide during a presentation, PowerPoint lets you automate the slide show by creating a slide show timing. You can even use slide show timings without audio to automatically navigate to subsequent slides during a live talk given by the presenter. As the speaker addresses the audience, the slide show can be on "autopilot," allowing the presenter to move away from the computer and interact more freely with the audience.

Determining Slide Timings

All it takes is a little math. If you can do simple division or have access to a calculator, you can time your presentation to your soundtrack and have both end at the same time. Assuming your audio begins on the first slide, and you want each slide displayed for an equal amount of time, follow the simple steps in the following table to determine the length of time to spend on each slide.

QUICK REFERENCE	DETERMINING SLIDE TIMINGS	
Task	**Procedure**	**Example**
Determine the length of the audio file in seconds	■ Select the audio icon on the slide. ■ Point at the right edge of the progress bar to see the total playing time of the audio file. ■ Convert this time to seconds.	A 2-minute 30-second audio file would be 150 seconds.
Divide the total seconds by the total slides	■ Use the Slides panel or Slide Sorter view to determine how many slides are in the presentation. ■ Divide the length of the audio in seconds by the total number of slides in the presentation.	A 150-second audio file used in a presentation containing 20 slides works out to 150 ÷ 20 = 7.5.
Determine the total time per slide	■ If your division works out to a whole number, that is the number of seconds to spend on each slide. ■ If your division works out to a decimal, you'll have to round off or use another creative solution.	The answer to the division was 7.5. You might display slide 1 for 7 seconds, slide 2 for 8 seconds, slide 3 for 7 seconds, slide 4 for 8 seconds, and so on. This averages to 7.5 seconds per slide.

Rehearsing Timings

PowerPoint's Rehearse Timings feature allows you to create an automated slide show. Use this feature to practice your speech and automatically have the slides advance as you speak, or time the presentation to a soundtrack so the audio ends just as the last slide appears.

QUICK REFERENCE	REHEARSING TIMINGS
Task	**Procedure**
Create a slide show that runs automatically	■ Choose Slide Show→Set Up→Rehearse Timings . ■ Click Next in the Rehearsal toolbar to advance the slides. ■ When you have reached the last slide, choose Yes to save or No to discard the timings.
Play a slide show with timings	■ Select the Use Timings checkbox in the Slide Show→Set Up command group.
Play a slide show manually	■ Remove the checkmark from the Use Timings checkbox in the Slide Show→Set Up command group.

Apply Rehearsed Timings to a Presentation

In this exercise, you will configure the slide show to run by itself with a soundtrack.

1. Save the presentation as `PP06-D05-Beneficiaries-[FirstInitialLastName]`.

2. Select the speaker icon on the title slide, and then choose **Audio Tools→Playback→Audio Styles→Play in Background** to automatically set the **Audio Options**.
   The sound will now start automatically and will continue to play as you navigate through the slides.

3. Point at the right edge of the progress bar to determine the total playing time for the audio file.
   The sound is about 1 minute and 17 seconds (01:17) in length.

4. Follow these steps to calculate the length of time to spend on each slide:
   - Determine the total number of slides in the presentation, in this case, 10.
   - Determine the length of the sound clip in seconds, in this case, 1:17 equals 77 seconds.
   - Divide the length of the sound by the total number of slides, in this case, you divide 77 by 10.
   - The total amount of time to spend on each slide is about 7.7 seconds.

5. Choose **Slide Show→Set Up→Rehearse Timings** and keep your eye on the timer.

6. Follow these steps to advance to the next slide at the correct time:

Ⓐ As soon as the timer shows **7 seconds**…

Ⓑ …click the **Next** button.

7. Click the **Next** button every 7 or 8 seconds, until you reach the last slide.

8. Choose **Yes** when prompted to save your timings.

9. Choose **Slide Show→Start Slide Show→From Beginning** and watch as the slide show autoplays with the soundtrack. Click anywhere on the black screen after the slide show ends.

Loop a Slide Show

10. Choose **Slide Show→Set Up→Set Up Slide Show**.

11. Place a checkmark in the **Loop Continuously Until 'Esc'** option box and click **OK**.

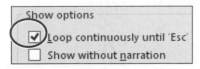

12. Choose **Slide Show→Start Slide Show→From Beginning** and notice that when the last slide is reached (Corky), the slide show starts over again.

13. Tap ⎡Esc⎤ to end the slide show and return to Normal view.

14. Save and close your presentation.

Using Video in Presentations

Video Library http://labyrinthelab.com/videos   Video Number: PP13-V0609

Similar to audio, PowerPoint allows you to insert online video or a video file from your computer. Online videos include video found via a Bing search (Bing is the Microsoft search engine, similar to Google, that is integrated into PowerPoint), and embedded video such as a video from YouTube.

Using Online Videos

You must always be careful when adding any kind of media—clip art images, audio, or video—to a presentation. Not all media found with an Internet search is free to use. PowerPoint may let you search for media with Bing, but that's not a guarantee that you are legally allowed to use the media clip. It is safest to research the license of any media you want to use and then verify that it is in the public domain (free to use), royalty free (absent of royalty or license fees), or carries the Creative Commons license (free to use and share). Finding this information is not always easy and usually involves finding out who the owner of the media is.

QUICK REFERENCE	INSERTING ONLINE VIDEO
Task	**Procedure**
Insert a video from a web search	■ Choose Insert→Media→Video→Online Video or click the Insert Video icon in a slide placeholder.
	■ Type a search term in the Search Bing box and tap ⎡Enter⎤.
	■ To preview a video, point at a video thumbnail, click the magnifying glass icon in the thumbnail's lower-right corner, and click the enlarged video.
	■ To stop a preview, click the X in the top-right corner of the video.
	■ Click a video thumbnail and then click the Insert button.
Insert a video from embed code	■ Navigate to a website that plays the video you want.
	■ Copy the embed code for the video from the website.
	■ For YouTube, select the Use Old Embed Code checkbox before copying.
	■ In PowerPoint, choose Insert→Media→Video→Online Video or click the Insert Video icon in a slide placeholder.
	■ Paste the embed code into the Paste Embed Code Here box and then click the Insert arrow on the right side of the box.

Using Video from Your Computer

You can create your own full-motion video movie files by using the video camera built in to a smart phone and video-editing software such as the free Windows Movie Maker available for Windows or third-party software such as Studio™ made by Pinnacle (http://www.pinnaclesys.com). You can also download videos from the Internet.

As with audio files, be sure you are not violating any copyright laws when downloading and using videos in a presentation. Always check a website's Terms and Conditions before using any downloaded multimedia content.

QUICK REFERENCE	INSERTING VIDEO FROM YOUR COMPUTER
Task	**Procedure**
Embed a video from your computer	■ Choose Insert→Media→Video→Video on My PC, or click the Insert Video icon in a slide placeholder and click Browse. ■ Navigate to the video's location on your computer. ■ Select the video and click Insert.
Link to a video from your computer	■ Follow the preceding three steps to select a video. ■ Click the arrow on the Arrow button menu and choose Link to File.

Video File Formats

Full-motion video, like a home movie of your trip to the beach, manifests in several file formats such as MPEG or AVI. MPEG files are generally smaller files compared to AVIs and are less problematic when playing on different computers. AVI files can be problematic because of missing codecs, as explained in the next section.

SUPPORTED VIDEO FILE TYPES	
Video Format	**File Extension**
Windows Media file	.asf
Windows video file	.avi
MP4 video file	.mp4, .m4v, .mov
Movie file	.mpg, .mpeg
Adobe Flash media	.swf
Windows Media Video file	.wmv

Codecs

Although you may think you're doing everything correctly by using a file with a supported file extension, your audio or video files may not play when the presentation is viewed on someone else's computer. This is most often due to a codec incompatibility.

The Role of Codecs

Audio and video multimedia files can be huge—sometimes several gigabytes. Software called a compressor is used to compress the file and make it smaller. To be played, the file must be decompressed or decoded—the job of more software called a decompressor. A codec, which is an abbreviation of **co**mpressor/**dec**ompressor, does both jobs.

If a multimedia file was created with a certain codec, that codec must be present on any computer wanting to successfully play the file. To confuse matters, many different codecs can create files with the same file extension, and they may not be compatible. For example, the I263, DivX, and Xvid codecs all create movie files with the .avi file extension.

Identifying a Codec

Don't assume that just because an AVI video file plays on your computer, it will also play on your friend's. Your computer may have the correct codec installed, while your friend's does not. This becomes an issue when using multimedia files compressed with codecs other than what Windows has installed by default—and is more of an issue with video than with audio. Software such as MediaInfo or AVIcodec—both free—can identify what codec is needed to play a certain video file.

See the student resource center for links to useful codec utilities such as the ones mentioned in the preceding paragraph.

Figuring Out a Codec

You will find that AVI video files downloaded from the Internet often contain nonstandard codecs. Also, some video-editing software may use nonstandard codecs when creating AVI files. The best advice is to simply try to play the video with Windows Media Player before inserting it in your presentation. If it plays in Windows Media Player, it will play in your presentation. If it fails to play, identify the codec by using software such as MediaInfo or AVIcodec. Then search the Internet for the codec, download it, and install it. The website VideoHelp.com is an excellent source for learning more about video and video codecs and offers a Tools section where you can download codecs and other helpful software.

When a Codec Is Missing

If you attempt to run a slide show with a multimedia file for which you do not have the correct codec, you will not receive any error. The media file will simply not play.

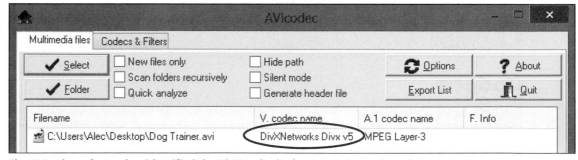

The AVIcodec software has identified the DivX codec in the Dog Trainer.avi movie.

Always make sure that your presentation computer has the necessary codecs for any movie to be played in your presentation.

QUICK REFERENCE	DEALING WITH AN EXOTIC VIDEO CODEC
Task	**Procedure**
Determine whether there is a problem	■ Attempt to play an AVI file with Windows Media Player. If it plays, there is no problem with a missing codec.
	■ If it fails to play or you receive a "missing codec" error message, proceed with the next steps to identify and install the missing codec.
Identify the codec	■ Use a program such as AVIcodec to identify the codec that was used to compress the video. A link to the AVIcodec website appears on the web page for this book.
Install the missing codec	■ Search the Internet for the codec identified in the previous step. Usually typing the name of the codec in a search engine provides the results you need.
	■ Download the codec installer to an easy-to-find location, such as your Desktop.
	■ Be sure you are running current antivirus software, antispyware software, and are downloading the codec from a reputable source!
	■ Double-click the downloaded file and follow the onscreen instructions to install the codec. Note that you may need to reboot your computer after installing.
	■ Attempt to play the video again.

DEVELOP YOUR SKILLS PP06-D06

Insert a Video from Your Computer

In this exercise, you will add a video from an existing external file.

1. Open **PP06-D06-Scholarship** from the **PP2013 Lesson 06** folder and save it as `PP06-D06-Scholarship-[FirstInitialLastName]`.

2. Choose **Home→Slides→New Slide** and type `Scholarship Recipient` as the title.

3. Click the **Insert Video** 🎞 icon on the slide and then click **Browse ▶**.

4. Navigate to your **PP2013 Lesson 06\Video** folder, select the **PP06-D07-Classical.mpg** video movie file, and click **Insert** to embed the video.

   Your computer may be configured to hide file extensions and may not display the .mpg portion of the filename. PowerPoint displays a message informing you that the video file must be optimized. Wait until the message box disappears.

5. Choose **Slide Show→Start Slide Show→From Beginning**.

6. Click anywhere to advance to the next slide.

7. Move your mouse around until the mouse pointer becomes visible.

8. Point at the video to display the control bar at the bottom and click the **Play** button to start the video.

9. Point at the video again to display the control bar and use the **Play/Pause** button to pause or resume the video.

10. When the movie ends, tap ⎡Esc⎤ to return to **Normal view**.

    You may have heard a clicking sound at the beginning and end of the video—a sound the video camera itself made. Such sounds can be removed.

11. Save your presentation.

Editing Videos

Video Library http://labyrinthelab.com/videos   Video Number: PP13-V0610

PowerPoint 2013 offers the ability to edit videos. While PowerPoint is not meant to replace a full video-editing suite, it offers basic editing functions. You can trim the start and end of a video (cut off the beginning or the end) and have it fade in or out. You can edit audio the same way. Any audio or video editing you perform in PowerPoint has no effect on the actual media file. The editing affects only how PowerPoint plays the media; therefore, the edits are nondestructive.

FROM THE RIBBON
Video Tools→Playback to access video editing tools

Trim Video lets you chop off the beginning or end of a video.

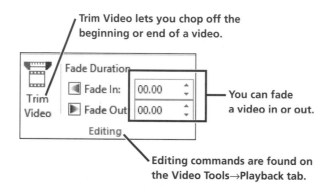

You can fade a video in or out.

Editing commands are found on the Video Tools→Playback tab.

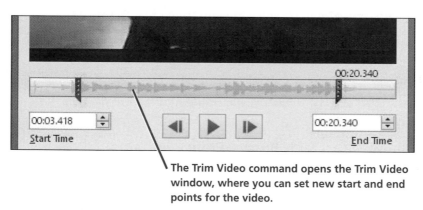

The Trim Video command opens the Trim Video window, where you can set new start and end points for the video.

Applying Video Effects

PowerPoint 2013 also offers the ability to apply video effects. Using the Video Styles gallery, you can easily format a video much like clip art.

FROM THE RIBBON
Video Tools→Format→ Video Styles to access video effects

You can choose a predefined style from the Video Styles gallery.

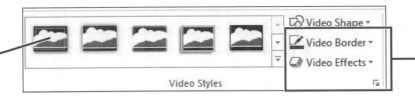

Create your own custom effect by using the Video Shape, Video Border, or Video Effects menus.

SCHOLARSHIP RECIPIENT

Slides can be spiced up with a simple Video Style.

PowerPoint 2013

DEVELOP YOUR SKILLS PP06-D07
Edit and Style a Video

In this exercise, you will trim a video. You will then apply a Video Style.

1. Save the presentation as **PP06-D07-Scholarship-[FirstInitialLastName]**.

2. Select the second slide, if necessary, and click the video to select it.

3. Choose **Video Tools→Playback→Editing→Trim Video**.

Remove an Unwanted Sound

4. Ensure that your speakers are turned on and click the **Play** button. As soon as you hear the popping sounds stop, click the **Stop** button.
   The Play button turns into a Stop button while the video is playing.

00:00			◀I	▶	I▶		00:24.241
Start Time							End Time

5. If necessary, drag the blue play head back to the start of the video and repeat step 4 until you can identify when the popping stops.

6. As the popping stops at about 1 second, drag the green trim control to the right until the number above it indicates that you are at about the 1 second mark. It doesn't have to be perfect, but should be close to 1 second.

7. Follow these steps to listen to the end of the video:

Ⓐ Click here toward the end of the video to set the play head.

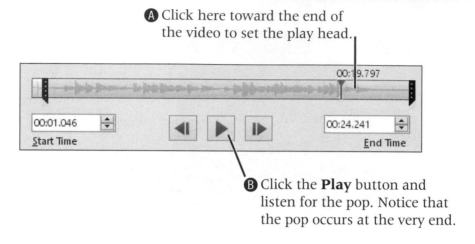

Ⓑ Click the **Play** button and listen for the pop. Notice that the pop occurs at the very end.

8. Follow these steps to trim the end of the video:

Ⓐ Drag the red trim control slightly to the left.

Ⓑ Click here toward the end of the video to set the play head.

Ⓒ Click the **Play** button and listen for the pop to have been removed.

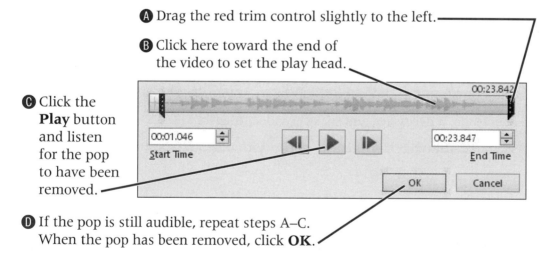

Ⓓ If the pop is still audible, repeat steps A–C. When the pop has been removed, click **OK**.

Apply a Video Style

9. Choose **Video Tools→Format→Video Styles→More** to display the Video Styles gallery.

10. Point at several styles to see them temporarily applied to the video on the slide, and then choose the **Intense→Monitor, Gray style**.

11. Choose **Slide Show→Start Slide Show→From Current Slide**.

    The slide displays the video with the three-dimensional style.

12. Move your mouse until the mouse pointer white arrow appears.

13. Point at the video on the slide and then click the **Play** button on the control bar.

    The popping sounds at the beginning and end of the video are no longer heard because the video has been trimmed.

14. Tap [Esc] to exit the slide show and return to **Normal view**.

15. Save your presentation.

Setting Video Options

Video Library   http://labyrinthelab.com/videos   Video Number: PP13-V0611

FROM THE RIBBON

Video Tools→
Playback→Video
Options

Just as with audio, there are several options you can apply to videos on a slide.

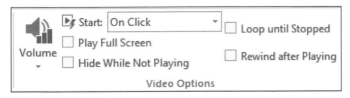

Video options are similar to the audio options.

PowerPoint 2013

- **Volume:** Just as the name indicates, you can set the volume for the audio playback of a video. This option sets the initial volume, which can be overridden by your computer speakers' volume control.

- **Start:** You can choose to automatically start the video when the slide loads, or require the video or Play button in the control bar to be clicked in order to play. Some online videos require a click to start playing even if they are set to start automatically.

- **Play Full Screen:** You can have the video play in full-screen mode, as shown in the following figure. When set to full-screen mode, the video appears as normal on the slide but enlarges to fill the screen when played. When the video is done, the size automatically reduces and the entire slide is once again visible.

- **Hide While Not Playing:** You can hide the video placeholder during a slide show. However, this will make it impossible to click the video to start it! Use this option when Start is set to Automatically. When the video ends, it disappears (hides) so your slide doesn't display a rectangular placeholder.

- **Loop Until Stopped:** The video can be configured to rewind and start over again and again until manually stopped.

Choosing the Options

There is no "wrong" or "right" when configuring these options. They are dependent on personal preference and the needs and expectations of the audience. For example, if your presentation were to play in a trade-show kiosk in a continuous loop to draw in a crowd, you would probably want video and audio to start automatically rather than requiring an icon to be clicked in order to start playback.

The same slide with a video playing normally (left) and full screen (right)

Set Video Playback Options

In this exercise, you will configure a video to play in full-screen mode.

1. Save the presentation as **PP06-D08-Scholarship-[FirstInitialLastName]**.

2. Select the **Scholarship Recipient** slide and then and select the existing movie there, if necessary.

3. Choose **Video Tools→Playback→Video Options**.

4. Place a checkmark in the **Play Full Screen** checkbox.

5. Choose **Slide Show→Start Slide Show→From Beginning**.

6. Navigate to the second slide and move your mouse around until the pointer becomes visible.

7. Click the movie to play it.

   The movie plays in full-screen mode. When the movie is done, it returns to normal size and the slide is visible again.

8. Tap Esc to end the slide show.

9. Save and close your presentation. Exit **PowerPoint**.

Concepts Review

To check your knowledge of the key concepts introduced in this lesson, complete the Concepts Review quiz by choosing the appropriate access option below.

If you are...	Then access the quiz by...
Using the Labyrinth Video Library	Going to http://labyrinthelab.com/videos
Using eLab	Logging in, choosing Content, and navigating to the Concepts Review quiz for this lesson
Not using the Labyrinth Video Library or eLab	Going to the student resource center for this book

Reinforce Your Skills

Work with Audio

In this exercise, you will add audio from an online source. You will also add audio that needs to be edited from your computer. Finally, you will apply rehearsed timings so the slide show can run unattended.

Insert an Online Audio Clip

1. Start **PowerPoint**. Open **PP06-R01-Tutoring** from your **PP2013 Lesson 06** folder and save it as `PP06-R01-Tutoring-[FirstInitialLastName]`.

2. Display **slide 2** and choose **Insert→Media→Audio→Online Audio**.

3. Type `yell` in the search box and tap Enter.

4. Point to several audio clip icons to preview them. When you find one you like, click it to select it and click **Insert**.

5. Drag the speaker icon to the bottom-left area of the slide so you can see it more easily.

6. Display **slide 3**. Search for an audio clip using the term `fanfare` and insert it on the slide.

Embed an Audio Clip from Your Computer

7. Display **slide 4** and choose **Insert→Media→Audio→Audio on My PC**.

8. Browse to your **PP2013 Lesson 06\Audio** folder, select **PP06-R01-Lunch**, and click **Insert**.

9. Drag the speaker icon next to the word *Lunch*.

10. Choose **Insert→Media→Audio→Audio on My PC**.

11. Browse to your **PP2013 Lesson 06\Audio** folder, select **PP06-R01-Castle**, and click **Insert**.

12. Drag the speaker icon next to the word *Castle*.

13. Choose **Insert→Media→Audio→Audio on My PC**.

14. Browse to your **PP2013 Lesson 06\Audio** folder, select **PP06-R01-Makeup**, and click **Insert**.

15. Drag the speaker icon next to the word *Makeup*.

Link to an Audio Clip from Your Computer

16. Choose **Insert→Media→Audio→Audio on My PC**.

17. Browse to your **PP2013 Lesson 06\Audio** folder, select the **PP06-R01-Library** audio file, and click **Insert menu ▼→Link to File**.

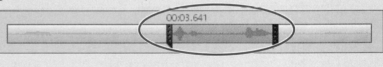

18. Drag the speaker icon next to the word *library*.

Set Audio Playback Options

19. Display **slide 2** and select the speaker icon on the slide.

20. Set the **Audio Tools→Playback→Audio Options→Start** option to **Automatically**.

21. Select the **Audio Tools→Playback→Audio Options→Hide During Show** checkbox.

22. Display **slide 3** and select the speaker icon on the slide.

23. Set the **Audio Tools→Playback→Audio Options→Start** option to **Automatically**.

24. Select the **Audio Tools→Playback→Audio Options→Hide During Show** checkbox.

Edit Audio

25. Display **slide 4** and select the **Lunch speaker icon**.

26. Choose **Audio Tools→Playback→Editing→Trim Audio**.

27. Click the **Play** button to play the audio and watch the blue play head move across the sound wave. Notice when the English word *Lunch* is spoken and when the French word for *Lunch* ends.

28. Drag the green trim control to the right until it is just before the large bump in the sound wave (the start of the English pronunciation of *Lunch*).

29. Drag the red trim control to the left until it is just after the second large bump in the sound wave (the end of the French pronunciation of *Lunch*).

30. Click **OK**.

31. Click a blank area on the right side of the slide to deselect the speaker icon.

32. Trim the unwanted sounds on from the beginning and end of the audio files on the remaining speaker icons.

Create Multimedia Folders

33. Save your presentation and minimize **PowerPoint**.

34. Choose **Start→Computer** from the lower-left corner of your screen.

35. Navigate to **PP2013 Lesson 06\Audio** and create a new folder named **French**.

Break and Repair a Link to a Media File

36. Drag these files into the **French folder**:

- PP06-R01-Castle
- PP06-R01-Library
- PP06-R01-Lunch
- PP06-R01-Makeup

37. Maximize **PowerPoint** and select the **Lunch speaker icon** on **slide 4**.

38. Click the **Play** button and notice that the audio plays fine because the Lunch audio file is embedded. Play the **Castle** and **Makeup** audio files, and notice that they also play fine.

39. Attempt to play the **Library** audio file. It fails to play because the link is broken.

40. Choose **File→Info→Edit Links to Files**.

41. Select the link to the **Library file** and click the **Change Source** button.

42. Browse to the **PP2013 Lesson 06\Audio\French** folder, select the **PP06-R01-Library** file, and click **Open**.

43. Close the **Links** dialog box.

44. Click the **Play** button and note that the Library audio now plays. If it doesn't, repair the broken link.

Apply Rehearsed Timings

45. Choose **Slide Show→Set Up→Rehearse Timings**.

46. When the timer reaches **5 seconds**, click **Next**.

47. After the **Math** slide has displayed for **10 seconds**, click **Next**.

48. After the **Humanities** slide has displayed for **15 seconds**, click **Next**.

49. After the **Language** slide has displayed for **30 seconds**, click **Next**.

50. Choose **Yes** to save the timings.

Run the Slide Show

51. Choose **Slide Show→Start Slide Show→From Beginning**.

52. Wait as the slide show runs automatically and displays the title slide for 5 seconds, the Math slide for 10 seconds, and the Humanities slide for 15 seconds.

53. When the **Language** slide appears, point to each speaker icon and click their **Play** button.

54. Tap Esc to end the slide show.

55. Save and close the file. Exit **PowerPoint**.

56. Submit your final file based on the guidelines provided by your instructor.

To view examples of how your file or files should look at the end of this exercise, go to the student resource center.

Work with Video

In this exercise, you will add video to a presentation. You will also trim a video and apply video effects and playback options.

Insert an Online Video from a Bing Search

1. Start **PowerPoint**. Open **PP06-R02-Math** from your **PP2013 Lesson 06** folder and save it as `PP06-R02-Math-[FirstInitialLastName]`.

2. Display **slide 2** and choose **Insert→Media→Video→Online Video**.

3. In the **Bing Video Search box**, type `Pythagorean Theorem` and tap Enter.

4. Point to a video thumbnail and click the magnifying glass icon to enlarge the thumbnail.

5. Click the enlarged video to play it.

6. When you've watched enough of the video, click the "X" in the upper-right corner of the video to close it.

7. Keep searching until you find a video you like. Then, select the thumbnail of your desired video and click **Insert**.

Insert an Online Video by Using Embed Code

The following steps work to embed a YouTube video at the time of this writing. YouTube may have changed the process. If these exact steps no longer work, you may have to research the process for getting the YouTube embed code for a video.

8. Display **slide 3** and minimize **PowerPoint**.

9. Start **Internet Explorer**, or the web browser of your choice, and navigate to http://www.youtube.com.

10. In the **YouTube search box**, type `Fibonacci Sequence` and tap Enter.

11. Click a video to watch it and continue previewing videos until you find one you like.

12. Once you find a video you like, click the **Share** link below the video.

13. Click the **Embed** link above the block of embed code.

PowerPoint 2013

14. Deselect all but the **Use Old Embed Code** checkbox.

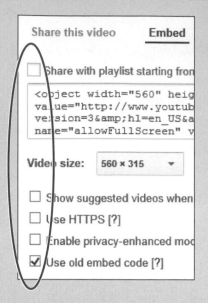

15. Click in the box containing the embed code and tap ⌈Ctrl⌉+⌈C⌉ to copy the code.

16. Close your web browser and maximize **PowerPoint**.

17. Choose **Insert→Media→Video→Online Video**.

18. Click in the embed code box and tap ⌈Ctrl⌉+⌈V⌉ to paste the copied embed code.

19. Click the **Insert** button on the right side of the embed code box.

Insert a Video from Your Computer

20. Display **slide 4** and choose **Insert→Media→Video→Video on My PC**.

21. Navigate to your **PP2013 Lesson 06\Video** folder, select **PP06-R02-ZeroPower**, and click **Insert**.

Wait while PowerPoint imports and optimizes the video.

Edit and Style a Video

22. Click the video on **slide 4** to select it, if necessary, and choose **Video Tools→Playback→Editing→Trim Video**.

23. Click the **Play** button and listen to the cough at the beginning of the video.

24. Drag the green trim control to the right of the cough so the cough no longer plays (about 2 seconds from the beginning).

25. Click the **Play** button to verify that the cough no longer plays and adjust the green trim control if necessary.

26. Click **OK**.

27. Choose **Video Tools→Format→Video Styles→More→Moderate→Compound Frame, Black**.

28. Apply the same video style to the videos on **slides 2 and 3**.

Set Video Playback Options

29. Display **slide 2** and click the video on the slide to select it.

30. Choose **Video Tools→Playback→Video Options→Start→Automatically**.

31. Display **slide 3** and set the video to start **Automatically**.

32. Display **slide 4** and set the video to start **Automatically**.

Run the Slide Show

33. Choose **Slide Show→Start Slide Show→From Beginning**.

34. Click the title slide to move to the **Pythagorean Theorem** slide.

35. Click the video to play it.

36. Tap [Esc] to stop the video and then click the slide to move to the **Fibonacci Sequence** slide.

37. Click the video to play it.

38. Tap [Esc] to stop the video and then click the slide to move to the **Power of Zero** slide.

39. Tap [Esc] two more times, once to stop the video and once to end the slide show.

40. Save and close the file. Exit **PowerPoint**.

41. Submit your final file based on the guidelines provided by your instructor.
    To view examples of how your file or files should look at the end of this exercise, go to the student resource center.

REINFORCE YOUR SKILLS PP06-R03
Work with Audio and Video

In this exercise, you will add audio and video to an automated presentation.

Insert Audio

1. Start **PowerPoint**. Open **PP06-R03-AudioBenefits** from your **PP2013 Lesson 06** folder and save it as `PP06-R03-AudioBenefits-[FirstInitialLastName]`.

2. Display **slide 1**, if necessary, and choose **Insert→Media→Audio→Audio on My PC**.

3. Navigate to the **PP2013 Lesson 06\Audio** folder and select the **PP06-R03-AudioBenefits** file.

4. Choose **Insert menu ▼→Link to File**.

Set Audio Playback Options

5. Choose **Audio Tools→Playback→Audio Style→Play in Background** to automatically set the audio options.

6. Deselect the **Audio Tools→Playback→Audio Options→Loop Until Stopped** checkbox.

Edit Audio

7. Choose **Audio Tools→Playback→Editing→Trim Audio**.

8. Click the **Play** button and note when the speaker says *Why should you join Kids for Change?*

9. Drag the green trim control to the right until it is just before *Why should you join Kids for Change?*

10. Click the sound wave at about **01:00.000** to place the blue play head toward the end of the file.

11. Click the **Play** button and note when the speaker says *Ok, is that it?*

12. Drag the red trim control to the left until it is just before *Ok, is that it?*

13. Click **OK**.

14. Click the **Play** button on the slide and ensure that the audio begins with *Why should you join Kids for Change?* Also ensure that it ends with *The reasons are obvious*. If necessary, trim the audio appropriately.

Create Multimedia Folders

15. Save your presentation and minimize **PowerPoint**.

16. Choose **Start→Computer** from the lower-left corner of your screen.

17. Navigate to **PP2013 Lesson 06\Audio** and create a new folder named **Benefits**.

Break and Repair a Link to a Media File

18. Drag **PP06-R03-AudioBenefits** and **PP06-R03-Video** into the **Benefits** folder.

19. Maximize **PowerPoint** and click the speaker icon on **slide 1** to select it.

20. Click the **Play** button and notice that the audio fails to play because the link is broken.

21. Choose **File→Info→Edit Links to Files**.

22. Select the link to the **Benefits** file and click **Change Source**.

23. Browse to the **PP2013 Lesson 06\Audio\Benefits** folder, select **PP06-R03-Benefits**, and click **Open**.

24. Close the **Links** dialog box.

25. Click the **Play** button and note that the audio now plays. If it doesn't, repair the broken link.

26. As necessary, trim the audio again now that the link has been repaired.

Apply Rehearsed Timings

27. Choose **Slide Show→Set Up→Rehearse Timings**.

28. Listen to the audio and click the **Next** button after you hear each of the following phrases:
   - Why should you join Kids for Change? There are many benefits.
   - …shows a college that you are not afraid to work for something worthwhile.
   - …translates to effective management skills, which are important for any job applicant.
   - …that you are willing to work hard to get the job done.
   - Why should you join Kids for Change? The benefits are obvious.

29. Choose **Yes** to save the timings.

Run the Slide Show

30. Choose **Slide Show→Start Slide Show→From Beginning**.

31. Watch as the slide show runs automatically and the slides match up to the narration.

32. When the slide show ends, click the screen to return to **Normal view**.

33. If necessary, choose **Slide Show→Set Up→Rehearse Timings** and re-create the timings to match up better with the audio.

Insert a Video

34. Display the last slide and choose **Home→Slides→New Slide**.

35. Choose **Home→Slides→Layout→Title and Content**.

36. Type **And It's Fun** as the slide title.

37. Display **slide 4** and choose **Insert→Media→Video→Video on My PC**.

38. Browse to the **PP2013 Lesson 06\Audio\Benefits** folder, select **PP06-R03-Video**, and click **Insert**.

Edit and Style a Video

39. Choose **Video Tools→Playback→Editing→Trim Video**.

40. Click in the middle of the sound wave to place the blue play head.

41. Drag the blue play head to the right and note when the camera starts to move away from the girl, at about 12 seconds.

42. Drag the red trim control to the left to cut off the end of the video where the camera moves, and then click **OK**.

43. Choose **Video Tools→Format→Video Styles→More→Intense→Reflected Bevel, White**.

Set Video Playback Options

44. Choose **Video Tools→Playback→Video Options→Start→Automatically**.

Run the Slide Show

45. Choose **Slide Show→Start Slide Show→From Beginning**.

46. Watch as the slide show plays automatically. When the last slide is displayed, the video should play automatically. When the video ends, tap Esc to end the slide show.

47. Save and close the file. Exit **PowerPoint**.

48. Submit your final file based on the guidelines provided by your instructor.

Apply Your Skills

Work with Audio

In this exercise, you will add audio from an online source. You will also add audio that needs to be edited from your computer. Finally, you will apply rehearsed timings so the slide show can run unattended.

Insert an Online Audio Clip

1. Start **PowerPoint**. Open **PP06-A01-Transportation** from your **PP2013 Lesson 06** folder and save it as **PP06-A01-Transportation-[FirstInitialLastName]**.

2. Add an online audio clip to **slide 1** of a car engine revving.

Link to an Audio Clip from Your Computer

3. On **slide 2**, link to (don't embed) **PP06-A01-TransportationNarration** from the **PP2013 Lesson 06\Audio** folder.

Set Audio Playback Options

4. Configure the audio on **slides 1 and 2** to start **Automatically**, **Play Across Slides**, and **Hide During Show**.

Edit Audio

5. Edit the audio on **slide 2** to remove the noise from the beginning of the file.

Create Multimedia Folders

6. Minimize **PowerPoint** and navigate to the **PP2013 Lesson 06\Audio** folder.

7. Create a new folder named **Universal**.

Break and Repair a Link to a Media File

8. Drag **PP06-A01-TransportationNarration** into the **Universal** folder.

9. Maximize **PowerPoint** and attempt to play the audio file on **slide 2**.

10. Edit the link to the file so that the audio on **slide 2** plays.

11. Trim the audio as necessary.

Apply Rehearsed Timings

12. Set up **Rehearsed Timings** so that **slide 2** displays after the car engine revving sound clip and each subsequent slide displays in time with the narration.

13. Choose **Slide Show→Set Up→Set Up Slide Show**, place a checkmark in the **Loop Continuously Until 'Esc'** option box, and click **OK**.

Run the Slide Show

14. Run the slide show and ensure that it plays automatically with slides timed to the narration.

15. Tap [Esc] to end the slide show.

16. Save and close the file. Exit **PowerPoint**.

17. Submit your final file based on the guidelines provided by your instructor.

    To view examples of how your file or files should look at the end of this exercise, go to the student resource center.

Work with Video

In this exercise, you will add video to a presentation. You will also trim a video and apply video effects and playback options.

Insert an Online Video from a Bing Search

1. Start **PowerPoint**. Open **PP06-A02-Entertainment** from your **PP2013 Lesson 06** folder and save it as **PP06-A02-Entertainment-[FirstInitialLastName]**.

2. Display **slide 2** and click the **Insert Video** icon in the left placeholder.

3. Use the **Bing** search to search for a video on **Line Dancing**.

Insert an Online Video by Using Embed Code

4. Minimize **PowerPoint** and use your web browser to navigate to http://www.youtube.com.

5. Find another line-dancing video and copy the embed code.

6. Close the web browser and maximize **PowerPoint**.

7. Click the **Insert Video** icon in the right placeholder on the slide.

8. Paste the embed code into the proper box and click **Insert**.

Insert a Video from Your Computer

9. Display **slide 3** and insert **PP06-A02-Band** from the **PP2013 Lesson 06\Audio** folder.

Edit and Style a Video

10. Edit the video on **slide 3** to remove the shaking at the beginning.

11. Apply the **Subtle→Simple Frame, White** video style to all three videos in the presentation.

Set Video Playback Options

12. Set all three videos to start when clicked.

Run the Slide Show

13. Run the slide show and verify that all three videos play when clicked. If necessary, delete a video from slide 2 and replace it with another line-dancing video found online.

14. Save and close the file. Exit **PowerPoint**.

15. Submit your final file based on the guidelines provided by your instructor.

    To view examples of how your file or files should look at the end of this exercise, go to the student resource center.

Work with Audio and Video

In this exercise, you will add audio and video to an automated presentation.

Insert Online Audio

1. Start **PowerPoint**. Open **PP06-A03-Invitations** from your **PP2013 Lesson 06** folder and save it as PP06-A03-Invitations-[FirstInitialLastName].

2. Add an online audio clip of classical music to **slide 1**. Make sure the audio is about 20 seconds.

3. Drag the speaker icon to the top-left corner of the slide.

Link to an Audio Clip from Your Computer

4. On **slide 1**, link to (don't embed) **PP06-A03-Invites** from the **PP2013 Lesson 06\Audio** folder.

5. Drag the speaker icon to the top-right corner of the slide.

Set Audio Playback Options

6. Configure the online audio clip (in the top-left corner) to start **Automatically, Play Across Slides, Hide During Show**, and **Loop Until Stopped**.

7. Configure the linked audio clip (in the top-right corner) to start **Automatically, Play Across Slides**, and **Hide During Show**.

Edit Audio

8. Edit the linked audio clip (in the top-right corner) to remove the noise from the beginning of the file.

Create Multimedia Folders

9. Minimize **PowerPoint** and navigate to the **PP2013 Lesson 06\Audio** folder on your file storage location.

10. Create a new folder named Invitations.

Break and Repair a Link to a Media File

11. Drag **PP06-A03-Invites** into the **Invitations** folder.

12. Maximize **PowerPoint** and attempt to play the linked audio file.

13. Edit the link to the file so that the linked audio file plays.

Apply Rehearsed Timings

14. Set up **Rehearsed Timings** so that each slide displays for about **4 seconds**.

Run the Slide Show

15. Run the slide show and ensure it plays automatically with both audio files. The narration should not get cut off at the end. If necessary, create new rehearsed timings to extend the length of the slide show.

16. Tap Esc to end the slide show.

Insert an Online Video from a Bing Search

17. Add a new slide to the end of the presentation by using the **Title and Content** layout.

18. Type Celebrations as the title of the new slide.

19. Insert an **Online Video** and use the **Bing** search to find a video on **Corporate Celebrations**.

Style a Video

20. Apply the **Intense→Perspective Shadow, White** video style.

Set Video Playback Options

21. Set the video to start when clicked.

Run the Slide Show

22. Run the slide show and verify that the video plays when clicked. If it doesn't, delete it from the slide and try another online video.

23. Save and close the file. Exit **PowerPoint**.

24. Submit your final file based on the guidelines provided by your instructor.

Extend Your Skills

In the course of working through the Extend Your Skills exercises, you will think critically as you use the skills taught in the lesson to complete the assigned projects. To evaluate your mastery and completion of the exercises, your instructor may use a rubric, with which more points are allotted according to performance characteristics. (The more you do, the more you earn!) Ask your instructor how your work will be evaluated.

PP06-E01 That's the Way I See It!

Create a blank presentation and save it in the **PP2013 Lesson 06** folder as `PP06-E01-Hobby-[FirstInitialLastName]`. Change the layout of the first slide to Title and Content. Think of one of your favorite active or creative hobbies, such as sports, music, or art. Title the first slide for your chosen hobby. If you have access to a video camera (many smart phones have a built-in video camera), take a short video of yourself explaining your hobby. Transfer the video to your computer and then insert the video on the first slide. Edit the video to trim off any unwanted beginnings or endings and apply a video style. Set it to play automatically. If you don't have a video camera, insert a clip art image depicting your hobby.

Create a second slide and insert an online video depicting your hobby. Apply a video style and set the video to play when clicked. Add an appropriate slide title. Finally, apply a design theme.

You will be evaluated based on the inclusion of all elements specified, your ability to follow directions, your ability to apply newly learned skills to a real-world situation, your creativity, and the relevance of your topic and/or data choice(s). Submit your final file based on the guidelines provided by your instructor.

PP06-E02 Be Your Own Boss

You are creating an automated slide show highlighting gardens created by Blue Jean Landscaping. Open **PP06-E02-BlueJean** from the **PP2013 Lesson 06** folder and save it as `PP06-E02-BlueJean-[FirstInitialLastName]`. Add online audio to slide 1 appropriate for a garden slide show (e.g., light classical or cool jazz). Set the audio to start automatically and ensure that it plays across all slides and loops until stopped. The speaker icon should not display during the slide show. Configure the slide show to run automatically, about 7 seconds per slide. Once reaching the last slide, the slide show should automatically start over and loop continuously until Esc is pressed. Save and close the presentation.

Create a second presentation with four slides and save it as `PP06-E02-HowTo-[FirstInitialLastName]`. On the title slide, add the title **Blue Jean Landscaping** and a subtitle of **How to Garden**. On each of the three remaining slides, insert an online video. Use the Bing search or find a video on the Internet you like and use the embed code. Set each video to start when clicked. Add an appropriate title to each slide and apply a design theme to the presentation. Apply the same video style to each of the three videos so the presentation has a consistent look. Run the slide show and verify that each video plays. If a video fails to play, replace it.

You will be evaluated based on the inclusion of all elements specified, your ability to follow directions, your ability to apply newly learned skills to a real-world situation, your creativity, and your demonstration of an entrepreneurial spirit. Submit your final file based on the guidelines provided by your instructor.

Transfer Your Skills

In the course of working through the Transfer Your Skills exercises, you will use critical-thinking and creativity skills to complete the assigned projects using skills taught in the lesson. To evaluate your mastery and completion of the exercises, your instructor may use a rubric, with which more points are allotted according to performance characteristics. (The more you do, the more you earn!) Ask your instructor how your work will be evaluated.

PP06-T01 Use the Web as a Learning Tool

Throughout this book, you will be provided with an opportunity to use the Internet as a learning tool by completing WebQuests. According to the original creators of WebQuests, as described on their website (WebQuest.org), a WebQuest is "an inquiry-oriented activity in which most or all of the information used by learners is drawn from the web." To complete the WebQuest projects in this book, navigate to the student resource center and choose the WebQuest for the lesson on which you are currently working. The subject of each WebQuest will be relevant to the material found in the lesson.

WebQuest Subject: Multimedia Conversion

Submit your files based on the guidelines provided by your instructor.

PP06-T02 Demonstrate Proficiency

To promote its cooking classes, Stormy BBQ wants to display a presentation on the restaurant television screens showing some of their favorite recipes. Create a blank presentation and save it to your **PP2013 Lesson 06** folder as `PP06-T02-Recipes-[FirstInitialLastName]`. Add an appropriate title, subtitle, and design theme. Create a second slide using the Title and Content layout.

Use the Internet to find a video showing how to cook something appropriate for a barbeque restaurant. Copy the embed code. (If the video does not have any embed code, search for a different video.) Insert the video, using the embed code, to the second slide and add an appropriate title. Apply a Video Style and set the video to play when clicked.

Add some online audio clips to slide 1 of people saying *mmmmm*, *yummy*, or making polite eating sounds. Set the audio to play automatically and hide the speaker icon during a slide show. Do not play the audio clips across all slides. Create Rehearsed Timings to display slide 1 for about 5 seconds, even if it cuts off the eating sounds. Make sure the timing for slide 2 is long enough to show the entire video.

Submit your final file based on the guidelines provided by your instructor.

POWERPOINT 2013

Using Tables in Presentations

LEARNING OBJECTIVES

After studying this lesson, you will be able to:

- Insert tables on slides
- Add and delete rows and columns in tables
- Format tables and cells
- Add nontext data over cells

Until now, you have been dealing mostly with bulleted text on slides. Quite often you will need to display tabular data—that is, text inside a table. In this lesson, you will work with tables. PowerPoint has tools to easily create and format tables. It also offers professionally designed, preformatted color schemes that match your document theme. A variety of custom colors and 3-D effects can be applied to your tables, allowing you total control over the look and feel of your slides.

Creating Tables in Presentations

The last Sunday of every month, Green Clean sponsors a family picnic complete with games and live entertainment. You feel it's a way to give back to the community and bond with staff and clients. You have the responsibility of creating a presentation to show during the awards ceremony, after the various picnic game competitions. You have a short time to complete these monthly presentations, because you typically create them on your laptop computer during the post-game picnic dinner. You use PowerPoint tables to present the day's events and competition results.

EVENTS	Team Competitions	
	Egg Toss	Tommy & Mary Derek & Isabella Ken & D'Andre
	Three-Legged Race	Tommy & Talos Derek & Ken Mary & D'Andre
	Wheelbarrow Race	Isabella & Talos Derek & Mary Ken & D'Andre
	Water Balloon Toss	Tommy & Derek Ken & Mary Isabella & D'Andre

This three-column table is formatted to match the presentation theme and lays out the day's competitions.

Using PowerPoint Tables

Video Library   http://labyrinthelab.com/videos   Video Number: PP13-V0701

Tables are useful for organizing information into rows and columns. PowerPoint has table layout features that make inserting tables into slides easy. After you insert a table, you can use various manual and automatic commands to format it, change column and row sizes, and make other adjustments.

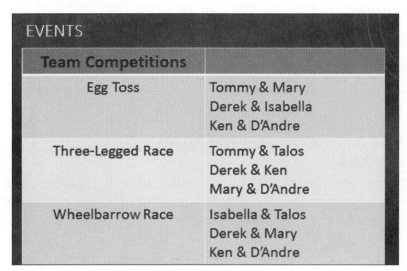

A table inserted on a PowerPoint slide

Inserting Tables

You can insert tables into slides with the table icon present on most slide layouts, or via the Ribbon. When you insert a new table, PowerPoint lets you specify the number of rows and columns it should contain.

QUICK REFERENCE	INSERTING TABLES
Task	**Procedure**
Insert a table from a slide icon	■ Click the Insert Table ⊞ icon if present on your slide layout. ■ Enter the desired number of columns and rows, and click OK.
Insert a table from the Ribbon	■ Choose Insert→Tables→Table ▼. ■ Drag with the mouse to indicate the desired number of rows/columns; release the mouse button.

Create a PowerPoint Table

In this exercise, you will create a PowerPoint table.

1. Start **PowerPoint** and maximize the program window.

2. Open **PP07-D01-Picnic** from your **PP2013 Lesson 07** folder and save it as **PP07-D01-Picnic-[FirstInitialLastName]**.

   Replace the bracketed text with your first initial and last name. For example, if your name is Bethany Smith, your filename would look like this: PP07-D01-Picnic-BSmith.

3. Select the title slide and choose **Home→Slides→New Slide**.

4. In the **Title placeholder**, type **Events**.

5. Click the **Insert Table** icon in the center of the slide.

   The Insert Table dialog box appears.

6. Enter **2** for the number of columns and **6** for the number of rows; click **OK**.

   PowerPoint creates a table with two columns and six rows on the slide. The table is already formatted with the color scheme of the document theme. You will enter data in the table in the next exercise.

7. Save your presentation.

Entering Data in Tables

Video Library   http://labyrinthelab.com/videos   Video Number: PP13-V0702

When you type text in a table cell, PowerPoint wraps the text to fit the cell. The cell height increases to accommodate the wrapped text. You can add text or numbers in table cells. You cannot insert pictures, clip art, other tables, SmartArt, or charts directly into a table cell. However, you will see how to accomplish a similar effect later in this chapter.

Navigating Table Cells

After inserting a new table on a slide, you will often want to enter information in each cell. Although you can click in the first cell, type your information, and then click in the next cell, type, click in the next, type, and so on, this method is not efficient because it requires you to move your hands away from the keyboard to use the mouse. Navigating table cells with the keyboard is a more efficient way to enter data initially.

Task	Procedure
Move to the next cell	■ Tap Tab. From the last cell of a row, this moves to the first cell in the next row.
Move to the previous cell	■ Tap Shift + Tab. From the first cell of a row, this moves to the last cell in the previous row.
Move to the next row	■ Tap ↓. This does not create a new row.
Move to the previous row	■ Tap ↑.
Add a new row for data entry	■ Move to the bottom-right table cell. ■ Tap Tab to create a new bottom row.

DEVELOP YOUR SKILLS PP07-D02

Enter Data into a PowerPoint Table

In this exercise, you will enter data into a PowerPoint table.

1. Save the presentation as **PP07-D02-Picnic-[FirstInitialLastName]**.

2. Click in the first cell of the first row, if necessary to display the insertion point, and type **Team Competitions**.

3. Tap the ↓ key once to move the insertion point to the first cell in the second row and type **Egg Toss**.

4. Tap Tab to move to the next cell and type the following:

   Tommy & Mary Enter
   Derek & Isabella Enter
   Ken & D'Andre

Team Competitions	
Egg Toss	Tommy & Mary Derek & Isabella Ken & D'Andre

5. Tap Tab and type **Three-Legged Race** in the first cell of the third row.

6. Tap Tab to move to the next cell and type the following:

   Tommy & Talos Enter
   Derek & Ken Enter
   Mary & D'Andre

7. Tap Tab to move to the next row, type **Wheelbarrow Race**, tap Tab, and type the names of the contestants in the next cell:

   Isabella & Talos Enter
   Derek & Mary Enter
   Ken & D'Andre

8. Complete the bottom two rows as shown.

Water Balloon Toss	Tommy & Derek Ken & Mary Isabella & D'Andre
Piggyback Race	Mary & Isabella D'Andre & Talos Ken & Tommy

The table extends off the bottom of the slide because there is so much text. You will fix that later.

9. Save your presentation.

Resizing and Moving Tables

Video Library   http://labyrinthelab.com/videos   Video Number: PP13-V0703

After you type text in a table, you may notice that the table has expanded and no longer fits on the slide, or a small table is not centered on the slide. You can adjust the table size manually by dragging the handles (white squares) along the table border, or autosize it to fit its contents. You can also drag the table to place it exactly where you like on the slide.

DEVELOP YOUR SKILLS PP07-D03
Resize and Move a Table

In this exercise, you will resize and move the table so it fits on the slide.

1. Save the presentation as **PP07-D03-Picnic-[FirstInitialLastName]**.

2. Point at the top border of the table until your mouse pointer displays a four-headed arrow and then drag the table up and right so it is top-aligned with the slide title and only the first few letters of the title are visible.

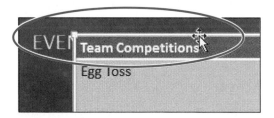

3. Point at the left-center handle of the table border until your mouse pointer displays a double-headed white arrow and then drag right until the entire slide title is visible.

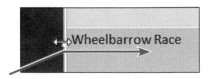

4. Save your presentation.

Aligning a Table

Video Library   http://labyrinthelab.com/videos   Video Number: PP13-V0704

Although you can drag the table to any location and eyeball it, you will achieve more-exact results with the Align option. Using the Align option lets you center the table perfectly in the middle of the slide, or align the table to any edge of the slide.

QUICK REFERENCE	ALIGNING A TABLE
Task	**Procedure**
Align a table to a specific location within a slide	■ Click in any cell so the table displays its border.
	■ Choose Table Tools→Layout→Arrange→Align.
	■ Choose Align to Slide to place a checkmark next to it, if necessary.
	■ Choose Table Tools→Layout→Arrange→Align again.
	■ Select Align Left, Align Center, or Align Right to shift the table horizontally.
	■ Select Align Top, Align Middle, or Align Bottom to shift the table vertically.

DEVELOP YOUR SKILLS PP07-D04
Align a Table to a Slide

In this exercise, you will position the table in the exact vertical center of the slide.

1. Save the presentation as **PP07-D04-Picnic-[FirstInitialLastName]**.

2. Click inside any table cell.

3. Choose **Table Tools→Layout→Arrange→Align→Align Middle**.

   Align to Slide is selected by default, so the table becomes centered vertically (top to bottom) on the slide.

4. Choose **Table Tools→Layout→Arrange→Align→Align Center**.

   The table becomes centered horizontally (side to side), but now overlaps the slide title.

5. Tap Ctrl + Z to undo the last alignment.

6. Save your presentation.

Formatting Data in Cells

Video Library   http://labyrinthelab.com/videos   Video Number: PP13-V0705

Table cells and their contents can be formatted in one of two ways—character formatting or cell formatting. Character formatting applies only to the selected text, whereas cell formatting applies to all text in the cell and any future text that is typed in the cell.

Character formatting is helpful when you wish to emphasize a single word or phrase. Cell formatting is helpful when you want all the text in a cell to look the same. In the following figure, character formatting was applied to the word *Winners*, so only that word was affected.

PowerPoint 2013

(A larger font size was applied.) Additionally, cell formatting was applied to color all text white, including any new text typed in the cell.

The word *Winners* is emphasized with character formatting.

Aligning and Formatting Cell Entries

Alignment is one form of cell formatting. You can align the contents of cells horizontally (side to side) and vertically (top to bottom). You can also add background color, textures, or pictures to tables or cells. You will learn more about this in the next topic.

You can align the contents of table cells horizontally and vertically.

QUICK REFERENCE	SELECTING TABLE CELLS
Task	**Procedure**
Select a single cell	Click in the cell, or point at the cell's left border until the mouse pointer changes to a thick diagonal arrow, and click.
Select multiple cells	Point at the first desired cell and drag to any other cell; or, click in any cell, press Shift, click in any other cell, and release Shift.
Select a single column	Point at the top of the table above any column until the mouse pointer turns into a thick down arrow then click; or, click in any cell and choose Table Tools→Layout→Table→Select→Select Column.
Select multiple adjacent columns	Point at the top of the table above the first desired column until the mouse pointer turns into a thick down arrow, and then click and drag across the remaining columns.
Select a single row	Point at the left of the table next to the desired row until the mouse pointer turns into a thick right arrow then click; or, click in any cell and choose Table Tools→Layout→Table→Select→Select Row.
Select multiple adjacent rows	Point at the left of the table next to the first desired row until the mouse pointer turns into a thick right arrow, and then click and drag up or down to the remaining rows.

Select Cells and Format Cell Content

In this exercise, you will select cells and apply character formatting and cell formatting.

1. Save the presentation as **PP07-D05-Picnic-[FirstInitialLastName]**.

2. Double-click the word *Egg* in the first cell of the second row.

3. Choose **Home→Font→Font Color ▼→Red**.
   Only the selected word turns red.

4. Click once to the right of the word *Toss* in the same cell, tap
   [Spacebar], and type **Contest**.
   The word Contest *is not red because character formatting applied only to the previously selected text.*

5. Tap [Backspace] repeatedly until the word *Contest* is deleted.

6. Follow these steps to format the cell:

Ⓐ Point at the bottom-left corner of the cell until your mouse pointer becomes a thick diagonal arrow then click.

Ⓑ Click the **Font Color ▼** on the Mini toolbar.

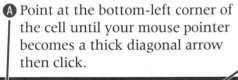

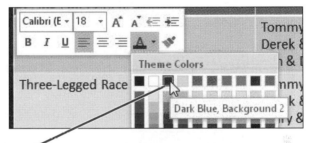

Ⓒ Choose the third themed color, **Dark Blue, Background 2**.

Ⓓ Tap [Esc] so the Mini toolbar disappears.

All text in the cell turns dark blue.

7. Click to the right of the word *Toss* in the same cell, tap [Spacebar], and type **Contest**.
   The word Contest *is automatically dark blue because cell formatting has been applied to the cell.*

8. Tap [Backspace] repeatedly until the word *Contest* is deleted.

9. Point at the left of the **Egg Toss** row until your mouse pointer turns into a thick right arrow.

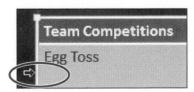

10. Drag down to the *Piggyback Race* row and then release the mouse button.
All but the top row (Team Competitions) *becomes selected.*

11. Choose **Home→Font→Font Color ▾→Standard Colors→Dark Blue**.

12. Click anywhere outside the table to deselect the highlighted rows.

13. Follow these steps to apply additional formatting to the cells:

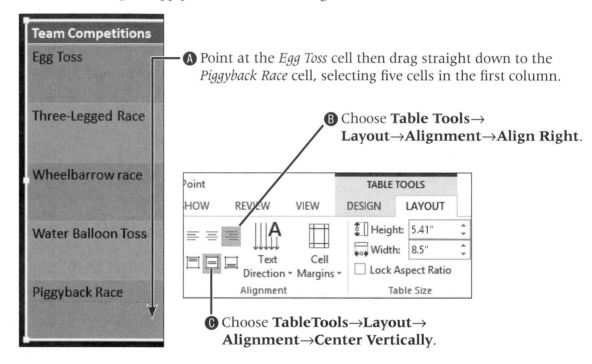

Ⓐ Point at the *Egg Toss* cell then drag straight down to the *Piggyback Race* cell, selecting five cells in the first column.

Ⓑ Choose **Table Tools→ Layout→Alignment→Align Right**.

Ⓒ Choose **TableTools→Layout→ Alignment→Center Vertically**.

The text in all five cells shifts to the right vertical centers of their cells.

14. Choose **Table Tools→Layout→Alignment→Align Bottom**.

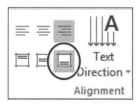

The text in all five cells shifts to the bottoms of their cells.

15. Choose Table **Tools→Layout→Alignment→Align Top**.

16. Click anywhere outside the table to deselect the highlighted cells.

17. Save your presentation.

Adjusting Column Widths and Row Heights

Video Library   http://labyrinthelab.com/videos   Video Number: PP13-V0706

Depending on your presentation design and your personal preference, you may want to reduce the extra space in a column or row by reducing the column width or row height. At other times, you may want to expand the width or height to create breathing room between cells. Another option is to set all columns to the same width or all rows to the same height. These adjustments can be made manually or automatically.

Team Competitions	
Egg Toss	Tommy & Mary Derek & Isabella Ken & D'Andre
Three-Legged Race	Tommy & Talos Derek & Ken Mary & D'Andre
Wheelbarrow Race	Isabella & Talos Derek & Mary Ken & D'Andre

Unequal column widths and row heights make the table unbalanced.

Team Competitions	
Egg Toss	Tommy & Mary Derek & Isabella Ken & D'Andre
Three-Legged Race	Tommy & Talos Derek & Ken Mary & D'Andre
Wheelbarrow Race	Isabella & Talos Derek & Mary Ken & D'Andre

Equal column widths and row heights create a more pleasing table.

QUICK REFERENCE	ADJUSTING COLUMN WIDTHS AND ROW HEIGHTS
Task	**Procedure**
Adjust a column width or row height manually	■ Point at a column or row border. ■ When the ⊹‖⊹ or ⊟ mouse pointer shape appears, drag the border to the desired width or height.
Adjust a column width automatically	■ Point at a column's right border until the ⊹‖⊹ mouse pointer appears, and then double-click.
Equalize column widths	■ Select the columns you wish to make equal. ■ Choose Table Tools→Layout→Cell Size→Distribute Columns ⊞.
Equalize row heights	■ Select the rows you wish to make equal. ■ Choose Table Tools→Layout→Cell Size→Distribute Rows ⊟.

DEVELOP YOUR SKILLS PP07-D06

Adjust Column Widths

In this exercise, you will automatically and manually change column widths.

1. Save the presentation as **PP07-D06-Picnic-[FirstInitialLastName]**.

2. Point at the column border between the two columns until your mouse pointer turns into a double-headed arrow.

3. Double-click to resize the left column.

   The column at the left of the border you double-clicked automatically resizes to the width of its longest contents.

4. Point at the right border of the table until the same double-headed arrow appears, and then double-click to adjust the size of the last column.

5. Follow these steps to manually adjust the width of the left column:

Ⓐ Point at the column border between the two columns until your mouse pointer turns into a double-headed arrow.

Ⓑ Drag the column border to the right, about halfway through the second column.

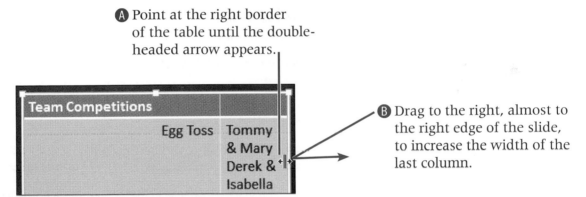

The left column widens, but the table does not. The additional space added to the left column was taken from the right column. The right column has become too narrow.

6. Follow these steps to manually widen the right column:

Ⓐ Point at the right border of the table until the double-headed arrow appears.

Ⓑ Drag to the right, almost to the right edge of the slide, to increase the width of the last column.

Equalize Column Widths

7. Point at the top of the left column until the mouse pointer becomes a thick down arrow, and then drag to the right to select both columns.

8. Choose **Table Tools→Layout→Cell Size→Distribute Columns**.
The column widths are made equal.

9. Click anywhere outside the table to deselect the highlighted cells.

10. Save your presentation.

Adding and Deleting Rows and Columns

Video Library   http://labyrinthelab.com/videos   Video Number: PP13-V0707

Adding rows to the bottom of a table is as simple as selecting the final cell and tapping the Tab key, but quite often you will want to add rows in the middle or top of the table or to add more columns. This is easily done from the Ribbon. You can also insert multiple rows and columns quickly.

Deleting Cells or Content

Deleting a row or column also deletes the content. A common mistake users make is to select a row or column and tap Delete. Although that deletes the content inside the cells, it leaves the cells themselves.

QUICK REFERENCE	ADDING AND DELETING ROWS AND COLUMNS
Task	**Procedure**
Insert a row	▪ Click in any cell you wish to place a row above or below. ▪ Choose Table Tools→Layout→Rows & Columns→Insert Above or Insert Below.
Insert multiple rows	▪ Select a number of rows equal to the number you wish to insert. ▪ Choose Table Tools→Layout→Rows & Columns→Insert Above or Insert Below.
Delete a row or multiple rows	▪ Click in any cell in the row you wish to delete, or select multiple rows. ▪ Choose Table Tools→Layout→Rows & Columns→Delete ▼→Delete Rows.
Insert a column	▪ Click in any cell you wish to place a column beside. ▪ Choose Table Tools→Layout→Rows & Columns→Insert Left or Insert Right.
Insert multiple columns	▪ Select a number of columns equal to the number you wish to insert. ▪ Choose Table Tools→Layout→Rows & Columns→Insert Left or Insert Right.
Delete a column or multiple columns	▪ Click in any cell in the column you wish to delete, or select multiple columns. ▪ Choose Table Tools→Layout→Rows & Columns→Delete ▼→Delete Columns.

DEVELOP YOUR SKILLS PP07-D07
Add and Delete Rows and Columns

In this exercise, you will delete a row and add a column.

1. Save the presentation as **PP07-D07-Picnic-[FirstInitialLastName]**.

2. Click once in the *Water Balloon Toss* cell.

3. Press Shift, click in the bottom-right cell, and then release Shift.
   The bottom two rows become selected.

4. Choose **Table Tools→Layout→Rows & Columns→Insert Below**.
   Because you selected two rows initially, two additional rows are inserted below your selection. As it happens, you don't need the bottom three rows at all. You will delete them in the next few steps.

Delete Rows

The Piggyback Race was cancelled, so its table row must be deleted.

5. Click once in the *Piggyback Race* cell.

6. Press ⎡Shift⎤, click in the bottom-right cell, and then release ⎡Shift⎤.
The bottom three rows become selected.

7. Choose **Table Tools→Layout→Rows & Columns→Delete ▼→Delete Rows**.
The Piggyback Race row and empty rows are deleted.

Add Columns

Clip art will add some visual excitement to the slide. A column is needed to hold the images.

8. Click once in the *Egg Toss* cell.

9. Choose **Table Tools→Layout→Rows & Columns→Insert Left**.
A new column is inserted to the left of the cell in which you clicked. Some cells in the last column may wrap to four lines.

10. Point at the column border to the right of the *Egg Toss* cell until your mouse pointer becomes a double-headed arrow, and then drag the border to the left of the word *Toss*.

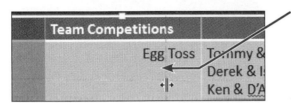

The middle column now has text that wraps.

11. Point at the column border to the left of the *Egg Toss* cell until your mouse pointer becomes a double-headed arrow, drag the border slightly to the left, and then release the mouse button.
The text in the middle column no longer wraps. If your text still wraps, drag the border a little more to the left. Your slide should resemble the following figure.

EVENTS		Team Competitions	
		Egg Toss	Tommy & Mary Derek & Isabella Ken & D'Andre
		Three-Legged Race	Tommy & Talos Derek & Ken Mary & D'Andre
		Wheelbarrow race	Isabella & Talos Derek & Mary Ken & D'Andre
		Water Balloon Toss	Tommy & Derek Ken & Mary Isabella & D'Andre

12. Click anywhere outside the table to deselect the highlighted cells.

13. Save your presentation.

Adding Nontext Data to Cells

Video Library   http://labyrinthelab.com/videos   Video Number: PP13-V0708

Only text you type at the keyboard can truly reside inside a table cell. If you attempt to insert a picture, chart, or some other object in a cell, it will simply sit on top of the table as an independent object. If you move the table, the overlapping object will not move with the table. If you resize a column or row, it will have no effect on the overlapping object. However, you can make it appear as though the object were inside the table cell by resizing and carefully positioning the object over the cell.

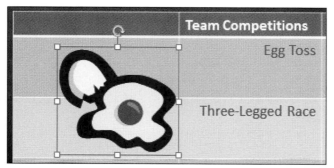

Clip art placed in a table cell actually sits on top of the table as an independent object (left). Reduced and repositioned artwork appears as if it is truly inside a cell (right).

DEVELOP YOUR SKILLS PP07-D08
Add Clip Art over a Cell

In this exercise, you will add clip art and make it appear as though the pictures are in the cells.

1. Save the presentation as **PP07-D08-Picnic-[FirstInitialLastName]**.

2. Choose **Insert→Images→Online Pictures**.

3. Type **broken egg** in the **Office.com** search box and tap Enter.

4. Select a clip art image and click **Insert**.

5. Follow these steps to move and scale the clip art image:

A Point at the middle of the picture (not at a handle), and drag with the four-headed arrow to the top-left cell.

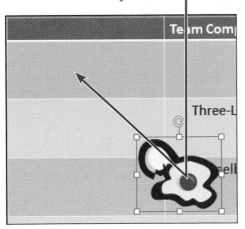

B Drag the bottom-right sizing handle until the picture fits in the cell.

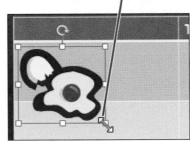

C Adjust the size and location of the picture to the vertical center of the cell.

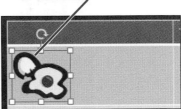

 Don't forget that the arrow (↑, ↓, etc.) keys are useful for adjusting the location of pictures. To make small adjustments, press the Ctrl key as you tap an arrow key.

6. Repeat steps 2–5 with the search term **belt** and position the picture to the left of the *Three-Legged Race* cell.

7. Repeat steps 2–5 with the search term **wheelbarrow** and position the picture to the left of the *Wheelbarrow Race* cell.

8. Repeat steps 2–5 with the search term **balloon** and position the picture to the left of the *Water Balloon Toss* cell.

Your table should resemble the following figure.

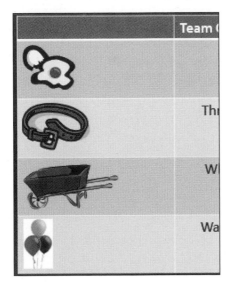

PowerPoint 2013

Adjust Column Widths

9. Point at the right border of the first column until your mouse pointer turns into a double-headed arrow and then drag the border to the left so the first column is as narrow as possible without cutting off the images.

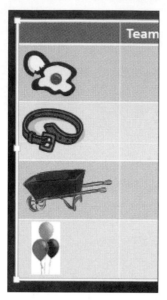

10. Point at the right border of the middle column until your mouse pointer turns into a double-headed arrow and then double-click to automatically size the middle column.

11. Point at the right border of the last column until your mouse pointer turns into a double-headed arrow and then double-click to automatically size the last column.

Team Competitions		
	Egg Toss	Tommy & Mary Derek & Isabella Ken & D'Andre
	Three-Legged Race	Tommy & Talos Derek & Ken Mary & D'Andre
	Wheelbarrow race	Isabella & Talos Derek & Mary Ken & D'Andre
	Water Balloon Toss	Tommy & Derek Ken & Mary Isabella & D'Andre

12. Save your presentation.

Merging and Splitting Cells

Video Library http://labyrinthelab.com/videos Video Number: PP13-V0709

Merging cells is the process of selecting multiple cells and combining them into one single larger cell that spans multiple rows or columns. Splitting cells is the opposite—cutting a single cell into several smaller cells.

Cells are often merged across the top row of a table to create a single long row that acts as a label for the table. It's easier to format the label text because it can be centered over the entire table rather than just in a single cell.

Team Competitions		
	Egg Toss	Tommy & Mary
		Derek & Isabella
		Ken & D'Andre

The top row contains three distinct cells. Although *Team Competitions* is centered in its cell, it is not centered over the entire table.

Team Competitions		
	Egg Toss	Tommy & Mary
		Derek & Isabella
		Ken & D'Andre

With the cells across the top row merged, *Team Competitions* can be centered over the entire table.

QUICK REFERENCE	MERGING AND SPLITTING CELLS
Task	**Procedure**
Merge cells	■ Select the cells you wish to merge. ■ Choose Table Tools→Layout→Merge→Merge Cells.
Split cells	■ Click in the single cell you wish to split. ■ Choose Table Tools→Layout→Merge→Split Cells. ■ Enter the number of columns and rows you wish to split the cell into, and then click OK.

DEVELOP YOUR SKILLS PP07-D09
Merge Cells

In this exercise, you will merge cells and finalize the cell alignment.

1. Save the presentation as **PP07-D09-Picnic-[FirstInitialLastName]**.

2. Click once in the top-left empty cell.

3. Press ⟨Shift⟩, click once in the top-right empty cell, and then release ⟨Shift⟩.
   All cells in the top row are selected.

4. Choose **Table Tools→Layout→Merge→Merge Cells**.
   The cells in the top row are merged into a single long cell. The text in this cell would look better if it were centered over the table.

5. Choose **Table Tools→Layout→Alignment→Center**.

6. Point at the **Egg Toss** cell and then drag down to the *Water Balloon Toss* cell.
   Four cells down the middle column become selected.

7. Choose **Table Tools→Layout→Alignment→Center**.
   The text becomes centered in its cells.

8. Click anywhere outside the table to deselect the highlighted cells.

9. Save your presentation.

Customizing Tables

Video Library   http://labyrinthelab.com/videos   Video Number: PP13-V0710

The contextual Design and Layout tabs on the Ribbon provide many commands with which to customize the appearance of tables and cells. You can apply borders and shading to cells in the table, change the alignment of text, add rows or columns, apply shadows, bevels, and other visual effects, and make many other adjustments.

Applying Table Styles

You can use table styles to quickly apply colors, shading, background patterns, bevels, and other special effects to tables and table cells. PowerPoint offers professionally created color schemes to complement your document theme, taking much of the guesswork out of applying color.

You can choose from several preset color schemes, which are organized in Light, Medium, Dark, and Best Match for Document categories. Additionally, table styles can be customized by designating certain rows or columns to receive a slightly different color. For example, the top row of a table may be a different color than the rest of the cells to emphasize the table's title. You can also add background colors, background pictures, gradients, textures, bevels, and shadows to tables. The following figures compare a simple table before and after table styles were applied.

	Sack Race	100-Yard Dash	Archery
1st place	Tommy	Mary	Derek
2nd place	Isabella	Ken	Jenna
3rd place	Nicole	Amy	Brian

Table with no formatting applied

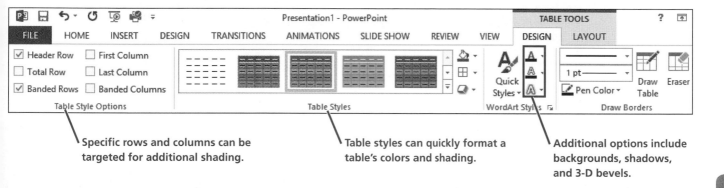

	Sack Race	100-Yard Dash	Archery
1st place	Tommy	Mary	Derek
2nd place	Isabella	Ken	Jenna
3rd place	Nicole	Amy	Brian

The same table with a table style and options applied

Specific rows and columns can be targeted for additional shading.

Table styles can quickly format a table's colors and shading.

Additional options include backgrounds, shadows, and 3-D bevels.

DEVELOP YOUR SKILLS PP07-D10
Apply Table Styles

In this exercise, you will create a new table and apply a table style to it.

1. Save the presentation as **PP07-D010-Picnic-[FirstInitialLastName]**.

2. If necessary, select the **Events** slide, and then choose **Home→Slides→New Slide**.

3. Type **Totals** as the slide title.

4. Click the **Insert Table** icon in the center of the slide.

   The Insert Table dialog box appears.

5. Enter **6** for the number of columns and **8** for the number of rows; click **OK**.

   PowerPoint creates a table with six columns and eight rows on the slide. The table is already formatted with the color scheme of the document theme.

PowerPoint 2013

6. Using Tab to navigate the cells, enter this table data:

	Egg Toss	Three-Legged Race	Wheelbarrow Race	Water Balloon Toss	Total
Tommy	5	5	0	5	15
Talos	0	5	5	0	10
Ken	1	3	1	3	8
Mary	5	1	3	3	12
D'Andre	1	1	1	1	4
Isabella	3	0	5	1	9
Derek	3	3	3	5	14

Some of the contest names wrap in an undesirable way. A smaller font and adjusted column widths will fix that.

7. Point at the border of the table until your mouse pointer becomes a four-headed arrow, and then click once to select the entire table.

The change on the screen is very subtle. The border still displays around the table, but the insertion point in the cell disappears, indicating that the entire table has been selected.

8. Choose **Home→Font→Font Size ▼→16**.

The font is reduced for the entire table, but the contest names still wrap. You will adjust the column widths to fix that.

9. Point at the right border of the *Wheelbarrow Race* column until your mouse pointer becomes a double-headed arrow, and then drag slightly to the right to manually fit the column.

You may have to drag, release the mouse button, drag, and release the mouse button several times to get it just right. Your table should resemble the following figure.

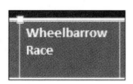

10. Continue to resize the other columns until your table resembles this figure.

	Egg Toss	Three-Legged Race	Wheelbarrow Race	Water Balloon Toss	Total

11. Click once in any cell and then choose **Table Tools→Design→Table Styles→More**.

The Table Styles gallery opens but covers your table.

12. Point at any of the table styles in the **Table Styles** gallery to see a Live Preview of the style on your slide.

Your table changes as you point at different styles, but your table is hidden behind the Table Styles gallery.

13. Tap Esc to close the **Table Styles** gallery without applying a style.

14. Follow these steps to preview table styles:

Ⓐ Point at any **Table Styles** thumbnail to preview the style on your slide.

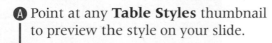

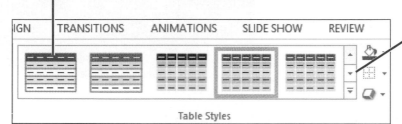

Ⓑ Click the scroll-down button to load the next row of table styles in the Ribbon.

Ⓒ Point at several more table styles to preview them on your slide.

Ⓓ Continue to use the scroll-down button to load more styles into the Ribbon and point at the thumbnails to preview them.

15. Follow these steps to apply a table style:

Ⓐ Click the scroll-down button to load more styles.

Ⓑ Continue to point at thumbnails until you find **Dark Style 1 – Accent 6**.

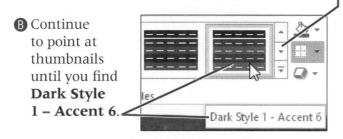

Dark Style 1 - Accent 6

Ⓒ Click **Dark Style 1 – Accent 6** to apply it.

PowerPoint applies your selection to the entire table.

16. Save your presentation.

Applying Table Style Options

Video Library   http://labyrinthelab.com/videos   Video Number: PP13-V0711

You are not stuck with the basic formatting applied by a table style. You can modify the table after applying a style to include additional shading or add backgrounds to the table cells.

	Egg Toss	Three-Legged Race	Wheelbarrow Race
Tommy	5	5	0
Talos	0	5	5
Ken	1	3	1
Mary	5	1	3

☑ Header Row   ☐ First Column
☐ Total Row   ☐ Last Column
☑ Banded Rows ☐ Banded Columns

Table Style Options

Use the Table Style Options command group to apply additional shading to specific rows or columns (left). The Header Row option applied a different color to the top row, while the Banded Rows option applied different colors to alternating rows (right).

APPLYING TABLE STYLE OPTIONS

Option	Where Additional Shading Is Applied
Header Row	Top row
Total Row	Bottom row
Banded Rows	Row colors alternate, with odd rows one shade and even rows a different shade
First Column	Left column
Last Column	Right column
Banded Columns	Column colors alternate, with odd columns one shade and even columns a different shade

DEVELOP YOUR SKILLS PP07-D11
Apply Table Style Options

In this exercise, you will customize your table's style. A 3-D bevel effect will make your data "pop."

1. Save the presentation as **PP07-D11-Picnic-[FirstInitialLastName]**.

2. Point at the left of the top row until your mouse pointer becomes a thick right arrow, and then click to select the entire top row.

3. Choose **Table Tools→Layout→Alignment→Center**.
   The text in the top row becomes center-aligned.

4. Point to the first cell in the second row, with the text *Tommy*.

5. Drag down to the last cell in the first column to select the seven cells with employee names.

6. Choose **Table Tools→Layout→Alignment→Align Right**.

The employee names are right-aligned in their cells.

7. Select all the cells in the body of the table that contain numbers.

8. Choose **Table Tools→Layout→Alignment→Center**.

Your table should resemble the following figure (yours may display white column lines if the table is selected).

	Egg Toss	Three-Legged Race	Wheelbarrow Race	Water Balloon Toss	Total
Tommy	5	5	0	5	15
Talos	0	5	5	0	10
Ken	1	3	1	3	8
Mary	5	1	3	3	12
D'Andre	1	1	1	1	4
Isabella	3	0	5	1	9
Derek	3	3	3	5	14

Apply Custom Shading

9. Place a checkmark in the **Table Tools→Design→Table Style Options→Last Column** checkbox.

The Totals column receives darker shading.

10. Select the seven cells in the first column containing employee names.

In the next step, you will create a visual effect called a gradient fill for the table.

11. Follow these steps to apply a gradient background to the cells:

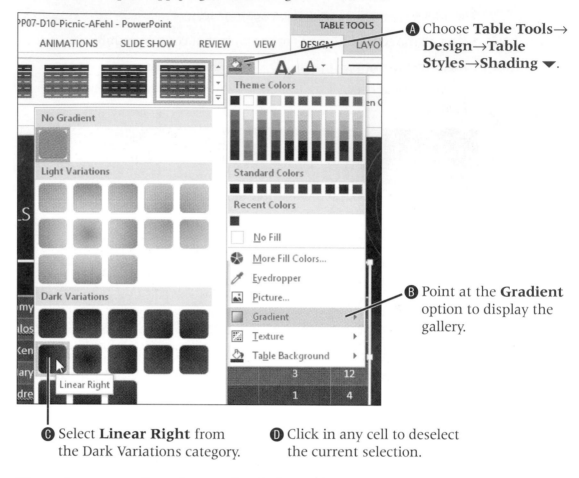

Ⓐ Choose **Table Tools→ Design→Table Styles→Shading ▼**.

Ⓑ Point at the **Gradient** option to display the gallery.

Ⓒ Select **Linear Right** from the Dark Variations category.

Ⓓ Click in any cell to deselect the current selection.

The employee name cells receive a gradient background.

Apply Custom Background Colors

You will color the Total cells to indicate first place, second place, and third place.

12. Click once inside *Tommy's Total* cell, the last cell in the second row.

13. Follow these steps to color Tommy's Total cell blue:

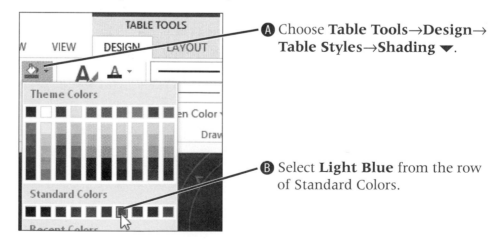

Ⓐ Choose **Table Tools→Design→ Table Styles→Shading ▼**.

Ⓑ Select **Light Blue** from the row of Standard Colors.

14. Click inside *Derek's Total* cell, with a score of 14.

15. Choose **Table Tools→Design→Table Styles→Shading ▼→Standard Colors→Red**.

16. Click inside *Mary's Total* cell, with a score of 12, and apply a background color of orange.

Apply 3-D Bevels

17. Point at the table border until your mouse pointer becomes a four-headed arrow, and then click to select the entire table.

18. Follow these steps to apply a 3-D bevel to the table cells:

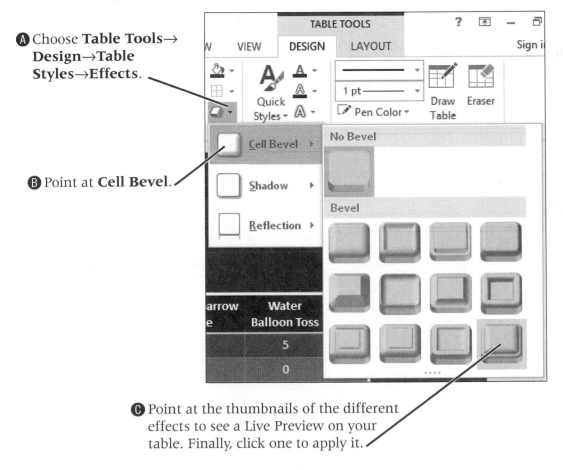

Ⓐ Choose **Table Tools→ Design→Table Styles→Effects**.

Ⓑ Point at **Cell Bevel**.

Ⓒ Point at the thumbnails of the different effects to see a Live Preview on your table. Finally, click one to apply it.

The effect is applied to all cells. However, it is barely noticeable along the top row because the row is black and the bevel shading cannot be seen.

19. Select all cells in the top row.

20. Choose **Table Tools→Design→Table Styles→Shading ▼→Theme Colors→Gold Accent 1**.

The 3-D bevel on the top row is now more visible. Your table should resemble the following figure.

	Egg Toss	Three-Legged Race	Wheelbarrow Race	Water Balloon Toss	Total
Tommy	5	5	0	5	15
Talos	0	5	5	0	10
Ken	1	3	1	3	8
Mary	5	1	3	3	12
D'Andre	1	1	1	1	4
Isabella	3	0	5	1	9
Derek	3	3	3	5	14

Center the Table

21. Choose **Table Tools→Layout→Arrange→Align→Align Center**.

The table is centered horizontally on the slide.

22. Save and close the file. Exit **PowerPoint**.

Concepts Review

To check your knowledge of the key concepts introduced in this lesson, complete the Concepts Review quiz by choosing the appropriate access option below.

If you are...	Then access the quiz by...
Using the Labyrinth Video Library	Going to http://labyrinthelab.com/videos
Using eLab	Logging in, choosing Content, and navigating to the Concepts Review quiz for this lesson
Not using the Labyrinth Video Library or eLab	Going to the student resource center for this book

Reinforce Your Skills

Add a Table

In this exercise, you will add a table to a slide to display a schedule for the Kids for Change Diversity Festival's Entertainment Stage. You will then add data and resize and position the table. Finally, you will format cell content and adjust column widths and row heights to accommodate the content.

Create a PowerPoint Table

1. Start **PowerPoint**. Create a new, blank presentation and save it as `PP07-R01-Schedule-[FirstInitialLastName]` in your **PP2013 Lesson 07** folder.

2. Type `Kids for Change` for the title and `Diversity Festival` for the subtitle.

3. Choose **Design→Themes→Integral**.

4. Choose **Design→Customize→Slide Size→Standard (4:3)** and then click **Ensure Fit**.

5. Choose **Home→Slides→New Slide**.

6. Type `Entertainment Schedule` as the title.

7. Click the **Insert Table** icon in the slide placeholder.

8. Enter **5** for the number of columns and **3** for the number of rows; click **OK**.

   A table with five columns and three rows is inserted on the slide.

Enter Data into a PowerPoint Table

9. Click in the second cell in the top row and type the following:

   `10 - 11` ⌷Tab⌷
   `11 - 12` ⌷Tab⌷
   `12 - 1` ⌷Tab⌷
   `1 - 2` ⌷Tab⌷

10. Type the following to complete the second row:

    `North Stage` ⌷Tab⌷
    `Alexander's Allstars` ⌷Tab⌷
    `Central Middle Cloggers` ⌷Tab⌷
    `Mr. Pamuk's Puppets` ⌷Tab⌷
    `The Amazing Yousef` ⌷Tab⌷

11. Type the following to complete the third row:

    `South Stage` ⌷Tab⌷
    `Butter Carving` ⌷Tab⌷
    `Native Dance` ⌷Tab⌷
    `World Music` ⌷Tab⌷
    `Animals of the World`

Resize a Table

12. Point to the left-center handle on the table border until your mouse pointer displays a double-headed white arrow and then drag the table border to the left until it touches the edge of the slide.

The table is widened and no longer centered on the slide.

Align a Table to a Slide

13. Choose **Table Tools→Layout→Arrange→Align→Align Center**.

The table is centered on the slide.

Select Cells and Format Cell Content

14. Point to the *North Stage* cell and drag down to the *South Stage* cell to select both cells.

15. Choose **Home→Font→Font Color→Theme Colors→Dark Green, Accent 5**.

16. Choose **Table Tools→Layout→Alignment→Align Right**.

17. Point to the *10 - 11* cell and drag down to the *Animals of the World* cell to select twelve cells.

18. Choose **Table Tools→Layout→Alignment→Center**.

Adjust Column Widths

19. Point to the border to the right of the first column until your mouse pointer displays a double-headed black arrow and then double-click to automatically size the first column.

20. Save and close the file. Exit **PowerPoint**.

21. Submit your final file based on the guidelines provided by your instructor.

To view examples of how your file or files should look at the end of this exercise, go to the student resource center.

REINFORCE YOUR SKILLS PP07-R02
Add Images and Format a Table

In this exercise, you will add images to a table. You will also format a table to add visual appeal.

Add Clip Art over a Cell

1. Start **PowerPoint**. Open **PP07-R02-Demonstrations** from your **PP2013 Lesson 07** folder and save it as `PP07-R02-Demonstrations-[FirstInitialLastName]`.

2. Display **slide 3** and choose **Insert→Images→Online Pictures**.

3. Type `Mexico Flag` in the **Office.com** search box and tap [Enter].

4. Select a clip art image of the Mexican flag and click **Insert**.

5. Drag any of the corner handles on the flag to reduce its size and then drag the flag to the cell to the left of Mexico.

6. Repeat steps 3–5, searching for **Cameroon Flag** to place a flag in the cell to the left of *Cameroon*.

7. Repeat steps 3–5, searching for **India Flag** to place a flag in the cell to the left of *India*. *Each country is represented by a flag.*

Merge Cells

8. Point to the cell containing the text *Demonstrations* and then drag to the top-right cell to select the last three cells in the top row.

9. Choose **Table Tools→Layout→Merge→Merge Cells**.

10. Choose **Table Tools→Layout→Alignment→Center**.
    The top cell now spans the width of the table, and its text is centered.

Apply Table Styles

11. Choose **Table Tools→Design→Table Styles→More→Medium→Medium Style 3, Accent 2**.

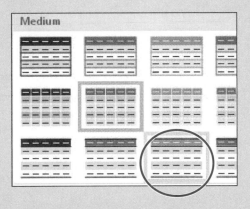

12. Point to the left of the second row until the mouse pointer displays a right-pointing black arrow and then click to select all cells across the second row.

13. Choose **Table Tools→Design→Table Styles→Shading→Theme Colors→Aqua, Accent 2**.

14. Point to the table border until the mouse pointer displays a four-headed arrow and then click to select the entire table.

15. Choose **Table Tools→Design→Table Styles→Effects ▼→Cell Bevel→Bevel→Divot**.

Apply Table Style Options

16. Place a checkmark in the **Table Tools→Design→Table Style Options→First Column** checkbox.

17. Save and close the file. Exit **PowerPoint**.

18. Submit your final file based on the guidelines provided by your instructor.

    To view examples of how your file or files should look at the end of this exercise, go to the student resource center.

REINFORCE YOUR SKILLS PP07-R03
Work with Tables

In this exercise, you will add and format a table to display Kids for Change events and participation of the top four volunteers.

Create a PowerPoint Table

1. Start **PowerPoint**. Open **PP07-R03-Volunteers** from your **PP2013 Lesson 07** folder and save it as `PP07-R03-Volunteers-[FirstInitialLastName]`.

2. Display **slide 2** and click the **Insert Table** icon in the slide placeholder.

3. Enter **5** for the number of columns and **10** for the number of rows; click **OK**.

   A 5x10 table is inserted on the slide.

Enter Data into a PowerPoint Table

4. Click in the second cell in the second row and type the following:

   ```
   Jen [Tab]
   TJ [Tab]
   Loni [Tab]
   Jo [Tab]
   ```

5. Type the following to complete the first column:

   ```
   iRecycling Day [↓]
   oy Collection [↓]
   Shave and a Haircut [↓]
   Diversity Festival [↓]
   Build-a-House [↓]
   Bully No More [↓]
   Adopt a Street [↓]
   Tutoring
   ```

Resize a Table

6. Point to the left-center handle on the table border until your mouse pointer displays a double-headed white arrow and then drag the table border left until it touches the edge of the slide.

   The table is no longer centered on the slide.

Align a Table to a Slide

7. Choose **Table Tools→Layout→Arrange→Align→Align Center**.

   The table is now centered on the slide.

Select Cells and Format Cell Content

8. Point to the *iRecycling Day* cell and drag down to the *Tutoring* cell to select eight cells.

9. Choose **Table Tools→Layout→Alignment→Align Right**.

10. Point to the *Jen* cell and drag right to the *Jo* cell to select four cells.

11. Choose **Table Tools→Layout→Alignment→Center**.

Adjust Column Widths

12. Point to the border to the right of the first column until your mouse pointer displays a double-headed black arrow and then double-click to automatically size the first column.

13. Point to the border to the right of the *Loni* cell until your mouse pointer displays a double-headed black arrow and then double-click to automatically size the fourth column.

14. Point to the top of the *Jen* column until your mouse pointer displays a downward black arrow and then drag to the last column to select the last four columns.

15. Choose **Table Tools→Layout→Cell Size→Distribute Columns**.

16. Choose **Table Tools→Layout→Arrange→Align→Align Center**.

Add Clip Art over a Cell

17. Choose **Insert→Images→Online Pictures**.

18. Type **Green Check** in the **Office.com** search box and tap Enter.

19. Select a clip art image of a green checkmark and click **Insert**.

20. Drag any of the corner handles on the image to reduce its size and then drag it to the cell directly under *Jen*.

21. Tap Ctrl + C to copy the image.

22. Tap Ctrl + V to paste the copied image.

23. Drag the copied image to the cell intersection of *Shave and a Haircut* and *Jen*.

24. Place checkmarks in the *Jen* column for *Diversity Festival* and *Tutoring*.

25. Place checkmarks in the *TJ* column for *Shave and a Haircut, Diversity Festival, Build-a-House, Bully No More,* and *Adopt a Street*.

26. Place checkmarks in the *Loni* column for *iRecycling Day, Toy Collection, Diversity Festival, Bully No More,* and *Tutoring*.

27. Place checkmarks in the *Jo* column for *Toy Collection, Diversity Festival, Build-a-House, Bully No More, Adopt a Street,* and *Tutoring*.

The matrix showing which person participated in which event is complete.

Merge Cells

28. Click in the top-left cell and type **Congratulations!**.

29. Point to the top-left cell and then drag to the top-right cell to select all cells in the top row.

30. Choose **Table Tools→Layout→Merge→Merge Cells**.

31. Choose **Table Tools→Layout→Alignment→Center**.

Apply Table Styles

32. Choose **Table Tools→Design→Table Styles→More→Dark→Dark Style 1, Accent 2**.

33. Point to the table border until the mouse pointer displays a four-headed arrow and then click to select the entire table.

34. Choose **Table Tools→Design→Table Styles→Effects ▼→Cell Bevel→Bevel→Hard Edge**.

Apply Table Style Options

35. Remove the checkmark in the **Table Tools→Design→Table Style Options→Banded Rows** checkbox.

36. Save and close the presentation. Exit **PowerPoint**.

37. Submit your final file based on the guidelines provided.

Apply Your Skills

Add a Table

In this exercise, you will add a table to display a vehicle maintenance schedule.

Create and Enter Data into a PowerPoint Table

1. Start **PowerPoint**. Create a new blank presentation and save it as **PP07-A01-Maintenance-[FirstInitialLastName]** in the **PP2013 Lesson 07** folder.

2. Type **Universal Corporate Events** for the title and **Employee Meeting** for the subtitle.

3. Choose **Design→Themes→Integral**.

4. Choose **Design→Customize→Slide Size→Standard (4:3)** and then click **Ensure Fit**.

5. Choose **Home→Slides→New Slide**.

6. Type **Vehicle Maintenance** as the title.

7. Insert a table with **5** columns and **5** rows.

8. Type the following across the first row, leaving the first cell empty:

	Oil Change	Tire Rotation	Interior Detailing	Clean and Wax

9. Type the following down the first column, leaving the top cell empty:

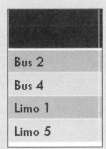

Bus 2
Bus 4
Limo 1
Limo 5

10. Type **Yes** in the cells as shown to complete the schedule:

	Oil Change	Tire Rotation	Interior Detailing	Clean and Wax
Bus 2	Yes	Yes		Yes
Bus 4	Yes			Yes
Limo 1	Yes	Yes	Yes	Yes
Limo 5		Yes	Yes	Yes

Resize a Table and Align It to a Slide

11. Drag the left border of the table to widen it until it touches the left edge of the slide.

12. Center the table on the slide, horizontally and vertically.

    The table is wide enough to comfortably display its content and it is centered on the slide.

Select and Format Cell Content; Adjust Column Widths and Row Heights

13. Right-align the text in the first column. Center-align all remaining cells.

14. Automatically resize all columns to fit their contents.

15. Center the table on the slide, horizontally and vertically.

16. Save and close the file. Exit **PowerPoint**.

17. Submit your final file based on the guidelines provided by your instructor.

    To view examples of how your file or files should look at the end of this exercise, go to the student resource center.

Format a Table

In this exercise, you will format a table.

Add Clip Art over a Cell and Merge Cells

1. Start **PowerPoint**. Open **PP07-A02-Lost** from your **PP2013 Lesson 07** folder and save it as **PP07-A02-Lost-[FirstInitialLastName]**.

2. Display **slide 2**.

3. Insert the **PP07-A02-Universal** picture from the **PP2013 Lesson 07** folder.

4. Resize and move the picture so it is roughly centered in the top-left cell.

5. Merge all cells along the bottom row.

6. Center the text in the bottom cell.

Apply Table Styles and Table Style Options

7. Apply the **Dark Style 1, Accent 3** table style.

8. Apply a shadow of your choice to the table.

9. Select the bottom cell and apply a bevel of your choice.

10. Turn on the **Last Column** option so the Total column stands out.

11. Save and close the file. Exit **PowerPoint**.

12. Submit your final file based on the guidelines provided by your instructor.

    To view examples of how your file or files should look at the end of this exercise, go to the student resource center.

APPLY YOUR SKILLS PP07-A03

Work with Tables

In this exercise, you will add and format a table showing an employee work schedule.

Create and Enter Data into a PowerPoint Table

1. Start **PowerPoint**. Open **PP07-A03-Work** from your **PP2013 Lesson 07** folder and save it as `PP07-A03-Work-[FirstInitialLastName]`.

2. Display **slide 2** and insert a table with **5** columns and **5** rows.

3. Click in the third cell in the first row and type the following:

4. Type the following to complete the second column:

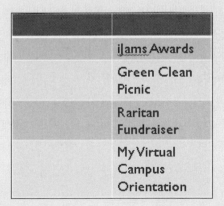

PowerPoint 2013

5. Type the following to complete the table content:

	Setup	Event Staff	Cleanup
rds	Chelsea & Brad	LaVell & Natasha	Colonna & Feim
an	Colonna & Feim	Chelsea & Brad	LaVell & Natasha
	LaVell & Natasha	Colonna & Feim	Chelsea & Brad
	Chelsea & Brad	LaVell & Natasha	Colonna & Feim
n			

Resize a Table and Align It to a Slide

6. Drag the bottom table border down until it touches the edge of the slide.

7. Choose **Table Tools→Layout→Arrange→Align→Align Center**.

Select Cells, Format Content, and Adjust Column Widths and Row Heights

8. Right-align all text in the second column. Center-align all remaining text.

9. Drag the border under the first row up so the first row is as short as possible while displaying its text.

10. Select all but the top row and distribute the rows so they have equal heights.

11. Drag the second column's left border to the right to reduce the width of the second column so that *iJams Awards* wraps to two lines. Be sure no other text is altered.

Add Clip Art over a Cell and Merge Cells

12. Insert the **PP07-A03-iJams** picture from the **PP2013 Lesson 07** folder.

13. Resize the picture and position it in the cell to the left of **iJams**.

14. Now insert **PP07-A03-GreenClean, PP07-A03-RaritanClinic**, and **PP07-A03-MyVirtualCampus** in their appropriate cells.

15. Merge the first two cells in the top row.

16. Type **Event** and center the text in the cell.

Apply Table Styles and Table Style Options

17. Apply the **Dark Style 1, Accent 2** table style.

18. Apply a shadow of your choice to the table.

19. Turn off the **Banded Rows** option.

20. Save and close the presentation. Exit **PowerPoint**.

21. Submit your final file based on the guidelines provided by your instructor.

Extend Your Skills

In the course of working through the Extend Your Skills exercises, you will think critically as you use the skills taught in the lesson to complete the assigned projects. To evaluate your mastery and completion of the exercises, your instructor may use a rubric, with which more points are allotted according to performance characteristics. (The more you do, the more you earn!) Ask your instructor how your work will be evaluated.

PP07-E01 That's the Way I See It

Create a presentation named **PP07-E01-Comparison-[FirstInitialLastName]** in **PP2013 Lesson 07**. Use **Comparison** as the title and your name as the subtitle. Add a second slide with the title **Food Comparison**. Insert a 5x5 table. Merge the cells in the top row and type **My Favorite Foods** as table title, centered. Complete the table as indicated.

Column	Content to Add
Food	List some foods you like
Photo	Find a picture to go with each food
Beverage	List a beverage to complement each food
Temperature	Indicate if the food is better served hot or cold
Preference	Rank the food, with 1 being your favorite

Resize the table and rows/columns and align the text for readability. Apply a Table Style and add shading, shadows, and/or bevels. Center the table horizontally on the slide; reposition pictures as necessary. Adjust the font size and apply Picture Styles as you like.

You will be evaluated based on the inclusion of all elements specified, your ability to follow directions, your ability to apply newly learned skills to a real-world situation, your creativity, and the relevance of your topic and/or data choice(s). Submit your final file based on the guidelines provided by your instructor.

PP07-E02 Be Your Own Boss

You are creating a slide show for Blue Jean Landscaping that highlights carnivorous plants. Create a new presentation and save it to **PP2013 Lesson 07** as **PP07-E02-Carnivorous-[FirstInitialLastName]**. Add the title **Blue Jean Landscaping** and the subtitle **Know Your Plants** to the title slide. Apply any design theme. Add a second slide with the Blank layout. Insert a 4x5 table and add the content to the left.

Carnivorous Plants			
Photo	Plant	Genus	Trapping Mechanism
	Pitcher Plant	Sarracenia	Pitfall
	Venus Flytrap	Dionaea	Rapid leaf movement
	Sundew	Drosera	Flypaper

Merge the cells across the top row. Resize the table to fill the slide then distribute the column widths equally. Center-align all cell content. Insert **PP07-E02-Pitcher**, **PP07-E02-Venus**, and **PP07-E02-Sundew** from **PP2013 Lesson 07**, resizing as necessary. Drag the horizontal row borders of the bottom three rows and drag each image to the left cell in its respective row. Distribute the row heights of the three bottom rows equally and adjust picture sizes as necessary. Apply a Table Style, and add a bevel and shadow. Adjust the font sizes and colors; add Picture Styles as appropriate.

You will be evaluated based on the inclusion of all elements specified, your ability to follow directions, your ability to apply newly learned skills to a real-world situation, your creativity, and your demonstration of an entrepreneurial spirit. Submit your final file based on the guidelines provided by your instructor.

Transfer Your Skills

In the course of working through the Transfer Your Skills exercises, you will use critical-thinking and creativity skills to complete the assigned projects using skills taught in the lesson. To evaluate your mastery and completion of the exercises, your instructor may use a rubric, with which more points are allotted according to performance characteristics. (The more you do, the more you earn!) Ask your instructor how your work will be evaluated.

PP07-T01 Use the Web as a Learning Tool

Throughout this book, you will be provided with an opportunity to use the Internet as a learning tool by completing WebQuests. According to the original creators of WebQuests, as described on their website (WebQuest.org), a WebQuest is "an inquiry-oriented activity in which most or all of the information used by learners is drawn from the web." To complete the WebQuest projects in this book, navigate to the student resource center and choose the WebQuest for the lesson on which you are currently working. The subject of each WebQuest will be relevant to the material found in the lesson.

WebQuest Subject: Shortcuts

Submit your files based on the guidelines provided by your instructor.

PP07-T02 Demonstrate Proficiency

As part of their cooking classes, Stormy BBQ wants to display a presentation on the kitchen television screens showing some basic cooking tips, including volume conversions.

Create a blank presentation and save it as `PP07-T02-Conversions-[FirstInitialLastName]` in your **PP2013 Lesson 07** folder. Add an appropriate title, subtitle, and design theme. Create a second slide using the Title and Content layout and add an appropriate slide title. Apply a theme of your choice. Insert a 5x5 table on the second slide. Populate the table with this conversion data.

	1 Teaspoon	1 Tablespoon	1 Ounce	1 Cup
Teaspoons	1	3	6	48
Tablespoons	1/3	1	2	16
Ounces	1/6	1/2	1	8
Cups	1/48	1/16	1/8	1

Resize each column so they are as narrow as possible without wrapping any text to a second line. Drag the top row's bottom border down to enlarge the height of the top row so that each top row cell is roughly a square. Center the top row text horizontally in the cells and vertically align them to the bottom. Align the remaining text in their cells so the data is easy to read.

Center the table on the slide. Insert the **PP07-T02-Stormy** picture from the **PP2013 Lesson 07** folder into the top-left cell. Resize the picture and column widths as needed. Apply a Table Style and add a bevel and shadow to the table. Make any final adjustments to the shading or Table Style Options you feel are necessary. Adjust the font sizes and colors and add Picture Styles as you see fit.

Submit your final file based on the guidelines provided by your instructor.

Customizing Themes and Slide Masters

LESSON OUTLINE

Customizing Document Themes

Using Slide Masters

Using Action Buttons

Concepts Review

Reinforce Your Skills

Apply Your Skills

Extend Your Skills

Transfer Your Skills

LEARNING OBJECTIVES

After studying this lesson, you will be able to:

- Customize a document theme
- Use the new Eyedropper tool
- Save and reuse a customized document theme
- Edit slide masters
- Insert and format action buttons

In this lesson, you will focus on customizing themes in PowerPoint 2013. You will learn how to customize color schemes and backgrounds, and then save a document theme as your own so you can reuse it as often as you like. In addition, you will edit slide masters to affect multiple slides at once. Finally, you will incorporate action buttons so you can add functionality to your slide show.

Saving Time with Themes

Green Clean is planning to expand. In their quest to secure more funding to help the new branches flourish, you need to create multiple presentations to deliver to various boards, committees, and conference attendees. You choose one of your favorite presentations to customize and save as a Green Clean Theme to help you establish a standard corporate image. Although you think it will be a chore, you find that customizing the document theme is easy. You change the color scheme of the original design to match the colors most used by Green Clean in their advertisements.

You plan to display the presentation at a kiosk during the upcoming EnviroProducts Trade Show. To make navigating through the slide show easy for the viewers, you add attractive action buttons on each slide. You discover that you can even add the action buttons to the slide master, saving tedious work.

These action buttons created on a slide master appear automatically on every slide of the presentation.

Customizing Document Themes

Video Library   http://labyrinthelab.com/videos   Video Number: PP13-V0801

PowerPoint 2013 comes with many built-in document themes that contain predesigned formats and color schemes you can apply to a presentation. Although this makes it easy to format a presentation with a consistent set of colors, fonts, and backgrounds, it may not always meet your needs. For example, you may like the slide background and fonts used in a certain document theme, but the colors may not match your company's official advertising colors used in the logo or other promotional materials. With PowerPoint's customization options, you can create custom color schemes or font schemes and apply them to any existing document theme. You can also use your custom colors, fonts, backgrounds, and effects to create an entirely new document theme.

Knowing What You Can Customize

There are several ways to customize any document theme, including:

- Color scheme
- Fonts
- Effects such as shadows and bevels
- Slide background

Customizations That Work Best

The best presentation document theme designs are simple, include a minimal number of fonts and background elements, make good use of white space, and have a pleasant color scheme.

Keeping the design simple ensures that the purpose of the slide is not lost.

Using Built-in Color Schemes

Although PowerPoint themes offer variants that change the color of the theme, the limited number of variants may not create the look or feel you want. You can further customize a theme by applying one of the many built-in color schemes.

Applying a built-in orange color scheme creates a custom theme unavailable with a default variant.

This theme offers a green, blue, pink, and dark green variant.

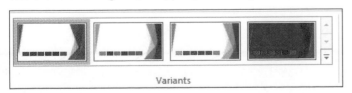

Variants

PowerPoint 2013

Apply a Built-in Color Scheme

In this exercise, you will apply a built-in color scheme.

1. Start **PowerPoint** and maximize the program window.

2. Open **PP08-D01-Custom** from the **PP2013 Lesson 08** folder and save it as **PP08-D01-Custom-[FirstInitialLastName]**.

   Replace the bracketed text with your first initial and last name. For example, if your name is Bethany Smith, your filename would look like this: PP08-D01-Custom-BSmith.

   The presentation has a variant of the Facet theme applied, which includes colors a little brighter than we want to use.

3. Follow these steps to apply a built-in color scheme:

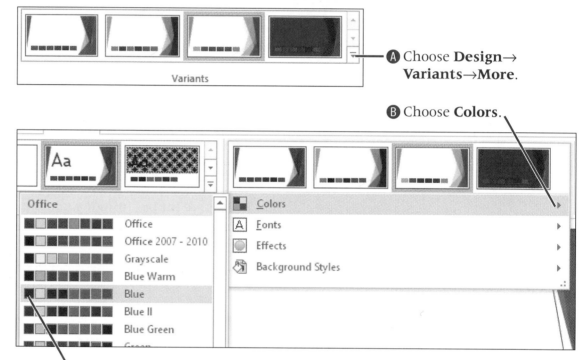

Ⓐ Choose **Design→ Variants→More**.

Ⓑ Choose **Colors**.

Ⓒ Point to several built-in color schemes to preview them and then choose **Blue**.

The color scheme on all slides has been changed from the bright pink of the Facet theme variant to dark blues.

4. Save your presentation.

Customizing the Color Scheme

Video Library   http://labyrinthelab.com/videos   Video Number: PP13-V0802

A color scheme is composed of twelve individual colors for text, backgrounds, hyperlinks, and various accents used for things such as bullets and slide titles. PowerPoint comes with many built-in color schemes. You can customize an existing color scheme by changing one color or all of the colors. You can base a new color scheme on any of the built-in color schemes; however, you cannot edit or delete the built-in color schemes themselves. When you create and save a new color scheme, PowerPoint automatically applies it to all the slides in the current presentation. After you create a custom color scheme, you can apply it to one slide or the entire presentation. The new color scheme is also available to other themes. You can also edit and delete custom color schemes.

New color schemes can be created by changing any of the 12 colors available in a document theme.

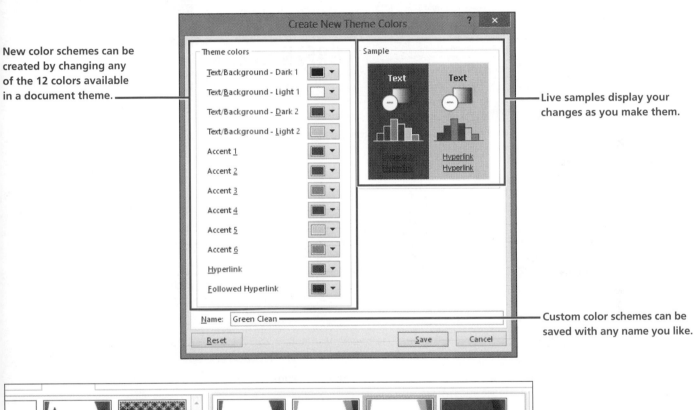

Live samples display your changes as you make them.

Custom color schemes can be saved with any name you like.

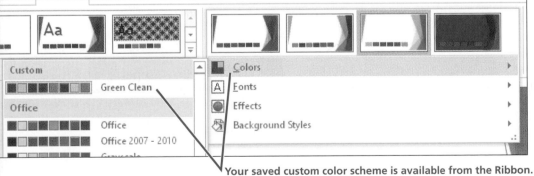

Your saved custom color scheme is available from the Ribbon.

PowerPoint 2013

Color Scheme Labels

PowerPoint has twelve fixed labels for all color scheme settings, as shown in the Theme Colors section in the preceding figure. Unfortunately, the colors are not labeled in such a way that makes sense. There is no *slide title* label or *bulleted text* label. You need to study the slide and then determine which colors in the dialog box affect the various objects on the slide. For example, some document themes use the Accent 4 color to color the slide title text, while another document theme may use the Accent 6 color.

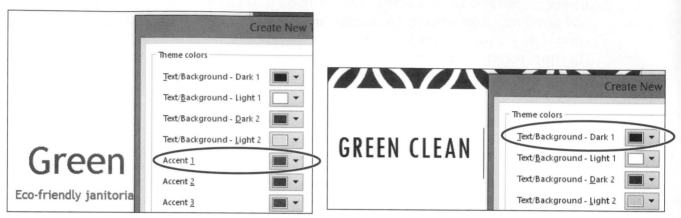

The Facet theme gets its slide title color from the Accent 1 setting, whereas the Integral theme gets its slide title color from the Text/Background – Dark 1 setting.

QUICK REFERENCE	WORKING WITH CUSTOM COLOR SCHEMES
Task	**Procedure**
Create a new custom color scheme	■ Choose Design→Variants→More→Colors→Customize Colors. ■ Choose a new color for any of the twelve theme colors. ■ Type a name for your custom color scheme and click Save. The new color scheme is immediately applied to all slides in the presentation.
Apply a custom color scheme	■ Choose Design→Variants→More→Colors. ■ Click the custom color scheme to apply it to all slides, or right-click the custom color scheme and choose Apply to Selected Slides.
Edit a custom color scheme	■ Choose Design→Variants→More→Colors. ■ Right-click the desired custom color scheme and choose Edit. ■ Change the colors as desired and click Save.
Delete a custom color scheme from the Ribbon	■ Choose Design→Variants→More→Colors. ■ Right-click the desired custom color scheme and choose Delete. If the custom color scheme was used on any slides, the slides will not be affected. The custom color scheme will simply no longer be available to apply to additional slides.

Create and Apply Custom Colors

In this exercise, you will create and apply a custom color scheme.

1. Save the presentation as **PP08-D02-Custom-[FirstInitialLastName]**.
    The Blue color scheme is close, but it is a bit dark for Green Clean. You will alter the color scheme in the next steps to use more green.

2. Choose **Design→Variants→More→Colors→Customize Colors**.
    The Create New Theme Colors dialog box opens.

3. Follow these steps to create a custom color scheme:

Ⓐ Click the **Accent 1** button.

Ⓑ Choose **Green, Accent 5, Lighter 40%** from the ninth column.

Ⓒ Click the **Text/Background – Dark 1** button.

Ⓓ Choose **Dark Blue, Background 2** from the top row.

Ⓔ Type **Green Clean Custom** and click **Save**.

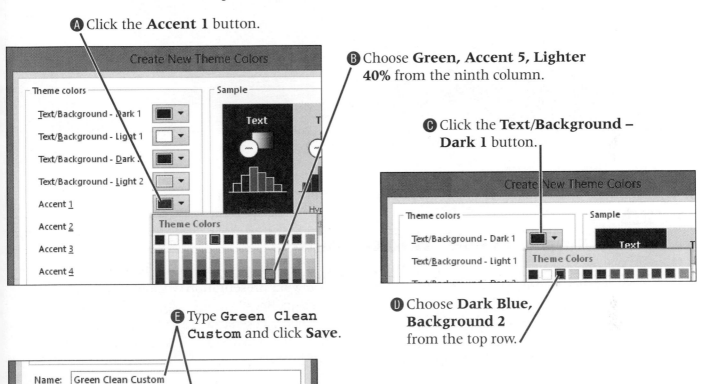

The custom color scheme is applied to all slides, and you see the new colors on the current slide.

4. Save your presentation.

Changing a Slide Background

Video Library http://labyrinthelab.com/videos Video Number: PP13-V0803

You can change the background for one slide or the entire presentation. You can choose from preset backgrounds tailored to your document theme, or you can create your own custom background that overrides the document theme. You might want to change the color, use an image, or add a textured look such as wood, marble, or fabric. You can also add color effects to vary the pattern and intensity of the color. For example, you can use a Gradient effect, which

PowerPoint 2013

fades from dark to light across a slide, or use a variety of Texture effects. You can experiment with custom backgrounds without fear of ruining your presentation because PowerPoint offers a Reset Slide Background command that resets the slide's background to the previous background.

The same slide with a gradient background (left) and a textured wood background (right).

 Avoid busy textures. They make your slide content hard to read.

Using a Preset Background

Each document theme comes with twelve preset, coordinated backgrounds. You can choose one of these preset backgrounds to modify the look of your presentation without worrying whether the background will clash with the rest of the design. Because the backgrounds are part of the document theme, they are designed to match. When you select a preset background, PowerPoint applies it to all slides in the presentation. Choosing a new document theme will change the background on all slides.

The twelve preset backgrounds match the current document theme.

The background applied to the selected slide is highlighted.

The Format Background command allows you to customize the background and override the document theme presets.

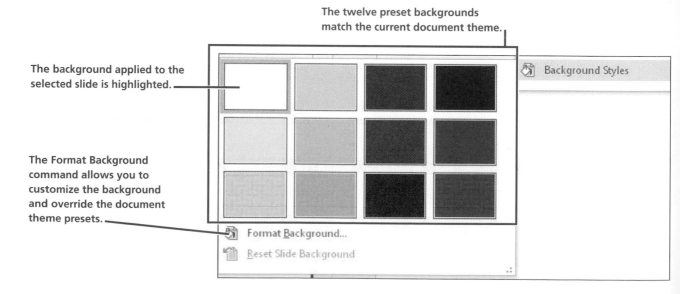

Apply a Preset Background

In this exercise, you will use the preset backgrounds included with the document theme.

1. Save the presentation as **PP08-D03-Custom-[FirstInitialLastName]**.

2. Display the second slide, **Our Services**.

3. Choose **Design→Variants→More→Background Styles**.

   PowerPoint displays the twelve background styles for the current theme.

4. Follow these steps to apply a preset background:

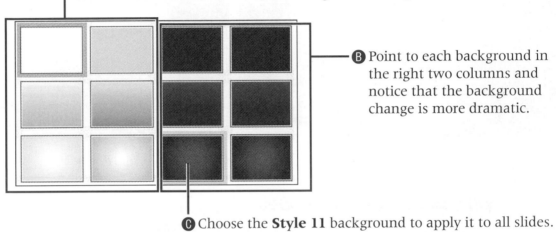

Ⓐ Point to (don't click on) each background in the left two columns and notice how the slide background changes.

Ⓑ Point to each background in the right two columns and notice that the background change is more dramatic.

Ⓒ Choose the **Style 11** background to apply it to all slides.

5. Choose **Design→Variants→More→Background Styles**.

   The Reset Slide Background command is not available because the current background is part of the document theme.

6. Click anywhere outside the drop-down menu to close it without applying any changes.

7. Choose **Design→Themes→More→Integral**.

   PowerPoint applies the Integral theme, and the slide backgrounds are reset to the Integral theme default.

8. Choose **Design→Themes→More→Facet** to reapply that document theme.

   The Facet theme is applied, but with its default color scheme. In effect, the reapplied Facet theme has replaced the manual customization you created earlier.

9. Choose **Design→Variants→More→Colors→Green Clean Custom**.

   PowerPoint applies your new custom color scheme.

10. Save your presentation.

PowerPoint 2013

Creating a Gradient Fill

Video Library   http://labyrinthelab.com/videos   Video Number: PP13-V0804

You can customize a background with a single solid color or with a gradient fill. A gradient fill consists of several colors that blend into one another. PowerPoint includes several preset gradients, but you can also create your own.

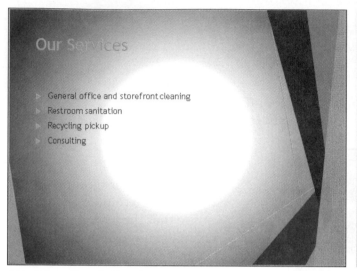 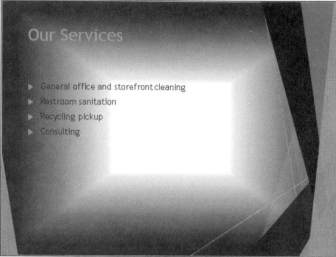

A Radial gradient (left) and a Rectangular gradient (right)

How Gradients Are Defined

Gradients in PowerPoint backgrounds may contain as few as two and as many as ten *stops*. A stop defines the color, position, brightness value, and transparency. Obviously, the color setting defines the color used. The position defines where the gradient occurs. The brightness defines how light or dark the color is. Increasing the brightness adds white to lighten the color, while decreasing the brightness adds black to darken the color. The transparency defines whether a color is fading out. A transparency of 0% means the color is not transparent at all and is at full color. A transparency of 100% means the color is invisible. A transparency of 50% means the color is very faded. Additional gradient settings include the shape (in what direction the colors blend, such as from the center out or diagonally) and the direction, which determines whether the colors blend from the top down, left to right, and so on.

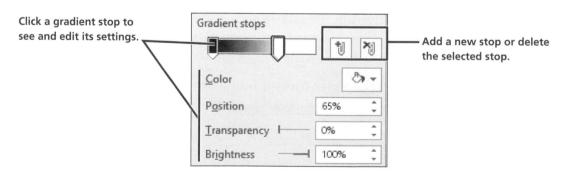

Click a gradient stop to see and edit its settings.

Add a new stop or delete the selected stop.

Setting Stop Positions

There are many ways to configure a custom gradient, and without a doubt, setting the stop position is the most confusing. One simple method is to always set the first stop to 0% and then set subsequent stop positions based on where the colors should stop blending. For example, consider a simple two-color gradient that blends from top to bottom. The first color is set to a position of 0%. The second color is set to a position of 50%. The gradient blend would occur entirely in the top half of the slide (from 0–50%). At 50%, the second color would be completely displayed with no more blend.

Stop 1 is set to black with a stop position of 0% so that the gradient blend begins immediately.

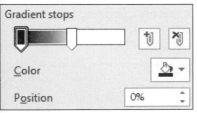

The gradient occurs from 0% to 50%. At 50%, the gradient stops and the slide is pure white.

Stop 2 is set to white with a stop position of 50% so that the blend stops and only the white remains.

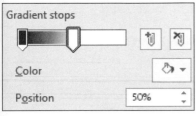

Stop 1 is set to black with a stop position of 25% so the top quarter of the slide is solid black. The gradient blend starts at 25%.

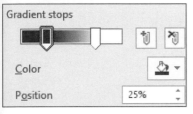

From 0%–25% the slide is pure black; from 25%–75% there is a gradient blend. At 75%, the gradient stops and the slide is pure white.

Stop 2 is set to white with a stop position of 75% so the gradient blend stops ¾ of the way down the slide.

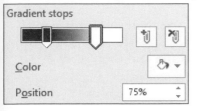

QUICK REFERENCE	APPLYING GRADIENT BACKGROUNDS
Task	**Procedure**
Apply a preset gradient as a custom background	■ Choose Design→Customize→Format Background. ■ Choose the Gradient Fill option. ■ Choose a gradient color scheme, a gradient type, and a direction. ■ Click Close (apply to selected slides) or click Apply to All.
Apply a custom gradient as a custom background	■ Choose Design→Customize→Format Background. ■ Choose the Gradient Fill option. ■ Click Add Gradient Stop or Remove Gradient Stop. ■ Click the left-most stop on the Gradient Stops bar and set a position, color, brightness, and transparency. ■ Choose the remaining stops and set options as desired. ■ Click Close (apply to selected slides) or click Apply to All.

DEVELOP YOUR SKILLS PP08-D04

Apply Gradient Backgrounds

In this exercise, you will apply a preset gradient and create a custom gradient background.

1. Save the presentation as **PP08-D04-Custom-[FirstInitialLastName]**.

2. If necessary, select the second slide, **Our Services**.

3. Choose **Design→Customize→Format Background**.

4. Follow these steps to apply a preset gradient:

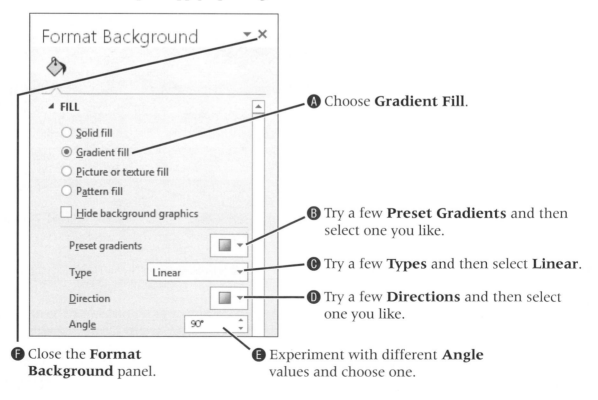

Ⓐ Choose **Gradient Fill**.

Ⓑ Try a few **Preset Gradients** and then select one you like.

Ⓒ Try a few **Types** and then select **Linear**.

Ⓓ Try a few **Directions** and then select one you like.

Ⓔ Experiment with different **Angle** values and choose one.

Ⓕ Close the **Format Background** panel.

Reset a Slide Background

5. Choose **Design→Variants→More→Background Styles→Reset Slide Background**.

   The slide background is reset to the previous background.

Create a Custom Gradient

Now you will create a simple custom gradient fill with just two stops.

6. Choose **Design→Customize→Format Background**.

7. Follow these steps to create exactly two stops:

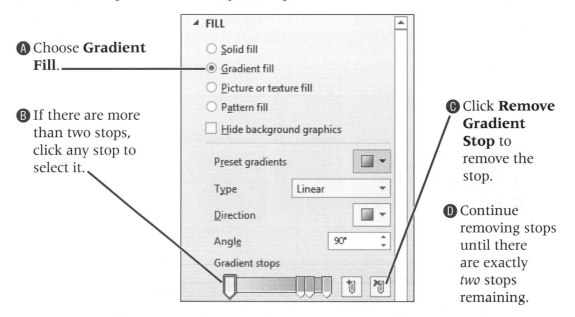

🅐 Choose **Gradient Fill**.

🅑 If there are more than two stops, click any stop to select it.

🅒 Click **Remove Gradient Stop** to remove the stop.

🅓 Continue removing stops until there are exactly *two* stops remaining.

8. Follow these steps to create a custom gradient:

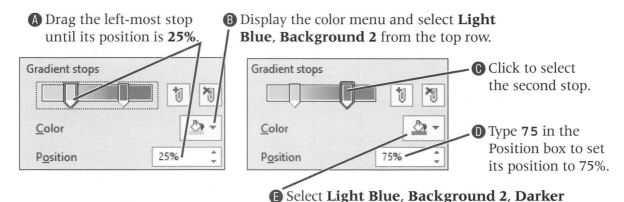

🅐 Drag the left-most stop until its position is **25%**.

🅑 Display the color menu and select **Light Blue**, **Background 2** from the top row.

🅒 Click to select the second stop.

🅓 Type **75** in the Position box to set its position to 75%.

🅔 Select **Light Blue**, **Background 2**, **Darker 25%** from the third column of the color menu.

PowerPoint displays the effects of the new stop settings. You could add still more stops, but instead let's see how the other gradient settings can work with just two stops.

9. Experiment with the Type, Direction, and Angle settings until you are satisfied with the custom gradient.

10. Click **Apply to All** to apply the gradient to all slides and then close the **Format Background** panel.

11. Save your presentation.

Using Pictures or Textures for Backgrounds

Video Library http://labyrinthelab.com/videos Video Number: PP13-V0805

PowerPoint offers 24 textures you can use as slide backgrounds, including wood, marble, and paper textures. You can also use clip art images or image files from your computer, such as a photo from a digital camera, as a slide background.

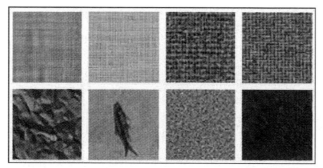

A few of the 24 textures provided with PowerPoint

Picture and Texture Background Settings

When you select a texture or insert a picture to use as a background, several settings allow you to control how the background looks. The main Tile Picture as Texture option determines which additional options are available.

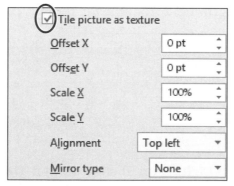
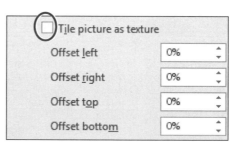

When Tile Picture as Texture is selected, a certain set of options appear (left). When deselected, the Offset options display (right).

Tile Picture as Texture

When the Tile Picture as Texture checkbox is selected, the image used for the background (texture, picture file, or clip art) repeats across the entire slide.

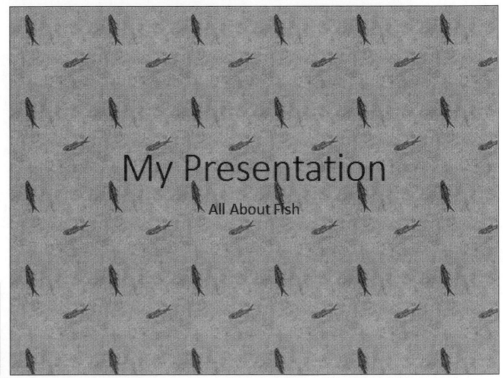

The image file (left) repeats across the slide (right).

When the Tile Picture as Texture option is selected, the available options include Offset, Scale, Alignment, and Mirror Type. Changing the Offset X option shifts the tiled background to the right (if a positive value is entered) or left (if a negative value is entered). The Offset Y option shifts the background up or down. The Scale X and Scale Y options resize the image being used as a tile (you cannot resize greater than 100%). The Alignment option can be used to further reposition the background on the slide, and is best used by experimentation. Last, the Mirror Type option flips the image horizontally or vertically as it's being tiled. This option also is best used by experimentation.

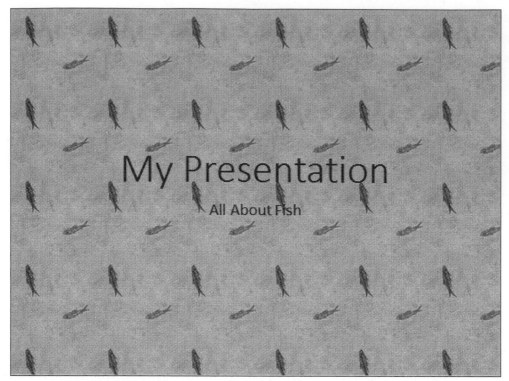

The original background

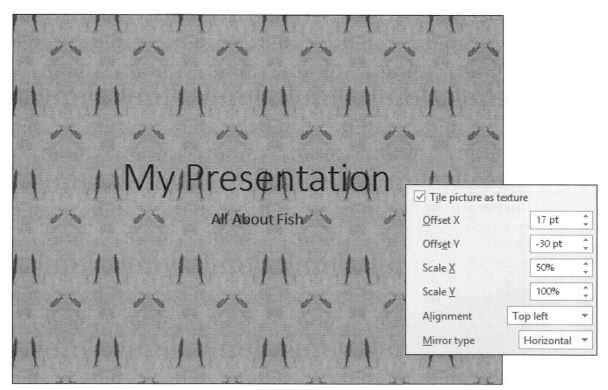

The altered background after the indicated settings have been made

Do Not Tile Picture as Texture

When the Tile Picture as Texture option is not selected, the image used for the background (texture, picture file, or clip art) resizes to fill the slide without repeating. If the picture is small, this can result in a blurry image, as in the following illustration.

The image file (above) enlarged to fill the slide (right)

When the Tile Picture as Texture option is not selected, the available options include a series of stretch offsets for left, top, right, and bottom. As these values are increased or decreased, the image stretches. For example, altering the Left offset works from the left side of the image. An offset of 0% results in the image being placed directly up against the left border. Positive values push the image into the slide, while negative values pull the image away from the slide. Similarly, increasing the Bottom offset squishes the image toward the top, while decreasing the Bottom offset stretches the image down toward the bottom.

Imagine you are standing in the computer screen next to the slide. A positive value in any of these offsets would instruct you to push the image away from you, toward the inside of the slide. A negative value would instruct you to pull the image toward you, out of the slide.

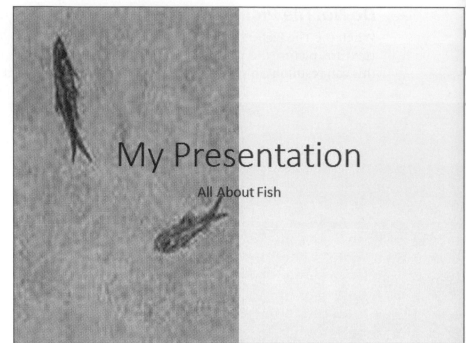

A Right offset of 50% pushes the picture from the right, halfway across the slide.

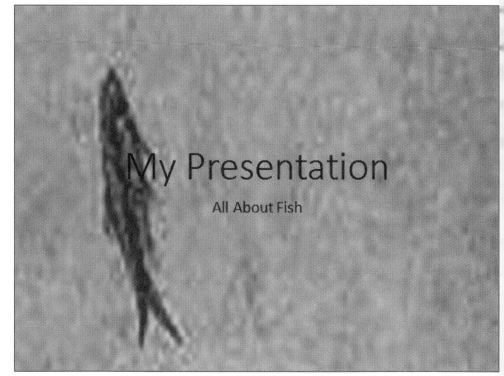

A Bottom offset of –100% pulls the picture down from the bottom.

Task	Procedure
Use a texture as a slide background	■ Choose Design→Customize→Format Background. ■ Choose the Picture or Texture Fill option. ■ Choose a texture from the Texture menu. ■ Click Close (apply to selected slides) or click Apply to All.
Use clip art as a slide background	■ Choose Design→Customize→Format Background. ■ Choose the Picture or Texture Fill option. ■ Click the Online button. Select a clip art image and click Insert. ■ Increase or decrease the Offset values to stretch the picture to fit the slide. ■ Click Close (apply to selected slides) or click Apply to All.
Use an image file as a slide background	■ Choose Design→Customize→Format Background. ■ Choose the Picture or Texture Fill option. ■ Click the File button. Browse to the desired image file and click Insert. ■ Increase or decrease the Offset values to stretch the picture to fit the slide. Negative values stretch or compress the picture off of the slide. Positive values stretch or compress the picture in toward the slide. ■ Click Close (apply to selected slides) or click Apply to All.

DEVELOP YOUR SKILLS PP08-D05

Apply Texture and Picture Backgrounds

In this exercise, you will apply a texture background and a clip art background.

1. Save the presentation as **PP08-D05-Custom-[FirstInitialLastName]**.

2. If necessary, select the second slide, **Our Services**.

3. Choose **Design→Customize→Format Background**:

A Choose **Picture or Texture Fill**.

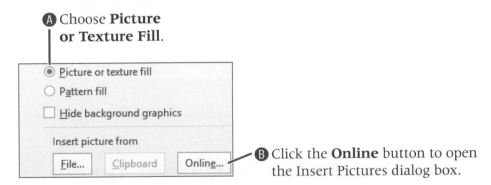

B Click the **Online** button to open the Insert Pictures dialog box.

4. Type **mop** in the **Office.com** search box and tap Enter.

5. Select an appropriate image and click **Insert**.

The clip art image is added as a slide background, but the Format Background panel remains open so you can change the settings.

6. Follow these steps to modify the background image by 50% of the original size:

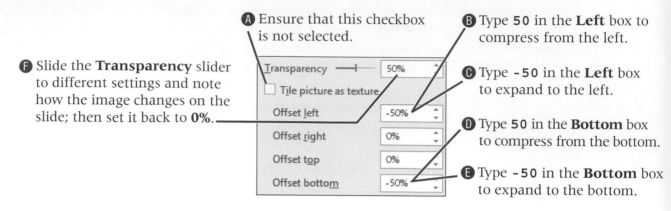

ⒶEnsure that this checkbox is not selected.

ⒷType **50** in the **Left** box to compress from the left.

ⒻSlide the **Transparency** slider to different settings and note how the image changes on the slide; then set it back to **0%**.

ⒸType **-50** in the **Left** box to expand to the left.

ⒹType **50** in the **Bottom** box to compress from the bottom.

ⒺType **-50** in the **Bottom** box to expand to the bottom.

A background image is too busy for this presentation. You will replace the clip art background with a textured background.

7. Follow these steps to apply a textured background:

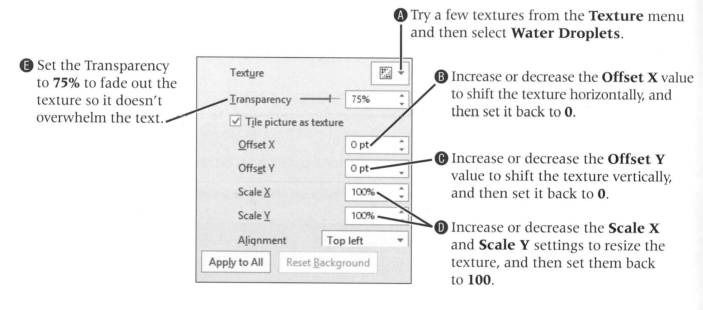

ⒶTry a few textures from the **Texture** menu and then select **Water Droplets**.

ⒺSet the Transparency to **75%** to fade out the texture so it doesn't overwhelm the text.

ⒷIncrease or decrease the **Offset X** value to shift the texture horizontally, and then set it back to **0**.

ⒸIncrease or decrease the **Offset Y** value to shift the texture vertically, and then set it back to **0**.

ⒹIncrease or decrease the **Scale X** and **Scale Y** settings to resize the texture, and then set them back to **100**.

8. Click **Apply to All**.

9. Close the **Format Background** panel.

10. Save your presentation.

Saving a Customized Document Theme

Video Library   http://labyrinthelab.com/videos   Video Number: PP13-V0806

After you have modified the color scheme, fonts, and/or background styles of a presentation, you may want to save your modified theme as a custom theme. The custom theme will be available to apply to new presentations just as with any built-in document theme. Your custom theme will even be available to other Microsoft Office applications. Your PowerPoint presentations can match your word processing documents created in Microsoft Word when your custom theme is applied to both.

Theme Location

Custom themes are saved to your computer in a folder associated with your Windows username. They are saved by default in the C:\Users\<username>\AppData\Roaming\Microsoft\ Templates\Document Themes folder.

Any custom themes saved in this location will be available directly from the Design→Themes command group on the Ribbon. You can also browse for and apply a custom theme stored somewhere else on your computer; however, such a theme won't be directly accessible from the Ribbon.

Many computer labs prevent saving a custom theme to the default location, but you can save your custom theme to your USB flash drive or other location. If you do this, remember that applying the theme would require a few more steps.

Deleting a Custom Theme

If your custom theme was saved to the default location, you can remove it from the Ribbon by deleting the theme file from the Document Themes folder. You can do this manually by navigating to the folder and deleting the file, or automatically from the Ribbon. Deleting the custom theme file will not affect any presentations that currently use the theme; you just won't be able to apply the custom theme to future presentations. Similarly, if you move a presentation with a custom theme to another computer that does not have the custom theme in the default location, your presentation will still use the custom theme.

QUICK REFERENCE	SAVING AND APPLYING A CUSTOM THEME
Task	**Procedure**
Save a custom theme to the default folder	■ Choose Design→Themes→More→Save Current Theme. ■ Name your theme and click Save. Your custom theme is saved to the default location and is available directly from the Design tab.
Save a custom theme to a different location	■ Choose Design→Themes→More→Save Current Theme. ■ Browse to an alternate location, such as your USB flash drive. ■ Name your theme and click Save. Your custom theme is saved to the alternate location and is not directly available from the Ribbon.
Apply a custom theme	■ If the custom theme was saved to the default location, choose Design→Themes and select your custom theme. ■ If the custom theme was saved to an alternate location, choose Design→Themes→More→Browse for Themes and navigate to the location. ■ Select the custom theme and click Apply.
Delete a custom theme from the default location	■ Choose Design→Themes→More. ■ Right-click your custom theme and choose Delete.

PowerPoint 2013

Save and Use a Custom Design Theme

In this exercise, you will save your custom document theme and apply it from the Ribbon.

Before You Begin: Check with your instructor to see whether you are able to save a custom theme to the default location or whether there is another specific location in which to save your custom theme.

1. Save your presentation as **PP08-D06-Custom-[FirstInitialLastName]**.
2. Choose **Design→Themes→More→Save Current Theme**.
3. In the File Name box, type **Green Clean Water**.
4. If you have permission to save in the default location, click **Save** and skip to step 6. Otherwise, continue with step 5.
5. Use the **Save Current Theme** dialog box to browse to the location suggested by your instructor and then click **Save**.

Apply a Custom Theme

6. Choose **File→New** and click the **Blank Presentation** icon to create a new presentation.
7. Type **Green Clean** for the slide title.
8. Type **Custom Theme** as the subtitle.
9. Choose **Design→Themes→More**.
10. If your custom theme was saved to the default location, continue with step 11. If your custom theme was saved to an alternate location, skip to step 16.

Default Location

11. Select your custom **Green Clean Water** theme from the **Custom** row.
12. Save your presentation as **PP08-D06-New-[FirstInitialLastName]**.
13. Choose **File→Close** to close the presentation and return to the previous presentation.
14. Apply the custom **Green Clean Water** theme to the current presentation.
15. Save the presentation.
    Skip the rest of this exercise and continue with the next topic.

Alternate Location

16. Click the **Browse for Themes** option at the bottom of the **Themes** menu.
17. Navigate to the location where you saved your custom theme.
18. Select your custom theme file and click **Apply**.
19. Save your presentation as **PP08-D06-New-[FirstInitialLastName]**.
20. Choose **File→Close** to close the presentation and return to the previous presentation.
21. Apply the custom **Green Clean Water** theme to the current presentation.
22. Save the presentation.

Using Slide Masters

Video Library http://labyrinthelab.com/videos Video Number: PP13-V0807

PowerPoint slide layouts and designs are based on master slides. The masters store all of the design elements, including the font styles and sizes, placeholder sizes, background design, and color schemes. Any changes made to a slide master are inherited by all the slides based on the master. This is a great way to easily insert a company logo or other design element on every slide in a presentation. For example, adding a logo to the slide master causes every slide based on that master to also display the logo.

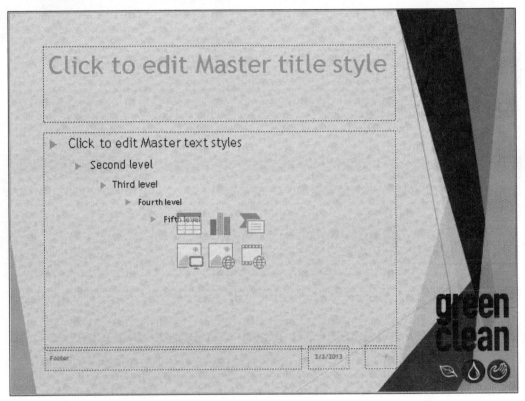

Slide master with a logo inserted in the bottom-right corner.

All slides based on the slide master display the logo that was inserted.

Using Slide Masters and Layout Masters

PowerPoint's document themes each have two types of master slides. There is one slide master and multiple layout masters. Both types of masters play specific roles.

- **Slide master:** This master is the basis from which all layout masters take their initial characteristics. Anything on the slide master is inherited by each of the eleven layout masters. However, layout masters can be further customized to be unique from each other (and from the slide master itself).

- **Layout masters:** These masters define what the various slide layouts look like, such as the Title Slide, Title and Content, or Two Content layouts.

Changes to master slides affect the current presentation only and do not permanently alter the document theme.

Slide Master View

You can view the slide masters in Master view, which is similar to Normal view with a scrollable slides panel on the left side of the screen. Pointing at any of the slide thumbnails displays a pop-up ToolTip with the number of slides in the current presentation using that particular master.

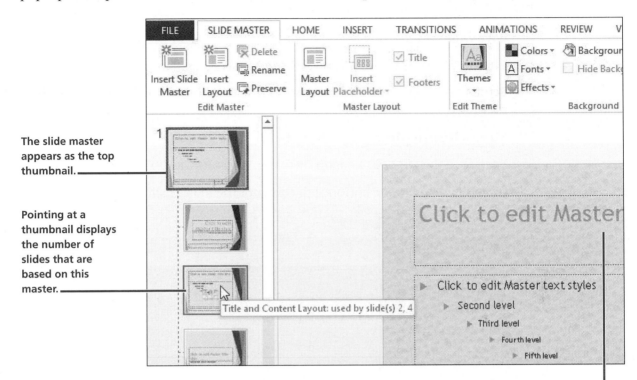

The slide master appears as the top thumbnail.

Pointing at a thumbnail displays the number of slides that are based on this master.

Title and Content Layout: used by slide(s) 2, 4

Changes made to a layout master affect all slides based on that layout.

QUICK REFERENCE	EDITING MASTER SLIDES
Task	**Procedure**
Edit a master slide	▪ Choose View→Master Views→Slide Master.
	▪ Select a master slide from the left side of the screen.
	▪ Make any changes you like to the slide master.
	▪ Choose Slide Master→Close→Close Master View.
Format a slide master background	▪ Choose View→Master Views→Slide Master.
	▪ Select a master slide from the left side of the screen.
	▪ Choose Slide Master→Background→Background Styles→Format Background.

Edit Slide Masters

In this exercise, you will edit slide masters to see the effect on presentation slides. You will display a logo on multiple slides by adding it to a slide master.

1. Save your presentation as `PP08-D07-Custom-[FirstInitialLastName]`.

2. Choose **View→Master Views→Slide Master**.

3. Scroll to the top of the **Slides panel** and select the **Green Clean Water Slide Master** slide.

4. Choose **Insert→Images→Pictures**.

5. Browse to the **PP2013 Lesson 08** folder, select **PP08-D07-Logo**, and click **Insert**.

6. Drag the image to the bottom-left corner of the master slide.

   The logo covers the slide footer. That is okay because the presentation does not use footers.

7. Click a few other slide masters on the left of your screen and notice that they all display the Green Clean logo image.

   Changes made to the first slide master affect all other slide masters and all slides in the presentation.

8. Choose **Slide Master→Close→Close Master View** to exit Master view.

9. Select each slide in Normal view and note that the logo appears on every slide.

10. Select the second slide, **Our Services**, and try to move the logo.

    You can't. The image exists on a master slide, so it can be moved or deleted only from the master slide.

11. Save your presentation.

Introducing the Eyedropper Tool

Video Library　http://labyrinthelab.com/videos　Video Number: PP13-V0808

Sometimes you need to select a color for text that matches a color from an image. Rather than guessing or "just getting close," you can use the *Eyedropper* tool to sample a color from an image—or from anywhere on a slide—and apply that sampled color to text. Unfortunately, the Eyedropper tool is not available from every color menu. For example, you can use the Eyedropper to choose a font color but not a color when editing a custom color scheme.

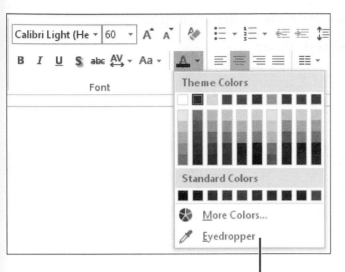

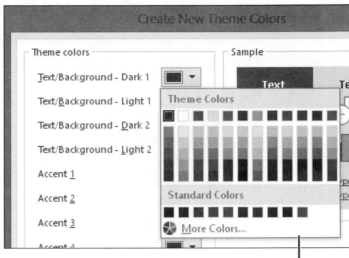

The Eyedropper is available on most color menus. | The Eyedropper is not available when editing theme color schemes. |

DEVELOP YOUR SKILLS PP08-D08
Use the Eyedropper Tool

In this exercise, you will use the Eyedropper tool to match the slide titles to a color from the logo.

1. Save your presentation as **PP08-D08-Custom-[FirstInitialLastName]**.

2. Choose **View→Master Views→Slide Master**.

3. Scroll to the top of the **Slides panel** and select the first slide, **Green Clean Water Slide Master**.

4. Click the border of the slide title to select the title placeholder.

5. Follow these steps to match the slide title font color to the Green Clean logo:

Ⓐ Choose **Home→ Font→Font Color→ Eyedropper**.

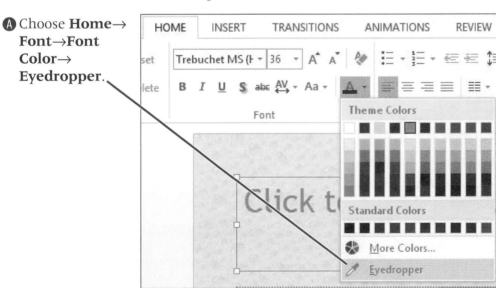

Ⓑ Click any part of the **Green Clean text** in the logo.

6. Click the border of the bulleted item placeholder to select the title placeholder.

7. Choose **Home→Font→Font Color→Eyedropper**.

8. Click any part of the green circle around the leaf on the logo.

9. Choose **Slide Master→Close→Close Master View**.

10. Display several slides in **Normal view** and notice that all the slides, except the title slide, use the new colors for the slide titles and bulleted text.

    The title slide layout is based on a different slide master. You will color the title slide layout in the next steps.

11. Display the title slide.

12. Choose **View→Master Views→Slide Master**.

    The correct slide master is preselected because you displayed the title slide in Normal view.

13. Click the border of the slide title to select the title placeholder.

14. Choose **Home→Font→Font Color→Eyedropper**.

15. Click any part of the **Green Clean text** on the logo.

16. Click the border of the slide subtitle to select the subtitle placeholder.

17. Choose **Home→Font→Font Color→Eyedropper**.

18. Click any part of the green circle around the leaf on the logo.

19. Choose **Slide Master→Close→Close Master View**.

20. Display **several slides** in **Normal view** and notice all slides, including the title slide, now use the new colors.

21. Save your presentation.

Using Action Buttons

Video Library   http://labyrinthelab.com/videos   Video Number: PP13-V0809

Action buttons allow you to add buttons to your presentations that can provide for slide navigation, opening of files, or other tasks. Action buttons contain widely recognized symbols for navigation and information commands, such as Next, Previous, Information, Document, and Sound. Action buttons are especially useful for creating a presentation that will be controlled by others, such as a presentation running on a sales table at a conference.

Action buttons for navigating a slide show at the bottom of a slide

Identifying Action Buttons

All action buttons, except custom buttons, have built-in functions that run whenever that button is clicked in Slide Show view. ToolTips make it easy to identify the function of an action button when you choose it from the menu.

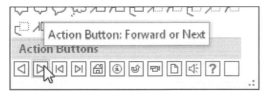

A ToolTip displays when you point to an action button on the Ribbon.

TIP

To quickly add action buttons to all slides in your presentation, place them on a master slide.

QUICK REFERENCE	USING ACTION BUTTONS
Task	**Procedure**
Insert an action button	■ Choose Insert→Illustrations→Shapes ▼.
	■ Point to an action button along the bottom row of the menu to see a ToolTip that identifies the action button.
	■ Click the action button to load your mouse pointer.
	■ Drag on the slide to draw the action button. The action button appears on your slide already formatted for the document theme.
	■ In the Action Settings dialog box, click OK to accept the default action associated with the button. Or, select a different action and click OK.
Change the action of an action button	■ Select the action button.
	■ Choose Insert→Links→Action.
	■ Choose a new action and click OK.

Formatting Action Buttons

Action buttons do not have a preset size. After you select an action button from the Ribbon, your mouse pointer changes to a crosshair icon resembling a plus sign (+) that you can use to draw a boundary for the action button. You can drag a small area to create a small button, or a large area to create a large button. Sometimes you will have several action buttons on a slide, and they will not all be drawn at the same size. PowerPoint has a variety of commands available from the Ribbon to size all the action buttons the same and to align them to each other.

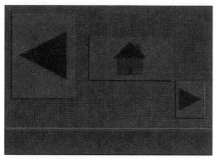 

Action buttons may initially be drawn at different sizes anywhere on the slide (left). Use Ribbon commands to make all the buttons the same size, aligned, and evenly distributed (right).

QUICK REFERENCE	FORMATTING ACTION BUTTONS
Task	**Procedure**
Make all action buttons the same size	■ Select one action button on the slide. ■ Hold down Shift, click the remaining action buttons, and release Shift. ■ Choose the Drawing Tools→Format tab. ■ In the Size command group, type values in the Shape Height and Shape Width boxes to make the buttons the same size.
Align action buttons to each other	■ Select one action button on the slide. ■ Hold down Shift, click the remaining action buttons, and release Shift. ■ Choose the Drawing Tools→Format→Arrange→Align ▼. ■ Select one of the top six align options.
Evenly space action buttons	■ Select one action button on the slide. ■ Hold down Shift, click at least two other action buttons, and then release Shift. ■ Choose the Drawing Tools→Format→Arrange→Align ▼. ■ Select Distribute Horizontally or Distribute Vertically.

DEVELOP YOUR SKILLS PP08-D09
Create Action Buttons

In this exercise, you will insert action buttons on a master slide to control movement forward and backward in your presentation.

1. Save your presentation as **PP08-D09-Custom-[FirstInitialLastName]**.

2. Choose **View→Master Views→Slide Master**.

   Remember, anything you place on a slide master appears on all of the slides based on that master.

3. Scroll to the top of the Slides panel and point at the first slide master, **Green Clean Water Slide Master**.

The ToolTip indicates that this master is being used by slides 1 through 4.

4. Click the first slide master, **Green Clean Water Slide Master**.

5. Choose the **Insert→Illustrations→Shapes** ▼.

PowerPoint displays a menu of available shapes. The action buttons are at the very bottom of the menu.

6. Follow these steps to place the Back action button on all the slides:

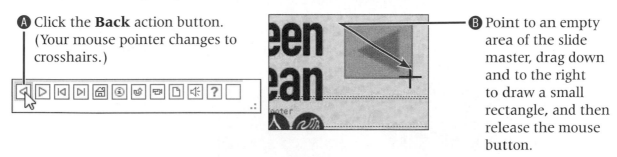

Ⓐ Click the **Back** action button. (Your mouse pointer changes to crosshairs.)

Ⓑ Point to an empty area of the slide master, drag down and to the right to draw a small rectangle, and then release the mouse button.

PowerPoint displays a dialog box with the preset action for this button. In this case, there's no need to modify the action.

7. Click **OK** to accept the default button action.

8. Now add a **Next** action button and a **Home** action button.

Don't worry if the action buttons aren't the same size or aligned—you will fix that in the next few steps. Your button size and location may differ from the following figure.

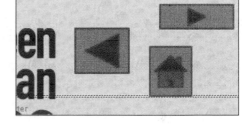

9. Select one of the action buttons, hold down Shift, click once on each of the remaining action buttons, and release Shift.

All three action buttons are selected (display handles).

10. Follow these steps to size the action buttons:

Ⓐ Choose **Drawing Tools→Format**.

Ⓑ Type **0.5** in the Shape Height box and then tap Enter.

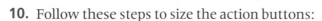

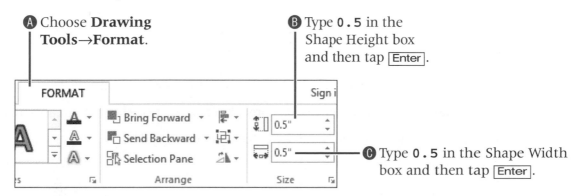

Ⓒ Type **0.5** in the Shape Width box and then tap Enter.

Ⓓ Click anywhere on the slide master to deselect the action buttons.

11. Drag the **Back** button to the right of the logo.

12. Drag the **Home** and **Next** buttons next to the Back button. (Don't worry about aligning the buttons perfectly. You will use a Ribbon command to align them.)

13. Using the Shift key, select all three buttons.

14. Choose **Drawing Tools→Format→Arrange→Align→Align Top**.
The buttons shift to become top-aligned.

15. Make sure all three buttons are still selected and, if necessary, drag them back down toward the bottom corner of the slide master.
Now that the buttons are in the desired general location, you will use a Ribbon command to distribute them evenly.

16. If necessary, use Shift to select all three buttons.

17. Choose **Drawing Tools→Format→Arrange→Align→Distribute Horizontally**.
PowerPoint spaces the buttons evenly.

18. Choose **Slide Master→Close→Close Master View**.

Test the Buttons

19. Choose **Slide Show→Start Slide Show→From Beginning**.

20. Click the **Next** action button (or anywhere on the title slide) to advance to the next slide.

21. Use the action buttons to navigate forward, back, and home.

22. Tap Esc to end the slide show.

23. Save the presentation.

Cleaning Up

Video Library   http://labyrinthelab.com/videos   Video Number: PP13-V0810

If you have created and saved a custom document theme to the default location, it is available directly from the Ribbon. If you have created and saved a custom color scheme, it is automatically available directly from the Ribbon. If you are using a shared computer such as one in a classroom or school computer lab, you should delete these customizations so other people can use PowerPoint in its default state.

DEVELOP YOUR SKILLS PP08-D10
Delete Customizations

In this exercise, you will delete custom color schemes and custom document themes that are directly available from the Ribbon.

1. Choose the **Design→Variants→More→Colors** menu and locate any custom color schemes listed at the top of the menu.

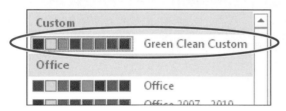

2. Right-click the custom color scheme and then choose **Delete** from the pop-up menu.

3. Choose **Yes** when prompted to delete the theme colors.
   The custom color scheme is deleted and is no longer available from the Ribbon.

4. Repeat steps 1–3 for any additional custom color schemes.

Remove Custom Document Themes

5. Choose **Design→Themes→More** to display the Themes menu.

6. Locate any custom themes listed at the top of the menu.

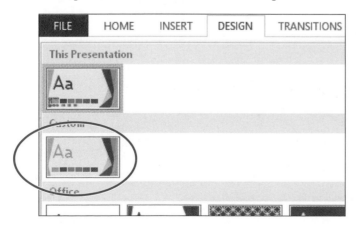

7. Right-click the custom document theme and choose **Delete**.

8. Choose **Yes** when prompted to delete the theme.

9. Repeat steps 5–8 for any additional custom themes.

10. Exit **PowerPoint**.

Concepts Review

To check your knowledge of the key concepts introduced in this lesson, complete the Concepts Review quiz by choosing the appropriate access option below.

If you are...	Then access the quiz by...
Using the Labyrinth Video Library	Going to http://labyrinthelab.com/videos
Using eLab	Logging in, choosing Content, and navigating to the Concepts Review quiz for this lesson
Not using the Labyrinth Video Library or eLab	Going to the student resource center for this book

Reinforce Your Skills

Create a Custom Design Theme

In this exercise, you will customize the background and colors of a design theme. You will then save the theme and apply it to another presentation.

Apply a Built-in Color Scheme

1. Start **PowerPoint**. Open **PP08-R01-Custom** from the **PP2013 Lesson 08** folder and save it as PP08-R01-Custom-[FirstInitialLastName].

2. Display the **Design** tab and note the color of the four variants.
   The organization leadership has asked for a yellow color scheme, but there is no yellow theme variant.

3. Choose **Design→Variants→More→Colors→Yellow**.
   Even though the Yellow color scheme is applied, the slide background is not yellow.

Create and Apply Custom Colors

4. Choose **Design→Variants→More→Colors→Customize Colors**.

5. Type Kids Custom in the **Name** box.

6. Click the **Text/Background – Light 1** color menu.

7. Choose **Yellow** from the bottom row of colors.

8. Click the **Accent 2** color menu.

9. Choose **Gold, Text 1, Lighter 40% 1** from the fifth column of colors.

10. Click **Save**.

11. Display **slide 2** and then display **slide 1** to see how they were changed.
    You will experiment with other slide backgrounds.

Apply a Preset Background

12. Choose **Design→Variants→More→Background Styles** and point to each of the twelve thumbnails to preview the effect on the slide.

13. Select the style at the bottom of the first column, **Style 9**.
    You will further customize the background gradient.

Apply Gradient Backgrounds

14. Choose **Design→Customize→Format Background**.

15. Click the **Type** menu and select **Radial**.

16. Click the **Direction** menu and select the third option, **From Center**.

17. Click the last gradient stop.

18. Click the **Color** menu and select **Yellow, Background 1, Darker 50%** from the bottom of the first column of colors.

19. Click **Apply to All**.

    Maybe a textured background would be more interesting.

Apply Texture and Picture Backgrounds

20. Select the **Picture or Texture Fill** option.

21. Click the **Texture** menu and select **Parchment** from the right side of the third row.

22. Slide the **Transparency** slider to **25%** to fade out the texture.

    The texture background is good for the title slide, but you prefer the gradient background for the rest of the presentation. Therefore, you will not apply the texture to all slides.

23. Close the **Format Background** panel.

Save and Use a Custom Design Theme

24. Choose **Design→Themes→More→Save Current Theme**.

25. Browse to your **PP2013 Lesson 08** folder, type `PP08-R01-CustomTheme-[FirstInitialLastName]` in the File Name box, and click **Save**.

26. Save and close the presentation.

27. Choose **File→New** and click **Blank Presentation**.

28. Type `Kids for Change` as the **title** and `Awards Ceremony` as the **subtitle**.

29. Choose **Home→Slides→New Slide** and title the slide `Agenda`.

30. Choose **Home→Slides→New Slide** and title the slide `Summary`.

31. Choose **Design→Themes→More**.

    Your custom theme is not available from the Ribbon because you saved it to your storage location rather than to PowerPoint's default theme location.

32. Choose **Browse for Themes**.

33. Navigate to your **PP2013 Lesson 08** folder, select **PP08-R01-CustomTheme-[FirstInitialLastName]**, and click **Open**.

    The theme is applied to the new presentation, but the custom background on the title slide was not applied. This is an unexpected behavior of PowerPoint that might be classified as a bug.

34. Save the presentation as `PP08-R01-Presentation2-[FirstInitialLastName]`.

Delete Customizations

35. Choose **Design→Variants→More→Colors**.

36. Right-click the **Kids Custom** color scheme and choose **Delete** from the pop-up menu.

37. Click **Yes** when prompted to delete the custom color scheme.

38. Delete any additional custom color schemes.

39. Save and close the file. Exit **PowerPoint**.

40. Submit your final files based on the guidelines provided by your instructor.

To view examples of how your final file or files should look at the end of this exercise, go to the student resource center.

Use Slide Masters

In this exercise, you will match slide colors to those in an image. You will also add action buttons to aid in slide show navigation.

Edit Slide Masters

1. Start **PowerPoint**. Open **PP08-R02-Kids** from your **PP2013 Lesson 08** folder and save it as PP08-R02-Kids-[FirstInitialLastName].

2. Choose **View→Master Views→Slide Master**.

3. Scroll to the top of the **Slides** panel and select the first slide, **Retrospect Slide Master**.

4. Choose **Insert→Images→Pictures**.

5. Navigate to the **PP2013 Lesson 08** folder, select **PP08-R02-KidsLogo**, and click **Insert**.

6. Locate the **Picture Tools→Format→Size** group.

7. Click in the **Height** box, type **1**, and tap Enter.

8. Drag the logo to the bottom-right corner of the slide, above the orange and brown colored bars.

You can see the logo in the corner of many of the thumbnails in the Slides panel, indicating the logo will appear on most, but not all, slide layouts.

9. Choose **Home→Clipboard→Copy**.

10. Display the second slide, **Title Slide Layout**, and choose **Home→Clipboard→Paste**.

The logo is pasted to the Title Slide Layout master slide in the same location.

Use the Eyedropper Tool

11. Display the first slide, **Retrospect Slide Master**.

12. Click the border of the slide title.

13. Choose **Home→Font→Font Color→Eyedropper**.

14. Click the green kids in the logo to match the title text color to the logo.

15. Click the border of the bulleted text placeholder.

16. Choose **Home→Font→Font Color→Eyedropper**.

17. Click the dark orange bar at the bottom of the slide to match the text color to it.

18. Display the second slide, **Title Slide Layout**.

19. Format the **Title Slide Layout**, formatting the subtitle area the same as the previous slide's bulleted text placeholder.

PowerPoint 2013

Create Action Buttons

20. Display the first slide, **Retrospect Slide Master**.

21. Choose **Insert→Illustrations→Shapes→Action Buttons→Back**.

22. Drag anywhere on the slide to create the **Back** button. Click **OK** to accept the default action.

23. Choose **Insert→Illustrations→Shapes→Action Buttons→Home**.

24. Drag anywhere on the slide to create the **Home** button. Click **OK** to accept the default action.

25. Choose **Insert→Illustrations→Shapes→Action Buttons→Next**.

26. Drag anywhere on the slide to create the **Next** button. Click **OK** to accept the default action.

27. With the Next button still selected, [Shift] +click the **Back** and **Home** buttons to select all three buttons.

28. Locate the **Picture Tools→Format→Size** group.

29. Click in the **Height** box, type **0.5**, and tap [Enter].

30. Click in the **Width** box, type **0.5**, and tap [Enter].

31. Click anywhere on the slide to deselect the action buttons.

32. Drag the **Back** button to the bottom-left area of the slide, above the orange bars.

33. Drag the **Home** button slightly to the right of the Back button.

34. Drag the **Next** button slightly to the right of the Home button.

35. With the Next button still selected, [Shift] +click the **Back** and **Home** buttons to select all three buttons.

36. Choose **Drawing Tools→Format→Arrange→Align→Align Bottom**.

37. Choose **Drawing Tools→Format→Arrange→Align→Distribute Horizontally**.

38. Click anywhere on the slide to deselect the action buttons.

39. Click the **Next** button to select it.

40. Choose **Home→Clipboard→Copy** to copy the logo.

41. Display the second slide, **Title Slide Layout**, and choose **Home→Clipboard→Paste**.
    The title slide needs only a Next button as there is no previous slide, and the title slide is the home *slide.*

42. Choose **Slide Master→Close→Close Master View**.

43. Save and close the file. Exit **PowerPoint**.

44. Submit your final file based on the guidelines provided by your instructor.
    To view examples of how your final file or files should look at the end of this exercise, go to the student resource center.

Work with Custom Design Themes

In this exercise, you will create a custom theme for Kids for Change.

Apply a Built-in Color Scheme

1. Start **PowerPoint**. Create a new, blank presentation and save it as `PP08-R03-KidsCustom-[FirstInitialLastName]` in the **PP2013 Lesson 08** folder.

2. Choose **Design→Themes→Wisp**.

3. Choose **Home→Slides→New Slide** twice to create two additional blank slides.

4. Display the third slide and choose **Home→Slides→Layout→Two Content**.

5. Choose **Design→Variants→More→Colors→Red**.

Create and Apply Custom Colors

6. Choose **Design→Variants→More→Colors→Customize Colors**.

7. Type `Kids New Custom` in the **Name** box.

8. Click the **Text/Background – Dark 1** color menu.

9. Choose **Dark Red** from the bottom row of colors.

10. Click the **Text/Background – Light 2** color menu.

11. Choose **White, Text 1** from the top row of colors. Click **Save**.

Apply a Preset Background

12. Choose **Design→Variants→More→Background Styles** and point to each of the twelve thumbnails to preview the effect on the slide.

13. Select the style at the top of the third column, **Style 3**.

Apply Gradient Backgrounds

14. Choose **Design→Customize→Format Background**.

15. Click the **Preset Gradients** menu and select **Radial Gradient – Accent 5** from the bottom of the fifth column.

16. Click the last gradient stop.

17. Click the **Color** menu and select **Gray - 80%, Background 2** from the top of the third column of colors.

18. Click **Apply to All**.

Apply Texture and Picture Backgrounds

19. Display the first slide.

20. Select the **Picture or Texture Fill** option.

21. Click the **File** button.

22. Browse to the **PP2013 Lesson 08** folder, select **PP08-R03-KidsLogo**, and click **Insert**.

23. Close the **Format Background** panel.

Edit Slide Masters

24. Choose **View→Master Views→Slide Master**.

25. Scroll to the top of the **Slides** panel and select the first slide, **Wisp Slide Master**.

26. Choose **Insert→Images→Pictures**.

27. Navigate to the **PP2013 Lesson 08** folder, select **PP08-R03-KidsLogo**, and click **Insert**.

28. Locate the **Picture Tools→Format→Size** group.

29. Click in the **Height** box, type **1**, and tap [Enter].

30. Drag the logo to the bottom-left corner of the slide.

Use the Eyedropper Tool

31. Display the first slide, **Wisp Slide Master**, and click the border of the slide title.

32. Choose **Home→Font→Font Color→Eyedropper**.

33. Click a blue portion of the Earth in the logo to match the title text color to the logo.

Create Action Buttons

34. Display the first slide, **Wisp Slide Master**, and choose **Insert→Illustrations→Shapes→Action Buttons→Back**.

35. Drag anywhere on the slide to create the **Back** button. Click **OK** to accept the default action.

36. Choose **Insert→Illustrations→Shapes→Action Buttons→Home**.

37. Drag anywhere on the slide to create the **Home** button. Click **OK** to accept the default action.

38. Choose **Insert→Illustrations→Shapes→Action Buttons→Next**.

39. Drag anywhere on the slide to create the **Next** button. Click **OK** to accept the default action.

40. With the Next button still selected, [Shift]+click the **Back** and **Home** buttons to select all three buttons.

41. Locate the **Picture Tools→Format→Size** group.

42. Click in the **Height** box, type **0.5**, and tap [Enter].

43. Click in the **Width** box, type **0.5**, and tap [Enter].

44. Click anywhere on the slide to deselect the action buttons.

45. Drag the **Back** button to the top-right corner of the slide.

46. Tap the [←] five times and then tap the [↓] five times to nudge the button away from the slide edges.

47. Drag the **Home** button slightly below the Back button.

48. Drag the **Next** button slightly below the Home button.

49. With the Next button still selected, Shift +click the **Back** and **Home** buttons to select all three buttons.

50. Choose **Drawing Tools→Format→Arrange→Align→Align Left**.

51. Choose **Drawing Tools→Format→Arrange→Align→Distribute Vertically**.

52. Choose **Slide Master→Close→Close Master View**.

53. Save the presentation.

Save and Use a Custom Design Theme

54. Choose **Design→Themes→More→Save Current Theme**.

55. Browse to your **PP2013 Lesson 08** folder, type `PP08-R03-KidsCustomTheme-[FirstInitialLastName]` in the File Name box, and click Save.

56. Save and close the presentation.

57. Choose **File→New** and click **Blank Presentation**.

58. Type `Kids for Change` as the title and `Monthly Review` as the subtitle.

59. Choose **Home→Slides→New Slide** and title the slide `Agenda`.

60. Choose **Home→Slides→New Slide** and title the slide `Last Month to This Month`.

61. Choose **Home→Slides→Layout→Two Content**.

62. Choose **Design→Themes→More**.

63. Choose **Browse for Themes**.

64. Navigate to your storage location, select **PP08-R03-KidsCustomTheme-[FirstInitialLastName]**, and click **Open**.

65. Save the presentation as `PP08-R03-KidsCustom2-[FirstInitialLastName]`.

Delete Customizations

66. Choose **Design→Variants→More→Colors**.

67. Right-click the **Kids New Custom** color scheme and choose **Delete**.

68. Click **Yes** when prompted to delete the custom color scheme.

69. Delete any additional custom color schemes.

70. Save and close all files. Exit **PowerPoint**.

71. Submit your final files based on the guidelines provided by your instructor.

Apply Your Skills

Create a Custom Design Theme

In this exercise, you will customize the background and colors of a design theme.
You will then save the theme and apply it to another presentation.

Apply a Built-in Color Scheme and Create and Apply Custom Colors

1. Start **PowerPoint**. Open **PP08-A01-Universal** from the **PP2013 Lesson 08** folder and save it as `PP08-A01-Universal-[FirstInitialLastName]`.

2. Apply the **Blue II** color scheme.

3. Create a custom color scheme named `Universal Colors`.

4. Change the **Accent 1** color to **Dark Teal, Background 2**.

5. Change the **Text/Background – Dark 2** color to **Dark Teal, Background 2, Darker 25%**.

Apply Backgrounds

6. Apply the Background Style, **Style 11**, to all slides.

7. Display **slide 2**.

8. Display the **Format Background** panel.

9. Adjust the existing gradient so the first gradient stop is at a position of **90%**. Then apply the edited gradient to all slides.

10. Display the title slide.

11. Format the background as a **Picture or Texture Fill**.

12. Use the **Denim** texture with a **Transparency** of **40%**.

13. Close the **Format Background** panel so the texture background applies only to the title slide.

Save and Use a Custom Design Theme

14. Save the custom theme to your **PP2013 Lesson 08** folder as `PP08-A01-UniversalTheme-[FirstInitialLastName]`.

15. Save and close the presentation.

16. Create a new, blank presentation with the title `Universal Corporate Events` and the subtitle `Committee Assignments`.

17. Apply **PP08-A01-UniversalTheme-[FirstInitialLastName]** from your **PP2013 Lesson 08** folder.

18. Add a new slide with the **title** `Welcome` and the **bulleted text** `Agenda` Enter `Refreshments`.

19. Save the presentation to your **PP2013 Lesson 08** folder as `PP08-A01-UniversalMeeting-[FirstInitialLastName]`.

Delete Customizations

20. Delete all custom color schemes.

21. Save and close all files. Exit **PowerPoint**.

22. Submit your final files based on the guidelines provided by your instructor.

    To view examples of how your final file or files should look at the end of this exercise, go to the student resource center.

Use Slide Masters

In this exercise, you will match slide colors to those in an image. You will also add action buttons to aid in slide show navigation.

Edit Slide Masters and Use the Eyedropper Tool

1. Start **PowerPoint**. Open **PP08-A02-UniversalColors** from your **PP2013 Lesson 08** folder and save it as **PP08-A02-UniversalColors-[FirstInitialLastName]**.

2. Display the **slide masters**.

3. Select the first slide master, **Quotable Slide Master**, and insert **PP08-A02-UniversalLogo** from the **PP2013 Lesson 08** folder.

4. Resize the logo to **1.1" tall** and **1" wide**.

5. Position the logo in the bottom-left corner of the slide.

6. Use the **Eyedropper** to color the slide title to match the gold at the top of the logo.

Create Action Buttons

7. Add **Back**, **Home**, and **Next** buttons to the master slide.

8. Resize the buttons to **0.4"**.

9. Position the **Next** button in the bottom-right corner of the slide.

10. Position the **Home** button on top of the Next button.

11. Position the **Back** button on top of the Home button.

12. Align the buttons and evenly space them.

13. Close **Master view**.

14. Save and close the presentation. Exit **PowerPoint**.

15. Submit your final files based on the guidelines provided by your instructor.

    To view examples of how your final file or files should look at the end of this exercise, go to the student resource center.

Work with Custom Design Themes

In this exercise, you will create a custom theme for Universal Corporate Events.

Apply a Built-in Color Scheme and Create and Apply Custom Colors

1. Start **PowerPoint**. Create a new, blank presentation and save it as **PP08-A03-UniversalCustom-[FirstInitialLastName]** in the **PP2013 Lesson 08** folder.

2. Type **Universal Corporate Events** for the slide title and **Theme Template** as the subtitle.

3. Apply the **Facet** theme.

4. Add a blank slide with the **Title & Content** layout, the title **Slide 2**, and the bulleted text **Item 1** Enter **Item 2**.

5. Add a blank slide with the **Two Content** layout, the title **Slide 3**, the left bulleted text **Left 1** Enter **Left 2**, and the right bulleted text **Right 1** Enter **Right 2**.

6. Apply the built-in **Yellow** color scheme.

7. Customize the color scheme and name it **Universal New Custom**.

8. Set the **Text/Background – Light 1** color to a light orange to change the slide title color.

9. Set the **Accent 1** color to purple.

10. Save the color scheme.

Apply Backgrounds

11. Apply the built-in **Style 5** background style.

12. Apply the **Papyrus** texture with a **Transparency** of **30%** to the title slide; close the **Format Background** panel.

Edit Slide Masters and Use the Eyedropper Tool

13. Edit the first slide master to include **PP08-A03-UniversalLogo** from the **PP2013 Lesson 08** folder.

14. Resize the logo to **1" wide** and position it in the top-right area of the slide master inside the orange strip.

15. Copy the logo and paste it to the second slide master so it appears on title slides.

16. Return to the first slide master and use the **Eyedropper** to set the bulleted text color to match the dark portion of the orange strip.

Create Action Buttons

17. Add **Back**, **Home**, and **Next** buttons to the master slide.

18. Resize the buttons to **0.3"**.

19. Position the **Back** button in the bottom-left corner of the slide under the footer.

20. Position the **Home** button to the right of the Back button.

21. Position the **Next** button to the right of the Home button.

22. Copy the **Next** button to the second slide master so the button appears on the title slide.

23. Align the buttons and evenly space them.

24. Close **Master view** and save the presentation.

Save and Use a Custom Design Theme

25. Save the theme to your **PP2013 Lesson 08** folder as `PP08-A03-UniversalCustomTheme-[FirstInitialLastName]`.

26. Save and close the presentation. Then create a new, blank presentation.

27. Add two slides, both using the **Title & Content** layout.

28. Apply **PP08-A03-UniversalCustomTheme-[FirstInitialLastName]** from the **PP2013 Lesson 08** folder.

29. Save the presentation as `PP08-A03-UniversalCustom2-[FirstInitialLastName]`.

Delete Customizations

30. Delete all custom color schemes.

31. Save and close all files. Exit **PowerPoint**.

32. Submit your final files based on the guidelines provided by your instructor.

Extend Your Skills

In the course of working through the Extend Your Skills exercises, you will think critically as you use the skills taught in the lesson to complete the assigned projects. To evaluate your mastery and completion of the exercises, your instructor may use a rubric, with which more points are allotted according to performance characteristics. (The more you do, the more you earn!) Ask your instructor how your work will be evaluated.

PP08-E01 That's the Way I See It!

Theme colors can be modified by creating custom color schemes or editing slide masters. Creating a custom color scheme can be frustrating because it's unclear and inconsistent how the different settings affect each slide. Having a theme guide can help. Create a new Word document named **PP08-E01-ColorGuide-[FirstInitialLastName]** and a new presentation named **PP08-E01-Colors-[FirstInitialLastName]**, both saved to **PP2013 Lesson 08**.

In the presentation, apply the Facet theme. Type **Facet** as the title and **Custom Colors** as the subtitle. Add a second slide with the Title & Content layout and **Title & Content** as the title. Add a few lines of bulleted text. Create one more slide for each layout, titling each with their layout name. Create a custom color scheme and change Text/Background – Dark 1 to red. Save the color scheme with a name of your choice. Examine each slide. In the Word document, describe what the Text/Background – Dark 1 setting affected. In PowerPoint, delete the custom color scheme. Repeat this process for the remaining colors, one at a time, until you have documented what each setting affects for the Facet theme. Delete all custom schemes.

You will be evaluated based on the inclusion of all elements specified, your ability to follow directions, your ability to apply newly learned skills to a real-world situation, your creativity, and the relevance of your topic and/or data choice(s). Submit your final file based on the guidelines provided by your instructor.

PP08-E02 Be Your Own Boss

Blue Jean Landscaping needs a custom theme for presentations. Create a new presentation and save it as **PP08-E02-BlueJean-[FirstInitialLastName]** in your **PP2013 Lesson 08** folder. Use **Blue Jean Landscaping** as the title and **Theme** as the subtitle. Create two additional slides; type any titles and a few lines of bulleted text. Apply the Ion theme and the Blue Warm color scheme. Edit the color scheme to make Text/Background – Light 2 white. Display the Master Slides and edit the Ion Slide Master background to achieve a light blue to gray radial gradient. Apply the gradient to all slide masters. Insert **PP08-E02-BlueJeanLogo** onto the Ion Slide Master; size and position as you see fit. Use the Eyedropper to color the bulleted text so it matches the dark blue of the logo. Save the presentation. Save the theme as **PP08-E02-BlueJeanTheme-[FirstInitialLastName]**. Delete all custom color schemes from the Ribbon.

You will be evaluated based on the inclusion of all elements specified, your ability to follow directions, your ability to apply newly learned skills to a real-world situation, your creativity, and your demonstration of an entrepreneurial spirit. Submit your final file based on the guidelines provided by your instructor.

Transfer Your Skills

In the course of working through the Transfer Your Skills exercises, you will use critical-thinking and creativity skills to complete the assigned projects using skills taught in the lesson. To evaluate your mastery and completion of the exercises, your instructor may use a rubric, with which more points are allotted according to performance characteristics. (The more you do, the more you earn!) Ask your instructor how your work will be evaluated.

PP08-T01 Use the Web as a Learning Tool

Throughout this book, you will be provided with an opportunity to use the Internet as a learning tool by completing WebQuests. According to the original creators of WebQuests, as described on their website (WebQuest.org), a WebQuest is "an inquiry-oriented activity in which most or all of the information used by learners is drawn from the web." To complete the WebQuest projects in this book, navigate to the student resource center and choose the WebQuest for the lesson on which you are currently working. The subject of each WebQuest will be relevant to the material found in the lesson.

WebQuest Subject: Themes and Templates

Submit your files based on the guidelines provided by your instructor.

PP08-T02 Demonstrate Proficiency

As part of their corporate branding and name recognition, Stormy BBQ wants all future presentations to use a consistent color scheme and basic design.

Create a blank presentation and save it as **PP08-T02-StormyTheme-[FirstInitialLastName]** in the **PP2013 Lesson 08** folder. Apply the design theme of your choice. Apply a color scheme that is appropriate for "smokiness" or "barbeque." Edit the slide masters so that **PPT08-T02-StormyLogo**, (find it in **PP2013 Lesson 08** folder) appears on every slide. Add Back, Home, and Next action buttons to the appropriate slide master so they appear on every slide. Change the text color of the master slides so slide titles match a color from the logo.

Save the presentation. Save the theme as **PP08-T02-ThemeTemplate-[FirstInitialLastName]** in the same location as the presentation. Delete any custom color schemes and any custom themes from the Ribbon.

Submit your final files based on the guidelines provided by your instructor.

Connecting and Broadcasting Presentations

LEARNING OBJECTIVES

After studying this lesson, you will be able to:

- Connect multiple presentations
- Use Object Linking and Embedding
- Broadcast a presentation over the Internet

Maintaining large presentations can be troublesome. Breaking them into smaller individual presentations and then linking them together makes it easy to delegate certain content to different people or departments. Using PowerPoint's linking and embedding features allows you to modularize your presentations. In this lesson, you will learn to link and embed small presentations to create a single large slide show. You will also learn to broadcast your presentations over the Internet.

Sharing a Presentation Online

Raritan Clinic East is a medical practice staffed by the finest clinical diagnosticians in the fields of pediatric general medicine, cardiology, orthopedics, pediatric emergency medicine, and neonatology. In an effort to attract the best and brightest from the nation's medical schools, you decide to make a promotional presentation about the facility to share with potential employees. You call Sarah, one of Raritan's technical support specialists, to ask whether it is possible to add a hyperlink to a file or to link one presentation to another. Sarah explains that with PowerPoint 2013, accomplishing this is a simple task. You tell Sarah you'd like to schedule a conference call with a few prospective employees across the country. You'd like to speak with them on the phone as you present the slide show over the Internet. Sarah tells you that PowerPoint 2013's broadcast feature is exactly what you are looking for.

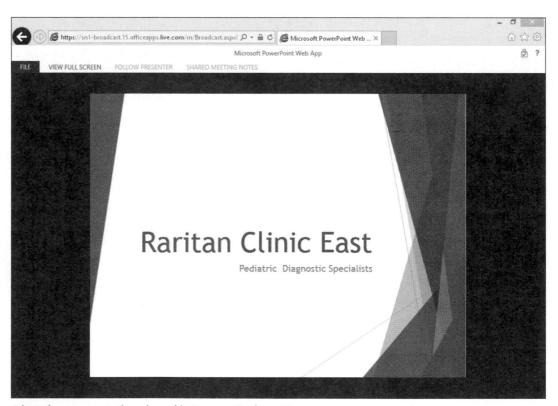

A broadcast presentation viewed in Internet Explorer 10.

Connecting Presentations

Video Library http://labyrinthelab.com/videos Video Number: PP13-V0901

The ability to connect multiple presentations is a powerful option in PowerPoint. For example, you may have several small presentations, each covering a specific topic, and need a larger presentation that incorporates all those topics. Or your workplace may have several departments—each responsible for its own small presentation. You can unify these small presentations into a single large presentation by connecting them.

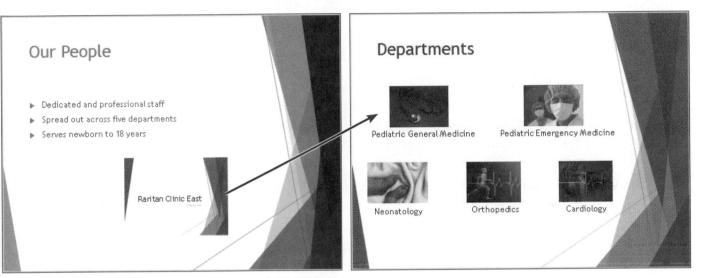

The main presentation connects to the Departments presentation.

The Hard Way: Copying and Pasting

One option for connecting presentations is to open each of the small presentations, copy the slides, and then paste the slides into the larger main presentation. Arranging the slides in the desired order would then be tedious and very confusing. A more efficient method is to simply link or embed the small presentations to connect them to the larger one.

CONNECTING PRESENTATIONS: COMPARING LINKING AND COPYING/PASTING	
Without Linking	**With Linking**
Open small presentation 1.	Open large presentation.
Copy all slides.	Link/embed small presentation 1.
Open large presentation.	Link/embed small presentation 2.
Paste all slides.	
Open small presentation 2.	
Copy all slides.	
Switch back to large presentation.	
Paste all slides.	

Choosing a Connection Technique

If you wish to connect presentations, you have the following three options. Each has its own unique benefits and drawbacks:

- Insert a hyperlink.
- Insert an action.
- Use Object Linking and Embedding.

Connecting Presentations with a Hyperlink

Video Library   http://labyrinthelab.com/videos   Video Number: PP13-V0902

You can create a hyperlink that navigates to another slide in the same presentation or that opens a different presentation entirely. You can even link to a specific slide in a different presentation. For example, imagine you will click a text link in the main presentation that opens a second presentation. However, you want to skip several slides at the beginning of the second presentation. You can specify that the target presentation initially open to the second, third, or any slide other than the title slide. Hyperlinks can be created from text, images, shapes, or charts.

After linking presentations, do not move them or change their filenames. Links will break if you do not maintain the relative locations of target presentations to the main presentation. This is similar to the way other linked documents work, such as linked charts and Excel spreadsheets.

The hyperlink in the main presentation may change color (depending on the document theme and color scheme) to indicate that the link has been clicked. The color will revert to its original color when viewed in a slide show.

Keep the main presentation file and all linked presentations in the same folder.

Task	Procedure
Connect presentations with a hyperlink	■ Select the text/object in the main presentation to turn into a hyperlink. ■ Choose Insert→Links→Hyperlink 🌐. ■ In the Link To option, select Existing File or Web Page. ■ Navigate to and select the other presentation. ■ To link to a specific slide, click Bookmark, select the slide, and click OK. ■ Click OK to close the Insert Hyperlink dialog box.
Connect presentations with an action	■ Select the text/object in the main presentation to turn into a hyperlink. ■ Choose Insert→Links→Action ⭐. ■ Choose Hyperlink To and then select Other PowerPoint Presentation. ■ Navigate to and select the other presentation; click OK. ■ Select a slide in the target presentation and click OK. ■ Click OK to close the Action Settings dialog box.
Use Object Linking and Embedding (OLE) to link or embed presentations	■ Choose Insert→Text→Object. ■ Choose the Create from File option. ■ Click Browse, navigate to the file/presentation to link, and click OK. ■ Select the Link checkbox for a linked presentation, or leave it deselected to embed the presentation. ■ Select the Display as Icon checkbox to display a generic file icon on the slide, or leave the box deselected to display a snapshot of the file contents.

PowerPoint 2013

DEVELOP YOUR SKILLS PP09-D01

Connect Presentations with Hyperlinks

In this exercise, you will hyperlink small presentations to a main presentation.

1. Start **PowerPoint** and maximize the program window.

2. Open **PP09-D01-Recruitment** from the **PP2013 Lesson 09** folder.

3. Navigate the slides to familiarize yourself with the presentation.

4. Close the presentation without saving any changes.

5. Open and explore the following presentations from the **PP2013 Lesson 09** folder one at a time. Close each without saving any changes when you are finished exploring.

   ■ PP09-D01-Departments

   ■ PP09-D01-Facility

   ■ PP09-D01-Services

   ■ PP09-D01-Staff

6. Open **PP09-D01-Facility** again and save it as `PP09-D01-Facility-[FirstInitialLastName]`.

   You will edit this presentation later in this lesson, so you must rename it. Replace the bracketed text with your first initial and last name. For example, if your name is Bethany Smith, your filename would look like this: PP09-D01-Facility-BSmith.

7. Open **PP09-D01-Recruitment** again and save it as `PP09-D01-Recruitment-[FirstInitialLastName]`.

8. On the second slide (Our Facility), select the text *State-of-the-art medical complex* and choose **Insert→Links→Hyperlink**.

9. Follow these steps to link to PP09-D01-Facility-[FirstInitialLastName]:

Ⓐ Choose **Existing File or Web Page**.

Ⓑ Browse to the **PP2013 Lesson 09** folder. (Your setting may differ from the figure.)

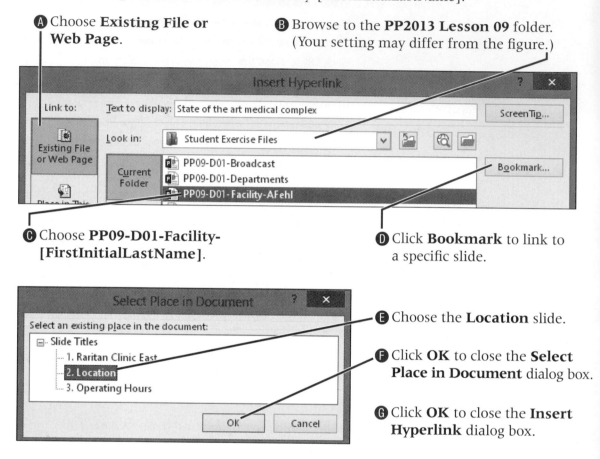

Ⓒ Choose **PP09-D01-Facility-[FirstInitialLastName]**.

Ⓓ Click **Bookmark** to link to a specific slide.

Ⓔ Choose the **Location** slide.

Ⓕ Click **OK** to close the **Select Place in Document** dialog box.

Ⓖ Click **OK** to close the **Insert Hyperlink** dialog box.

10. Select the text *Open 24 x 7 x 365* and add a hyperlink to the **Operating Hours** slide in **PP09-D01-Facility-[FirstInitialLastName]**.

11. Save your presentation.

Connecting Presentations with an Action

Video Library http://labyrinthelab.com/videos   Video Number: PP13-V0903

Actions, like hyperlinks, can also link to other presentations. In fact, actions create hyperlinks. It is a good idea to keep the main presentation and all linked presentations in the same folder, as this makes it easier to keep track of them.

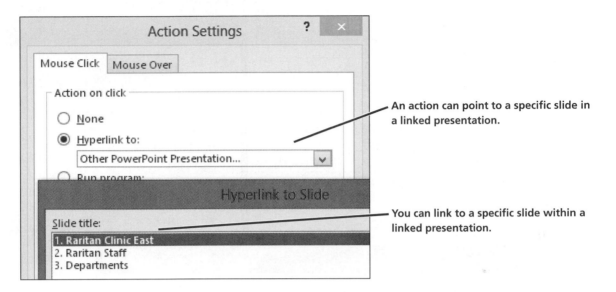

An action can point to a specific slide in a linked presentation.

You can link to a specific slide within a linked presentation.

DEVELOP YOUR SKILLS PP09-D02
Connect Presentations with Actions

In this exercise, you will connect presentations with an action.

1. Save the presentation as **PP09-D02-Recruitment-[FirstInitialLastName]**.

2. Select the text *Variety of patient and community services* and then choose **Insert→Links→Action**.

3. Follow these steps to link to a presentation with a mouse-click action:

Ⓐ Choose **Hyperlink To**.

Ⓑ Scroll down the list and choose **Other PowerPoint Presentation**.

Ⓒ If necessary, browse to the **PP2013 Lesson 09** folder.

Ⓓ Select **PP09-D01-Services** and click **OK**.

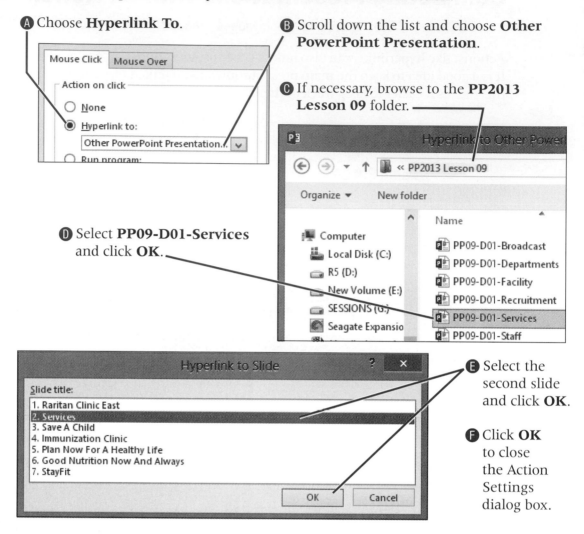

Ⓔ Select the second slide and click **OK**.

Ⓕ Click **OK** to close the Action Settings dialog box.

The new action links directly to slide 2 of the connected presentation.

4. Display slide 3, **Our People**.

5. Create an action that links the text *Dedicated and professional staff* to the second slide of **PP09-D01-Staff**.

6. Save your presentation.

Connecting Presentations with Object Linking and Embedding

Video Library http://labyrinthelab.com/videos Video Number: PP13-V0904

Object Linking and Embedding (OLE) works in a similar way as hyperlinks or actions, but it inserts its own icon on the slide rather than turning text, an existing image, or a chart into a hyperlink. As the name indicates, OLE can either link or embed the targeted files.

Linking Versus Embedding

A few differences exist between linking and embedding. Each has its use, and your choice depends largely on personal preference:

- Linked presentations should not be renamed or moved, or the link will be broken. Embedded presentations can be renamed and moved with no effect on the main presentation.
- Linked presentations can be edited, and the changes are immediately visible when accessed via a link from the main presentation. Remember, embedding a presentation places a copy of it in the main presentation. Changes you make in the original file are not transferred to the embedded copy, and the opposite also is true.
- Linking presentations does not increase the size of the main presentation. Embedding presentations does increase its size.

Linking with OLE

Files linked through OLE behave just as if they were linked with a hyperlink or action. Be aware of the filenames and locations, and store all the files in the same folder just as you would if you were using a hyperlink or action. Linking with OLE creates an icon on the slide that, when clicked, opens the linked file. You can set the icon to appear as a generic icon or as a snapshot of the actual file contents. You should choose OLE linking over hyperlinks or actions when you want a file icon or snapshot on the slide rather than a typical hyperlink or button.

OLE linked file displayed as a generic icon   **OLE linked file displayed as a document snapshot**

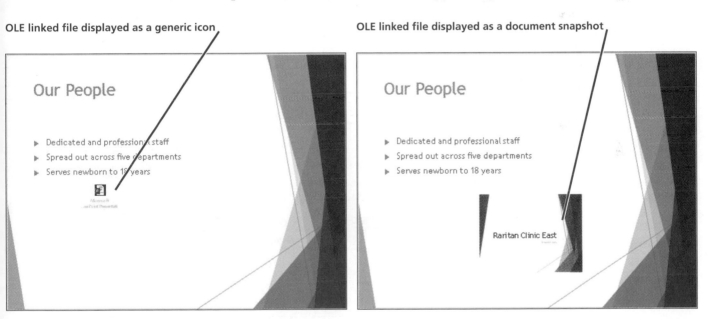

Embedding with OLE

OLE embedding works just like OLE linking except a copy of the file is embedded in the presentation rather than linked. With OLE embedding, you connect the files the same way as with OLE linking and can select from a generic file icon or a snapshot of the actual file contents. The difference is that the connected file will be absorbed into the main presentation, increasing the overall size of the presentation.

You can also embed Word documents, Excel workbooks, and other types of files into a PowerPoint presentation by using OLE embedding.

Formatting an Embedded File's Icon

When an OLE file is placed on a slide, you can choose to display it as a PowerPoint icon or as a thumbnail of the file contents. If you choose to use a generic icon, you can change the caption under the icon. PowerPoint also offers several icon variations.

┌ You can display the
  OLE file as an icon.

You can choose from several
icons and change the caption.

┌ Here is a slide displaying an
  altered OLE icon and caption.

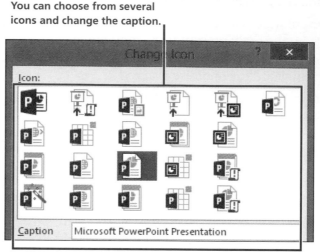

DEVELOP YOUR SKILLS PP09-D03

Connect Presentations with OLE

In this exercise, you will use Object Linking and Embedding to embed a small presentation in a main presentation.

1. Save the presentation as **PP09-D03-Recruitment-[FirstInitialLastName]**.

2. Select the third slide, **Our People**.

3. Choose **Insert→Text→Object** 🔲.

4. Follow these steps to embed the event calendar presentation:

Ⓐ Choose **Create from File**.

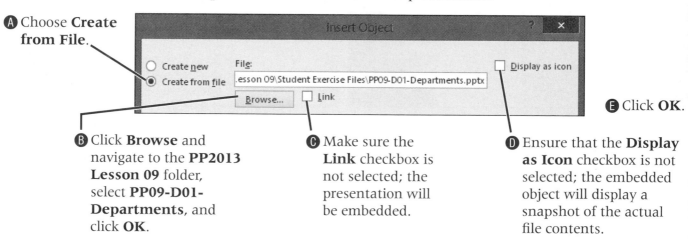

Ⓔ Click **OK**.

Ⓑ Click **Browse** and navigate to the **PP2013 Lesson 09** folder, select **PP09-D01-Departments**, and click **OK**.

Ⓒ Make sure the **Link** checkbox is not selected; the presentation will be embedded.

Ⓓ Ensure that the **Display as Icon** checkbox is not selected; the embedded object will display a snapshot of the actual file contents.

A copy of the PP09-D01-Departments presentation is embedded. There is no link from the main presentation to the PP09-D01-Departments presentation. Changes made to the original PP09-D01-Departments presentation will have no effect on the embedded copy.

5. Follow these steps to resize the embedded presentation:

Ⓐ Point to the top-left corner of the embedded presentation until your mouse pointer becomes a double-headed arrow.

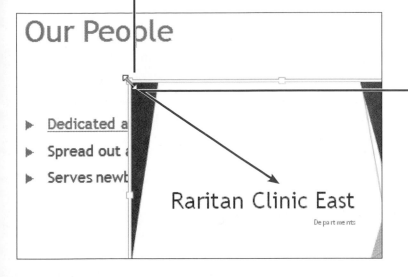

Ⓑ Drag down and to the right to shrink the embedded presentation to your liking.

Ⓒ Drag the embedded presentation to the lower-right area of the slide.

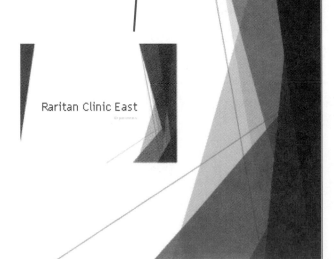

6. Save your presentation.

Navigating Connected Presentations

Video Library   http://labyrinthelab.com/videos   Video Number: PP13-V0905

A connected presentation ends differently when it is connected with a hyperlink or action as opposed to using OLE. A hyperlinked or action-connected presentation displays the black End of Slide Show screen, which can interrupt the mood you've set with your document theme. OLE-connected presentations—linked or embedded—do not display the black screen. Instead, you are returned immediately to the current slide in the main presentation after a connected presentation ends.

The linked and embedded presentations are optional during a slide show. You can choose to click the hyperlinks or OLE objects to display the connected presentations or ignore them.

DEVELOP YOUR SKILLS PP09-D04
View Connected Presentations

In this exercise, you will navigate a slide show and its connected presentations.

1. Choose **Slide Show→Start Slide Show→From Beginning**.

2. Navigate to the second slide, **Our Facility**, and click the hyperlink for *State-of-the-art medical complex*.

   The PP09-D01-Facility-[FirstInitialLastName] presentation opens.

3. Click through to the end of **PP09-D01-Facility-[FirstInitialLastName]** until the black **End of Slide Show** screen appears. Click to end the linked presentation.

4. Click the *Open 24 x 7 x 365* hyperlink and navigate the linked slide show, resuming the main slide show when the linked presentation ends.

5. View the final linked presentation on the **Our Facility** slide and resume the slide show when it is through.

6. Advance to the **Our People** slide and click the **OLE object** to display the embedded **PP09-D01-Departments** presentation.

7. Navigate through **PP09-D01-Departments** and return to the **Our People** slide.

   Notice that the black End of Slide Show screen does not display with OLE-connected presentations but just returns to the Our People slide when complete.

8. Tap Esc to exit the slide show and return to **Normal** view.

Editing Linked and Embedded Presentations

Video Library   http://labyrinthelab.com/videos   Video Number: PP13-V0906

No presentation lasts forever. Edits must be made to keep presentation content current. Fortunately, you can access linked and embedded presentations right from the main presentation, which makes the editing process a little easier.

Editing Linked Presentations

Remember that when presentations (or any files) are linked, a pointer to the original file is created. If the original file is edited, the changes are seen when the link is clicked.

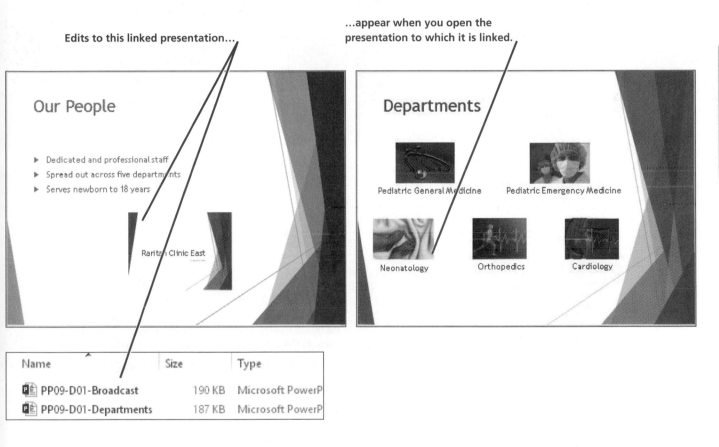

Edits to this linked presentation...

...appear when you open the presentation to which it is linked.

Editing Embedded Presentations

When presentations (or any files) are embedded, a copy of the original file is absorbed into the main presentation. Editing the original file has no effect on the embedded copy in the main presentation. Embedded files must be edited directly from the main presentation.

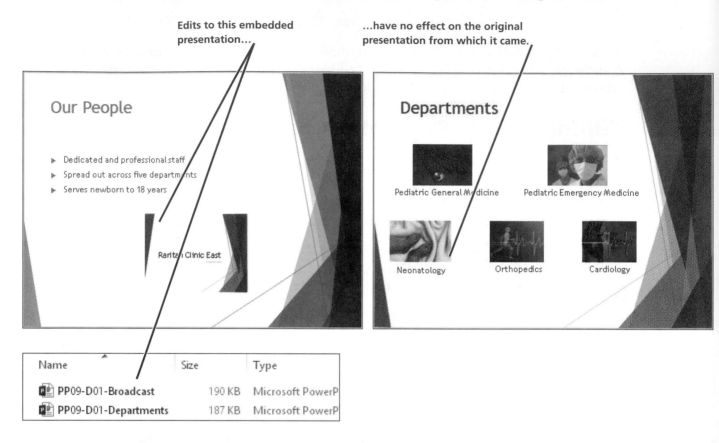

Edits to this embedded presentation...

...have no effect on the original presentation from which it came.

QUICK REFERENCE	EDITING A LINKED OR EMBEDDED PRESENTATION
Task	**Procedure**
Edit a linked presentation	■ Choose File→Open, navigate to and select the original linked file, and click Open; or right-click the hyperlink in the main presentation and choose Open Hyperlink.
	■ Make the changes to the linked presentation and then save and close it.
Edit an OLE linked presentation	■ Double-click the OLE object icon in the main presentation; or open the linked presentation normally with File→Open.
	■ Make the changes to the linked presentation and then save and close it.
Edit an OLE embedded presentation	■ Double-click the OLE object icon in the main presentation.
	■ If the OLE object displays as a generic icon, the embedded presentation will open in full screen just as a linked presentation does. Make the changes to the embedded presentation and close it. Changes are automatically saved.
	■ If the OLE object displays as a snapshot of the file contents, the embedded presentation becomes editable in a small window inside the current slide. Make the changes to the embedded presentation and then click anywhere on the main slide.

Edit Linked and Embedded Presentations

In this exercise, you will edit the linked and embedded presentations.

1. Save the presentation as **PP09-D05-Recruitment-[FirstInitialLastName]**.

Edit a Linked Presentation

2. Select the second slide, **Our Facility**.

3. Right-click the *Open 24 x 7 x 365* hyperlink and choose **Open Hyperlink**.

   The linked PP09-D01-Facility-[FirstInitialLastName] presentation opens.

4. Select the third slide, **Operating Hours**, if necessary, and change *12:00 a.m.* to **midnight**.

5. Save and close **PP09-D01-Facility-[FirstInitialLastName]**.

   The color of the hyperlink on the Our Facility slide changes to indicate that the hyperlink has been visited. If this bothers you, you may save, close, and reopen the presentation to reset the hyperlink color.

6. Choose **File→Open**.

7. Navigate to the **PP2013 Lesson 09** folder and open **PP09-D01-Facility-[FirstInitialLastName]**.

8. Navigate to the third slide, **Operating Hours**, and notice that *12:00 a.m.* has been changed to *midnight*.

   Editing the linked document affected the original.

9. Close **PP09-D01-Facility-[FirstInitialLastName]**. Choose **Don't Save** if prompted to save any changes.

Edit an Embedded Presentation

10. Navigate to the third slide, **Our People**.

11. Double-click the **embedded object**.

   The PowerPoint window changes. The File tab is gone, a small menu bar appears above the Ribbon, and the Save command in the Quick Access toolbar is disabled. The OLE object displays its own set of scroll bars.

12. Use the **OLE object** scroll bars to scroll to the second slide in the embedded presentation, **PP09-D01-Departments**.

   The embedded presentation is too small to edit comfortably.

13. Click the **Zoom In** button at the bottom-right of the PowerPoint window repeatedly until you can see the text below each of the pictures in the embedded presentation.

14. Double-click the word *Neonatology* and type **Neonatal Care**.

15. Click anywhere on the **Our People** main slide, outside the OLE object.

   The PowerPoint window resets itself, and the OLE object scroll bars disappear.

PowerPoint 2013

16. Click the **Fit Slide to Current Window** button at the bottom-right of the PowerPoint window so you can see the whole Our People slide.

17. Choose **File→Open**.

18. Navigate to the **PP2013 Lesson 09** folder and open **PP09-D01-Departments**.

19. Navigate to the second slide, **Departments**, and notice that the changes do not appear here in the original presentation.

    Editing the embedded document had no effect on the original.

20. Close **PP09-D01-Departments**. Choose **Don't Save** if prompted to save any changes.

21. Save and close **PP09-D05-Recruitment-[FirstInitialLastName]**.

Broadcasting Presentations

Video Library   http://labyrinthelab.com/videos   Video Number: PP13-V0907

Microsoft offers the PowerPoint Broadcast Service. This free service allows users to broadcast their presentations over the Internet. The service provides you with a link to the broadcast that you can share with friends or colleagues. Anyone with the link and an Internet connection can view the broadcast, even if they don't have PowerPoint, as the broadcasted presentation runs in a web browser. Although the service is free, it requires a Microsoft account, sometimes called a Microsoft Account ID.

Creating a Microsoft Account ID

A Microsoft account, or Microsoft Account ID, is a free account with one of the many Microsoft services, such as an Outlook.com email account. Many Microsoft services are free but require a Microsoft Account ID to log in. Only the person broadcasting the presentation needs a Microsoft Account ID. To view the broadcast, you need only the link.

You can sign in or create a new free Microsoft Account ID at any of the following Microsoft websites:

- http://www.live.com
- http://www.outlook.com
- http://www.skydrive.com

DEVELOP YOUR SKILLS PP09-D06
Create a Microsoft Account ID

In this exercise, you will create a Microsoft Account ID.

You must have an Internet connection to complete this exercise. Web pages change often. The Outlook.com web page may have changed and may no longer exactly match this exercise. However, the steps to create a Microsoft Account ID should be similar no matter what changes Microsoft has made to the Outlook.com page.

1. Start your web browser and navigate to **http://www.outlook.com**.

   The Outlook.com page loads, but you are redirected to another Microsoft URL in the address bar.

2. Click the **Sign Up Now** link on the right side of the page.

3. Complete the form on the **Sign Up** page. Feel free to use a fake name, address, and birth date. Microsoft doesn't need to know your personal information!

   Be sure to remember your Microsoft Account ID and password, as you will need them later. It is not secure to write down this information, unless you can guarantee storing it in a safe place. If you forget your Microsoft Account ID or password, it is easy enough to simply create a new one.

Broadcasting a Presentation

Video Library   http://labyrinthelab.com/videos   Video Number: PP13-V0908

Once you have a Microsoft Account ID, you can broadcast your presentation for free to anyone with an Internet connection. You begin setting up the broadcast in Backstage view, and PowerPoint walks you through the remaining steps.

QUICK REFERENCE	BROADCASTING A PRESENTATION
Task	**Procedure**
Broadcast a presentation	■ Choose File→Share→Present Online→Present Online.
	■ Sign in with your Microsoft Account ID. PowerPoint will connect to the service, upload your presentation, and create a unique link you can share.
	■ Copy the link and email it to people with whom you would like to share the presentation.
	■ Click Start Presentation to broadcast it.
End a broadcast	■ Click through the slide show until the black End of Slide Show screen appears and then click the black screen. Tap Esc to end the slide show at any time.
	■ Choose Present Online→Present Online→End Online Presentation.
	■ Click End Online Presentation to confirm the end or click Cancel to keep the broadcast alive.
Sign out	■ Choose File→Account.
	■ Click Sign Out; click Yes to confirm.
	■ Tap Esc to exit Backstage view.
	■ Save your work, close PowerPoint, and log out of Windows.

Security Considerations

Once you sign in with a Microsoft Account ID, PowerPoint keeps you logged in even after the broadcast presentation has ended. This is a security risk, because anyone who has access to the computer you have used can then use your account to access Microsoft services. It is recommended that you sign out after ending an online presentation. Microsoft recommends that after signing out, you close all programs and log out of Windows to completely clear the login information that PowerPoint saved.

DEVELOP YOUR SKILLS PP09-D07
Broadcast a Presentation

In this exercise, you will work with another student to broadcast a presentation.

You must have an Internet connection, a Microsoft Account ID, access to email, and a partner at another computer to complete this exercise.

1. Find a student partner and decide who will be **Student A** and who will be **Student B**.
   Student A will broadcast a presentation to Student B. You will reverse roles at the end of this exercise.

Student A
Only Student A should complete the steps in this section.

2. Choose **File→Open**.
3. Navigate to your **PP2013 Lesson 09** folder and open **PP09-D07-Broadcast**.
4. Choose **File→Share→Present Online**.
5. Click the **Present Online** button in the right column of Backstage view.
6. Enter your **Microsoft Account ID** and password in the dialog box and click **Sign In**.
7. Click **Copy Link**.

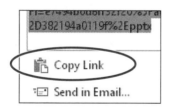

8. Start your email program. If you use a webmail service such as Outlook.com, Yahoo!, or Gmail, launch your web browser and sign in to your email page.
   You are not able to minimize PowerPoint yet because the Broadcast Slide Show dialog box is still open.
9. Compose an email to **Student B**. You will have to ask for **Student B**'s email address.
10. Type the subject `PPT Broadcast` for the email's subject.
11. Click in the message body area, type `Use this link to view my PPT broadcast`, tap Enter to create a new line, and tap Ctrl+V to paste the copied link.
12. Tap Enter again to create a blank line under the pasted link.

13. Send the email and then close your email program (or web browser).

   The PowerPoint window appears, and the Broadcast Slide Show dialog box is still open.

14. Click **Start Presentation**.

Student B
Only Student B should complete the steps in this section.

15. Start your email program and check your email.

16. Open the message from **Student A** and click the link in the email to the **PowerPoint Broadcast**.

   Your web browser opens a window with the broadcast presentation loaded.

17. Watch your screen as **Student A** delivers the slide show.

Student A
Only Student A should complete the steps in this section.

18. Navigate through the slide show as normal.

   As you navigate the slide show, the presentation runs for Student B.

19. End the slide show, choose **Present Online→Present Online→End Online Presentation**, and click **End Online Presentation** when prompted to confirm.

   The slide show ends for both students.

20. Choose **File→Account**.

21. Click **Sign Out** and then click **Yes** when prompted.

Students A and B
Both students should complete the steps in this section.

22. Close all programs and return to your **Windows Desktop**.

23. Repeat this exercise and reverse roles so that **Student B** broadcasts the presentation to **Student A**.

24. When you are through, close all programs and return to the **Windows Desktop**.

25. Log out of **Windows** to completely clear your Microsoft Account ID from PowerPoint.

Concepts Review

To check your knowledge of the key concepts introduced in this lesson, complete the Concepts Review quiz by choosing the appropriate access option below.

If you are...	Then access the quiz by...
Using the Labyrinth Video Library	Going to http://labyrinthelab.com/videos
Using eLab	Logging in, choosing Content, and navigating to the Concepts Review quiz for this lesson
Not using the Labyrinth Video Library or eLab	Going to the student resource center for this book

Reinforce Your Skills

Connect Presentations

In this exercise, you will connect presentations developed by different people within the Kids for Change organization.

Connect Presentations with Hyperlinks

1. Start **PowerPoint**. Open **PP09-R01-Main** from the **PP2013 Lesson 09** folder and save it as `PP09-R01-Main-[FirstInitialLastName]`.

2. Display slide 2, **Events**.

3. Select the text *iRecycling Day*.

4. Choose **Insert→Links→Hyperlink**.

5. From the **Link To** buttons, choose **Existing File or Web Page**.

6. In the **Look In** menu, browse to the **PP2013 Lesson 09** folder.

7. Click **PP09-R01-iRecycle** to select it and then click **OK**.
   The text iRecycling Day *becomes a hyperlink.*

Connect Presentations with Actions

8. Select the text *Build-a-House*.

9. Choose **Insert→Links→Action** and then choose **Hyperlink To**.

10. From the **Hyperlink To** menu, choose **Other PowerPoint Presentation**.

11. Navigate to the **PP2013 Lesson 09** folder, choose **PP09-R01-Houses**, and click **OK**.
    The Hyperlink to Slide dialog box displays, prompting you to select a slide in the target presentation.

12. Ensure that the first slide, **Kids for Change**, is selected and click **OK**.

13. Click **OK** to close the Actions Settings dialog box.
    The text Build-a-House *becomes a hyperlink.*

Connect Presentations with OLE

14. Choose **Insert→Text→Object**.

15. Choose **Create from File**.

16. Click **Browse** and navigate to the **PP2013 Lesson 09** folder. Choose **PP09-R01-Volunteers** and click **OK**.

17. Click **OK** to close the Insert Object dialog box.

18. Drag any of the corners of the **OLE embedded presentation** toward the center to shrink the image.

19. Drag the **OLE image** to the side of the slide so it does not overlap any text.

View Connected Presentations

20. Choose **Slide Show→Start Slide Show→From Beginning**.

21. Navigate to the second slide.

22. Click the **iRecycling Day** link to open the linked presentation.

23. Click through the **iRecycling Day** presentation until it ends and you see a black **End of Slide Show** screen.

24. Click the black screen to close the linked presentation and return to the main presentation.

25. Click the **Build-a-House** link to open the linked presentation.

26. Click through the **Build-a-House** presentation until it ends and you see a black **End of Slide Show** screen.

27. Click the black screen to close the linked presentation and return to the main presentation.

28. Click the **OLE image** to open the embedded presentation.

29. Click through the **Top Volunteers** presentation until it ends and you return to the **Events** slide of the main presentation.

    Remember that presentations linked or embedded with OLE do not display the black End of Slide Show screen.

30. Tap [Esc] to end the slide show.

31. Save the presentation and exit **PowerPoint**.

32. Submit your final files based on the guidelines provided by your instructor.

    To view samples of how your file or files should look at the end of this exercise, go to the student resource center.

REINFORCE YOUR SKILLS PP09-R02

Edit Connected Presentations and Present Online

In this exercise, you will edit linked and embedded presentations. You will also present a slide show online.

Connect Presentations with Hyperlinks

1. Start **PowerPoint**. Open **PP09-R02-Editing** from your **PP2013 Lesson 09** folder and save it as `PP09-R02-Editing-[FirstInitialLastName]`.

2. Open **PP09-R02-Toy** from your **PP2013 Lesson 09** folder save it as `PP09-R02-Toy-[FirstInitialLastName]`. Close the presentation.

3. Display slide 2, **Events**.

4. Select the text *Toy Collection* and then choose **Insert→Links→Hyperlink**.

5. From the **Link To** buttons, choose **Existing File or Web Page**.

6. In the **Look In** menu, browse to the **PP2013 Lesson 09** folder.

7. Choose **PP09-R02-Toy-[FirstInitialLastName]** and click **OK**.

    The text Toy Collection *becomes a hyperlink.*

Edit Linked and Embedded Presentations

8. Right-click the **Toy Collection** link and choose **Open Hyperlink**.
   The linked presentation opens in a new PowerPoint window.

9. Display slide 3, **When?**.

10. Add a new third bullet with the text `Collection 3 from Oct 1 - Dec 1`.

11. Save and close the **Toy** presentation.

12. Double-click the picture of the embedded presentation.

13. Scroll the embedded presentation to the last slide (**Locations?**).

14. Use the **Zoom slider** at the bottom of the PowerPoint window to zoom in until you can easily read the text in the embedded presentation.

15. Click after the word *August*, tap Enter, and then tap Tab.

16. Type `Sycamore Rd` Enter `Spooner St` Enter `Clinton Way` Enter `Beacon St`.

17. Click on the slide, outside the embedded presentation.

18. Fit the slide to the window.

19. Save the presentation.

Create a Microsoft Account ID

20. If you have not yet created a Microsoft Account ID, start your web browser, navigate to `http://www.live.com`, and click **Sign Up Now**. Follow the steps on the web page to create a Microsoft Account ID and then close the web browser. If you have already created a Microsoft Account ID, continue with step 21.

Broadcast a Presentation

21. Find another student with whom to partner.

22. Choose **File→Share→Present Online**.

23. Click the **Present Online** button in the right column of **Backstage view**.

24. Enter your **Microsoft Account ID** and password in the dialog box and click **Sign In**.

25. Click **Copy Link**.

26. Start your email program. If you use a webmail service such as Outlook.com, Yahoo!, or Gmail, launch your web browser and sign in to your email page.

27. Compose an email to your partner. You will have to ask for your partner's email address.

28. Type the subject `Editing Broadcast` for the email's subject.

29. Click in the message body area, type **Use this link to view my PPT broadcast**, tap Enter to create a new line, and tap Ctrl + V to paste the copied link.

30. Tap Enter again to create a blank line under the pasted link.

31. Send the email and then close your email program (or web browser).

32. Click **Start Presentation**.

33. Have your partner check his/her email, open your message, and click the link in the email to the PowerPoint broadcast.

34. Navigate your slide show and ensure that your partner sees it on his/her screen.

35. End the slide show and choose **Present Online→Present Online→End Online Presentation**. Click **End Online Presentation** when prompted to confirm.

36. Choose **File→Account**.

37. Click **Sign Out** and then click **Yes** when prompted.

38. Save the presentation and then log out of **Windows** to completely clear your **Microsoft Account ID** from **PowerPoint**.

39. Submit your final files based on the guidelines provided by your instructor.
    To view examples of how your final file or files should look at the end of this exercise, go to the student resource center.

REINFORCE YOUR SKILLS PP09-R03
Work with Connected Presentations

In this exercise, you will connect presentations. You will also edit connected presentations and broadcast a presentation online.

Connect Presentations with Hyperlinks

1. Start **PowerPoint**. Open **PP09-R03-Kids** from your **PP2013 Lesson 09** folder and save it as **PP09-R03-Kids-[FirstInitialLastName]**.

2. Open **PP09-R03-College** from your **PP2013 Lesson 09** folder and save it as **PP09-R03-College-[FirstInitialLastName]**. Close the presentation.

3. Display slide 2, **Events**, and select the text *Details*.

4. Choose **Insert→Links→Hyperlink**.

5. From the **Link To** buttons, choose **Existing File or Web Page**.

6. In the **Look In** menu, browse to the **PP2013 Lesson 09** folder.

7. Choose **PP09-R03-Details** and click **OK**.
   The text Details *becomes a hyperlink.*

Connect Presentations with Actions

8. Display slide 4, **Program Benefits**, and select the text *College application*.

9. Choose **Insert→Links→Action**.

10. Choose the **Hyperlink To** option.

11. From the **Hyperlink To** menu, choose **Other PowerPoint Presentation**.

12. Navigate to the **PP2013 Lesson 09** folder, select **PP09-R03-College-[FirstInitialLastName]**, and click **OK**.

    The Hyperlink to Slide dialog box displays, prompting you to select a slide in the target presentation.

13. Ensure that the first slide, **Applying for College**, is selected and click **OK**.

14. Click **OK** to close the **Actions Settings** dialog box.

    The text College application *becomes a hyperlink.*

Connect Presentations with OLE

15. Display slide 3, **Next Event**.

16. Choose **Insert→Text→Object**.

17. Choose **Create from File**.

18. Click **Browse** and navigate to the **PP2013 Lesson 09** folder. Then choose **PP09-R03-June** and click **OK**.

19. Click **OK** to close the **Insert Object** dialog box.

20. Drag the **OLE image** so it is positioned on the slide to your liking.

View Connected Presentations

21. Choose **Slide Show→Start Slide Show→From Beginning**.

22. Navigate to the second slide.

23. Click the **Details** link to open the linked presentation.

24. Click through the linked presentation until you see a black **End of Slide Show** screen. Click the black screen to close the linked presentation and return to the main presentation.

25. Navigate to the **Next Event** slide.

26. Click the **OLE image** to open the embedded presentation.

27. Click through the **June Event** presentation until it ends and you return to the **Next Event** slide of the main presentation.

    Remember that presentations linked or embedded with OLE do not display the black End of Slide Show screen.

28. Navigate to the **Program Benefits** slide.

29. Click the **College application** link to open the linked presentation.

30. Click through the **Applying for College** presentation until it ends and you see a black **End of Slide Show** screen.

31. Click the black screen to close the linked presentation and return to the main presentation.

32. Tap Esc to end the slide show.

Edit Linked and Embedded Presentations

33. Display slide 4, **Program Benefits**.

34. Right-click the **College application** link.

35. Choose **Open Hyperlink** from the pop-up menu.

The linked presentation opens in a new PowerPoint window.

36. Display slide 2, **General Steps**.

37. Add a new sixth bullet with the text `Investigate financial aid`.

38. Save and close the **College** presentation.

39. Display slide 3, **Next Event**.

40. Double-click the picture of the embedded presentation.

41. Scroll the embedded presentation to the second slide.

42. Use the **Zoom slider** at the bottom of the PowerPoint window to zoom in until you can easily read the text in the embedded presentation.

43. Correct the spelling of the last word in the last bullet.

44. Click on the slide outside the embedded presentation.

45. Fit the slide to the window.

46. Save the presentation.

Create a Microsoft Account ID

47. If you have not yet created a Microsoft Account ID, start your web browser, navigate to `http://www.live.com`, and click the **Sign Up Now** link. Follow the steps on the web page to create a Microsoft Account ID and then close the web browser. If you have already created a Microsoft Account ID, continue to step 48.

Broadcast a Presentation

48. Find another student with whom to partner.

49. Choose **File→Share→Present Online**.

50. Click the **Present Online** button in the right column of **Backstage view**.

51. Enter your **Microsoft Account ID** and password in the dialog box when prompted and click **Sign In**.

52. Click **Copy Link**.

53. Start your email program. If you use a webmail service such as Outlook.com, Yahoo!, or Gmail, launch your web browser and sign in to your email page.

54. Compose an email to your partner. You will have to ask for your partner's email address.

55. Type the subject `Kids Broadcast` for the email's subject.

56. Click in the message body area and type `Use this link to view my PPT broadcast`, tap ⌷Enter⌷ to create a new line, and then tap ⌷Ctrl⌷+⌷V⌷ to paste the link that was copied in a previous step.

57. Tap ⌷Enter⌷ again to create a blank line under the pasted link.

58. Send the email and then close your email program (or web browser).

59. Click **Start Presentation**.

60. Have your partner check his/her email, open your message, and click the link in the email to the PowerPoint broadcast.

61. Navigate your slide show and ensure that your partner sees it on his/her screen.

62. End the slide show and choose **Present Online→Present Online→End Online Presentation**, and then click **End Online Presentation** when prompted to confirm.

63. Choose **File→Account**.

64. Click **Sign Out** and then click **Yes** when prompted.

65. Save the presentation and then log out of **Windows** to completely clear your **Microsoft Account ID** from **PowerPoint**.

66. Submit your final files based on the guidelines provided by your instructor.

Apply Your Skills

Connect Presentations

In this exercise, you will connect presentations developed by different people within the Universal Corporate Events organization.

Connect Presentations with Hyperlinks and Actions

1. Start **PowerPoint**. Open **PP09-A01-Main** from the **PP2013 Lesson 09** folder and save it as `PP09-A01-Main-[FirstInitialLastName]`.

2. Display slide 2, **Event Types**, and use a hyperlink to link the text *Celebrations* to **PP09-A01-Celebrations** in the **PP2013 Lesson 09** folder.
   The text Celebrations *becomes a hyperlink.*

3. Display slide 3, **Services**, and use an action to link the text *Catering* to the first slide of **PP09-A01-Catering** in the **PP2013 Lesson 09** folder.
   The text Catering *becomes a hyperlink.*

Connect Presentations with OLE

4. Display the last slide and use OLE to embed **PP09-A01-Specialties** in the **PP2013 Lesson 09** folder. Ensure that the embedded presentation displays as a thumbnail of the presentation rather than as a generic PowerPoint icon.

5. Size and position the embedded object to your liking.

View Connected Presentations

6. View the **Main** presentation as a slide show and test each of the three linked presentations.

7. End the slide show.

8. Save the presentation. Exit **PowerPoint**.

9. Submit your final files based on the guidelines provided by your instructor.
   To view examples of how your file or files should look at the end of this exercise, go to the student resource center.

Edit Connected Presentations and Present Online

In this exercise, you will edit linked and embedded presentations. You will also present a slide show online.

Connect Presentations with Hyperlinks

1. Start **PowerPoint**. Open **PP09-A02-Editing** from your **PP2013 Lesson 09** folder and save it as **PP09-A02-Editing-[FirstInitialLastName]**.

2. Open **PP09-A02-Stage** from your **PP2013 Lesson 09** folder and save it as **PP09-A02-Stage-[FirstInitialLastName]**. Close the presentation.

3. Display slide 3, **Services**, and use a hyperlink to link the text *Stage and sound equipment* to **PP09-A02-Stage-[FirstInitialLastName]** in the **PP2013 Lesson 09** folder.

    The text Stage and sound equipment *becomes a hyperlink.*

Edit Linked and Embedded Presentations

4. Open the **Stage and sound equipment** link.

5. Display the last slide and, in the title, change **Stooges** to **Stages**.

6. Save and close the **Stages** presentation.

7. Display the last slide and double-click the embedded presentation.

8. Display the last slide of the embedded presentation, zooming if necessary, and in the first bullet, change the word *certifiable* to **certified**.

9. Click on the slide, outside the embedded presentation, and save the presentation.

Create a Microsoft Account ID and Broadcast a Presentation

10. If you have not yet created a Microsoft Account ID, start your web browser, navigate to **http://www.live.com**, and click the **Sign Up Now** link. Follow the steps on the web page to create a Microsoft Account ID and then close the web browser.. If you have already created a Microsoft Account ID, continue to step 11.

11. Find another student with whom to partner.

12. Choose the **Present Online** option from **Backstage view**, sign in with your **Microsoft Account ID**, and copy the broadcast link.

13. Send an email to your partner that includes the link to your broadcasted presentation.

14. Start the broadcast.

15. Have your partner check his/her email, open your message, and click the link in the email to the PowerPoint broadcast.

16. Navigate your slide show and ensure that your partner sees it on his/her screen.

17. End the slide show and then end the online broadcast.

18. Sign out of your Microsoft Account ID.

19. Save the presentation and then log out of **Windows** to completely clear your **Microsoft Account ID** from **PowerPoint**.

20. Submit your final files based on the guidelines provided by your instructor.

    To view examples of how your file or files should look at the end of this exercise, go to the student resource center.

Work with Connected Presentations

In this exercise, you will connect presentations. You will also edit connected presentations and broadcast a presentation online.

Connect Presentations with Hyperlinks and Actions

1. Start **PowerPoint**. Open **PP09-A03-Universal** from the **PP2013 Lesson 09** folder and save it as **PP09-A03-Universal-[FirstInitialLastName]**.

2. Open **PP09-A03-Invitations** from your **PP2013 Lesson 09** folder and save it as **PP09-A03-Invitations-[FirstInitialLastName]**. Close the presentation.

3. Display slide 2, **In Focus**, and use a hyperlink to link the text *Invites* to **PP09-A03-Invitations-[FirstInitialLastName]** in the in **PP2013 Lesson 09** folder.

    The text Invites *becomes a hyperlink.*

4. Use an action to link the text *Transportation comfort* to the first slide of **PP09-A03-Transportation** in the **PP2013 Lesson 09** folder.

    The text Transportation comfort *becomes a hyperlink.*

Connect Presentations with OLE and View Connected Presentations

5. Use OLE to embed **PP09-A03-Catering** from the **PP2013 Lesson 09** folder. Ensure that the embedded presentation displays as a thumbnail of the presentation rather than as a generic PowerPoint icon.

6. Size and position the embedded object to your liking.

7. View the presentation as a slide show and test each of the three linked presentations.

8. End the slide show.

Edit Linked and Embedded Presentations

9. Open the **Invites** link.

10. Display **slide 3** and drag the top-right image down so that it overlaps the other image and no longer covers the text.

11. Save and close the **Invitations** presentation.

12. Double-click the embedded presentation.

13. Display slide 3, Vegan, of the embedded presentation, zooming if necessary, and in the first bullet, change the word **Been** to **Bean**.

14. Click on the slide, outside the embedded presentation, and save the presentation.

Create a Microsoft Account ID and Broadcast a Presentation

15. If you have not yet created a Microsoft Account ID, start your web browser, navigate to `http://www.live.com`, and click the **Sign Up Now** link. Follow the steps on the web page to create a Microsoft Account ID and then close the web browser. If you have already created a Microsoft Account ID, continue to step 16.

16. Find another student with whom to partner.

17. Choose the **Present Online** option from **Backstage view**, sign in with your **Microsoft Account ID**, and copy the **broadcast link**.

18. Send an email to your partner that includes the link to your broadcasted presentation.

19. Start the broadcast.

20. Have your partner check his/her email, open your message, and click the link in the email to the PowerPoint broadcast.

21. Navigate your slide show and ensure that your partner sees it on his/her screen.

22. End the slide show and then end the online broadcast.

23. Sign out of your Microsoft Account ID.

24. Save the presentation and then log out of **Windows** to completely clear your **Microsoft Account ID** from **PowerPoint**.

25. Submit your final files based on the guidelines provided by your instructor.

Extend Your Skills

In the course of working through the Extend Your Skills exercises, you will think critically as you use the skills taught in the lesson to complete the assigned projects. To evaluate your mastery and completion of the exercises, your instructor may use a rubric, with which more points are allotted according to performance characteristics. (The more you do, the more you earn!) Ask your instructor how your work will be evaluated.

PP09-E01 That's the Way I See It!

Everyone has their own opinion. Some people prefer chocolate to vanilla. Some would rather listen to classical than heavy metal music. Some like cats; some like dogs. Think of a question for which people usually have a preference between two answers, for example, "What is better—hot pizza or cold pizza?"

Create a presentation named **PP09-E01-Option1-[FirstInitialLastName]** that has at least three slides and shows why you believe the first answer is the best. Then create a second presentation named **PP09-E01-Option2-[FirstInitialLastName]** that has at least three slides and shows why you believe the second answer is the best. Finally, create a third presentation named **PP09-E01-Question-[FirstInitialLastName]**. Present the question on the title slide. Create a second slide that contains text or pictures that connect to the other two presentations. Connect to the presentations using hyperlinks, actions, or OLE. Format all three presentations with design themes of your choice and add anything else that you think enhances the presentations, such as pictures, additional text, animation, or audio/video. Arrange a time with your instructor to broadcast your presentation online using a Microsoft Account ID.

You will be evaluated based on the inclusion of all elements specified, your ability to follow directions, your ability to apply newly learned skills to a real-world situation, your creativity, and the relevance of your topic and/or data choice(s). Submit your final files based on the guidelines provided by your instructor.

PP09-E02 Be Your Own Boss

In this exercise, you will connect supporting presentations to a main Blue Jean Landscaping presentation. Open **PP09-E02-Blue** and **PP09-E02-Plants** from the **PP2013 Lesson 09** folder and save them as **PP09-E02-Blue-[FirstInitialLastName]** and **PP09-E02-Plants-[FirstInitialLastName]**, respectively. Close the Plants presentation.

On the *Services* slide, link *Lawn Care* to the **PP09-E02-Lawn** presentation and *Edible Gardens* to the **PP09-E02-Plants-[FirstInitialLastName]** presentation. Use OLE to embed the **PP09-E02-Custom** presentation next to the text *Garden Design*. From the main presentation, edit the linked **Edible Gardens** presentation and remove *Golden Chanterelle Mushrooms* from the list. Edit slide 5 of the embedded presentation so that the photo is centered on the slide like the others. Run the slide show and test the links. Use your Microsoft Account ID to broadcast the presentation to your instructor, another student, or the class.

You will be evaluated based on the inclusion of all elements specified, your ability to follow directions, your ability to apply newly learned skills to a real-world situation, your creativity, and your demonstration of an entrepreneurial spirit.

Transfer Your Skills

In the course of working through the Transfer Your Skills exercises, you will use critical-thinking and creativity skills to complete the assigned projects using skills taught in the lesson. To evaluate your mastery and completion of the exercises, your instructor may use a rubric, with which more points are allotted according to performance characteristics. (The more you do, the more you earn!) Ask your instructor how your work will be evaluated.

PP09-T01 Use the Web as a Learning Tool

Throughout this book, you will be provided with an opportunity to use the Internet as a learning tool by completing WebQuests. According to the original creators of WebQuests, as described on their website (WebQuest.org), a WebQuest is "an inquiry-oriented activity in which most or all of the information used by learners is drawn from the web." To complete the WebQuest projects in this book, navigate to the student resource center and choose the WebQuest for the lesson on which you are currently working. The subject of each WebQuest will be relevant to the material found in the lesson.

WebQuest Subject: Online Meetings

Submit your final file(s) based on the guidelines provided by your instructor.

PP09-T02 Demonstrate Proficiency

Stormy BBQ is creating a series of presentations to present online. Rather than have one person create the entire presentation, employees have created their own individual presentations showcasing their favorite barbeque recipe. The individual presentations must now be connected to a main presentation.

Open **PP09-T02-Carol** and **PP09-T02-Stormy** from the **PP2013 Lesson 09** folder and save them as `PP09-T02-Carol-[FirstInitialLastName]` and `PP09-T02-Stormy-[FirstInitialLastName]`, respectively. Close the Carol presentation. On the Stormy presentation, use hyperlinks or actions to connect the text on slide 2 to their respective presentations in the **PP2013 Lesson 09** folder, linking each presentation to their second slides (Ingredients). Embed Mini's recipe as an OLE object on the last slide. From the main Stormy presentation, edit Carol's recipe to indicate 2 tablespoons of chili power instead of 24 and edit Mini's recipe to simmer for 30 minutes rather than for 300. Run the slide show and test the links. Use your Microsoft Account ID to broadcast the presentation to your instructor, another student, or the class.

Submit your final file based on the guidelines provided by your instructor.

POWERPOINT 2013

Collaborating with Others Online

LEARNING OBJECTIVES

After studying this lesson, you will be able to:

- Send a presentation for review via email
- Attach, edit, review, and delete comments
- View multiple presentations at once
- Combine presentations
- Store, access, and edit files with Microsoft SkyDrive and Office Web Apps

PowerPoint 2013 allows you to collaborate on presentations by sharing your presentations with reviewers and having them add comments. You can then incorporate recommendations from multiple reviewers. PowerPoint also includes commands to automatically arrange several open presentations on the screen so you can easily compare versions and copy and paste between them. In this lesson, you will learn how to use the collaboration tools that PowerPoint 2013 offers and the document-sharing services available from Microsoft.

Working with Reviewers

Your latest presentation for Raritan Cinic East is ready for review, and you have learned that Microsoft offers some very powerful collaboration tools. Before leaving town for a medical conference, you ask the department chiefs to review the presentation, add comments, and make changes directly to it. You can later review their changes and, when finished, compare and incorporate the desired changes into the original presentation. You know that even though some of the department chiefs don't have PowerPoint, they can use Microsoft SkyDrive and Office Web Apps to review, edit, and comment on the presentation. Additionally, you are confident that while out of town and without your laptop, you can use Office Web Apps to make minor edits to the presentation from a computer at an Internet café in the conference hotel.

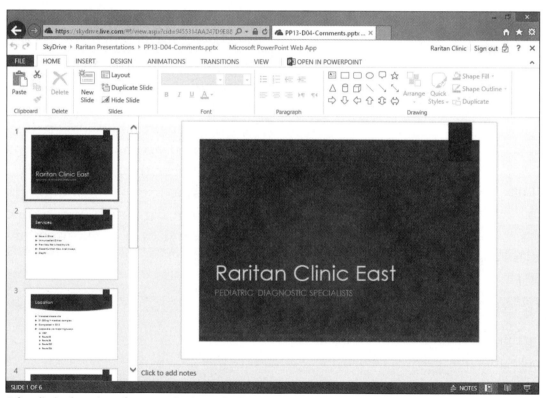

A free limited version of PowerPoint is available as a web app.

Collaborating Online

Video Library http://labyrinthelab.com/videos Video Number: PP13-V1001

If you have ever worked on a team presentation project, you know the havoc created as a presentation is passed from person to person for review. PowerPoint 2013 incorporates a commenting feature that allows reviewers to attach comments that can be read by anyone working on the presentation. The presentation creator can then read through all the comments and incorporate any desired changes into the presentation. Alternatively, a presentation can be shared via Microsoft SkyDrive. And when SkyDrive is used with Office Web Apps, reviewers can leave comments in a central location that can be read online rather than being attached to the actual presentation.

Setting Up a Review Cycle

The first steps in setting up a review cycle are to decide how you want to receive feedback from the reviewers and what your goals are. For example, do you want reviewers to make actual changes to the presentation or to simply write comments? Should the comments be attached to the presentation or should there be a centralized list of comments online that reviewers can simply add to? You indicate your preference in the email message that accompanies the presentation (assuming you are emailing the presentation to your reviewers) or the link to the presentation (if you are using SkyDrive). If you want to request the reviewers to make changes directly in the presentation, you should send them a copy of the presentation with a slightly different name so you can later identify who made the changes. You can then copy and paste the desired changes into your original presentation.

Following the Review Cycle Process

Regardless of the method you choose for collaborating, there is a standard review cycle process, which is shown in the following table.

THE REVIEW CYCLE PROCESS	
Process Step	**Performed By**
Send the presentation for review.	Original author
Review the presentation, making changes or adding comments.	Reviewer(s)
Return the presentation to the original author.	Reviewer(s)
Compare, merge, and finalize the reviewed presentation.	Original author

Sharing Files

Video Library   http://labyrinthelab.com/videos   Video Number: PP13-V1002

Before reviewers can do their job and edit or comment on a presentation, you must decide how to get the presentation to them. Copying a presentation to a CD and mailing it is slow. Instead, you can use the speed of the Internet to share your presentation several ways, including these:

- Email
- SkyDrive and Office Web Apps

Sharing Files via Email

Sharing files via email is a simple procedure, but as with any process, it has its own strengths and weaknesses.

STRENGTHS AND WEAKNESSES OF SHARING FILES VIA EMAIL	
Strengths	**Weaknesses**
■ No Microsoft Account ID is required. ■ Most users are already familiar with using email. ■ Attaching a presentation to an email is a simple process. ■ As reviewers must have PowerPoint, they can add comments directly to the presentation.	■ Managing several versions of the same presentation can be time-consuming. ■ Large presentations containing video, audio, or other linked files can be problematic to email. ■ Each reviewer must have PowerPoint installed to edit the presentation or insert comments.

Selecting an Email Program

When you use the option to send via email directly from PowerPoint, your email message is automatically created and the presentation automatically attached to the message. PowerPoint works with any email program or webmail service that you can select from the Windows Control Panel. If you want to change the default email service, you should make this selection before starting PowerPoint. Some email services (for example, most webmail services) don't support attaching the presentation automatically, so you must do so manually.

QUICK REFERENCE	SETTING THE DEFAULT EMAIL PROGRAM
Task	**Procedure**
Set the default email program (Windows 8)	■ Tap the Windows key, if necessary, to display the Desktop. ■ Press Windows+C. ■ Click Settings. ■ Click Control Panel. ■ Click Programs. ■ Click Set Your Default Programs. ■ Select your preferred email program from the list at the left. ■ Click Set This Program as Default in the right column.
Set the default email program (Windows 7)	■ Choose Start→Control Panel. ■ Click Programs. ■ Click Set Your Default Programs. ■ Select your preferred email program from the list at the left. ■ Click Set This Program as Default in the right column.

Using the Send Using Email Pane

The Share tab of Backstage view contains an Email pane that includes commands to attach the current presentation as a regular PowerPoint file, a PDF, an XPS document, or as an Internet fax. When you choose this command, PowerPoint immediately displays an email window with the file attached. You just need to address the email and type your message. You can also change the subject line, which defaults to the name of the file you are sending.

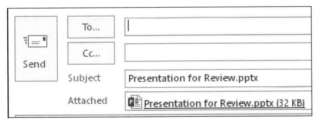

The Outlook 2013 message window (with presentation automatically attached) waiting to be addressed

Clicking the Send button in the Outlook window does not actually send the message. It simply saves it to your Outlook Outbox, where it remains until you start Outlook.

SEND USING EMAIL OPTIONS

Option	Explanation
Send as Attachment	▪ The file is attached in its current format. For example, if you have a PPTX file open (the default file format for PowerPoint), that PPTX file is attached to the email.
Send as PDF	▪ The presentation is converted to the PDF file format, and the PDF is attached to the email. ▪ The recipient must have the free Adobe Acrobat Reader or other PDF reader to open the attached PDF.
Send as XPS	▪ The presentation is converted to the XPS file format, and the XPS is attached to the email. ▪ XPS files can be opened with Internet Explorer.
Send as Internet Fax	▪ You must sign up with a fax service provider before using this option.

Naming Reviewer Copies

Experience shows that it works best to name each copy of a presentation sent out for review with the reviewer's name. Then as the presentations are returned from review, it's easy to track which reviewer sent each one.

Save all reviewer copies in a single folder to keep them together.

QUICK REFERENCE	SENDING A PRESENTATION VIA EMAIL
Task	**Procedure**
Send a presentation for review with Outlook, Windows 8 Mail, or Windows Live Mail	▪ Open the presentation in PowerPoint. ▪ (Optional but recommended) Choose File→Save As, rename the presentation, indicating which reviewer is to review this copy, and click Save. (A copy of the presentation is now saved with a new name and is currently open in PowerPoint.) ▪ Choose File→Share→Email→Send as Attachment. (The presentation is automatically attached to the email.) ▪ Enter the recipient's email address and, if desired, revise the Subject line. ▪ Click the Send button in the message window. ▪ Open your email program to actually send the message. ▪ Repeat the preceding steps for each reviewer.
Send a presentation for review by using another email program	▪ Open your email program and address a message for the first reviewer. ▪ Use your email program's procedure to attach the saved copy of the presentation and click Send.

Attach a Presentation to an Email Message

In this exercise, you will play the part of the original presentation author as you use PowerPoint to automatically attach the presentation to an email message you want to send to a reviewer.

Outlook must be configured for an email account or have been set up to function without an email account. Check with your instructor.

1. Start PowerPoint and maximize the program window.

2. Open **PP10-D01-Comments** from the **PP2013 Lesson 10** folder and save it as **PP10-D01-Comments-[FirstInitialLastName]**.

   Replace the bracketed text with your first initial and last name. For example, if your name is Bethany Smith, your filename would look like this: PP10-D01-Comments-BSmith.

   The original presentation is closed and the renamed copy remains open, ready to be emailed.

3. Choose **File→Share→Email→Send as Attachment**.

   The Outlook message window opens with the presentation already attached. At this stage, you could address the message, change the subject line if desired, and type the body of the message. Because these are familiar email tasks, we will skip them and simply close this new message.

4. Close the message window. Choose **No** if prompted to save the message.

5. Exit **PowerPoint** and choose **No** if prompted to save changes to the presentation.

   All programs should be closed, and you should be returned to your Desktop.

Opening an Attached Presentation

Video Library   http://labyrinthelab.com/videos   Video Number: PP13-V1003

With Outlook, Windows 8 Mail, or Windows Live Mail as the default email program, the recipient can open the attached presentation directly from the email message window. However, if any changes are made to a presentation opened directly from an email message, the presentation must be saved to the hard drive or the changes will be lost.

Use Save As to save the attached presentation immediately after opening it, and then make your changes.

PowerPoint 2013

Open and Save the Attached Presentation

In this exercise, you will play the part of a reviewer who has received a presentation to review. You will open and save a presentation attached to an email.

1. Starting from your Desktop, navigate to the **PP2013 Lesson 10** folder and double-click the Outlook message file named **PP10-D02-Review**.

   The message opens just as if you had received it normally.

2. Double-click the attached file to view it.

   Your screen may differ from the figure.

3. Click **Enable Editing** to enable the Ribbon commands.

   For security purposes, PowerPoint disables the Ribbon when an email attachment is opened.

> 🛡 PROTECTED VIEW Be careful—email attachments can contain viruses. Unless you need to edit, it's safer to stay in Protected View. ⬜ Enable Editing

4. Review the presentation, looking for comments and other changes.

   You will not make any changes now but will save the presentation to your hard drive so you can make changes later.

5. Close **PowerPoint** and choose **Don't Save** if prompted to save changes.

   The presentation attached to the email closes, and the Outlook window is visible.

   You will save the presentation so you can make and save changes to it later.

6. Right-click the attached file and choose **Save As** from the pop-up menu.

7. If necessary, navigate to the **PP2013 Lesson 10** folder from the Save Attachment dialog box.

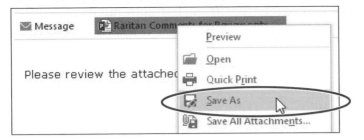

8. Name the file `PP10-D02-Review-[FirstInitialLastName]` and click **Save**.

9. Choose **File→Close** to close the email message window.

10. If necessary, choose **File→Exit** to close Outlook.

Working with Comments

Video Library   http://labyrinthelab.com/videos   Video Number: PP13-V1004

Attaching a comment in a PowerPoint presentation is the electronic equivalent of passing a printed copy of the presentation with a yellow sticky note on it to a team member and asking for a response. By using comments, you can send the presentation with your notes, questions, or concerns regarding individual slides to a reviewer and have that person add comments and return the presentation to you for review. With this method, reviewers do not make changes directly to the slides.

A comment on a slide. →

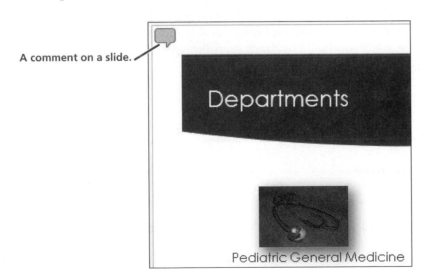

Reading Comments

Comments are visible only in Normal view. Slides containing a comment display a small speech bubble icon. Comments cannot be read directly on the slide, but instead display in the new Comments panel.

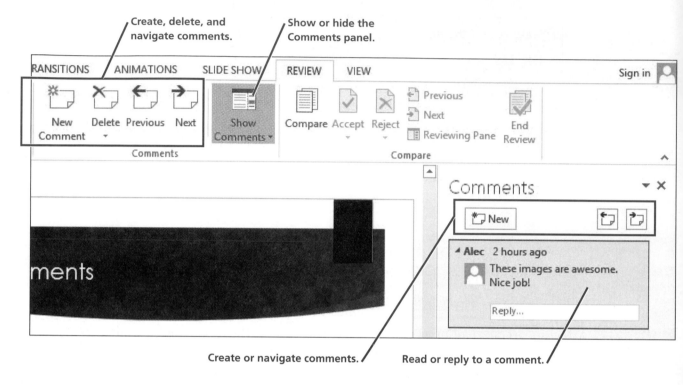

Create, delete, and navigate comments.

Show or hide the Comments panel.

Create or navigate comments.

Read or reply to a comment.

Setting the Comment Name

Each comment is identified by a name, which should be the name of the person who created the comment, but that's not always the case. Your name may be Alec, but how does PowerPoint know that? You may create a comment and discover it is labeled as Alec, even though that is not your name. Therefore, it's a good idea to check your PowerPoint options and ensure that PowerPoint is configured with your name.

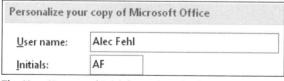

The User Name and Initials settings in the PowerPoint Options dialog box...

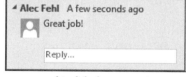

...are used to label comments.

Any comments you attach are labeled with your name as specified in the PowerPoint Options dialog box.

Personalize PowerPoint

In this exercise, you will personalize PowerPoint with your name and initials.

1. Start PowerPoint and maximize the program window.

   You must create or open a presentation so the File tab, Backstage, and PowerPoint options are available.

2. Click **Blank Presentation**.

   You will not save this blank presentation. You created it only to gain access to the File tab.

3. Choose **File→Options**.

4. Locate the **Personalize Your Copy of Microsoft Office** section in the PowerPoint Options dialog box and write down the current settings for User Name and Initials here:

   ■ User Name: _____

   ■ Initials: _____

   You will refer to these settings later so you can reset the PowerPoint options for other students.

5. Type your name in the **User Name** box.

6. Type your initials in the **Initials** box.

7. Click **OK**.

   Any comments you add or edit will be labeled with your name.

8. Choose **File→Close** to close the blank presentation. Choose **Don't Save** if prompted to save it.

Attaching Comments

Video Library   http://labyrinthelab.com/videos   Video Number: PP13-V1005

Comments can be added in three ways:

■ **Comment on selected text:** You can select text and then add a comment that appears beside the selection.

■ **Comment on a selected object:** You can select an object such as a chart or picture and then add a comment that appears beside the object.

■ **Comment on a slide:** When comments are attached to the slide as a whole, the comment appears in the top-left corner of the slide.

No matter where a comment appears, you can always drag it to a new location on the slide.

FROM THE RIBBON
Review→Comments→
New Comment

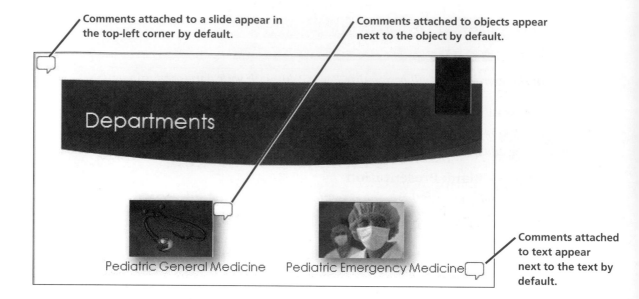

Comments attached to a slide appear in the top-left corner by default.

Comments attached to objects appear next to the object by default.

Comments attached to text appear next to the text by default.

Departments

Pediatric General Medicine   Pediatric Emergency Medicine

Navigating Comments

In large presentations with many slides, navigating from slide to slide searching for comments can be tedious. This can result in a huge waste of time. Imagine a 100-slide presentation with comments on slides 2 and 92. There would be no point in displaying slides 3–91 if all you were interested in were the comments. PowerPoint's Previous and Next commands allow you to skip to the next or previous comment in the presentation without having to view all the slides in between.

QUICK REFERENCE	USING COMMENTS IN PRESENTATIONS
Task	**Procedure**
Personalize PowerPoint with your name and initials	■ Choose File→Options. ■ Type your name and initials in the appropriate boxes in the Personalize Your Copy of Microsoft Office section. Click OK.
Attach a comment	■ Display the slide to receive the comment. ■ Select the text, picture, or other object to receive the comment; or click the slide on the Slide pane. ■ Choose Review→Comments→New Comment. ■ Type the comment then click outside the comment box.
Edit a comment	■ Select the comment indicator then open the Comments panel. ■ Click in the comment text, type the edit, and then click outside the comment box.
Delete a comment	■ Click the comment indicator to select it. ■ Choose Review→Comments→Delete; or point to the comment in the Comments panel and click the X in the top-right corner of the comment.
Navigate comments	■ Display any slide. ■ Choose Review→Comments→Previous or Next to navigate to the previous or next slide with a comment; or use the Previous and Next buttons in the Comments panel.

Attach Comments

In this exercise, you will attach comments in the Raritan Comments presentation.

1. Open **PP10-D04-Comments** from the **PP2013 Lesson 10** folder and save it as `PP10-D04-Comments-[FirstInitialLastName]`.

2. Display the fourth slide, **Operating Hours**.

3. Select the text *12:00 a.m.*

4. Choose **Review→Comments→New Comment**.

   A comment icon is placed next to the selected text, and the Comments panel opens, ready for you to type a comment.

5. In the comment box, type this text: **Should this be "midnight" instead of 12am?**

6. Click in an empty area outside the comment box.

7. Choose **Review→Comments→New Comment**.

   A comment icon is placed in the top-left corner of the slide, because no text or object was selected.

8. Type **Should we state we are open on holidays?** in the comment box, and then click outside the comment box.

Navigate and Read Comments

9. Display the title slide from the Slides pane.

   The Comments panel indicates there are no comments on this slide.

10. Choose **Review→Comments→Next**.

    The Operating Hours slide displays with the first comment highlighted in the Comments panel.

11. Continue clicking **Review→Comments→Next**, pausing to read each comment as it displays, until the end-of-presentation message appears.

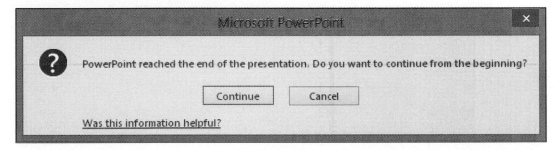

12. Click **Cancel**.

    You started searching for comments on the title slide, so there is no need to search for comments from the beginning again.

13. Save the presentation.

Editing and Deleting Comments

Video Library   http://labyrinthelab.com/videos   Video Number: PP13-V1006

FROM THE RIBBON
Review→Comments→
Delete

When presentations are undergoing a review process, it is typical for the presentation to be emailed back and forth between reviewers, each reading and commenting on previous comments. For example, the first reviewer may leave a comment such as *Should this list be sorted?* The original author may respond to that comment with *Alphabetically or by date?* The reviewer can respond with *By date.* By editing an existing comment, reviewers can enter into a dialogue.

After a comment has been read, the author can decide to honor the comment and make a change to the slide, or ignore the comment. Either way, the comment can be deleted when it is no longer needed.

Writing Effective Comments

Nobody likes to be attacked, berated, or made to feel inadequate. When leaving comments for others to read, try to be supportive and offer constructive criticism where appropriate. A comment such as *That color is awful* may hurt the reader's feelings and cause hostility or a stressful work environment. A more productive comment might be *That color is hard on the eyes— how about a light blue instead?* Try to offer suggestions for things you think need to be changed. Additionally, don't underestimate the power of compliments. Sometimes a simple comment such as *Good Job!* inspires a coworker's creativity and productivity.

DEVELOP YOUR SKILLS PP10-D05
Reply to and Delete Comments

In this exercise, you will reply to and delete comments.

1. Save the presentation as **PP10-D05-Comments-[FirstInitialLastName]**.

2. Click the comment indicator in the top-left corner of the **Departments** slide to highlight the comment in the Comments panel.

3. Click in the **Reply** box under the comment and type **Thank you**.

4. Click outside the comment box.

   The reply is indented and contained within the same comment box as the original comment. This makes it easy to keep track of which reply goes with an original comment. Notice that the top-left corner of the slide displays two overlapped comment icons, indicating a comment with a reply.

Delete Comments

5. Display slide 4, **Operating Hours**.

6. Click the comment indicator in the top-left corner of the slide to highlight the comment in the Comments panel.

7. Read the comment.

8. Point to the comment until an **X** appears in the top-right corner of the comment box.

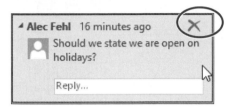

9. Click the **X** to delete the comment.

You could have deleted the comment from the Ribbon, but it is easier to delete it from the Comments panel because your eyes are already focused on the comment in the Comments panel.

10. Save your presentation.

Comparing and Merging Presentations

Video Library   http://labyrinthelab.com/videos   Video Number: PP13-V1007

When you receive reviewed presentations, you will compare them to the original and decide which changes you want to incorporate into the final presentation. If you use Outlook, Windows 8 Mail, or Windows Live Mail to check your email, you can open the presentation from the attached file in the email message by double-clicking it. If you use another email program, you may have to save the attached file to your hard drive before opening it in PowerPoint.

Viewing Multiple Presentations

The View→Window command group offers several commands that automate the process of arranging multiple open presentations on the screen. There are two automatic layouts you can use to quickly view more than one presentation at a time:

■ **Cascade (overlapped):** You can overlap presentations by using the Cascade command. When presentations are overlapped, you can see a large version of the presentation while easily switching from presentation to presentation. However, you can see only one presentation at a time.

■ **Arrange All (side by side):** When you display presentations side by side, the slide views are smaller but you can see several presentations at once.

Whichever command you use, you can always manually resize and reposition the presentation windows to your liking. The preceding Ribbon commands simply get you started.

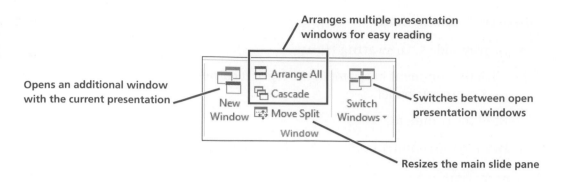

Opens an additional window with the current presentation

Arranges multiple presentation windows for easy reading

Switches between open presentation windows

Resizes the main slide pane

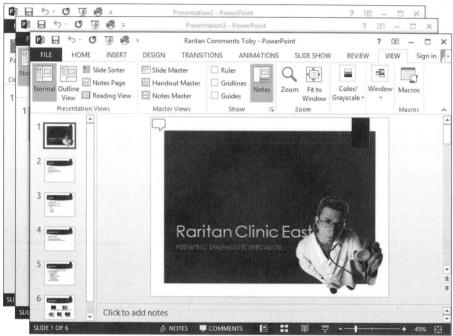

The Cascade command overlaps presentations, making it easy to switch among them.

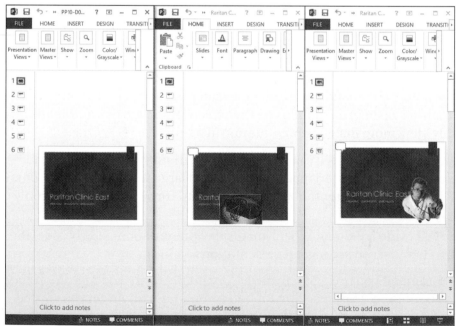

The Arrange All command positions presentations side by side, making it easy to compare them.

COMMANDS IN THE WINDOW COMMAND GROUP

Command	What It Does
New Window	■ Creates an additional window for the current presentation ■ Useful to work on two slides in the same presentation at once
Arrange All	■ Arranges all open presentations side by side ■ Useful to compare open presentations
Cascade	■ Overlaps all open presentations ■ Useful to quickly see which presentations are open
Move Split	■ Enables the use of the arrow keys on the keyboard to adjust the size of the Slides pane within a single PowerPoint window
Switch Windows	■ Used to switch between open presentations ■ An alternative to using the Windows taskbar to switch between PowerPoint windows

DEVELOP YOUR SKILLS PP10-D06
Compare Reviewed Presentations

In this exercise, you will compare two reviews of a presentation to the original, and incorporate some of their changes into the presentation.

1. Save the presentation as **PP10-D06-Comments-[FirstInitialLastName]**.

2. If necessary, display the title slide.

3. Open **PP10-D06-Rene** and **PP10-D06-Toby** from the **PP2013 Lesson 10** folder.

   You now have three versions of the presentation open—your original and the ones reviewed by Rene and Toby.

4. Choose **View→Window→Arrange All**.

   The three presentations are arranged side by side and are easy to compare.

Compare the Title Slides

5. Click the title slide in Toby's presentation (with the photo of the doctor), click the comment in the top-left corner, and read the comment in the Comments panel.

6. Close the **Comments panel** so you can see the slide again.

7. Click the title slide in Rene's presentation (with the photo of the doctor's bag), click her comment, and read it in the Comments panel.

   Both reviewers suggested a picture on the title slide. Toby's choice is more appropriate.

8. Close the **Comments panel**.

9. Click anywhere in Toby's presentation to make it active, select the picture, and choose **Home→Clipboard→Copy**.

10. Click the title slide in the original **PP10-D06-Comments-[FirstInitialLastName]** presentation and choose **Home→Clipboard→Paste**.

   The image is pasted to the same location on the original presentation.

Compare the Services Slide

11. Use the **Slides** panel to select the second slide in each of the three presentations so you can compare them.

    Only Toby has comments on slide 2.

12. Click anywhere in Toby's presentation to make it active, and then click his comment to read it.

    Toby has suggested alphabetizing the list of services. You will do just that.

13. Close the **Comments panel**.

14. Click anywhere in the original **PP10-D06-Comments-[FirstInitialLastName]** presentation to make it active.

    The slide is too small to work comfortably with the text.

15. Maximize the PowerPoint window for the original **PP10-D06-Comments-[FirstInitialLastName]** presentation.

16. Follow these steps to alphabetize the list of services:

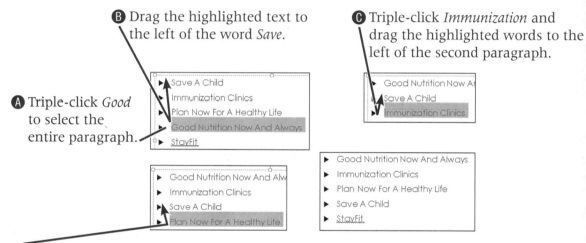

Ⓐ Triple-click *Good* to select the entire paragraph.

Ⓑ Drag the highlighted text to the left of the word *Save.*

Ⓒ Triple-click *Immunization* and drag the highlighted words to the left of the second paragraph.

Ⓓ Triple-click *Plan* and drag the highlighted paragraph so it becomes the third bullet point.

Ⓔ The paragraphs should be ordered as shown here.

The list of services is alphabetized.

17. Choose **View→Windows→Arrange All** to view all three presentations again side by side.

    The order of presentation windows from left to right may have changed.

Compare the Remaining Slides

18. Use the **Slides** panel to display the third slide in each presentation.

19. Read the comment in Rene's presentation and then close the **Comments panel**.

    You agree that this slide works better as a two-column layout.

20. Maximize the original **PP10-D06-Comments-[FirstInitialLastName]** presentation.

21. Choose slide 3, **Location**, if necessary.

22. Choose **Home→Slides→Layout→Two Content**.

23. Follow these steps to move the highway information to the new column:

Ⓐ Point to the left of *Accessible*.

Ⓑ Drag down and to the right to highlight all the highways.

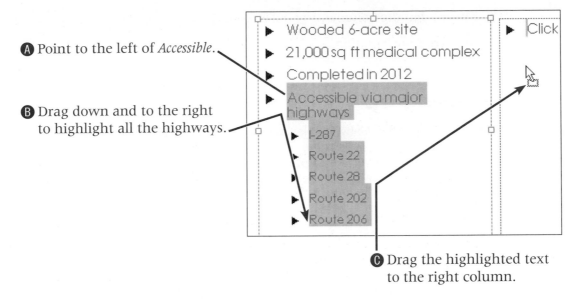

Ⓒ Drag the highlighted text to the right column.

The text is moved to the right column.

24. Choose **View→Windows→Arrange All**.
The order of presentation windows from left to right may have changed.

25. Display the fourth slide in each presentation and check for comments.
The fourth slide of each presentation contains the same comment from the original author. You will make the suggested change.

26. Maximize the original **PP10-D06-Comments-[FirstInitialLastName]** presentation.

27. Click the comment to read it and leave the Comments panel open.

28. Drag to select the text *12:00 a.m.* and then type `midnight`.

29. Point to the comment in the **Comments panel** and then click the **X** in the top-right corner of the comment to delete it.

30. Close the **Comments panel**.

Close the Reviewers' Presentations

31. Choose **View→Window→Switch Windows→PP10-D06-Toby**.
Toby's presentation displays in a smaller window than that of the original presentation.

32. Choose **File→Close** from Toby's presentation. If asked to save changes, choose **Don't Save**.

33. Choose **View→Window→Switch Windows→PP10-D06-Rene**.
Rene's presentation displays in a smaller window than that of the original presentation.

34. Choose **File→Close** from Rene's presentation. If asked to save changes, choose **Don't Save**.
Only the PP10-D06-Comments-[FirstInitialLastName] presentation is open.

35. Display the final slide and delete the comment in the top-left corner.

36. Ensure that the Comments panel is closed.

37. Save your presentation.

Cleaning Up

Video Library   http://labyrinthelab.com/videos   Video Number: PP13-V1008

It's nice to set any PowerPoint options you have changed back to the default settings so other students can use PowerPoint in its default state.

DEVELOP YOUR SKILLS PP10-D07
Reset PowerPoint Options

In this exercise, you will reset the User Name and Initials settings you changed earlier.

1. Choose **File→Options**.

2. Locate the **Personalize Your Copy of Microsoft Office** section in the PowerPoint Options dialog box.

3. Change the User Name and Initials settings back to the default settings you wrote down earlier in **Develop Your Skills PP10-D03**.

4. Click **OK**.

5. Close **PowerPoint**.

Using SkyDrive and Office Web Apps

Video Library   http://labyrinthelab.com/videos   Video Number: PP13-V1009

You may not always be at your computer or have access to your hard drive when you need to edit a file. For example, you may need to edit an important work document from home, but have no access to your work computer. With Microsoft SkyDrive™, you can store your files online so they are available from any computer with an Internet connection. With Office Web Apps, you can edit those files residing on SkyDrive even if you don't have the actual Microsoft Office programs installed on your computer.

Storing Files on SkyDrive

SkyDrive is a free service provided by Microsoft that allows you to store your files online. There are several benefits to this:

■ You can access your files from any computer with an Internet connection.

■ You don't need to worry about your hard drive crashing or USB drive breaking because your files are stored on the SkyDrive servers.

Task	Procedure
Save a presentation to SkyDrive if you are not already signed in	■ Open your presentation in PowerPoint. ■ Choose File→Save As and then choose SkyDrive. ■ Click Sign In and sign in with your Microsoft Account ID. ■ Choose [YourName] SkyDrive. ■ Click Browse and navigate to the desired folder on SkyDrive. ■ Name the file, click Save, and wait as the presentation is uploaded.
Sign in first and then save to SkyDrive	■ Open your presentation in PowerPoint. ■ Click Sign In and sign in with your Microsoft Account ID. ■ Choose File→Save As. ■ Choose [YourName] SkyDrive. ■ Click Browse and navigate to the desired folder on SkyDrive. ■ Name the file, click Save, and wait as the presentation is uploaded.
Access a file stored on SkyDrive	■ Start your web browser, navigate to http://skydrive.com, and sign in with your Microsoft Account ID. ■ Click the folder containing the file you want to access. ■ Click a file to view it. Or point to the file you want to access, select the checkbox in the file block's top-right corner, and click an action at the top of the web page.
Create a new file on SkyDrive	■ Start your web browser, navigate to http://skydrive.com, and sign in with your Microsoft Account ID. ■ Click Create at the top of the web page and choose the desired file type. ■ Type a filename and click Create. The file is ready for editing.
Open a file stored on SkyDrive from PowerPoint	■ Start PowerPoint and click Open Other Presentations. ■ Click SkyDrive and then click Sign In. ■ Sign in with your Microsoft Account ID. ■ Click SkyDrive and browse to the folder containing your presentation. ■ Double-click the desired presentation and wait for it to download and open.

PowerPoint 2013

DEVELOP YOUR SKILLS PP10-D08

Save a Presentation to SkyDrive

WebSim PP13-W1008

In this exercise, you will save a presentation to SkyDrive.

1. Type the URL for the student resource center into the address bar of your web browser and tap Enter.

   The student resource center URL is printed on the inside front cover of your book.

2. From the left navigation bar, click **Lessons 9–12**. Click the link for **PP10** and then **DYS PP13-W1008 Save a Presentation to SkyDrive**.

   The WebSim loads. The Raritan Final presentation is open in PowerPoint.

3. Work your way through the onscreen exercise instructions.

4. Click the **Back to Course** link.

Editing Files with Office Web Apps

Video Library http://labyrinthelab.com/videos   Video Number: PP13-V1010

Files that have been saved to SkyDrive can be edited online using Office Web Apps. These can be thought of as free online versions of Microsoft Office programs, but with limited functionality. Currently, Microsoft plans to support editing only PowerPoint, Word, Excel, and OneNote documents with Office Web Apps. Microsoft may add features to Web Apps just as they make changes to their website. The current version of the Web Apps may feature different capabilities than those found in the WebSim exercises.

The PowerPoint Web App features a Ribbon similar to the full version of PowerPoint, but lacks much of the functionality. Notice the absence of the Review and Slide Show tabs.

STRENGTHS AND WEAKNESSES OF OFFICE WEB APPS	
Strengths	**Weaknesses**
■ Files can be edited from any computer with an Internet connection.	■ The program requires a Microsoft Account ID.
■ Microsoft Office does not need to be installed.	■ Fewer features and capabilities are available than in the full Microsoft Office application.
■ Presentations display full color, backgrounds, and fonts.	

DEVELOP YOUR SKILLS PP10-D09
Edit a Presentation with Office Web Apps

WebSim PP13-W1009

In this exercise, you will edit a presentation with Office Web Apps.

1. From the left navigation bar, click **Lessons 9–12**. Click the link for **PP10** and then **DYS PP13-W1009 Edit a Presentation with Office Web Apps**.

   The WebSim loads, and the SkyDrive start page appears. The computer represented in the WebSim does not have PowerPoint installed. You will edit the presentation by using Office Web Apps.

2. Work your way through the onscreen exercise instructions.

3. Click the **Back to Course** link.

Sharing Files with SkyDrive

Video Library http://labyrinthelab.com/videos Video Number: PP13-V1011

In addition to editing files stored on SkyDrive yourself with Office Web Apps, you can share files and allow others to edit or comment on them. Alternatively, you can share files and allow others to only view or comment on them.

The default view does not indicate which folders are shared.

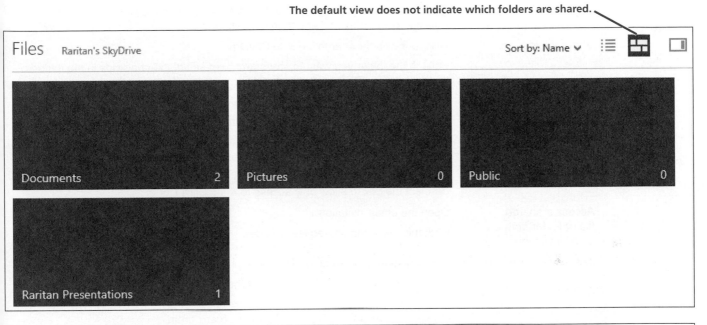

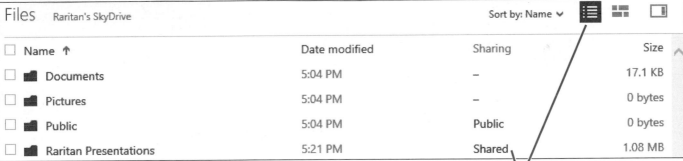

You can change to Detail view to see which folders are shared.

SkyDrive Shares

You can share individual files stored on SkyDrive, or entire folders. When you share a folder, all files inside the folder are automatically shared. You can easily create additional SkyDrive folders to more easily manage permissions. For example, you can create one folder that stores files you allow others to edit, and create another folder that stores files you allow the same people to only view.

QUICK REFERENCE	WORKING WITH SKYDRIVE FOLDERS
Task	**Procedure**
Create a folder and add files	■ Use your web browser to log in to SkyDrive. ■ Choose Create→Folder from the web page menu bar above the SkyDrive folder icons. ■ Type a name for your new folder and tap [Enter]. ■ Drag documents from your computer onto the folder in the web page window; or click the folder to open it and then click Upload.
Share a folder	■ Use your web browser to log in to SkyDrive. ■ Point to the folder you want to share and then select the checkbox in the folder's top-right corner. Repeat to select additional folders if desired. ■ Click Sharing at the top of the web page. ■ Enter the email address of the person with whom you would like to share the folder(s). ■ Type a message to include in the invitation email and click Share. ■ Leave the Can Edit checkbox selected to allow the user to edit the shared files, or deselect the box to allow only access to read. Click Done.
Access a shared file or folder from an email invitation	■ Open the email invitation. ■ Click the link to the shared file or folder.
Access a shared file or folder from within SkyDrive	■ Use your web browser to log in to SkyDrive. ■ Click the Shared link on the left side of the web page to view all files and folders others have shared with you. ■ Click any of the shared files or folders to access them.

DEVELOP YOUR SKILLS PP10-D10
Create a SkyDrive Folder

WebSim   PP13-W1010

In this exercise, you will create a SkyDrive folder to store shared documents.

1. From the left navigation bar, click **Lessons 9–12**. Click the link for **PP10** and then **DYS PP13-W1010 Create a SkyDrive Folder**.

   The WebSim loads, and the SkyDrive start page appears. You are already logged in as DrJacksonFromRaritan@hotmail.com.

2. Work your way through the onscreen exercise instructions.

3. Click the **Back to Course** link.

Moving Files

Video Library http://labyrinthelab.com/videos   Video Number: PP13-V1012

You may find it necessary to move files from one SkyDrive folder to another. For example, you may have a shared folder with documents that are being reviewed. Once the review process is complete, you may wish to move some files into a *final versions* folder.

DEVELOP YOUR SKILLS PP10-D11
Move Files

WebSim PP13-W1011

In this exercise, you will move a file from one SkyDrive folder to another.

1. From the left navigation bar, click **Lessons 9–12**. Click the link for **PP10** and then **DYS PP13-W1011 Move Files**.

   The WebSim loads, and the SkyDrive start page appears. You are already logged in as DrJacksonFromRaritan@hotmail.com.

2. Work your way through the onscreen exercise instructions.

3. Click the **Back to Course** link.

Setting Folder Permissions

Video Library http://labyrinthelab.com/videos   Video Number: PP13-V1013

Once a folder is created, you can set its permissions, allowing others to view or edit the files inside. SkyDrive lets you set global permissions and share a folder with the general public, or you can specify individuals by their email address. Any files stored in the folder will inherit the folder's permissions.

DEVELOP YOUR SKILLS PP10-D12
Share a Folder

WebSim PP13-W1012

In this exercise, you will share a SkyDrive folder and all the files within.

1. From the left navigation bar, click **Lessons 9–12**. Click the link for **PP10** and then **DYS PP13-W1012 Share a Folder**.

   The WebSim loads, and the SkyDrive page appears, displaying the contents of the For Review folder. You are already logged in as DrJacksonFromRaritan@hotmail.com.

2. Work your way through the onscreen exercise instructions.

3. Click the **Back to Course** link.

Accessing Shared Files

Once a file has been shared with you, accessing it is simple. You click the link to the file or folder in the invitation email, log in with your Microsoft Account ID if prompted, and edit the file just as if it were one of your own files on SkyDrive. If you no longer have the invitation email, you can still access files and folders that were shared with you via the Shared link on the SkyDrive main page.

The invitation email identifies who shared their files with you.

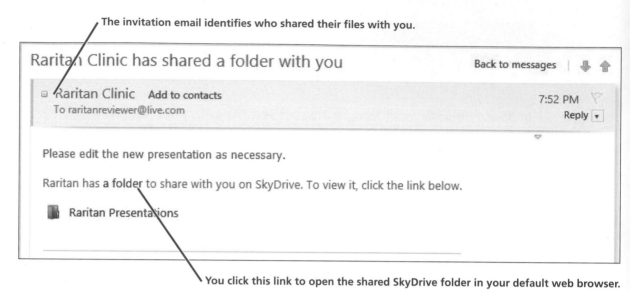

Raritan Clinic has shared a folder with you | Back to messages

⊟ Raritan Clinic   Add to contacts   7:52 PM
   To raritanreviewer@live.com   Reply ▾

Please edit the new presentation as necessary.

Raritan has **a folder** to share with you on SkyDrive. To view it, click the link below.

📁 Raritan Presentations

You click this link to open the shared SkyDrive folder in your default web browser.

Using Reference Tools

Video Library   http://labyrinthelab.com/videos   Video Number: PP13-V1014

PowerPoint offers thesaurus and translation capabilities, making it easy to find just the right word for your presentation. By default, PowerPoint supports English, French, and Spanish.

Using the Research and Thesaurus Panels

The reference tools are accessed through the Research and Thesaurus panels. You can drag the border of the panel to make it wider and easier to read the content. The Thesaurus panel helps you find alternatives for words, while the Research panel helps you translate words in addition to using the thesaurus.

The Research pane shows a translation of the word *Medicine* from English to French.

Use the Thesaurus and Research Panels

In this exercise, you will use the various tools provided in the Research panel.

1. Start PowerPoint. Open **PP10-D06-Comments-[FirstInitialLastName]** from your **PP2013 Lesson 10** folder and save it as `PP10-D13-Comments-[FirstInitialLastName]`.

2. Display the fifth slide, **Raritan Staff**, and double-click the word *specialists* at the bottom of the slide to select it.

   Selecting a word or phrase first saves you from having to type it in the Research panel.

3. Choose **Review→Proofing→Thesaurus**.

4. Follow these steps to replace the word *specialists* with one from the thesaurus:

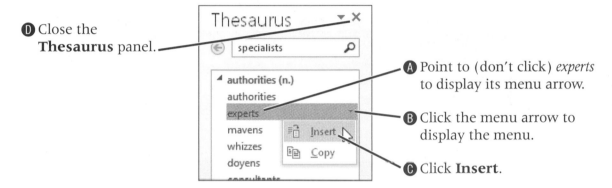

D Close the **Thesaurus** panel.

A Point to (don't click) *experts* to display its menu arrow.

B Click the menu arrow to display the menu.

C Click **Insert**.

The word experts *replaces the word* specialists *on the slide.*

Use the Translation Feature

5. Double-click the word *experts* at the bottom of the slide to select it.

6. Choose **Review→Proofing→Research**.

7. Follow these steps to perform a translation of the word *experts:*

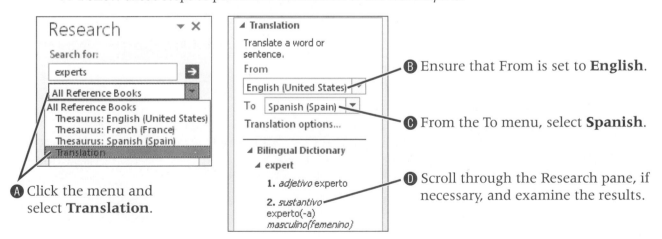

A Click the menu and select **Translation**.

B Ensure that From is set to **English**.

C From the To menu, select **Spanish**.

D Scroll through the Research pane, if necessary, and examine the results.

PowerPoint 2013

8. Close the **Research** pane.

9. Save your changes and close the file. Exit **PowerPoint**.

Concepts Review

To check your knowledge of the key concepts introduced in this lesson, complete the Concepts Review quiz by choosing the appropriate access option below.

If you are...	Then access the quiz by...
Using the Labyrinth Video Library	Going to http://labyrinthelab.com/videos
Using eLab	Logging in, choosing Content, and navigating to the Concepts Review quiz for this lesson
Not using the Labyrinth Video Library or eLab	Going to the student resource center for this book

Reinforce Your Skills

Work with Comments

In this exercise, you will work with email to exchange presentations. You will also add, reply to, and delete comments as you compare reviewed presentations.

Attach a Presentation to an Email Message

1. Start **PowerPoint** and maximize the program window.

2. Open **PP10-R01-Comments** from the **PP2013 Lesson 10** folder.

3. Choose **File→Share→Email→Send as Attachment**.

4. In the **To** box, type **raritanreviewer@live.com**.

5. In the **Message** box, type this text: **Please review this latest presentation. Thanks!**

   You would normally click Send at this point, but you will not actually send the email in this exercise. Instead, you will save the message so that you can submit it to your instructor later.

6. Save the message to your **PP2013 Lesson 10** folder as **PP10-R01-Comments-[FirstInitialLastName]**.

7. Choose **File→Close** and click **No** when prompted to save changes.

   The Outlook windows closes, and the email is neither sent nor placed in Outlook's Outbox.

8. Close **PowerPoint**.

Open and Save the Attached Presentation

9. Starting from your Desktop, navigate to the **PP2013 Lesson 10** folder and double-click the Outlook message file named **PP10-R01-Review**.

10. Double-click the attached presentation to view it.

11. Click **Enable Editing** to enable the Ribbon commands.

12. Review the presentation, looking for comments and other changes.

13. Close **PowerPoint** and choose **Don't Save** if prompted to save changes.

14. Right-click the attached file in the Outlook message and choose **Save As** from the pop-up menu.

15. If necessary, navigate to the **PP2013 Lesson 10** folder from the Save Attachment dialog box.

16. Name the file **PP10-R01-Review-[FirstInitialLastName]** and click **Save**.

17. Choose **File→Close** to close the email message window.

18. If necessary, choose **File→Exit** to close Outlook.

Personalize PowerPoint

19. Starting from your Desktop, navigate to the **PP2013 Lesson 10** folder and double-click **PP10-R01-Review-[FirstInitialLastName]**.

20. Click **Enable Editing** to enable the Ribbon commands.

21. Choose **File→Options**.

22. Locate the **Personalize Your Copy of Microsoft Office** section in the PowerPoint Options dialog box and write down the current settings for User Name and Initials here:

User Name: _____

Initials: _____

You will refer to these settings later so you can reset the PowerPoint options for other students.

23. Type your name in the **User Name** box and your initials in the **Initials** box. Click **OK**.

Attach Comments

24. Display the title slide, if necessary.

25. Choose **Review→Comments→New Comment**.

26. Type **I like the background** and then click the slide to deselect the comment.

Reply to and Delete Comments

27. Choose **Review→Comments→Next**.
The title slide comment is displayed.

28. Choose **Review→Comments→Next**.
The comment on slide 2 is displayed.

29. Read the comment and then click the **X** in the comment box to delete it.
The suggested change is a good one.

30. Double-click the word *Reasons* and type **Purpose** to replace it.

31. Choose **Review→Comments→Next**.

32. Read the comment and then click the **X** in the comment box to delete it.
The suggested change is a good one.

33. Change the word *house* to **House** so that it is capitalized.

34. Choose **Review→Comments→Next**.

35. Read the comment and then click in the **Reply** box.

36. Type **Yes. All locations are still planned.**

37. Close the **Comments panel**.

38. Save the presentation.

Compare Reviewed Presentations

39. Choose **File→Open**, browse to the **PP2013 Lesson 10** folder, and open **PP10-R01-Merilyn**.

40. Choose **View→Windows→Arrange All**.

41. Display the title slide in each presentation.

42. Click the comment on each title slide and read the comment in each presentation.
The original green color scheme is preferred.

43. Click the **Next** button in Merilyn's Comments panel.

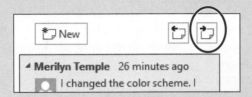

44. Read Merilyn's comment and then close the **Comments panel**.
Her comment refers to the word March *on slide 4.*

45. Click the original presentation to make it active and then close the **Comments panel**.

46. Display **slide 4** in the original presentation.

47. Double-click the word *March* and type **April**.

48. Click the comment in Merilyn's presentation to show the Comments panel and then click the **Next** button to display her next comment.

49. Read her comment and note that the **Slides** panel indicates this comment is on **slide 5**.

50. Display **slide 5** in the original presentation and add **M&M Construction** to the bottom of the bulleted list.

51. Click the **Next** button in Merilyn's Comments panel to view the next comment.
There are no more comments in her presentation.

52. Click **Cancel**.

53. Choose **File→Close** in Merilyn's presentation to close it.
Only the original presentation is open.

54. Maximize the PowerPoint window.

55. Choose **Review→Comments→Delete menu ▼→Delete All Comments and Ink in This Presentation** and then click **Yes** to confirm.
The Comments panel opens and indicates no comments exist.

56. Close the **Comments panel**.

Reset PowerPoint Options

57. Choose **File→Options**.

58. Locate the **Personalize Your Copy of Microsoft Office** section in the **PowerPoint Options** dialog box.

59. Change the **User Name** and **Initials** settings back to the default settings you wrote down earlier in this exercise.

60. Click **OK**.

Use the Thesaurus

61. Display slide 3, **Purpose**.

62. Double-click the word *responsibility*.

63. Choose **Review→Proofing→Thesaurus**.

64. In the **Thesaurus panel**, point to the word *obligation* and then click the arrow menu to display the option for *obligation*.

65. Choose **Insert**.

The word responsibility *is replaced with the word* obligation.

66. Close the **Thesaurus panel**.

67. Save and close the presentation. Exit **PowerPoint**.

68. Submit your final file based on the guidelines provided by your instructor.

To view examples of how your final file or files should look at the end of this exercise, go to the student resource center.

REINFORCE YOUR SKILLS PP10-R02
Use SkyDrive and Web Apps

WebSim   PP13-WR1002

In this exercise, you will use SkyDrive to store a presentation and the Office Web Apps to edit it.

1. If necessary, type the URL for the student resource center into the address bar of your web browser and tap Enter.

The student resource center URL is printed on the inside front cover of your book.

2. From the left navigation bar, click **Lessons 9–12**. Click the link for **PP10** and then **RYS PP13-WR1002 Use SkyDrive and Web Apps**.

The WebSim loads, and the SkyDrive start page appears. The computer represented in the WebSim does not have PowerPoint installed. You will edit the presentation by using Office Web Apps.

3. Work your way through the onscreen exercise instructions.

4. Click the **Back to Course** link.

Review Presentations

In this exercise, you will use PowerPoint comments to aid in the review process of a presentation. You will also use SkyDrive and Office Web Apps to share and edit a presentation.

Attach a Presentation to an Email Message

1. Start **PowerPoint** and maximize the program window.

2. Open **PP10-R03-KidsComments** from the **PP2013 Lesson 10** folder.

3. Choose **File→Share→Email→Send as Attachment**.

4. In the **To** box, type `raritanreviewer@live.com`.

5. In the **Message** box, type this text: `Please review this latest presentation and then send it on to the team. Thanks!`
   You would normally click Send at this point, but you will not actually send the email in this exercise.

6. Save the message to your **PP2013 Lesson 10** folder as `PP10-R03-KidsComments-[FirstInitialLastName]`.

7. Choose **File→Close** and click **No** when prompted to save changes.
   The Outlook window closes, and the email is neither sent nor placed in Outlook's Outbox.

8. Close **PowerPoint**.

Open and Save the Attached Presentation

9. Starting from your Desktop, navigate to the **PP2013 Lesson 10** folder and double-click the Outlook message file named **PP10-R03-Review**.

10. Double-click the attached presentation to view it.

11. Click **Enable Editing** to enable the Ribbon commands.

12. Review the presentation, looking for comments and other changes.

13. Choose **File→Save As**, browse to the **PP2013 Lesson 10** folder, and save the presentation as `PP10-R03-Review-[FirstInitialLastName]`.

14. Click the **Outlook button** in the **Windows taskbar**.

15. Chose **File→Close** to close the Outlook email window.

Personalize PowerPoint

16. In PowerPoint, choose **File→Options**.

17. Locate the **Personalize Your Copy of Microsoft Office** section in the PowerPoint Options dialog box and write down the current settings for User Name and Initials here:

    User Name: _____

    Initials: _____
    You will refer to these settings later so you can reset the PowerPoint options for other students.

18. Type your name in the **User Name** box and your initials in the **Initials** box. Click **OK**.

PowerPoint 2013

Attach Comments

19. Display the title slide, if necessary.

20. Choose **Review→Comments→New Comment**.

21. Type `I love the blue theme!` and then click the slide to deselect the comment.

Reply to and Delete Comments

22. Choose **Review→Comments→Next**.

The title slide comment is displayed.

23. Choose **Review→Comments→Next**.

The comment on slide 2 is displayed.

24. Read the comment and then click the **X** in the comment box to delete it.

You will address this suggestion later, after comparing the presentations of other reviewers.

25. Choose **Review→Comments→Next**.

26. Read the comment and then click the **X** in the comment box to delete it.

The suggested change is a good one.

27. Select the **1 + 1 = 2 picture** and tap Delete.

28. Choose **Review→Comments→Next**.

29. Read the comment and then click in the **Reply** box.

30. Type `Yes. See my comment on the first slide!`.

31. Close the **Comments panel**.

32. Save the presentation.

Compare Reviewed Presentations

33. Choose **File→Open**, browse to the **PP2013 Lesson 10** folder, and open **PP10-R03-Malcolm**.

34. Choose **File→Open**, browse to the **PP2013 Lesson 10** folder, and open **PP10-R03-Marita**.

35. Choose **View→Windows→Arrange All**.

36. Display the title slide in each presentation.

37. Click the comment on each title slide and read the comment in each presentation.

The original green-blue scheme is preferred.

38. Click the **Next** button in Malcolm's Comments panel.

39. Read Malcolm's comment.

His comment refers to the word Better *on slide 2. You can see slide 2 is selected in Malcolm's Slides panel. You will address this comment later.*

40. Click the **Next** button in Malcolm's Comments panel.

His comment refers to the word picture *on slide 3.*

41. Close Malcolm's Comments panel so you can see the picture on which he commented.

42. Click Malcolm's comment to display the **Comments panel** and then click **Next Comment**.

43. Click **Cancel** when prompted to search for more comments starting at the title slide.

44. Close Malcolm's presentation and choose **Don't Save** if prompted to save changes.

45. Maximize the original presentation and then choose **View→Window→Arrange All** to redistribute the two open presentations.

46. Read the comment on Marita's title slide.

    The original green-blue scheme is preferred.

47. Click the **Next** button in Marita's Comments panel.

48. Read Marita's comment, and then close Marita's Comments panel so you can see the period to which she refers.

    The period is in the last bulleted paragraph, which is fine, because it is a sentence, whereas the others are not. As this comment was on the last slide, you can close the presentation.

49. Choose **File→Close** in Marita's presentation to close it.

    Only the original presentation is open.

50. Maximize the PowerPoint window.

51. Close the **Comments panel**.

Reset PowerPoint Options

52. Choose **File→Options**.

53. Locate the **Personalize Your Copy of Microsoft Office** section in the **PowerPoint Options** dialog box.

54. Change the **User Name** and **Initials** settings back to the default settings you wrote down earlier in this exercise.

55. Click **OK**.

Use the Thesaurus

56. Display slide 2, **Benefits**.

57. Double-click the word *Better* in the first paragraph.

58. Choose **Review→Proofing→Thesaurus**.

59. In the **Thesaurus panel**, point to the word *Improved* and then click the arrow menu to display the option for *Improved*.

60. Choose **Insert**.

    The word Better *is replaced with the word* Improved.

61. Double-click the word *Better* in the second paragraph.

62. In the **Thesaurus panel**, scroll down until you can see the word *Enhance*.

63. Point to the word *Enhance* and then click the arrow menu to display the option for *Enhance*.

64. Choose **Insert**.

    The word Better *is replaced with the word* Enhance.

65. Type **d** so the word on the slide becomes *Enhanced*.

66. Close the **Thesaurus panel**.

67. Save the presentation and close **PowerPoint**.

Use SkyDrive and Office Web Apps

WebSim PP13-WR1003

68. If necessary, type the URL for the student resource center into the address bar of your web browser and tap Enter.

    The student resource center URL is printed on the inside front cover of your book.

69. From the left navigation bar, click **Lessons 9–12**. Click the link for **PP10** and then **RYS PP13-WR1003 Use SkyDrive and Office Web Apps**.

    The WebSim loads, and the SkyDrive start page appears. The computer represented in the WebSim does not have PowerPoint installed. You will edit the presentation by using Office Web Apps.

70. Work your way through the onscreen exercise instructions.

71. Click the **Back to Course** link.

Apply Your Skills

APPLY YOUR SKILLS PP10-A01

Work with Email and Comments

In this exercise, you will exchange a presentation with a review via email so that you may compare presentations and work with comments.

Attach, Open, and Save an Email Message Attachment

1. Start **PowerPoint**. Open **PP10-A01-Maintenance** from the **PP2013 Lesson 10** folder.

2. Attach the presentation to an email from within PowerPoint, using `raritanreviewer@live.com` as the recipient's address and a message of your choice.

3. In the Outlook window, choose **File→Save As** and save the email message as `PP10-A01-Maintenance-[FirstInitialLastName]`.

4. Close **Outlook** and do not save changes if prompted. Close **PowerPoint**.

5. Starting from your Desktop, navigate to the **PP2013 Lesson 10** folder and open the Outlook message file named **PP10-A01-Review**.

6. Open the attached presentation, save it to the **PP2013 Lesson 10** folder as `PP10-A01-Review-[FirstInitialLastName]`, and close Outlook.

Personalize PowerPoint and Work with Comments

7. View the PowerPoint options and write down the current settings for User Name and Initials here:

   User Name: _____

   Initials: _____
   You will refer to these settings later so you can reset the PowerPoint options for other students.

8. Change the options to use your name and initials.

9. Add a comment to the title slide that says `Should we change the subtitle to "Maintenance Meeting"?`

10. Read the other comment on the title slide and then delete it.

11. Read the comment on **slide 2** and reply to it with the message `I agree. Interior detailing on Limo 2 is a must!`

12. In the table cell for **Limo 2's Interior Detailing**, type `Yes`.

Compare Reviewed Presentations and Reset PowerPoint Options

13. Open **PP10-A01-Chelsea** from the **PP2013 Lesson 10** folder and view both presentations side by side.

14. Read the comment on Chelsea's title slide.

15. Apply the **Ion Boardroom** theme to the original presentation.

16. Read the next comment in Chelsea's presentation.

    No action is required for this comment, because you already made the change based on a previous comment.

17. Close Chelsea's presentation, maximize the remaining presentation, and close the **Comments panel**.

18. Access **PowerPoint's options** and change the **User Name** and **Initials** settings back to the default settings you wrote down earlier in this exercise.

Use the Thesaurus

19. Select the word *Maintenance* in the title of **slide 2** and use the **Thesaurus panel** to find an alternate word.

20. Use the **Thesaurus panel** to replace *Maintenance* with a word of your choice and then close the **Thesaurus panel**.

21. Save and close the presentation. Exit **PowerPoint**.

22. Submit your final files based on the guidelines provided by your instructor.

    To view examples of how your file or files should look at the end of this exercise, go to the student resource center.

APPLY YOUR SKILLS PP10-A02

Use SkyDrive and Web Apps

WebSim PP13-WA1002

In this exercise, you will use SkyDrive to store a presentation and the Office Web Apps to edit it.

1. If necessary, type the URL for the student resource center into the address bar of your web browser and tap Enter.

   The student resource center URL is printed on the inside front cover of your book.

2. From the left navigation bar, click **Lessons 9–12**. Click the link for **PP10** and then **AYS PP13-WA1002 Use SkyDrive and Web Apps**.

   The WebSim loads, and the SkyDrive start page appears. The computer represented in the WebSim does not have PowerPoint installed. You will edit the presentation by using Office Web Apps.

3. Work your way through the onscreen exercise instructions.

4. Click the **Back to Course** link.

Review Presentations

In this exercise, you will use PowerPoint comments to aid in the review process of a presentation. You will also use SkyDrive and Office Web Apps to share and edit a presentation.

Attach, Open, and Save an Email Message Attachment

1. Start **PowerPoint**. Open **PP10-A03-Work** from the **PP2013 Lesson 10** folder.

2. Attach the presentation to an email from within PowerPoint, using `raritanreviewer@live.com` as the recipient's address and a message of your choice.

3. In the Outlook window, choose **File→Save As** and save the email message as `PP10-A03-Work-[FirstInitialLastName]`.

4. Close **Outlook** and do not save changes if prompted. Close **PowerPoint**.

5. Starting from your Desktop, navigate to the **PP2013 Lesson 10** folder and open the Outlook message file named **PP10-A03-Review**.

6. Open the attached presentation, save it to the **PP2013 Lesson 10** folder as `PP10-A03-Review-[FirstInitialLastName]`, and then close Outlook.

Personalize PowerPoint and Work with Comments

7. View the PowerPoint options and write down the current settings for User Name and Initials here:

   User Name: _____

   Initials: _____

   You will refer to these settings later so you can reset the PowerPoint options for other students.

8. Change the options to use your name and initials.

9. Add a comment to the title slide that says `Should we add a photo in the big blue space?`

10. Read the next comment (on **slide 2**) and then type `Customers` in the empty table cell above the logos.

11. Read the next comment about the addition of the logos and then delete the comment.

12. Close the **Comments panel**.

Compare Reviewed Presentations and Reset PowerPoint Options

13. Open **PP10-A03-Salvador** from the **PP2013 Lesson 10** folder and view both presentations side by side.

14. Read the first comment on Salvador's title slide.

15. Add a space between the words *Corporate* and *Events* in the slide title.

16. Read the next comment on **Salvador's title slide**.

17. Change the word *Working* in the subtitle to **Work**.

18. Read the next comment in Salvador's presentation.

19. Display **slide 2** in the original presentation and change each of the four instances of *Brad* to **Josh**.

20. Close Salvador's presentation, maximize the remaining presentation, and close the **Comments panel**.

21. Access **PowerPoint's options** and change the **User Name** and **Initials** settings back to the default settings you wrote down earlier in this exercise.

Use the Thesaurus

22. Select the word *Customers* in the first column of the table on **slide 2** and use the **Thesaurus panel** to find an alternate word.

23. Use the **Thesaurus panel** to replace *Customers* with the word **Clients** and then close the **Thesaurus panel**.

24. Save and close the presentation. Exit **PowerPoint**.

Use SkyDrive and Office Web Apps

WebSim   PP13-WA1003

25. If necessary, type the URL for the student resource center into the address bar of your web browser and tap [Enter].

    The student resource center URL is printed on the inside front cover of your book.

26. From the left navigation bar, click **Lessons 9–12**. Click the link for **PP10** and then **AYS PP13-WA1003 Use SkyDrive and Office Web Apps**.

    The WebSim loads, and the SkyDrive start page appears. The computer represented in the WebSim does not have PowerPoint installed. You will edit the presentation by using Office Web Apps.

27. Work your way through the onscreen exercise instructions.

28. Click the **Back to Course** link.

Extend Your Skills

In the course of working through the Extend Your Skills exercises, you will think critically as you use the skills taught in the lesson to complete the assigned projects. To evaluate your mastery and completion of the exercises, your instructor may use a rubric, with which more points are allotted according to performance characteristics. (The more you do, the more you earn!) Ask your instructor how your work will be evaluated.

PP10-E01 That's the Way I See It!

Go to Yahoo.com, create a new (free) Yahoo account, and spend some time navigating the email interface. Sign out of Yahoo. Then create a new (free) Outlook.com email account. Explore the interface then sign out of Outlook.com.

Create a presentation named **PP10-E01-EmailCompare-[FirstInitialLastName]** and saved to the **PP2013 Lesson 10** folder. Create a title slide indicating that the presentation compares Yahoo to Outlook.com. Create four more slides: one listing three things you like about Yahoo, one listing three things you dislike about it, one listing three things you like about Outlook.com, and one that states three things you dislike about Outlook.com. Add a comment to the title slide that shows your new Yahoo and Outlook.com email addresses. Apply a design theme and add graphical elements to enhance it. Save a copy of the presentation to SkyDrive by using your Outlook.com account login as the Microsoft Account ID. Share the presentation with your instructor (ask for your instructor's email address).

You will be evaluated based on the inclusion of all elements specified, your ability to follow directions, your ability to apply newly learned skills to a real-world situation, your creativity, and the relevance of your topic and/or data choice(s). Submit your final file based on the guidelines provided by your instructor.

PP10-E02 Be Your Own Boss

In this exercise, you will partner with a classmate and exchange presentations via SkyDrive. You must have a Microsoft Account ID and be able to access SkyDrive.com. You will also need your partner's email address.

Search the Internet for common garden pests and environmentally friendly ways to control them. Create a presentation with at least four slides that describe a few garden pests and methods of controlling them. Format the presentation to be visually appealing and save it to SkyDrive in a folder named **Gardening** as **PP10-E02-Blue-[FirstInitialLastName]**. Share the folder with your partner. Close PowerPoint. Access your partner's shared folder and edit that presentation in the PowerPoint Web App. Using the Comments panel, add at least two edits. Send your partner an email when your review is complete.

Start PowerPoint and, using the File tab, open your presentation from SkyDrive. Reply to each comment from your partner and edit your presentation as you see fit. Use the Thesaurus panel to change one word and add a comment noting the change. Save the presentation. Save a copy of it to the **PP2013 Lesson 10** folder as **PP10-E02-Blue-[FirstInitialLastName]**.

You will be evaluated based on the inclusion of all elements specified, your ability to follow directions, your ability to apply newly learned skills to a real-world situation, your creativity, and your demonstration of an entrepreneurial spirit. Submit your final file based on the guidelines provided by your instructor.

Transfer Your Skills

In the course of working through the Transfer Your Skills exercises, you will use critical-thinking and creativity skills to complete the assigned projects using skills taught in the lesson. To evaluate your mastery and completion of the exercises, your instructor may use a rubric, with which more points are allotted according to performance characteristics. (The more you do, the more you earn!) Ask your instructor how your work will be evaluated.

PP10-T01 Use the Web as a Learning Tool

Throughout this book, you will be provided with an opportunity to use the Internet as a learning tool by completing WebQuests. According to the original creators of WebQuests, as described on their website (WebQuest.org), a WebQuest is "an inquiry-oriented activity in which most or all of the information used by learners is drawn from the web." To complete the WebQuest projects in this book, navigate to the student resource center and choose the WebQuest for the lesson on which you are currently working. The subject of each WebQuest will be relevant to the material found in the lesson.

WebQuest Subject: Cloud Storage

Submit your final file(s) based on the guidelines provided by your instructor.

PP10-T02 Demonstrate Proficiency

Stormy BBQ is finalizing its presentation that features employee recipes. Two employees have reviewed the presentation and have offered comments. You need to compare these presentations, make changes as necessary, and add your own comment before emailing your version to the restaurant.

Open **PP10-T02-Benji** from the **PP2013 Lesson 10** folder and save it as **PP10-T02-Recipe-[FirstInitialLastName]**. Then open **PP10-T02-Jenice** and arrange both presentations side by side. Read the comments on both presentations and edit **PP10-T02-Recipe-[FirstInitialLastName]** as you see fit. When you are finished, delete all comments in **PP10-T02-Recipe-[FirstInitialLastName]**. Add a new comment to the title slide of **PP10-T02-Recipe-[FirstInitialLastName]** indicating that you are finished with your edits.

Attach the presentation to an Outlook email addressed to **stormy@example.com**. Write an appropriate message. Rather than sending the email, save it as **PP10-T02-Email-[FirstInitialLastName]** in your **PP2013 Lesson 10** folder.

Submit your final files based on the guidelines provided by your instructor.

Transporting Presentations

LESSON OUTLINE

Transporting the Presentation

Preparing the Meeting Room

Following the Presentation Setup Checklist

Preparing for Success

Targeting Your Audience

Concepts Review

Reinforce Your Skills

Apply Your Skills

Extend Your Skills

Transfer Your Skills

LEARNING OBJECTIVES

After studying this lesson, you will be able to:

- Package a presentation
- Transfer a presentation to a USB flash drive
- Use the PowerPoint Viewer
- Burn a presentation to a CD
- Prepare a meeting room

In this lesson, you will learn about transporting presentations from your computer to another computer. This lesson also addresses other vital components of a successful presentation, such as setting up the meeting room and preparing everything from the lights to the hardware and software. The checklists and guides presented in this lesson will assist you with these all-important tasks in addition to helping you target your audience. Finally, a practice workshop will require you to create and deliver a presentation to a live audience, which will undoubtedly provide you with essential presentation skills.

Transporting a Presentation

Raritan Clinic East

Pediatric Diagnostic Specialists

You are satisfied with the final version of your recruitment presentation. You plan on mailing CDs of the presentation to various medical schools, but want to ensure that recipients can view the presentation if they don't have PowerPoint. You decide to include a short note explaining how to install and use the PowerPoint Viewer.

Additionally, you plan on delivering the presentation to the department chiefs. For this task, you decide to copy the presentation to a USB flash drive so you can use the presentation in the conference room rather than holding the meeting in your office. Finally, you give some serious thought as to how you can keep the attention of the meeting attendees using the PEER-LESS guidelines.

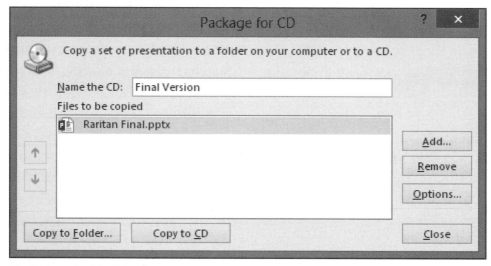

The Package for CD dialog box

Transporting the Presentation

Video Library   http://labyrinthelab.com/videos   Video Number: PP13-V1101

If you are using a notebook computer to create and deliver your presentation, you have a self-contained unit that holds the PowerPoint application, images, fonts, and all linked files for the presentation. But if you need to deliver the presentation on a computer other than the one on which it was created (that is, you may be presenting at a conference, a school, a client site, or another branch of your office), those essential files will not be present. To be sure you have the files you need, store the presentation and accompanying files on a USB flash drive, portable external hard drive, or compact disc (CD) to use at the presentation site. Whether you choose to use a USB (or other) drive or a CD depends on your personal preference. Either way, you will use the Package Presentation for CD feature to organize and copy your presentation files.

How Package Presentation for CD Works

The Package Presentation for CD feature collects all the elements required for your presentation to run smoothly. These elements include the presentation file, fonts, and any linked files. After all options are set, Package Presentation for CD will copy all the files to your CD or to a folder you specify.

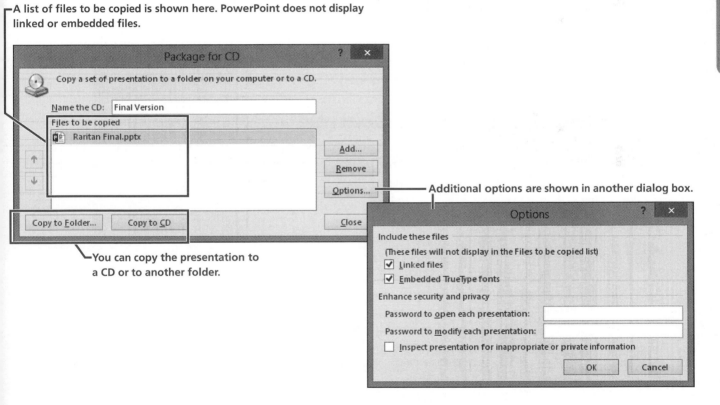

A list of files to be copied is shown here. PowerPoint does not display linked or embedded files.

Additional options are shown in another dialog box.

You can copy the presentation to a CD or to another folder.

PowerPoint 2013

Using Font Embedding

You should be aware of potential problems with fonts if you are going to run a presentation on a computer other than your own. If a font specified in your presentation is not available, PowerPoint will substitute the closest match it can find. However, even fonts that appear quite similar may differ in width and relative height. This could make your lines wrap incorrectly and cause other problems with the display of your presentation.

Example

In the following example, both lines are identical except for the font. Notice how much longer the lower line is.

• Both of these lines contain the same text. ──────── This line uses the 24 pt Times New Roman font.

• Both of these lines contain the same text. ──────── This line uses the 24 pt Georgia font.

Benefit of Embedding

If you use font embedding in your packaged presentation, it won't matter if the target computer doesn't have the fonts used in your presentation. You can use any custom fonts you like without worrying whether the other computer has them. The downside is that embedding fonts will slightly increase the file size. The benefit of being able to use custom fonts outweighs this negligible increase in file size. Unless you have very little storage space left on your USB drive or CD, you should choose to embed the fonts.

Displaying Linked Content

Files linked through hyperlinks or actions can be copied to the package folder to be distributed with your presentation. This means the links on your slides will still work, because the linked files will be copied to the USB drive or CD along with the presentation.

QUICK REFERENCE	TRANSPORTING A PRESENTATION
Task	**Procedure**
Pack a presentation for transport to another computer by using Package Presentation for CD	▪ Open the presentation you wish to package. ▪ Choose File→Export→Package Presentation for CD→Package for CD. Be sure there is a USB drive in the computer or a writable CD in your CD drive. (Your CD drive must also be capable of burning CDs.) ▪ Click Options, select the desired options from the Options dialog box, and click OK. ▪ To copy to a USB drive, select Copy to Folder, browse to the desired folder on your USB drive, and click OK. ▪ To copy to a CD, select Copy to CD.

Copying Files to a CD

Most new computers sold today include a drive capable of writing files to a CD. You can write a presentation to a CD directly from PowerPoint with no additional CD burning software installed. Because CDs can safely and durably hold up to 700 MB of data, they make an ideal long-term storage medium.

Types of Writable CDs

There are two types of compact discs to which you can write files:

- **Write Once (Standard CD-R):** These CDs allow you to write files to discs but not erase files from them. Although you can write files to a standard CD on several occasions, each file uses up more of the CD's storage capacity. After the storage capacity is reached, you can no longer write new files to the CD. Files written to a standard CD can last 30 years or more.
- **Rewritable CDs (Erasable CD-RW):** These CDs allow you to erase files as well as write to them. In general, writing files to a rewritable CD-RW is slower than writing files to a standard CD-R. However, you can erase individual files from the CD-RW or reformat it to erase all files. This type of CD makes a useful short-term backup medium. CD-RW discs are not suitable for the long-term storage of files.

DEVELOP YOUR SKILLS PP11-D01
Write Files to a Compact Disc

`WebSim` PP13-W1101

In this exercise, you will run a simulation of writing files to a CD. This WebSim features Windows 8, but the steps are similar for Windows 7.

1. Type the URL for the student resource center into the address bar of your web browser and tap Enter.

   The student resource center URL is printed on the inside front cover of your book.

2. From the left navigation bar, click **Lessons 9–12**. Click the link for **PP11** and then **DYS PP13-W1101 Write Files to a Compact Disc**.

   The WebSim loads as if a blank CD is already in the CD writing drive.

3. Work your way through the onscreen instructions.

4. Click the **Back to Course** link.

Viewing a Packaged Presentation from CD

Video Library   http://labyrinthelab.com/videos   Video Number: PP13-V1102

If you are sending a presentation on CD to someone, you may want to include a note explaining how to view the presentation, because the procedure may not be obvious to the CD recipient. The first thing to determine is whether the recipient has PowerPoint. If they don't, they will need the free PowerPoint Viewer to view the presentation. The second thing to determine is whether AutoPlay is enabled for the CD—this setting can differ from computer to computer. If AutoPlay is enabled, the CD may automatically prompt the recipient to open a file. If AutoPlay is disabled, the recipient will have to open the CD manually and locate the appropriate files. If the AutoPlay dialog box appears after a CD is inserted, AutoPlay is enabled.

Using AutoPlay with the PowerPoint Viewer

The AutoPlay feature causes Windows to automatically open a file on a CD, named AUTORUN. INF. The AUTORUN file includes instructions for Windows to open additional files or programs. In the case of a packaged presentation CD, the AUTORUN file tells Windows to open a web page on the CD, which in turn includes a download link for the PowerPoint Viewer.

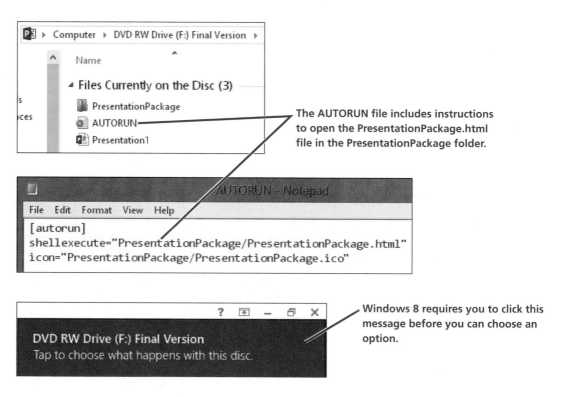

The AUTORUN file includes instructions to open the PresentationPackage.html file in the PresentationPackage folder.

Windows 8 requires you to click this message before you can choose an option.

DVD RW Drive (F:) Final Ve...

Choose what to do with this disc.

Install or run program from your media

 Run PresentationPackage.html
Publisher not specified

Other choices

 Open folder to view files
File Explorer

 Take no action

You can open the **HTML** file or open the CD to view its contents.

The PresentationPackage.html file includes a link to download the PowerPoint Viewer.

Final Version

Presentation1
Microsoft PowerPoint Presentation

Download Viewer

QUICK REFERENCE	USING AUTOPLAY WITH THE POWERPOINT VIEWER WHEN POWERPOINT IS NOT INSTALLED
Task	**Procedure**
Download the PowerPoint Viewer	■ Make sure your computer is connected to the Internet. ■ Place the CD in your computer's CD drive and click the Tap to Choose message. Or, for Windows 7, wait for the AutoPlay prompt. ■ Click Run PresentationPackage.html. ■ Click Download Viewer on the PresentationPackage.html web page. ■ Follow the instructions to download and install the PowerPoint Viewer.
View the presentation with the PowerPoint Viewer in Windows 8	■ Tap the [Windows] key to display the Desktop, if necessary. ■ Click the File Explorer button on the taskbar. ■ In the left column, click the CD drive to display its contents. ■ Double-click the presentation file to view it by using the PowerPoint Viewer.
View the presentation with the PowerPoint Viewer in Windows 7	■ Close any open windows and return to the Desktop. ■ Choose Start→Computer. ■ Right-click the CD drive and choose Open from the pop-up menu. (Do not simply double-click the CD drive, which causes the AutoPlay dialog box to open.) ■ Double-click the presentation file to view it by using the PowerPoint Viewer.

View a CD Presentation with AutoPlay and the PowerPoint Viewer

WebSim PP13-W1102

In this exercise, you will simulate downloading and installing the PowerPoint Viewer. You will then view a presentation burned to CD. This WebSim features Windows 8, but the steps are similar in Windows 7.

1. From the left navigation bar, click **Lessons 9–12**. Click the link for **PP11** and then **DYS PP13-W1102 View a CD Presentation with AutoPlay and the PowerPoint Viewer**.

   The WebSim loads as if you have just inserted a presentation CD burned from PowerPoint. The simulation computer does not have PowerPoint installed.

2. Work your way through the onscreen instructions.

3. Click the **Back to Course** link.

Using the PowerPoint Viewer Without AutoPlay

Video Library http://labyrinthelab.com/videos   Video Number: PP13-V1103

It may be the case that PowerPoint is not installed, AutoPlay is disabled, and the CD recipient needs to use the PowerPoint Viewer. In this case, when the CD is inserted, no AutoPlay dialog box appears and, therefore, no Download Viewer link is available. The following table outlines the steps to deal with this situation.

QUICK REFERENCE	DOWNLOADING THE POWERPOINT VIEWER WITHOUT AUTOPLAY
Task	**Procedure**
Download the PowerPoint Viewer	■ Make sure your computer is connected to the Internet.
	■ Insert the CD to your computer's CD drive.
	■ Display the contents of the CD.
	■ Double-click the PresentationPackage folder to open it.
	■ Double-click the PresentationPackage.html file to open it.
	■ Click the Download Viewer link and follow the instructions on the download page to download and install the PowerPoint Viewer.

Copying Files to a Folder

Video Library http://labyrinthelab.com/videos   Video Number: PP13-V1104

If you are transporting the presentation to another location so that you may present it at another computer, it is easier to copy the presentation files to a portable USB drive rather than writing the files to a CD. It is also more cost-effective, as files on a USB drive can simply be deleted and new files copied.

Copy a Presentation to a Folder

WebSim PP13-W1103

In this exercise, you will simulate copying a presentation to a folder on a USB drive. This WebSim features Windows 8, but the steps are similar for Windows 7.

1. From the left navigation bar, click **Lessons 9–12**. Click the link for **PP11** and then **DYS PP13-W1103 Copy a Presentation to a Folder**.

   The WebSim loads as if you have just inserted a USB drive, and the AutoPlay dialog box is displayed.

2. Work your way through the onscreen instructions.

3. Click the **Back to Course** link.

Viewing a Packaged Presentation from a Folder

Video Library http://labyrinthelab.com/videos Video Number: PP13-V1105

When you have copied a presentation to a folder, the AUTORUN file is copied to the presentation folder rather than to the root of the USB drive. The PresentationPackage.html file (with the link to download the PowerPoint Viewer) will open automatically only if the AUTORUN.INF file is at the *root*, or starting, folder of the USB drive. Therefore, AutoPlay will not help to automatically open the HTML file. When working with a presentation copied to a folder, it is easiest to close the AutoPlay dialog box if it appears and access the presentation file or PresentationPackage. html file manually.

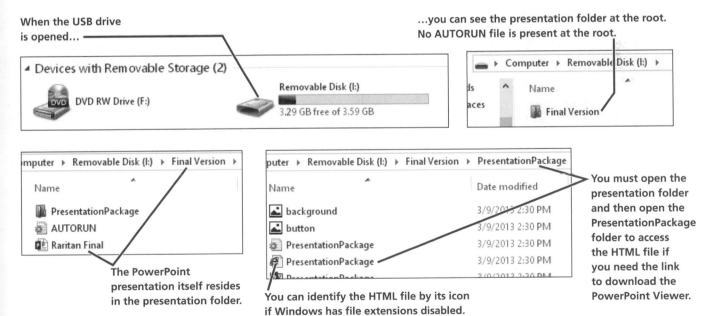

When the USB drive is opened...

...you can see the presentation folder at the root. No AUTORUN file is present at the root.

The PowerPoint presentation itself resides in the presentation folder.

You can identify the HTML file by its icon if Windows has file extensions disabled.

You must open the presentation folder and then open the PresentationPackage folder to access the HTML file if you need the link to download the PowerPoint Viewer.

PowerPoint 2013

QUICK REFERENCE	VIEWING A PRESENTATION FROM A FOLDER
Task	**Procedure**
Install the PowerPoint Viewer from a presentation folder	■ Make sure your computer is connected to the Internet. ■ Insert the USB drive. ■ If the AutoPlay dialog box appears, choose Open Folder to View Files. ■ If the AutoPlay dialog box does not appear, display the Computer contents and then double-click the USB drive to open it. ■ Browse to the presentation folder. ■ Double-click the PresentationPackage folder to open it. ■ Double-click the PresentationPackage.html file to open it. ■ Click the Download Viewer link and follow the instructions on the download page to download and install the PowerPoint Viewer.
View a presentation from a folder	■ Insert the USB drive. ■ If the AutoPlay dialog box appears, choose Open Folder to View Files. ■ If the AutoPlay dialog box does not appear, display the Computer contents and then double-click the USB drive to open it. ■ Browse to the presentation folder. ■ Double-click the presentation file. The presentation will open in PowerPoint if it is installed. If the PowerPoint Viewer is installed, the presentation will open in that instead.

DEVELOP YOUR SKILLS PP11-D04

View a Presentation from a Folder

WebSim   PP13-W1104

In this exercise, you will simulate viewing a presentation from a folder on a USB drive. The PowerPoint Viewer is installed on the WebSim computer. This WebSim features Windows 8, but the steps are similar to those for Windows 7.

1. From the left navigation bar, click **Lessons 9–12** . Click the link for **PP11** and then **DYS PP13-W1104 View a Presentation from a Folder**.

   The WebSim loads as if you have just inserted a USB drive, and the Tap to Choose dialog box displays.

2. Work your way through the onscreen instructions.

3. Click the **Back to Course** link.

Comparing Copy to CD and Copy to Folder

Video Library   http://labyrinthelab.com/videos   Video Number: PP13-V1106

The option you choose (Copy to CD or Copy to Folder) largely depends on what you plan to do with the presentation package. Copying to a CD works best if you are giving the CD to someone else so they can view the presentation—and they don't have PowerPoint installed. AutoPlay is enabled on Windows by default, so this makes it very easy for the recipient to download and install the PowerPoint Viewer. However, recipients still need instruction on how to view the presentation. (Open the CD and double-click the presentation file.)

Copy to Folder works best if you plan on transporting the presentation to another computer yourself, as you will be familiar with the location of the presentation file on the USB drive. Additionally, as the PowerPoint expert, you will know how to deal with the situation where PowerPoint is not installed and the PowerPoint Viewer must be downloaded—without the benefit of AutoPlay.

It's a good idea to download and copy the PowerPoint Viewer installer to your USB folder, as you may not have Internet access on the presentation computer.

Preparing the Meeting Room

Video Library   http://labyrinthelab.com/videos   Video Number: PP13-V1107

When you take a presentation on the road, you may have limited control over many details. It is important to clearly specify all the equipment and room setup requirements for your presentation ahead of time. Several critical details are described in the following topics.

Setting Up a Slide Show

PowerPoint allows you to set up variations on a slide show. Now that you have developed your PowerPoint skills, examine the Set Up Show dialog box once more in the following illustration. The Set Up Slide Show command displays a dialog box with several adjustable settings.

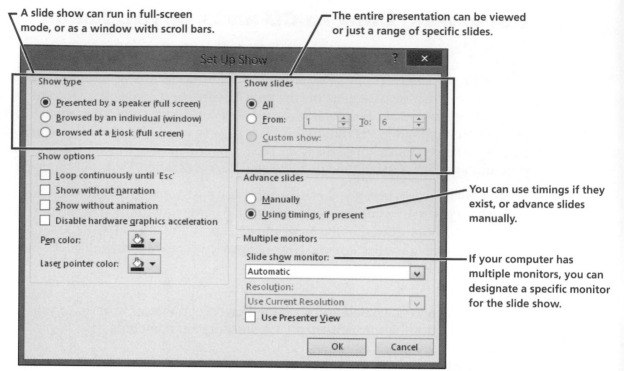

A slide show can run in full-screen mode, or as a window with scroll bars.

The entire presentation can be viewed or just a range of specific slides.

You can use timings if they exist, or advance slides manually.

If your computer has multiple monitors, you can designate a specific monitor for the slide show.

The Set Up Show dialog box allows you to control the display of a slide show.

SLIDE SHOW OPTIONS	
Option Category	**What It Affects**
Show Type	▪ You can choose between running the slide show in full-screen mode or in a window. ▪ If run in full-screen mode, no scroll bars are visible and slides are advanced by clicking the Slide Show toolbar or by using the keyboard. Also, the Minimize, Restore, and Close buttons in the top-right corner of the window are not visible. ▪ If run in a window, slides can be advanced only by right-clicking and choosing Advance, or by using the optional scroll bar. Also, the Minimize, Restore, and Close buttons in the top-right corner of the window are visible across the top of the slide show.
Show Options	▪ You can choose to loop the slide show repeatedly until manually stopped, to disable narration or animation, and to set the default pen color for ink annotations.
Show Slides	▪ Displays all slides or a specified range of slides in the presentation during the slide show.
Advance Slides	▪ You can choose to advance slides manually through mouse clicks or the keyboard, or use timings if they are present.
Multiple Monitors	▪ If the presentation computer has multiple monitors, you can choose which monitor will display the slide show. You can also enable or disable Presenter View.

Specifying the Equipment Setup

It is always a good idea to know as much as possible about the equipment that will be available in the presentation room. Telephone the owner of the computer or send an email to ask questions and verify that the available equipment meets your needs. Ask whether a technician who understands the equipment will be available, or bring a knowledgeable friend.

Using Sound Amplification and Speakers

If you are making a presentation to a large audience, or if you have some audio content in the presentation, you will need some sort of amplification system and speakers. You should not count on notebook computer speakers being loud enough for an audience greater than two or three. Likewise, if you will have a self-running presentation at a vendor table or kiosk, you should use external speakers to provide good sound quality—something few notebook computers can provide unassisted.

Choosing a Projection Display

Unless your audience is quite small, you will need a projection display to show the presentation on a screen, wall, or large computer monitor. Most computer screen projection systems fit one of the following descriptions:

PowerPoint 2013

- **Computer projection display:** These are projectors designed to project computer video from the computer directly to a screen or wall. These units usually offer a bright picture that is visible in a variety of lighting conditions.

- **Overhead projection display:** You use this older style of display with a standard overhead projector. These displays tend to be far less bright than projectors. The room must be completely dark for the audience to see the presentation. If the room has many windows, make sure curtains or shades block out any direct sunlight.

 If you do not use Presenter View, every motion you make on the presentation computer is displayed on the big screen, which the participants will see. There are no secrets from the participants!

Considering Screen Size

An important consideration for successful projection is the resolution (screen size) of the projector and the presentation computer. Too low a resolution will compromise the quality of your design, but not all projectors support the higher resolutions. If you will present on your own notebook computer, be sure to check the capabilities of the projection display you will use. Older projection displays may be able to project only a 640 x 480 pixel screen, which may result in substandard quality of your slide text and graphics. This also means you may not be able to display as much material legibly on the screen. Many notebook computer screens display satisfactorily only at a resolution of 1024 x 768 or greater. Therefore, you should look for a projection display that supports at least a 1024 x 768 resolution (which most modern projectors do).

 Check the manual for the projection display, because some require that the presentation computer and projection display are set for the same screen size—otherwise, the projection display may not work.

The following table provides a translation for the alphabet soup of screen-resolution standards.

STANDARD SCREEN RESOLUTIONS			
Acronym	**Resolution**	**Acronym**	**Resolution**
VGA	640 x 480	UGXA	1600 x 1200
SVGA	800 x 600	WUXGA	1920 x 1200
XGA	1024 x 768	QXGA	2048 x 1536
SXGA+	1400 x 1050	WQXGA	2560 x 1600

Changing Resolution

Sometimes it is necessary to adjust the resolution of the presentation computer before it will work with the projection display. This is where the projection display's user manual comes in handy! Windows offers a simple slider to control the screen resolution, but finding this slider can be tricky.

Older Versions of Windows

Although PowerPoint 2013 will not run on any version of Windows older than Windows 7, you might find yourself having to run a presentation on an older version of Windows using an old version of PowerPoint or the PowerPoint Viewer. Therefore, it is good to know how to change the screen resolution on versions of Windows as old as Windows XP.

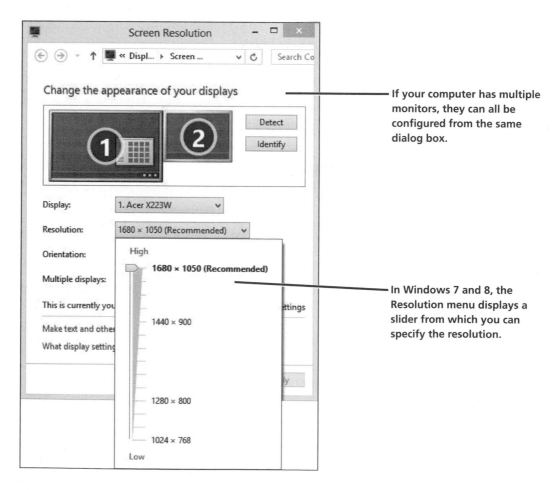

If your computer has multiple monitors, they can all be configured from the same dialog box.

In Windows 7 and 8, the Resolution menu displays a slider from which you can specify the resolution.

QUICK REFERENCE	SETTING UP A SLIDE SHOW
Task	**Procedure**
Set up a slide show	■ Open the presentation you will be running.
	■ Choose Slide Show→Set Up→Set Up Slide Show from the Ribbon.
	■ Configure your options and click OK.
Set the screen size on the presentation computer	■ Windows 7 and 8
	◆ Right-click a clear area of the Desktop and choose Screen Resolution.
	◆ Click the Resolution menu.
	◆ Use the slider to adjust the screen size.
	◆ Click anywhere outside the slider menu to close it; click OK.
	◆ Choose Keep Changes or Revert.
	■ Windows Vista
	◆ Right-click a clear area of the Desktop and choose Personalize.
	◆ Click the Display Settings link.
	◆ If necessary, use the slider control to adjust the screen size; click OK.
	◆ Choose Yes or No to keep or discard the changes made.
	■ Windows XP
	◆ Right-click a clear area of the Desktop and choose Properties.
	◆ Click the Settings tab.
	◆ If necessary, use the slider control to adjust the screen size; click OK.
	◆ Choose Yes or No to keep or discard the changes made.
Check the screen size setting on a projection display (generic steps)	■ Obtain a copy of the instruction manual and check the features page, the index, or the specifications page.
	■ The screen size setting is commonly referred to as the *resolution* of the projection display.
	■ Find the menu button on the body of the projection unit or its remote control. Search for a resolution setting on the control menu.

If there is no resolution setting on the menu, the unit is probably capable of projecting a screen size of only 640 x 480 pixels.

Preparing the Presentation Computer

If you will not make the presentation on your notebook computer, you should ask several questions regarding the computer you will be using:

■ **Does the computer run the same family of operating system as the computer on which I created the presentation?** If you used Windows 7 or 8 to create the presentation and the package, the presentation computer should also run Windows (XP, Vista, 7, or 8). If it runs a different operating system (such as Mac OS X), you may have trouble playing the presentation.

■ **Does the computer have PowerPoint or the PowerPoint Viewer?** If not, you should plan on installing the PowerPoint Viewer so you can display your presentation. You will need to log on to the presentation computer with a user account that has permission to install software. Otherwise, you will need to request that the software is preinstalled for you.

■ **Does the computer have the fonts I need?** If not, be sure to use the Package for CD feature and configure the option to embed your fonts.

- **Does the computer have an Internet connection?** If you use hyperlinks to web pages in your presentation, be sure to verify that the computer you will use has a working Internet connection. If you are delivering the presentation in a college or school, ask if you can connect to the Internet. If there is no Internet connection on the presentation computer and you need to install the PowerPoint Viewer, you should download the installer and copy it to your USB drive so you can install it without an Internet connection.

- **Do I need a password or ID to open PowerPoint?** Many company and school computers require a username and password. Be sure you know the password for the computer you will use and for the computer your participants will use (if this is a hands-on presentation).

- **Does the computer have the hardware I need?** Not all computers have a CD drive or available USB port. If your presentation is packaged on CD or USB, you need to make sure you can access your files on the presentation computer.

Following the Presentation Setup Checklist

Video Library   http://labyrinthelab.com/videos   Video Number: PP13-V1108

Make a copy of the following checklist and use it to help prepare for your next presentation.

Configuring Presentation Computer Software

___   The computer has PowerPoint installed.
___   Download and copy the PowerPoint Viewer installer to the USB drive or CD.
___   The computer has any other programs I need to run installed (for example, Word and Excel).

Setting Up the Computer Display Projector/Panel

Record the computer display projector/panel setting in the following table.

COMPUTER DISPLAY PROJECTOR/PANEL SETTINGS	
Projection Display Screen Size	**Presentation Computer Screen Size**
___ 640 x 480	___ 640 x 480
___ 800 x 600	___ 800 x 600
___ 1024 x 768	___ 1024 x 768
___ Other _____	___ Other _____

___   The focus is clear and can be seen from any area in the room.
___   The projector is stable and balanced (if it is not a ceiling mount) so the slide show will not be skewed.
___   The audio equipment for the projection unit is active and not muted.

Checking Room Lighting

___ The room can be dimmed for the presentation.

___ Dim lights are available for attendees to take notes during the presentation.

___ The projection display is powerful enough to be easily visible at the time of day planned for the presentation.

Preparing Audio and Video

___ The computer can play audio files.

___ The presentation computer can be connected to an audio system.

___ External speakers are available for the presentation computer.

___ The computer can play AVI and/or MPEG video files.

___ The computer can play video with sound.

Switching Programs During Slide Shows

Video Library   http://labyrinthelab.com/videos   Video Number: PP13-V1109

FROM THE KEYBOARD
Alt + Tab to switch programs

PowerPoint 2013

Windows allows you to switch between various programs by clicking the appropriate taskbar button. However, the taskbar is not visible during a slide show. Windows also lets you switch between programs via the keyboard. This technique can be quite useful when you need to switch to other programs during a PowerPoint slide show.

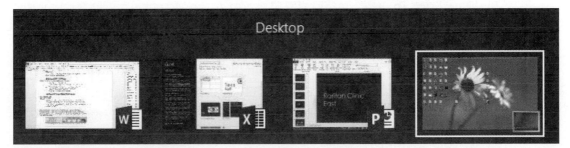

The selection window pops up when you hold down Alt and then tap Tab.

QUICK REFERENCE	SWITCHING PROGRAMS DURING A PRESENTATION
Task	**Procedure**
Switch between programs during a presentation	■ Hold down the Alt key. ■ Tap the Tab key until a box appears around the desired program icon. ■ Release the Alt key.

Using Alt + Tab has no effect if only one program is running, such as PowerPoint.

Switch Programs During a Presentation

In this exercise, you will switch between programs while viewing a slide show.

1. Start **PowerPoint** and maximize the program window.

2. Open **PP10-D05-Final** from the **PP2013 Lesson 11** folder.

3. Start **Microsoft Excel 2013** and maximize the program window.

4. Open **PP10-D05-Schedule** from the **PP2013 Lesson 11** folder.

   This spreadsheet shows the upcoming February schedule, still in progress.

5. Click the taskbar button for **PowerPoint** to make PowerPoint the active program.

Switch Between Programs by Using the Keyboard

6. Choose **Slide Show→Start Slide Show→From Beginning**.

7. Navigate to the **Services** slide.

   You will display the upcoming February schedule, which is still being planned in Excel.

   In the next step, you will use Alt + Tab *to display the selection window. It contains icons for each running program.*

8. While holding down the Alt key, tap the Tab key until the **Excel** icon is chosen in the program-switching window as shown in the following image. Release the Alt and Tab keys when you are finished.

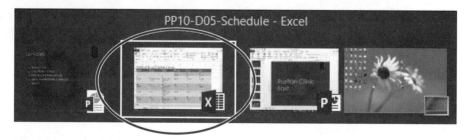

   Your computer may display different icons. Excel becomes the active program.

9. Use Alt + Tab to return to the PowerPoint slide show.

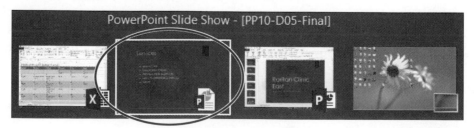

   Your computer may display different icons. The slide show becomes active.

10. Tap [Esc] to end the slide show and return to Normal view.

11. Use the **taskbar** to return to **Excel**.

12. Close **Excel**.

13. Close **PowerPoint**.

All programs are closed, and you are returned to the Desktop.

Preparing for Success

Video Library http://labyrinthelab.com/videos   Video Number: PP13-V1110

With the projection unit ready, and your presentation and the computer you will use synchronized for screen resolution and effects, don't forget to run through a checklist of your own. Usually, if you are narrating the presentation and delivering it to an audience, you will have created handouts for them and speaker notes for yourself. Use the following checklist to ensure that you are fully prepared so that the minute the first participants enter the room, you can give them your full attention.

Checking a List Prior to Leaving Your Office

Before leaving your office, check that you have the following with you:

___ A CD or USB flash drive with your presentation and all accompanying files. Also, a second CD or USB flash drive as a backup.

___ Handouts you prepared for the participants. (Be sure you have enough handouts so you don't have to scurry to a copier at the last moment—be prepared!)

___ Speaker notes that you can use as a guide as you deliver the presentation.

___ Items that you want to give to the participants (such as a business card or CD that contains a copy of the presentation).

___ Paper notepad, pens, and business cards to use after the presentation.

Allowing Yourself Time

Always arrive at the meeting site at least one-half hour before the presentation begins. If this is the first time you have used the computer or been to the meeting site, allow one hour to give yourself time to find the location and make any adjustments necessary before the participants arrive. Traditionally, participants arrive 15–20 minutes before the presentation is scheduled to begin.

Preparing for the Workshop

When you arrive at the meeting place, do the following:

___ Verify that your CD or USB thumb drive works on the presentation computer and contains all the files necessary.

___ Step through the checklists.

___ Run the presentation in its entirety.

___ Note where the light switches are located so you can smoothly turn them on and off. Check whether there is a remote control unit to do this for you.

___ Bring a laser pointer with you or check whether the projection remote control is equipped with a pointer feature.

___ Practice using the projection remote control (if provided with one).

___ Place the handouts on a table nearby for easy access.

___ If you are displaying a resource table, lay out the resources so participants can browse through them.

___ Be generous in supplying resources, whether they are handouts, CDs, or souvenirs that will remind them of the presentation.

___ Bring candy or souvenirs to give out for participation rewards.

Greeting the Participants

Greet participants with a smile and take some time to talk with each of them.

___ Explain a general timeline so they know what to expect—for example, that you will be letting them out sometime in the morning and afternoon for a break, and if they are "really good," you might even let them out for lunch. Finally, let them know that they will be out of there no later than…

___ Ask questions of the participants and reward answers.

___ Request that they ask questions and explain that there are "no dumb questions."

___ Devise and use an icebreaker for introductions if the group is small.

There are plenty of books and websites devoted to giving creative presentations, including icebreakers, energizers, and other tips and tricks.

Targeting Your Audience

Video Library   http://labyrinthelab.com/videos   Video Number: PP13-V1111

It is important to know your audience when creating the PowerPoint presentation. Finding out the day of the presentation is too late. For example, you would create two completely different presentations if your audience were managers versus clerical staff.

Using PEER Guidelines

How you present the information on each slide makes the difference between an engaging and an unsuccessful presentation. Lead your audience. Help them focus on the message of your presentation, not on you as the presenter. Use the following **PEER** guidelines to deliver an effective presentation:

- **Pace:** Maintain a moderate pace. Speaking too fast will exhaust your audience, and speaking too slowly may put them to sleep.
- **Emphasis:** Pause for emphasis. As you present, use a brief pause to emphasize your points. The pause you take will give your audience time to absorb the message.
- **Eye contact:** Address your audience. Always face your audience while speaking. A common mistake is to speak while walking or facing the projection screen. If you are speaking from a lectern or desk, resist the temptation to lean on it. Stand tall and make eye contact. Use the 3-second rule: look somewhere different after 3 seconds—any longer than that is staring. At the same time, don't dart your eyes around continuously.
- **Relax:** You are enthusiastic and want to convey that tone to the audience. When you speak, avoid fast movement, pacing, or rushed talking because your audience will be drawn to your movements and miss the point. So speak clearly and maintain a steady pace.

Using LESS Guidelines

In addition to the PEER guidelines, consider the following **LESS** guidelines to help you deliver your presentation **PEERLESS**ly.

- **Limit questions:** This depends on the type of presentation you are giving. If the presentation is just that—a presentation versus a training session—you may request the audience to delay asking their questions until you complete a topic or the entire presentation. However, if it is a particularly long presentation and you're not allowing questions, you must have energizers prepared to keep your audience with you. Nothing is more boring than just sitting and listening hour after hour. If the presentation is a training session, invite questions. If a question is not relevant, you can say you'll address it later in private. Or, if the question is coming up on the next slide, just say something like, "Oh, I'm so glad you asked; that's coming next," and continue.
- **Engage your audience:** An interactive presentation is not a free-for-all for the audience, but includes you asking a brief question or two during and after the presentation to be sure the audience understands your points. Do something different every 20 minutes or you risk losing your audience. For example, lecture, ask a hypothetical question, lecture, give a "pop quiz" on the material, lecture, ask for a question, and so forth.

PowerPoint 2013

- **Stay focused:** If you are given 20 minutes to deliver your presentation, do not go over your allotted time! Even if you have an unlimited amount of time to deliver, don't presume that the audience has nothing else to do but listen to your presentation. As captivating as the presentation may seem, be considerate of their time constraints.

- **Seek feedback:** After the presentation is over but before the audience leaves the room, ask for feedback from them. Use their feedback to improve the presentation the next time it is delivered.

Concepts Review

To check your knowledge of the key concepts introduced in this lesson, complete the Concepts Review quiz by choosing the appropriate access option below.

If you are...	Then access the quiz by...
Using the Labyrinth Video Library	Going to http://labyrinthelab.com/videos
Using eLab	Logging in, choosing Content, and navigating to the Concepts Review quiz for this lesson
Not using the Labyrinth Video Library or eLab	Going to the student resource center for this book

Reinforce Your Skills

Use a CD to Package a Presentation

WebSim PP13-WR1101

In this exercise, you will simulate using the Package for CD feature to copy a presentation to a CD while working at the Development *computer. You will then simulate using the PowerPoint Viewer to view the presentation on the* Presentation *computer.*

1. If necessary, type the URL for the student resource center into the address bar of your web browser and tap [Enter].

   The student resource center URL is printed on the inside front cover of your book.

2. From the left navigation bar, click **Lessons 9–12**. Click the link for **PP11** and then **RYS PP13-WR1101 Use a CD to Package a Presentation**.

   The WebSim loads as if a blank CD is already in the CD writing drive of the Development computer.

3. Work your way through the onscreen exercise instructions.

4. Click the **Back to Course** link.

Use a Folder to Package a Presentation

WebSim PP13-WR1102

In this exercise, you will simulate using the Package for CD feature to copy a presentation to a folder on a USB *drive while working at the* Development *computer. You will then simulate using the PowerPoint Viewer to view the presentation on the* Presentation *computer.*

1. From the left navigation bar, click **Lessons 9–12**. Click the link for **PP11** and then **RYS PP13-WR1102 Use a Folder to Package a Presentation**.

   The WebSim loads as if you have just inserted a USB drive, and the Tap to Choose message is displayed. You are at the Development computer.

2. Work your way through the onscreen exercise instructions.

3. Click the **Back to Course** link.

Package a Presentation

WebSim PP13-WR1103

In this exercise, you will use the Package for CD feature to copy a presentation to a CD and then to a USB drive. You will then use the PowerPoint Viewer to view the presentation. Throughout the WebSim, you will simulate going back and forth between the Development computer (used to create the presentation) and the Presentation computer (used to view the presentation).

1. If necessary, type the URL for the student resource center into the address bar of your web browser and tap Enter.

   The student resource center URL is printed on the inside front cover of your book.

2. From the left navigation bar, click **Lessons 9–12**. Click the link for **PP11** and then **RYS PP13-WR1103 Package a Presentation**.

   The WebSim loads as if a blank CD is already in the CD writing drive of the Development computer.

3. Work your way through the onscreen exercise instructions.

4. Click the **Back to Course** link.

Apply Your Skills

Package a Presentation to CD

WebSim   PP13-WA1101

In this exercise, you will simulate using the Package for CD feature to copy a presentation to a CD while working at the Development *computer. You will then simulate using the PowerPoint Viewer to view the presentation on the* Presentation *computer.*

1. If necessary, type the URL for the student resource center into the address bar of your web browser and tap Enter.

   The student resource center URL is printed on the inside front cover of your book.

2. From the left navigation bar, click **Lessons 9–12**. Click the link for **PP11** and then **AYS PP13-WA1101 Package a Presentation for CD**.

   The WebSim loads as if a blank CD is already in the CD writing drive of the Development computer.

3. Work your way through the onscreen exercise instructions.

4. Click the **Back to Course** link.

Package a Presentation to USB

WebSim   PP13-WA1102

In this exercise, you will simulate using the Package for CD feature to copy a presentation to a folder on a USB drive while working at the Development *computer. You will then simulate using the PowerPoint Viewer to view the presentation on the* Presentation *computer.*

1. From the left navigation bar, click **Lessons 9–12**. Click the link for **PP11** and then **AYS PP13-WA1102 Package a Presentation to USB**.

   The WebSim loads as if you have just inserted a USB drive, and the Tap to Choose message is displayed. You are at the Development computer.

2. Work your way through the onscreen exercise instructions.

3. Click the **Back to Course** link.

Package a Presentation

WebSim PP13-WA1103

In this exercise, you will use the Package for CD feature to copy a presentation to a CD and then to a USB drive. You will then use the PowerPoint Viewer to view the presentation. Throughout the WebSim, you will simulate going back and forth between the Development computer (used to create the presentation) and the Presentation computer (used to view the presentation).

1. If necessary, type the URL for the student resource center into the address bar of your web browser and tap Enter.

   The student resource center URL is printed on the inside front cover of your book.

2. From the left navigation bar, click **Lessons 9–12**. Click the link for **PP11** and then **AYS PP13-WA1103 Package a Presentation**.

   The WebSim loads as if a blank CD is already in the CD writing drive of the Development computer.

3. Work your way through the onscreen exercise instructions.

4. Click the **Back to Course** link.

Extend Your Skills

In the course of working through the Extend Your Skills exercises, you will think critically as you use the skills taught in the lesson to complete the assigned projects. To evaluate your mastery and completion of the exercises, your instructor may use a rubric, with which more points are allotted according to performance characteristics. (The more you do, the more you earn!) Ask your instructor how your work will be evaluated.

PP11-E01 · That's the Way I See It!

Before You Begin: You must have computer permissions to be able to install fonts. You must also be able to burn CDs or use a USB drive.

The type of font used in a presentation can make all the difference to its visual appeal. Unfortunately, the fonts installed on a computer by default are rather uninteresting. However, there are many free resources for those wishing to spice up their fonts. First, use a website such as dafont.com or fontsquirrel.com to find and download a font you like. Make sure the font is licensed as free for personal use. Next, research the Internet for instructions on installing a font on your computer. Once the font is installed, start PowerPoint and create a presentation using the new font on your slides. The presentation can be on any topic you like, but make sure the font is used throughout.

Save the presentation as **PP11-E01-Fonts-[FirstInitialLastName]**. Copy the presentation to a CD or a folder on a USB drive, making sure to embed the fonts. View the presentation on a different computer that does not have your font installed and verify that the embedded font still displays in the presentation.

You will be evaluated based on the inclusion of all elements specified, your ability to follow directions, your ability to apply newly learned skills to a real-world situation, your creativity, and the relevance of your topic and/or data choice(s). Submit your final file based on the guidelines provided by your instructor

PP11-E02 · Be Your Own Boss

In this exercise, you will practice delivering a slide show to a live audience. Review the PEER and LESS guidelines in this lesson before you begin.

Use the Internet to research recommendations for growing a specific fruit or vegetable. Aside from garden care, be sure to take note of the required climate. Choose a fruit or vegetable that can be grown and harvested in your region.

Using the skills you have gained in this class, create a presentation that helps you explain how to successfully grow your chosen fruit or vegetable. Save the presentation as **PP11-E02-Garden-[FirstInitialLastName]**.

Present the slide show to your class as if they were attendees at an organic gardening conference and make sure to use the PEER and LESS guidelines.

You will be evaluated based on the inclusion of all elements specified, your ability to follow directions, your ability to apply newly learned skills to a real-world situation, your creativity, and your demonstration of an entrepreneurial spirit. Submit your final file based on the guidelines provided by your instructor.

Transfer Your Skills

In the course of working through the Transfer Your Skills exercises, you will use critical-thinking and creativity skills to complete the assigned projects using skills taught in the lesson. To evaluate your mastery and completion of the exercises, your instructor may use a rubric, with which more points are allotted according to performance characteristics. (The more you do, the more you earn!) Ask your instructor how your work will be evaluated.

PP11-T01 Use the Web as a Learning Tool

Throughout this book, you will be provided with an opportunity to use the Internet as a learning tool by completing WebQuests. According to the original creators of WebQuests, as described on their website (WebQuest.org), a WebQuest is "an inquiry-oriented activity in which most or all of the information used by learners is drawn from the web." To complete the WebQuest projects in this book, navigate to the student resource center and choose the WebQuest for the lesson on which you are currently working. The subject of each WebQuest will be relevant to the material found in the lesson.

WebQuest Subject: Preparing for Success

Submit your final files based on the guidelines provided by your instructor.

PP11-T02 Demonstrate Proficiency

Stormy BBQ is sponsoring a local barbeque competition. As part of the festivities, the company will present a short history of barbeque. Use the Internet to research the history of barbeque and prepare a 5-minute presentation based on what you learn, using the skills you have learned in this class. Save the presentation as `PP11-T02-History-[FirstInitialLastName]`.

Practice presenting the slide show to friends or family to ensure that your presentation lasts 5 minutes. (Your instructor may wish to allow a 30-second grace period for a presentation between 4 min 30 sec and 5 min 30 sec.) Present the slide show to your class as if they were spectators at the barbeque competition and make sure to use the PEER and LESS guidelines.

Submit your final file based on the guidelines provided by your instructor.

Integrating with Other Office Programs

LESSON OUTLINE

Maintaining Compatibility with Previous Versions of Office

Working with Word Integration

Working with Excel Integration

Integrating with Outlook

Concepts Review

Reinforce Your Skills

Apply Your Skills

Extend Your Skills

Transfer Your Skills

LEARNING OBJECTIVES

After studying this lesson, you will be able to:

- Explain the significance of the PowerPoint 2013 and earlier file formats

- Save and open presentations in nonnative file formats

- Integrate the use of PowerPoint with Word, Excel, and Outlook

Microsoft Office 2013 includes several programs that specialize in a variety of tasks, such as working with email and calendars, performing word processing, making spreadsheet calculations, and creating dynamic presentations. By using the power of the other programs in the Office 2013 suite, you will efficiently accomplish tasks that extend beyond the capabilities of PowerPoint. In this lesson, you will learn about integrating PowerPoint with other Microsoft Office 2013 applications. You will also learn how to share your presentation files with users of previous versions of PowerPoint.

Reviewing a Year of Success

Raritan Clinic East

Pediatric Diagnostic Specialists

As the year draws to an end, you plan a Year in Review presentation for the next staff meeting to remind department chiefs of all the success that their hard work over the last year has produced. You feel so proud of the company's success that you want to share the presentation with your old college roommate—a user of PowerPoint 2003. You ask Sarah, one of the technical support specialists, to help create the presentation and send her a Microsoft Word document that outlines the topics for your presentation. Sarah knows she can easily convert this Word outline to a presentation. After it is complete, you insert the presentation into your Outlook Tasks to remind yourself to print speaker notes before the presentation.

- Raritan Clinic East
  - A Year of Success
- Community Service Success
  - Over 200 children treated through Save a Child
  - Over 600 free immunizations given
  - StayFit classes now offer spinning
- Record Financial Success
- New Construction
  - Construction on west facility under way
  - Residential wing to be completed early next year
- Thank You!
  - Our Success Is Your Success

Record Financial Success

General Medicine	$120
Emergency Medicine	$90
Neonatal	$132
Orthopedics	$117
Cardiology	$121
Total	$580

A Microsoft Word outline used to create presentation slides (left) and an embedded Excel spreadsheet that automatically updates the total if any other value is changed (right)

Maintaining Compatibility with Previous Versions of Office

Video Library http://labyrinthelab.com/videos Video Number: PP13-V1201

By default, presentations created in PowerPoint 2013 are compatible with PowerPoint 2007, but not with earlier versions. This means that if you try to open a presentation created with PowerPoint 2013 in PowerPoint 97 through 2003, the file will not open. You will not be able to edit the presentation or view a slide show. Of course, there are ways around this. You can save your 2013 presentation in a format compatible with PowerPoint 97 through 2003. Similarly, users of PowerPoint 97 through 2003 can download and install a patch allowing them to open PowerPoint 2013 presentations.

About File Formats

A file format describes the way a file is saved by a program. Different programs use different file formats, and generally a file can be opened only by a program that understands its file format. For example, PowerPoint saves files in the PowerPoint file format so that only PowerPoint can open them. You can't open a PowerPoint file in Microsoft Word! File formats are identified in Windows by a file extension—usually a three-character suffix at the end of a filename. (Recent Office versions create files with a four-character suffix.) Windows hides the file extension by default, so unless you have changed your computer configuration, you won't actually see the file extension. However, Windows also associates a file's icon with its file extension and file format. Even if you can't see the file extension, you can still identify a file format by its icon.

The default file extension for PowerPoint 2013 presentations is .pptx.

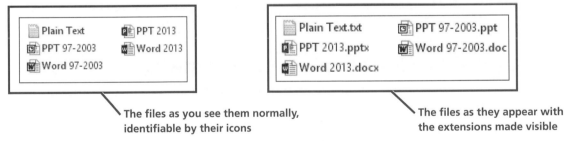

The files as you see them normally, identifiable by their icons

The files as they appear with the extensions made visible

Native File Formats

A native file format is the one that a program uses by default. In PowerPoint 2013, the native file format is a PowerPoint 2013 presentation file. When you save a new presentation in PowerPoint 2013, the program saves the file in the native file format unless you instruct it differently (such as saving in the PowerPoint 97-2003 format or PDF format).

Older PowerPoint File Formats

Older versions of PowerPoint (from 1997–2003) use a common file format that PowerPoint 2013 can open but that is not its native file format. The older 2003 version of PowerPoint cannot open native PowerPoint 2013 presentation files unless you install the Microsoft Office Compatibility Pack (described later in this lesson).

PowerPoint 2007 and 2010 use the same native file format as PowerPoint 2013, so presentations created in 2007 or 2010 can be opened by 2013, and vice versa, without installing additional software.

Open XML

Technically, Microsoft refers to the file formats used by Office 2007 through 2013 applications as Open XML formats. The Microsoft website has a lot of information about exactly what Open XML format is, and if you are technically inclined, you may find it interesting to read. The short version is that the Open XML file formats used by Office 2007 through 2013 applications provide the following advantages over the PowerPoint 97-2003 format:

- Greater compression (files are 50%–75% smaller than in previous versions of Office)
- Improved recoverability of corrupted files
- Several other more advanced features beyond the scope of this book

 The website FILExt—The File Extension Source—is a great source for figuring out what program is needed to open a particular file format. A link to this website is on the web page for this book.

Nonnative File Formats

A nonnative file format is one that an application can understand but does not use as its default, or native, file format. For example, PowerPoint can open text files (with the .txt file extension). Therefore, the Text file format is usable by PowerPoint, but it is nonnative.

Opening Nonnative File Formats

When you choose Open from within most programs such as PowerPoint, you are shown a filtered list of files in the current folder. By default, most programs show you only the native or most popular formats supported by the program. You can use the File of Type menu in the Open dialog box to display and open nonnative file formats.

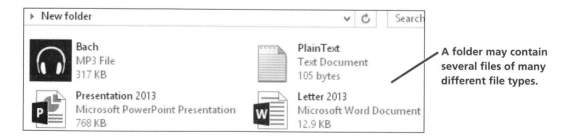

A folder may contain several files of many different file types.

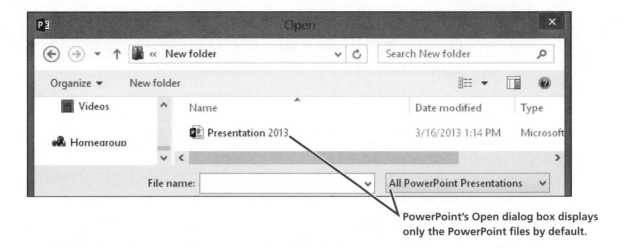

PowerPoint's Open dialog box displays
only the PowerPoint files by default.

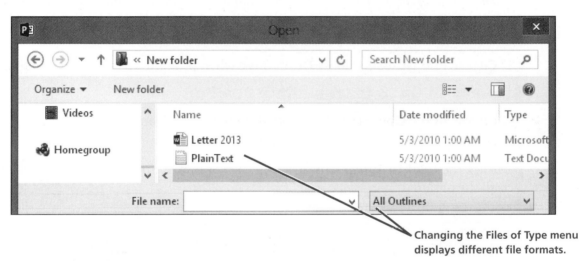

Changing the Files of Type menu
displays different file formats.

Open Various File Formats

*In this exercise, you will open (or attempt to open) native, nonnative, and incompatible file formats with
PowerPoint 2013.*

1. Start **PowerPoint** and maximize the program window.

2. Choose 📂 Open Other Presentations and then navigate to the **PP2013 Lesson 12** folder from
   your file storage location.

   *The Open dialog box displays only PowerPoint presentations because that is what the Files of Type
   menu is set to.*

3. Open **PP12-D01-2013**.

   *The file opens because the file format is compatible with PowerPoint. In fact, it is the native file format
   of PowerPoint.*

4. Choose **File→Close**. Choose **Don't Save** if prompted to save any changes.

Open Nonnative File Formats

5. Choose **File→Open** and navigate to the **PP2013 Lesson 12** folder.

6. Choose **All Outlines** from the Files of Type menu.

The All Outlines option includes Word 2013 documents and text files, among others. The Open dialog box now displays Microsoft Word and text files in the PP2013 Lesson 12 folder.

7. Open **PP12-D01-PlainText**.

The text file opens in PowerPoint but looks a little odd. Remember that text files are not native to PowerPoint and contain no formatting. If the text file contained useful text, you could cut and paste the text into a bulleted text area on a slide.

8. Choose **File→Close**. Choose **Don't Save** when prompted to save the presentation.

Attempt to Open Incompatible File Formats

9. Choose **File→Open** and navigate to the **PP2013 Lesson 12** folder.

PowerPoint remembers your previous setting and shows you All Outlines.

10. Click the **Files of Type** menu and read each option. Remember to use the scroll bar to read all the options.

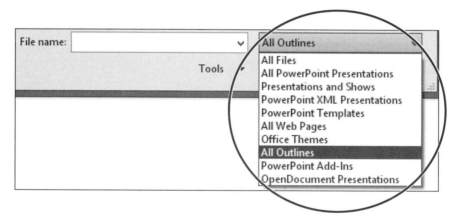

Note that there is no option for MP3 sound files. Although you can embed an MP3 sound file on a slide, this file format cannot be directly opened by PowerPoint.

11. Choose **All Files** from the top of the **Files of Type** menu.

PowerPoint displays all files in the folder, even those that are not compatible with PowerPoint.

12. Open the MP3 sound file **PP12-D01-Bach**.

An error box appears, indicating that you attempted to open an incompatible file format.

13. Click **OK** to close the error box.

Compatibility with Previous PowerPoint Versions

Video Library   http://labyrinthelab.com/videos   Video Number: PP13-V1202

If users of PowerPoint 97-2003 attempt to open your PowerPoint 2013 files, they will receive an error similar to the one you received in the previous exercise when you attempted to open the MP3 sound file. PowerPoint 2013 files are compatible with PowerPoint 2007, but not with earlier versions. This can be problematic if you need to share presentation files with other users. Not to worry. PowerPoint 2013 offers a command that saves your presentation in a format compatible with PowerPoint 97, PowerPoint 2000, PowerPoint XP, and PowerPoint 2003.

The Compatibility Checker

If there are elements of the presentation that cannot be edited in earlier versions of PowerPoint, the Microsoft Office PowerPoint Compatibility Checker displays a dialog box giving you the details when both of the following are true:

- You are saving the presentation for an older version of PowerPoint.
- There are features that aren't supported by the older version.

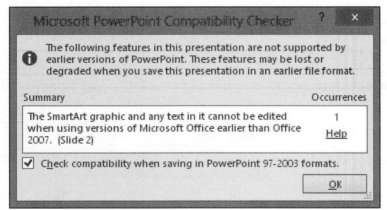

The Microsoft Office PowerPoint Compatibility Checker displays incompatibilities in the presentation with earlier versions of PowerPoint.

The Microsoft Office Compatibility Pack

If you send a colleague your PowerPoint 2013 file not realizing she is using PowerPoint 2003, don't worry. Even if you didn't save your presentation in the 97-2003 format, she can still open the 2013 file in PowerPoint 2003 provided she has installed the compatibility pack from Microsoft.

The Compatibility Pack, officially dubbed the *Microsoft Office Compatibility Pack for Word, Excel, and PowerPoint File Formats*, is a free download from the Microsoft website allows users of Office 2000/XP/2003 to open and work with the 2007 and 2013 file formats.

A link to the Microsoft Office Compatibility Pack for Word, Excel, and PowerPoint appears on the student resource center for this book.

PowerPoint 97 Support

The Microsoft Office Compatibility Pack does not provide support for PowerPoint 97. To make your presentation compatible with PowerPoint 97, use the Change File Type command.

QUICK REFERENCE	OPENING AND SAVING NONNATIVE FILES
Task	**Procedure**
Open a nonnative compatible file	■ Choose Open Other Presentations from the Start screen and navigate to the desired location, or choose File→Open. ■ Select the file format from the Files of Type menu. ■ Select the desired file and click OK.
Save a presentation to be compatible with PowerPoint 97-2003	■ Open the presentation you wish to make compatible. ■ Choose File→Export→Change File Type→PowerPoint 97-2003 Presentation→Save As. ■ Name and save your file.

DEVELOP YOUR SKILLS PP12-D02

Save a 2013 Presentation in a Compatible Format

In this exercise, you will save a PowerPoint 2013 presentation so that it is compatible with PowerPoint 97–2003.

1. Choose **File→Open** and navigate to the **PP2013 Lesson 12** folder from your file storage location.

2. Choose **All PowerPoint Presentations** from the Files of Type menu.

Displaying only PowerPoint presentations makes the Open dialog box less cluttered and makes it easier to focus on the files you want.

3. Open **PP12-D02-Final** and save it as `PP12-D02-Final-[FirstInitialLastName]`.
   You will save the presentation in a format that can be opened by earlier versions of PowerPoint.

4. Follow these steps to save the presentation in the PowerPoint 97-2003 format:

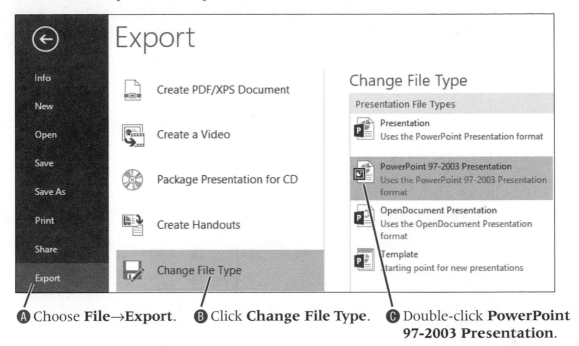

Ⓐ Choose **File→Export**. Ⓑ Click **Change File Type**. Ⓒ Double-click **PowerPoint 97-2003 Presentation**.

The Save As dialog box opens with the Save as Type menu already set to the PowerPoint 97-2003 Presentation file format.

5. Ensure that the default filename of *PP12-D02-Final-[FirstInitialLastName]* has not changed, and then click **Save**.

If any presentation elements could not be edited in earlier versions of PowerPoint, the Microsoft Office PowerPoint Compatibility Checker would have displayed an information dialog box giving you those details. No problems were found in this presentation.

You now have two files that appear to have the same name— PP12-D02-Final-[FirstInitialLastName]. Remember that your computer may be configured to hide the file extensions. The actual names of the files are PP12-D02-Final-[FirstInitialLastName].pptx and PP12-D02-Final-[FirstInitialLastName].ppt. They are, in fact, different.

6. Choose **File→Close**.

7. Choose **File→Open**, navigate to the **PP2013 Lesson 12** folder, and ensure that the Files of Type menu is set for **All PowerPoint Presentations**.

*Notice that two files appear to have the same name—PP12-D02-Final-[FirstInitialLastName].
Can you identify which one is the 2013 format and which one is the format compatible with earlier
versions of PowerPoint? In the space below each icon, write **2013** or **97-2003** to match the icon
with the correct version of PowerPoint.*

   _____      _____

8. Click **Cancel**.

Working with Word Integration

Video Library   http://labyrinthelab.com/videos   Video Number: PP13-V1203

Microsoft Word is an excellent word processing program that easily integrates with PowerPoint.
Two primary integration tasks are useful with Word and PowerPoint:

■ Drafting an outline in Word and then converting it to a PowerPoint presentation

■ Completing a PowerPoint presentation and then creating handouts in Word with more
options than PowerPoint's Print Handouts option

Creating a Presentation Outline in Word

Word's powerful outlining tool makes setting up and modifying outlines easy. You can create an
outline in Word and import it to PowerPoint. To use Word outlines in PowerPoint, you must
apply the appropriate styles to the paragraphs in the Word document prior to importing the
outline. PowerPoint converts the Word outline by using these rules:

■ All Level 1 paragraphs translate to Titles in a PowerPoint slide.

■ All Level 2 paragraphs translate to Level 1 Body Bullets in a PowerPoint slide.

■ All Level 3 paragraphs translate to Level 2 Body Bullets in a PowerPoint slide.

After a Word outline is imported into PowerPoint, you can promote or demote the bullets, apply
layouts and a design template, and make other enhancements.

This Word outline...   ...creates these PowerPoint slides.

Create a Presentation and Import a Word Outline

In this exercise, you will start a new Raritan presentation, create an outline in Word, and modify the resulting presentation.

Create an Outline in Word

1. Start **Word** and click **Blank Document**.

   In the next few steps, you will type and apply Word styles to paragraphs.

2. With the blank document opened, choose **View→Views→Outline**.

3. Type **Raritan Clinic East** [Enter].

4. Type [Tab] **A Year of Success** [Enter].

   Typing [Tab] *increases the list level and creates a Level 2 style.*

5. Type [Shift]+[Tab] **Community Service Success** [Enter].

   Typing [Shift]+[Tab] *decreases the list level and returns the text to a Level 1 style.*

6. Type the following to create Level 2 style text that will be converted in PowerPoint to text bullets:

   [Tab] **Over 200 children treated through Save a Child** [Enter]
   Over 600 free immunizations given [Enter]
   StayFit classes now offer spinning [Enter]
   [Shift]+[Tab]

   Pressing [Shift]+[Tab] *returns you to a Level 1 style, and you are ready to continue typing the rest of the outline.*

7. Continue typing the outline as follows:

   Record Financial Success [Enter]
   New Construction [Enter]
   [Tab] **Construction on west facility under way** [Enter]
   Residential wing to be completed early next year [Enter]
   [Shift]+[Tab] **Thank You!** [Enter]
   [Tab] **Our Success Is Your Success**

   Your outline should match the following figure.

   ⊕ Raritan Clinic East
       ⊖ A Year of Success
   ⊕ Community Service Success
       ⊖ Over 200 children treated through Save a Child
       ⊖ Over 600 free immunizations given
       ⊖ StayFit classes now offer spinning
   ⊖ Record Financial Success
   ⊕ New Construction
       ⊖ Construction on west facility under way
       ⊖ Residential wing to be completed early next year
   ⊕ Thank You!
       ⊖ Our Success Is Your Success

8. Choose **File→Save As** and save the outline to the **PP2013 Lesson 12** folder as `PP12-D03-Outline-[FirstInitialLastName]`.

9. Close **Word**.
   Word closes, and PowerPoint is visible.

Import the Outline

10. Restore **PowerPoint** from the **Windows taskbar**.

11. Choose **File→New** and then click **Blank Presentation**.

12. Choose **Design→Themes→More [=]→Retrospect**.

13. Choose **Home→Slides→New Slide menu ▼→Slides from Outline**.

14. Use the **Insert Outline** dialog box to navigate to the **PP2013 Lesson 12** folder.
    Note that the Files of Type menu is already set to All Outlines. The Insert Outline dialog box displays nonnative but compatible files.

15. Choose **PP12-D03-Outline-[FirstInitialLastName]** and click **Insert**.
    PowerPoint takes a moment to import the outline. Note that the first slide is blank because PowerPoint inserted the slides from the outline after the existing blank title slide.
    Each slide is formatted with blue text because Word formatted the heading styles as blue.

16. Choose **View→Presentation Views→Outline View** and examine the PowerPoint outline.

    Observe that each Level 1 paragraph from the outline has become a slide title, and each Level 2 paragraph has become a bulleted paragraph under the appropriate title.

    1 ☐
    2 ☐ **Raritan Clinic East**
       A Year of Success
    3 ☐ **Community Service Success**
       Over 200 children treated throu

17. Choose **View→Presentation Views→Normal**.

18. Choose the first slide (the blank slide) and tap [Delete] to remove it.
    The blank slide is deleted, and the Raritan Clinic East slide becomes selected.

Change a Layout and Apply a Design Template

19. Choose **Home→Slides→Layout menu ▼→Title Slide**.
    The layout of the selected slide changes.

20. Select the final slide, **Thank You**, and choose **Home→Slides→Layout menu ▼→ Section Header**.

Reset the Slide Formatting

21. Select the first slide, **Raritan Clinic East**, and choose **Home→Slides→Reset**.
    The text formatting is removed and returns to the default setting for the current document theme.

22. Select the second slide, press [Shift], select the **last slide**, and release [Shift].
    Slides 2–5 become selected.

23. Choose **Home→Slides→Reset** to reformat the text on the selected slides with the document theme formatting.

24. Save the presentation as `PP12-D03-OutlinePresentation-[FirstInitialLastName]` in the **PP2013 Lesson 12** folder.

Creating Presentation Handouts in Word

Video Library http://labyrinthelab.com/videos   Video Number: PP13-V1204

To create presentation handouts for attendees, PowerPoint offers several formats. However, only the 3 Slides per Page option includes lines for note taking. By sending the presentation to Word to create handouts, you have more options for including areas for note taking. In addition, you have the opportunity in Word to format any text on the handouts. Finally, you can edit the slide thumbnails in Word without affecting the presentation slides. This is helpful when you wish to remove or add portions of a slide on the handouts only.

More layout options are available when you create handouts in Word.

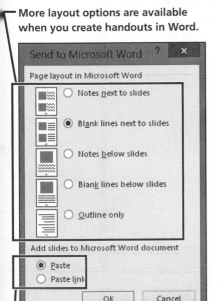

The handout as created in Word.

Paste embeds the slides in the Word document, whereas Paste Link links the slides.

QUICK REFERENCE	INTEGRATING WORD WITH POWERPOINT
Task	**Procedure**
Import an outline from Word	■ Open a presentation or create a new, blank one.
	■ Choose Home→Slides→New Slide→Slides from Outline.
	■ Delete any blank slides, if necessary.
	■ Select the imported slides and choose Home→Slides→Reset to reset the text formatting to match the document theme.
Create handouts in Word	■ Open the presentation for which you wish to create handouts.
	■ Choose File→Export→Create Handouts→Create Handouts.
	■ Select the desired layout.
	■ Choose Paste to embed the slides or choose Paste Link to link the slides, and then click OK.
	■ Edit the slides or format text in Word as desired, and then print.

PowerPoint 2013

Create Handouts in Word

In this exercise, you will create presentation handouts in Microsoft Word.

1. Choose **File→Export→Create Handouts→Create Handouts** to open the **Send to Microsoft Word** dialog box.

2. Follow these steps to create the handouts:

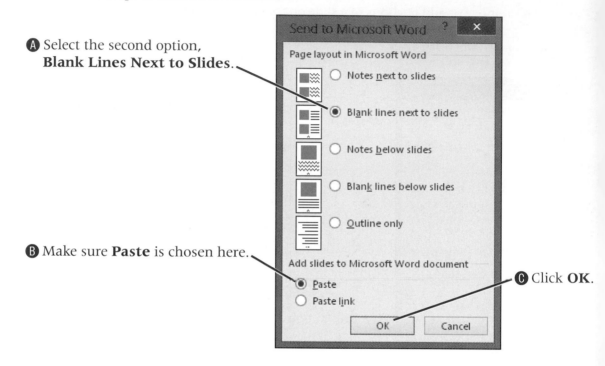

Ⓐ Select the second option, **Blank Lines Next to Slides**.

Ⓑ Make sure **Paste** is chosen here.

Ⓒ Click **OK**.

Word opens and creates the handouts.

3. If necessary, use the taskbar to display **Word**.

4. In **Word**, scroll to the third slide.

   This slide contains only a title and no bulleted text. An Excel spreadsheet will be placed on the actual slide later. You will edit the slide thumbnail in the handout.

5. Double-click the slide thumbnail in the **Word document**.

   The slide becomes editable just as if you were in PowerPoint. In fact, the Ribbon has changed to the PowerPoint Ribbon.

6. Click in the bulleted text area of the slide and type **Excel spreadsheet displaying yearly totals appears in the actual slide show.**

7. Drag to select the text, and then choose **Home→Font→Font Size menu ▼→44**.

8. Click on the **Word document**, outside the slide. The PowerPoint Ribbon is replaced by the Word Ribbon, and your document should match this illustration.

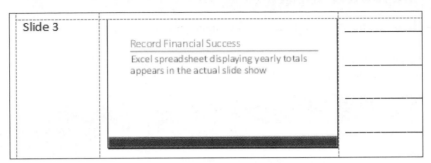

9. Save the document as `PP12-D04-Handouts-[FirstInitialLastName]` to the **PP2013 Lesson 12** folder.

   You will save the document for later printing in case you need to make more changes.

10. Close **Word**.

Working with Excel Integration

Video Library   http://labyrinthelab.com/videos   Video Number: PP13-V1205

You should already know that PowerPoint can integrate with Excel by inserting a chart that links to Excel data. The integration doesn't stop there. By incorporating Object Linking and Embedding (OLE), you can embed an entire Excel worksheet into your presentation.

Embedding a Worksheet

By embedding an Excel worksheet in a slide, you have full access to the Excel data just as if it resided in an external document. Of course, with an embedded spreadsheet, you never have to worry about breaking links by changing the name of a file or moving it to a different location.

DEVELOP YOUR SKILLS PP12-D05
Embed an Excel Worksheet

In this exercise, you will embed an entire Excel worksheet on a slide.

1. Save the presentation as `PP12-D05-OutlinePresentation-[FirstInitialLastName]`.

2. Display the third slide, **Record Financial Success**.

3. Click the dotted border of the bulleted text area to select it. The border will become solid when correctly selected.

4. Tap ⌈Delete⌋ to delete the text block from the slide.

5. Choose **Insert→Text→Object**.

6. Follow these steps to embed an Excel worksheet:

Ⓐ Make sure the **Create New** option is chosen.

Ⓑ Scroll down the list and choose **Microsoft Excel Worksheet**.

Ⓒ Click **OK**.

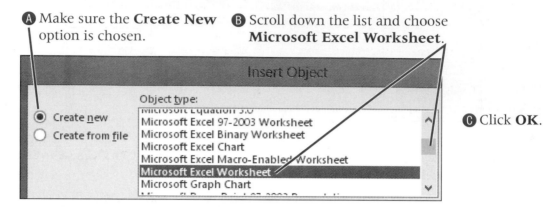

PowerPoint places the worksheet on the slide, and the PowerPoint Ribbon is replaced by the Excel Ribbon.

Enter Data and Apply Formatting

7. Follow these steps to enter data in the worksheet:

Ⓐ Type the categories in **column A**.

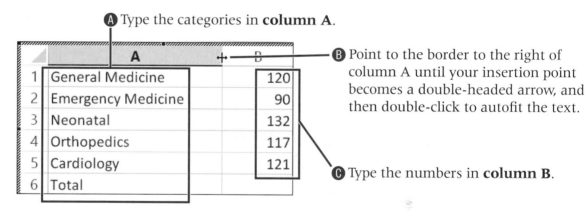

Ⓑ Point to the border to the right of column A until your insertion point becomes a double-headed arrow, and then double-click to autofit the text.

Ⓒ Type the numbers in **column B**.

8. Follow these steps to format the money in column B:

Ⓐ Point to **cell B1** and then drag down to **cell B6** to select six cells.

Ⓑ Right-click any of the selected cells in column B and choose **Format Cells** from the context menu.

Ⓒ Choose **Currency** from the Category list.

Ⓓ Set the Decimal Places to zero.

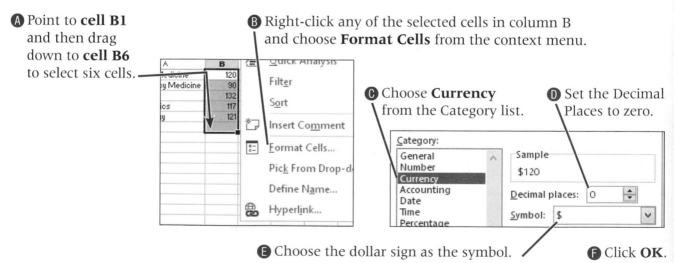

Ⓔ Choose the dollar sign as the symbol.

Ⓕ Click **OK**.

9. Choose **Home→Editing→AutoSum** Σ.

   The sum of cells B1 through B5 is displayed in cell B6. Your spreadsheet may display a repeated # symbol to indicate that the cell is not wide enough to display the entire number.

10. If **cell B6** displays a repeated # symbol instead of the actual number, double-click the border to the right of column B to autofit the cell contents.

11. Point to **cell A6** and drag across to **cell B6** to select both bottom cells.

12. Choose **Home→Styles→Cell Styles menu ▼→Accent 1**.

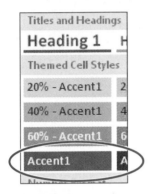

13. Point to **cell A1** and drag diagonally down to **cell B5** to select ten cells.

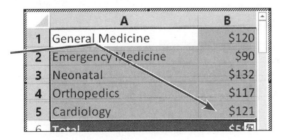

14. Choose **Home→Styles→Cell Styles menu ▼→60% – Accent 1**.

15. Click anywhere on the slide, outside the spreadsheet.

    The PowerPoint Ribbon reappears. The spreadsheet has a lot of wasted space.

16. Double-click the spreadsheet again and follow these steps to resize it for optimal display:

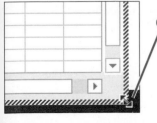

Ⓐ Point to the bottom-right corner of the spreadsheet until your pointer becomes a double-headed arrow.

Ⓑ Drag up and to the left to reduce the size of the spreadsheet. Drag close to the content cells and then release the mouse.

17. Click anywhere on the slide, outside the spreadsheet.

    The spreadsheet appears on the slide but is much too small.

18. Point to the bottom-right corner of the spreadsheet and drag down and to the right to enlarge it.

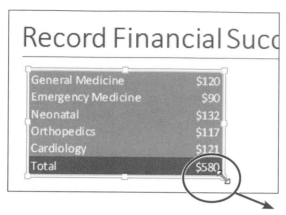

19. Drag the spreadsheet so it is centered on the slide.

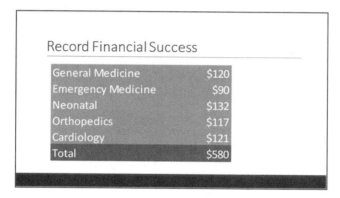

Edit an Embedded Spreadsheet

20. Double-click the spreadsheet.

21. Click once in **cell B2** and type **190**, and then click anywhere outside the spreadsheet.

    Cell B2 changes to $190 because the currency formatting was applied earlier. The Total amount has been updated to accommodate for the higher value in cell B2.

22. Save your presentation and close **PowerPoint**.

Integrating with Outlook

Video Library   http://labyrinthelab.com/videos   Video Number: PP13-V1206

Microsoft Outlook is much more than a simple email program. It provides several other advanced features, including a calendar and task list. By integrating PowerPoint with Outlook, you can schedule reminders for yourself and never miss an important presentation.

Setting Calendar Reminders

Outlook's calendar lets you schedule appointments or set up simple reminders. For example, if you had an important presentation to deliver, you might schedule reminders in the Outlook calendar for tasks such as printing handouts and speaker notes in addition to the time and location of the presentation. Doing this would ensure you were on time with all your materials.

Attaching Files

You can also attach files, such as a PowerPoint presentation, to an appointment. When the reminder alarm pops up, you can open the file and print from the alarm reminder. Files attached to appointments are embedded, so changes to the embedded presentation do not appear in the originally attached presentation.

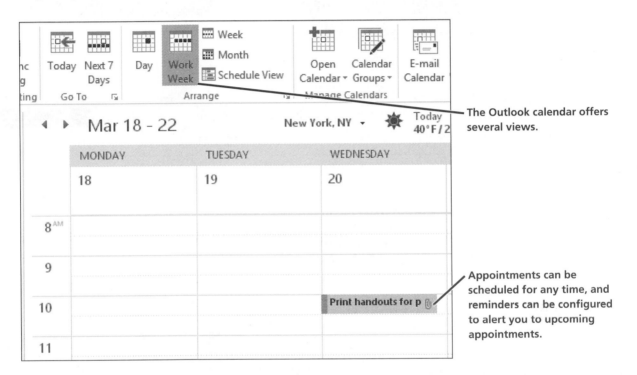

The Outlook calendar offers several views.

Appointments can be scheduled for any time, and reminders can be configured to alert you to upcoming appointments.

DEVELOP YOUR SKILLS PP12-D06
Schedule a Reminder in Outlook

In this exercise, you will schedule a reminder to print handouts in Outlook. You will also attach the PowerPoint file to the appointment for easy printing.

Before You Begin: Outlook must be configured to open without prompting you to create an account. Check with your instructor to verify that Outlook is configured to work with this exercise.

1. Start **Outlook** and maximize the program window.

2. Choose **Calendar** from the bottom-left area of the Outlook window.

3. Choose **Home→Arrange→Work Week**.

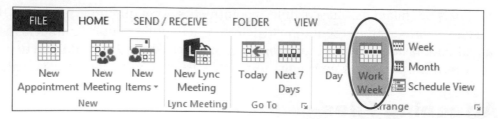

Outlook highlights the current day.

4. Double-click in the **9:00 AM cell** for tomorrow's date to add a new appointment.

	MONDAY	TUESDAY	WEDNESDAY	THURSDAY	F
	18	19	20	21	2
8 ᴬᴹ					
9				▬▬▬▬▬	

Your screen will show the current date and will differ from the illustration.

5. Follow these steps to create an appointment:

Ⓐ Type **Raritan presentation** as the subject.

Ⓑ Verify that the **Start** and **End** dates are set for tomorrow's date.

Ⓒ Set the Start and End times for **9:00 AM** and **10:00 AM**, respectively. (You may have to deselect the All Day Event checkbox first.)

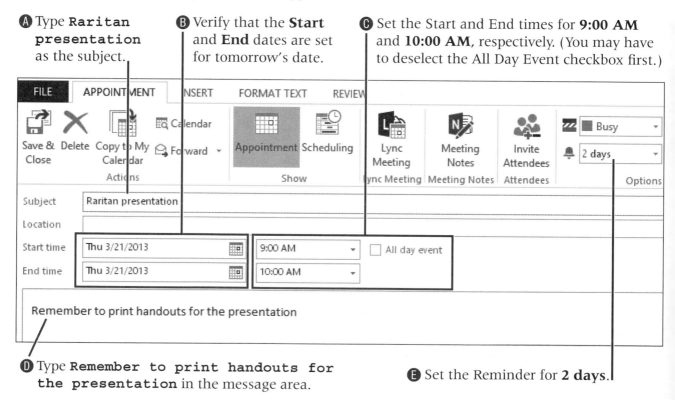

Ⓓ Type **Remember to print handouts for the presentation** in the message area.

Ⓔ Set the Reminder for **2 days**.

Attach a Presentation to an Appointment

6. Follow these steps to attach the presentation to the appointment:

Ⓐ Choose **Insert→**
Include→Attach File.

Ⓑ Navigate to the **PP2013 Lesson 12** folder,
select **PP12-D06-Final**, and click **Insert**.

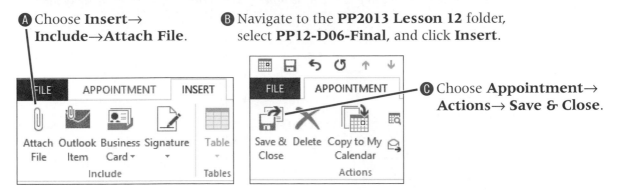

Ⓒ Choose **Appointment→**
Actions→ Save & Close.

*The Reminder will pop up because the appointment is for 9:00 AM tomorrow and you set a reminder
for two days.*

Open an Attached File from an Appointment Reminder

7. Follow these steps to temporarily close the reminder:

Ⓐ Type **1 minute** because that option
is not available from the menu.

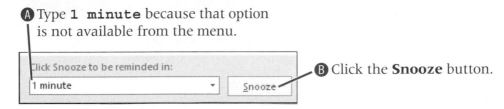

Ⓑ Click the **Snooze** button.

*Normally you would choose a longer snooze time, but you probably don't want to wait an entire day
to finish this exercise! After 1 minute, the reminder pops up again.*

8. In the **Reminder** box, double-click the **Raritan presentation** item.

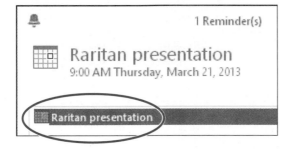

The appointment opens, and you can read your message.

9. Double-click the attached **PP12-D06-Final.pptx** file.

*The presentation opens. Any changes to the presentation would have no effect on the original
presentation that was attached. Normally, you would print your handouts and exit PowerPoint.*

10. Close **PowerPoint**.

11. Choose **File→Close** to close the appointment window.

12. Choose **Dismiss** in the **Reminder window** to cancel the reminder permanently.

13. Right-click the appointment in the calendar window and choose **Delete** from the pop-up menu.

    You are deleting the appointment so other students can complete this activity later.

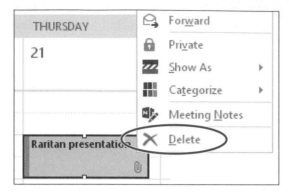

14. Choose **File→Exit** to close Outlook.

Concepts Review

To check your knowledge of the key concepts introduced in this lesson, complete the Concepts Review quiz by choosing the appropriate access option below.

If you are...	Then access the quiz by...
Using the Labyrinth Video Library	Going to http://labyrinthelab.com/videos
Using eLab	Logging in, choosing Content, and navigating to the Concepts Review quiz for this lesson
Not using the Labyrinth Video Library or eLab	Going to the student resource center for this book

Reinforce Your Skills

Use Compatible File Formats and Integrate with Word

In this exercise, you will explore various file formats and create a new presentation from a Word outline.

Open Various File Formats

1. Start **PowerPoint**. Open **PP12-R01-Old** from the **PP2013 Lesson 12** folder and save it as **PP12-R01-Old-[FirstInitialLastName]**.

   The presentation is in the old PowerPoint 97-2003 PPT file format, but it is native to PowerPoint 2013 so it opens without issue.

2. Choose **File→Open** and navigate to the **PP2013 Lesson 12** folder.

3. Change the **Files of Type** menu to **All Files**.

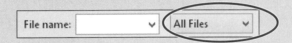

4. Click the **PP12-R01-House** picture and click **Open**.

   You receive an error because the JPG file format is an incompatible file type. JPG pictures can be inserted on a slide, but not opened directly from PowerPoint.

5. Click **OK** to close the error box.

6. On the last slide, **Summary**, choose **Insert→Images→Pictures**.

7. Navigate to the **PP2013 Lesson 12** folder, select **PP12-R01-House**, and click **Insert**.

8. Drag the picture to the bottom-right corner of the slide.

Save a Presentation in a Compatible Format

9. Display the second slide, **Agenda**.

10. Choose **Insert→Illustrations→SmartArt**.

11. Select the **Process** category and double-click the first SmartArt graphic.

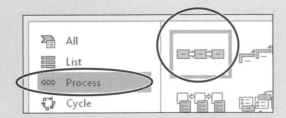

12. Click in the first SmartArt text box and type **Purpose**.

13. Click in the middle SmartArt text box and type **Goals**.

14. Click in the last SmartArt text box and type **Sponsors**.

15. Choose **File→Save**.

The Compatibility Checker summary appears and informs you that the SmartArt graphic is not compatible with the old PPT file format. You can still save the presentation, but you won't be able to edit the SmartArt graphic in PowerPoint 97–2003.

16. Click **Continue**.

The file is saved in its original old PPT format.

17. Close **PowerPoint**.

Create a Presentation and Import a Word Outline

18. Start **Word** and click **Blank Document**.

19. Choose **View→Views→Outline**.

20. Type the following:

```
Kids for Change Enter
Tab  New Houses Enter
Shift + Tab  98 Brookline Enter
Tab  LEED certified Enter
Geothermal Enter
South patio Enter
Shift + Tab  101 Riverside Enter
Tab  LEED certified Enter
Natural well Enter
Shift + Tab  28 Tacoma Enter
Tab  LEED certified Enter
Solar panels Enter
Organic garden
```

21. Save the outline to the **PP2013 Lesson 12** folder as **PP12-R01-Outline-[FirstInitialLastName]**.

22. Close **Word**. Then start **PowerPoint** and click **Blank Presentation**.

23. Choose **Design→Themes→More→Slice**.

24. Choose **Home→Slides→New Slide menu ▼→Slides from Outline**.

25. Navigate to the **PP2013 Lesson 12** folder.

26. Choose **PP12-R01-Outline-[FirstInitialLastName]** and click **Insert**.

27. Choose the first slide (the blank slide) and tap Delete to remove it.

28. Choose **Home→Slides→Layout menu ▼→Title Slide**.

29. Press Shift, select the last slide, and release Shift.

30. Choose **Home→Slides→Reset** to reformat the text on the selected slides with the document theme formatting.

31. Save the presentation as **PP12-R01-Houses-[FirstInitialLastName]**.

Create Handouts in Word

32. Choose **File→Export→Create Handouts→Create Handouts**.

33. Select the **Blank Lines Next to Slides** option.

34. Ensure that the **Paste** option is selected and click **OK**.

35. If necessary, use the **taskbar** to display **Word**.

36. Save the file as `PP12-R01-Handouts-[FirstInitialLastName]` to the **PP2013 Lesson 12** folder.

37. Exit **Word** and **PowerPoint**.

38. Submit your final files based on the guidelines provided by your instructor.

    To view examples of how your final file or files should look at the end of this exercise, go to the student resource center.

Integrate with Excel and Outlook

In this exercise, you will embed an OLE worksheet and create an appointment reminder in Outlook.

Embed an Excel Worksheet

1. Start **PowerPoint**. Open **PP12-R02-Kids** from your **PP2013 Lesson 12** folder and save it as `PP12-R02-Kids-[FirstInitialLastName]`.

2. Display the last slide, **Donations**.

3. Choose **Insert→Text→Object**.

4. Ensure that **Create New** is selected. Then scroll down the list, select **Microsoft Excel Worksheet**, and click **OK**.

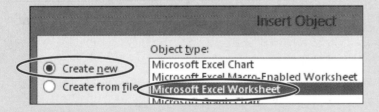

5. Type the following data, double-clicking the border to the right of the A and B column headers as necessary to autofit the contents:

	A	B
1	Builder Mart	$40,000
2	Pinky's Power Tool World	$35,000
3	Lorenzo's Lumber	$65,000
4	Total	

6. Click **cell B4**, choose **Home→Editing→Sum**, and tap [Enter].

7. Double-click the border to the right of **column B** to autofit the contents.

8. Select the first three cells in columns A and B and choose **Home→Styles→Cell Styles→40% Accent 2**.

9. Select the two **Total cells** and choose **Home→Styles→Cell Styles→Accent 2**.

10. Drag the bottom-right corner of the worksheet up and left to hide as many blank cells as you can.

11. Click on the slide, outside the worksheet.

12. Drag the lower-right corner of the worksheet to enlarge it and then drag the worksheet from the center to position it on the slide.

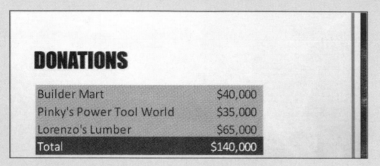

13. Save the presentation and close **PowerPoint**.

Schedule a Reminder in Outlook

14. Start **Outlook** and click **Calendar** at the bottom of the Outlook window.

15. Choose **Home→Arrange→Work Week**.

16. Double-click in the **10:30 AM cell** for tomorrow's date to add a new appointment.

17. Type `Kids Presentation` as the appointment subject.

18. Verify that the start and end dates are for tomorrow, and that the start and end times show **10:30** to **11:00**.

19. Type `Don't forget handouts` in the message area.

20. Set the reminder to **3 days**.

21. Choose **Insert→Include→Attach Files** and attach the **PP12-R02-Kids-[FirstInitialLastName]** presentation.

22. Choose **File→Save As**.

23. Type `PP12-R02-iCal-[FirstInitialLastName]` and save the appointment file to the **PP2013 Lesson 12** folder.
    You have saved the appointment in the iCal file format so that you can submit it to your instructor.

24. Choose **Appointment→Actions→Save & Close**.

25. Wait until the reminder pops up and then click **Dismiss**.

26. Close **Outlook**.

27. Submit your final files based on the guidelines provided by your instructor.
    To view examples of how your final file or files should look at the end of this exercise, go to the student resource center.

Work with Other Office Programs

In this exercise, you will use Word and Excel to create and enhance a presentation.

Open Various File Formats

1. Start **PowerPoint**. Open **PP12-R03-Final** from the **PP2013 Lesson 12** folder and save it as `PP12-R03-Final-[FirstInitialLastName]`.

   The presentation is in the native PPTX file format, so it opens without issue.

2. Choose **File→Open** and navigate to the **PP2013 Lesson 12** folder.

3. Change the **Files of Type** menu to **All Files**.

4. Click the **PP12-R03-KidsLogo** picture and then click **Open**.

   You receive an error because the JPG file format is an incompatible file type. JPG pictures can be inserted on a slide, but not opened directly from PowerPoint.

5. Click **OK** to close the error box.

6. Display the last slide and choose **Insert→Images→Pictures**.

7. Navigate to the **PP2013 Lesson 12** folder, select **PP12-R03-KidsLogo**, and click **Insert**.

8. Drag the picture to the top-right corner of the slide.

Save a Presentation in a Compatible Format

9. Display the last slide.

10. Choose **Insert→Illustrations→SmartArt**.

11. Select the **Cycle** category and then double-click the **first SmartArt graphic**.

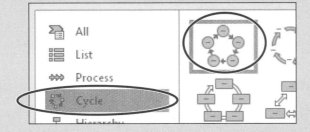

12. Click in the top SmartArt text box and type `Recycling`.

13. Click in the next SmartArt text box and type `Toys`.

14. Click in the next SmartArt text box and type `Diversity`.

15. Click in the next SmartArt text box and type `Bullies`.

16. Click in the next SmartArt text box and type `Tutoring`.

PowerPoint 2013

17. Drag the **SmartArt** graphic by its border to the top-left corner of the slide so the circles of the SmartArt don't cover the slide title.

18. Save the presentation.

    You will now save the presentation in the old PPT format for users of PowerPoint 97–2003.

19. Choose **File→Export→Change File Type** and double-click **PowerPoint 97-2003 Presentation**.

20. Ensure that the file name does not change from **PP12-R03-Final-[FirstInitialLastName]**.

21. Click **Save**.

    The Compatibility Checker summary appears and informs you that the SmartArt graphic is not compatible with the old PPT file format. You can still save the presentation, but you won't be able to edit the SmartArt graphic in PowerPoint 97–2003.

22. Click **Continue**.

    The file is saved in the old PPT format, and the title bar at the top of the PowerPoint window indicates the presentation is now saved in Compatibility Mode.

23. Close **PowerPoint**.

Create a Presentation and Import a Word Outline

24. Start **Word** and click **Blank Document**.

25. Choose **View→Views→Outline**.

26. Type the following:

    Kids for Change `Enter`
    `Tab` Recruitment `Enter`
    `Shift`+`Tab` Schools `Enter`
    `Tab` Cannon Middle School `Enter`
    Spencer High School `Enter`
    Wynn School of the Arts `Enter`
    `Shift`+`Tab` Presentations `Enter`
    `Tab` May 3 `Enter`
    May 21 `Enter`
    `Shift`+`Tab` Prizes `Enter`
    `Tab` New iPad Mini `Enter`
    $50 iTunes gift card `Enter`
    $25 Stormy BBQ gift certificate

27. Save the outline to the **PP2013 Lesson 12** folder as `PP12-R03-Outline-[FirstInitialLastName]`.

28. Close **Word**. Then start **PowerPoint** and click **Blank Presentation**.

29. Choose **Design→Themes→More→Organic**.

30. Choose **Home→Slides→New Slide menu ▼→Slides from Outline**.

31. Navigate to the **PP2013 Lesson 12** folder, choose **PP12-R03-Outline-[FirstInitialLastName]**, and click **Insert**.

32. Choose the first slide (the blank slide) and tap ⌷Delete⌷ to remove it.

33. Choose **Home**→**Slides**→**Layout menu ▼**→**Title Slide**.

34. Press ⌷Shift⌷, select the last slide, and release ⌷Shift⌷.

35. Choose **Home**→**Slides**→**Reset** to reformat the text on the selected slides with the document theme formatting.

36. Save the presentation as `PP12-R03-Recruitment-[FirstInitialLastName]`.

Create Handouts in Word

37. Choose **File**→**Export**→**Create Handouts**→**Create Handouts**.

38. Select the **Blank Lines Next to Slides** option.

39. Ensure that the **Paste** option is selected and click **OK**.

40. If necessary, use the **taskbar** to display **Word**.

41. Save the document as `PP12-R03-Handouts-[FirstInitialLastName]` to the **PP2013 Lesson 12** folder.

42. Close **Word**.

Embed an Excel Worksheet

43. If necessary, use the **Windows taskbar** to display **PowerPoint**.

44. Add a new slide to the end of the presentation with the title `Top Recruiters`.

45. Click the border of the bulleted text placeholder and tap ⌷Delete⌷.

46. Choose **Insert**→**Text**→**Object**.

47. Ensure that **Create New** is selected. Then scroll down the list, select **Microsoft Excel Worksheet**, and click **OK**.

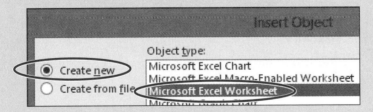

48. Type this data, double-clicking the border to the right of the A and B column headers as necessary to autofit the contents:

	A	B
1	Mike B	8
2	Tanisha D	7
3	Rolf V	4
4	Total	

49. Click **cell B4**, choose **Home**→**Editing**→**Sum**, and tap ⌷Enter⌋.

50. Double-click the border to the right of the **column B** header to autofit the contents.

51. Select the first three cells in columns A and B and choose **Home→Styles→Cell Styles→40% Accent 4**.

52. Select the two **Total cells** and choose **Home→Styles→Cell Styles→Accent 4**.

53. Drag the bottom-right corner of the worksheet up and left to hide as many blank cells as you can.

54. Click on the slide, outside the worksheet.

55. Drag the lower-right corner of the worksheet to enlarge it and then drag the worksheet from the center to position it on the slide to your liking.

56. Save the presentation and close **PowerPoint**.

Schedule a Reminder in Outlook

57. Start **Outlook** and click **Calendar** at the bottom of the Outlook window.

58. Choose **Home→Arrange→Work Week**.

59. Double-click in the **8:00 AM cell** for tomorrow's date to add a new appointment.

60. Type `Recruiting Presentation` as the appointment subject.

61. Verify that the start and end dates are for tomorrow and that the start and end times show **8:00 AM** to **8:30 AM**.

62. Type `Don't forget the prizes` in the message area.

63. Set the reminder to `1 week`.

64. Choose **Insert→Include→Attach Files** and attach the **PP12-R03-Recruitment-[FirstInitialLastName]** presentation.

65. Choose **File→Save As**.

66. Type `PP12-R03-iCal-[FirstInitialLastName]` and save the appointment file to the **PP2013 Lesson 12** folder.

    You have saved the appointment in the iCal file format so that you can submit it to your instructor.

67. Choose **Appointment→Actions→Save & Close**.

68. Wait until the reminder pops up and then click **Dismiss**.

69. Close **Outlook**.

70. Submit your final files based on the guidelines provided by your instructor.

Apply Your Skills

Use Compatible File Formats and Integrate with Word

In this exercise, you will explore various file formats and create a new presentation from a Word outline.

Open Various File Formats and Save in a Compatible Format

1. Start **PowerPoint**. Open **PP12-A01-Old** from the **PP2013 Lesson 12** folder and save it as **PP12-A01-Old-[FirstInitialLastName]**.

   The presentation is in the old PowerPoint 97-2003 PPT file format, but it is native to PowerPoint 2013 so it opens without issue.

2. Choose **File→Open** and attempt to open **PP12-A01-Hands** from the **PP2013 Lesson 12** folder.

   You receive an error because the PNG file format is an incompatible file type. PNG pictures can be inserted on a slide, but not opened directly from PowerPoint.

3. Close the error box, and insert **PP12-A01-Hands** in the yellow box on the title slide.

4. Display the second slide, **Agenda**.

5. Click anywhere in the bulleted text to display its border, and then delete it.

6. Click the border of the text placeholder and tap [Delete].

7. Insert the **Varying Width List SmartArt**, which is in the second row of the List category.

8. In the top SmartArt text box, type **Catering**.

9. In the middle SmartArt text box, type **Line Dancing**.

10. In the bottom SmartArt text box, type **Transportation**.

11. Drag the SmartArt graphic to center it on the slide.

12. Save the file.

    The Compatibility Checker summary appears and informs you that the SmartArt graphic is not compatible with the old PPT file format. You can still save the presentation, but you won't be able to edit the SmartArt graphic in PowerPoint 97–2003.

13. Click **Continue**.

    The file is saved in its original old PPT format.

14. Close **PowerPoint**.

Import a Word Outline and Create Handouts in Word

15. Start **Word** and click **Blank Document**.

16. Switch to **Outline view**.

17. Type the following:

```
Universal Corporate Events [Enter]
[Tab] Let us be your guide [Enter]
[Shift]+[Tab] Transportation [Enter]
[Tab] Bus [Enter]
Limo [Enter]
Ferry [Enter]
[Shift]+[Tab] Bus [Enter]
[Tab] Seats 40 [Enter]
Air-conditioned [Enter]
Restroom
[Shift]+[Tab] Limos [Enter]
[Tab] Privacy glass [Enter]
Widescreen television [Enter]
[Shift]+[Tab] Ferry [Enter]
[Tab] 3 levels [Enter]
Restrooms [Enter]
Wrap-around seating
```

18. Save the outline to the **PP2013 Lesson 12** folder as `PP12-A01-Outline-[FirstInitialLastName]` and then close **Word**.

19. Start **PowerPoint** and create a new **Blank Presentation**.

20. Apply the **Ion Boardroom** theme.

21. Create slides from **PP12-R01-Outline-[FirstInitialLastName]**.

22. Delete the first blank slide and then apply the **Title Slide** layout to the new first slide.

23. Reset all slides so they are formatted by the PowerPoint theme rather than by the Word outline.

24. Save the presentation as `PP12-A01-Guide-[FirstInitialLastName]`.

25. Create handouts in Word by using the **Blank Lines Below Slides** option and save the handouts document as `PP12-A01-Handouts-[FirstInitialLastName]` to the **PP2013 Lesson 12** folder.

26. Exit **Word** and **PowerPoint**.

27. Submit your final files based on the guidelines provided by your instructor.

    To view examples of how your final file or files should look at the end of this exercise, go to the student resource center.

Integrate with Excel and Outlook

In this exercise, you will embed an OLE worksheet and create an appointment reminder in Outlook.

Embed an Excel Worksheet

1. Start **PowerPoint**. Open **PP12-A02-Universal** from your **PP2013 Lesson 12** folder and save it as `PP12-A02-Universal-[FirstInitialLastName]`.

2. Insert a **Microsoft Excel Worksheet object** on the **Popularity** slide.

3. Type this data, double-clicking the border to the right of columns A and B as necessary to autofit the contents:

	A	B
1	Category	Orders
2	Vegetarian	87
3	Vegan	12
4	Kosher	45
5	Meat	87
6	Total	

4. Apply the **Sum** function to the Total cell in column B and autofit the cell contents.

5. Apply **Accent 2** to the cells in **rows 1 and 6** and apply **20% Accent 2** to **rows 2–5**.

6. Resize the worksheet to hide as many blank cells as you can.

7. Click on the slide, outside the worksheet, and resize the worksheet so it is easy to read and centered on the slide.

8. Save the presentation and close **PowerPoint**.

Schedule a Reminder in Outlook

9. Start **Outlook** and display the **Calendar** as a **Work Week**.

10. Create a new appointment in the **11:00 AM cell** for tomorrow's date.

11. Type `Universal Presentation` as the appointment subject and type `Don't forget samples` in the message area.

12. Verify that the start and end dates are for tomorrow and that the start and end times show **11:00** to **11:30**.

13. Set the reminder to `4 days` and attach the **PP12-A02-Universal-[FirstInitialLastName]** presentation.

14. Save the appointment as `PP12-A02-iCal-[FirstInitialLastName]` in the **PP2013 Lesson 12** folder.

    You have saved the appointment in the iCal file format so that you can submit it to your instructor.

PowerPoint 2013

15. Choose **Appointment→Actions→Save & Close**.

16. Dismiss the reminder and close **Outlook**.

    To view examples of how your final file or files should look at the end of this exercise, go to the student resource center.

Work with Other Office Programs

In this exercise, you will use Word and Excel to create and enhance a presentation.

Open Various File Formats and Save in a Compatible Format

1. Start **PowerPoint**. Open **PP12-A03-UCE** from the **PP2013 Lesson 12** folder and save it as `PP12-A03-UCE-[FirstInitialLastName]`.

   The presentation is in the native PPTX file format, so it opens without issue.

2. Choose **File→Open** and attempt to open **PP12-A03-UCELogo** from the **PP2013 Lesson 12** folder.

   You receive an error because the JPG file format is an incompatible file type. JPG pictures can be inserted on a slide, but not opened directly from PowerPoint.

3. Close the error box and insert **PP12-A03-UCELogo** below the subtitle.

4. Insert the **Basic Process SmartArt**, which is first in the Process category.

5. In the left SmartArt text box, type `Excellent`.

6. In the middle SmartArt text box, type `Customer`.

7. In the right SmartArt text box, type `Service`.

8. Drag the **SmartArt graphic** to center it below the logo.

9. Choose **File→Export→Change File Type** and double-click **PowerPoint 97-2003 Presentation**.

10. Save the presentation to the **PP2013 Lesson 12** folder.

    The Compatibility Checker summary appears and informs you that the SmartArt graphic is not compatible with the old PPT file format. You can still save the presentation, but you won't be able to edit the SmartArt graphic in PowerPoint 97–2003.

11. Click **Continue** and then close **PowerPoint**.

Import a Word Outline and Create Handouts in Word

12. Start a new, **blank Word document** and display it in **Outline view**.

13. Type the following:

Universal Corporate Events [Enter]
[Tab] Event Specialists [Enter]
[Shift]+[Tab] Services [Enter]
[Tab] Planning [Enter]
Catering [Enter]
Entertainment [Enter]
Transportation [Enter]
[Shift]+[Tab] Planning [Enter]
[Tab] Venue scouting [Enter]
Booking [Enter]
[Shift]+[Tab] Catering [Enter]
[Tab] Healthy choices [Enter]
Allergy accommodations [Enter]
[Shift]+[Tab] Entertainment [Enter]
[Tab] Dancing [Enter]
Bands [Enter]
[Shift]+[Tab] Transportation [Enter]
[Tab] Bus [Enter]
Ferry [Enter]
Limo [Enter]

14. Save the outline to the **PP2013 Lesson 12** folder as `PP12-A03-Outline-[FirstInitialLastName]` and then close **Word**.

15. Start **PowerPoint**, create a new blank presentation, and apply the **Ion** theme.

16. Create slides from **PP12-A03-Outline-[FirstInitialLastName]**.

17. Delete the first blank slide and then apply the **Title Slide** layout to the new first slide.

18. Reset all slides so they are formatted by the PowerPoint theme rather than by the Word outline.

19. Save the presentation as `PP12-A03-Specialists-[FirstInitialLastName]`.

20. Create handouts in Word by using the **Blank Lines Below Slides** option and save the handouts document as `PP12-A03-Handouts-[FirstInitialLastName]` to the **PP2013 Lesson 12** folder.

21. Close **Word**.

Embed an Excel Worksheet

22. Add a new blank slide at the end of the presentation, type **Events by Year** as the title, and delete the bulleted text placeholder.

23. Insert a **Microsoft Excel Worksheet object** on the **Events by Year** slide.

24. Type this data, double-clicking the border to the right of columns A and B as necessary to autofit the contents:

	A	B
1	Year	Events
2	2012	410
3	2011	350
4	2010	348
5	2009	250
6	Total	

25. Apply the **Sum** function to the Total cell in column B and autofit the cell contents.

26. Apply **Accent 5** to the cells in **rows 1 and 6** and apply **20% Accent 5** to **rows 2–5**.

27. Resize the worksheet to hide as many blank cells as you can.

28. Click on the slide, outside the worksheet, and resize the worksheet so it is easy to read and centered on the slide.

29. Save the presentation and close **PowerPoint**.

Schedule a Reminder in Outlook

30. Start **Outlook** and display the **Calendar** as a **Work Week**.

31. Create a new appointment in the **1:00 PM cell** for tomorrow's date.

32. Type **Universal Services Presentation** as the appointment subject and type **Remember handouts** in the message area.

33. Verify that the start and end dates are for tomorrow and that the start and end times show **1:00** to **1:30**.

34. Set the reminder to **3 days** and attach the **PP12-A03-UCE-[FirstInitialLastName]** presentation.

35. Save the appointment with the name **PP12-A03-iCal-[FirstInitialLastName]** to the **PP2013 Lesson 12** folder.
    You have saved the appointment in the iCal file format so that you can submit it to your instructor.

36. Choose **Appointment→Actions→Save & Close**.

37. Dismiss the reminder and close **Outlook**.

38. Submit your final files based on the guidelines provided by your instructor.

Extend Your Skills

In the course of working through the Extend Your Skills exercises, you will think critically as you use the skills taught in the lesson to complete the assigned projects. To evaluate your mastery and completion of the exercises, your instructor may use a rubric, with which more points are allotted according to performance characteristics. (The more you do, the more you earn!) Ask your instructor how your work will be evaluated.

PP12-E01 That's the Way I See It!

Different Microsoft Office 2013 suites include different programs. In this exercise, you will figure out the different combinations. In Word, create an outline listing all Office 2013 suite editions and the programs included in each. Indicate retail prices. Organize the information as you see fit and ensure that the outline is formatted to create slides (including a title slide) with appropriate titles and bulleted paragraphs when imported to PowerPoint. Save the outline as **PP12-E01-Outline-[FirstInitialLastName]**. Import the outline into a new presentation named **PP12-E01-Presentation-[FirstInitialLastName]**. Delete any unnecessary slides and ensure that the first slide uses the Title Slide layout. Apply a theme and reset the slides so they inherit the theme's formatting.

Add a final slide and insert a new Excel worksheet OLE object. In the first worksheet column, enter the name of each individual program in the Office Professional suite. In the second column, enter the price for the individual program (if not purchased as part of a suite). Create a Total row beneath your entries that automatically sums individual program prices. Format the worksheet so it's color-coordinated and no blank cells are visible. Save the presentation. Save a second copy (same name) in the 97-2003 format. Save all files in the **PP2013 Lesson 12** folder.

You will be evaluated based on the inclusion of all elements specified, your ability to follow directions, your ability to apply newly learned skills to a real-world situation, your creativity, and the relevance of your topic and/or data choice(s). Submit your final files based on the guidelines provided by your instructor.

PP12-E02 Be Your Own Boss

In this exercise, you will create and enhance a presentation for Blue Jean Landscaping. Create a Word outline saved as **PP12-E02-BlueJeanOutline-[FirstInitialLastName]** that organizes examples of three types of plantings (such as Vegetables, Ground Cover, and Flowering Shrubs) and three or four examples of each. The outline should include text for a title slide. Use the outline to generate slides in a blank presentation. Delete any unnecessary slides, ensure that the first slide uses the Title Slide layout, and format each slide to match the theme. Add an embedded OLE Excel worksheet that displays the cost of one planting in each category and include a Total row that calculates the total price. Format the Excel data on the slide so no blank cells are visible and the rows are color-coordinated with the slide theme. Save the presentation as **PP12-E02-BlueJeanPresentation-[FirstInitialLastName]**. Save a copy for users of PowerPoint 97 named **PP12-E02-BlueJeanPresentation97-[FirstInitialLastName]**. Store all files in the **PP2013 Lesson 12** folder.

You will be evaluated based on the inclusion of all elements specified, your ability to follow directions, your ability to apply newly learned skills to a real-world situation, your creativity, and your demonstration of an entrepreneurial spirit. Submit your final files based on the guidelines provided by your instructor.

Transfer Your Skills

In the course of working through the Transfer Your Skills exercises, you will use critical-thinking and creativity skills to complete the assigned projects using skills taught in the lesson. To evaluate your mastery and completion of the exercises, your instructor may use a rubric, with which more points are allotted according to performance characteristics. (The more you do, the more you earn!) Ask your instructor how your work will be evaluated.

PP12-T01 Use the Web as a Learning Tool

Throughout this book, you will be provided with an opportunity to use the Internet as a learning tool by completing WebQuests. According to the original creators of WebQuests, as described on their website (WebQuest.org), a WebQuest is "an inquiry-oriented activity in which most or all of the information used by learners is drawn from the web." To complete the WebQuest projects in this book, navigate to the student resource center and choose the WebQuest for the lesson on which you are currently working. The subject of each WebQuest will be relevant to the material found in the lesson.

WebQuest Subject: OneNote

Submit your final files based on the guidelines provided by your instructor.

PP12-T02 Demonstrate Proficiency

Stormy BBQ is finalizing its customer satisfaction survey. Create a Word outline that organizes customer quotes into the categories Food, Service, Cost, and Atmosphere. Create two to four customer quotes (just make them up) for each category. Do not include text for a title slide, as you will create that manually. Save the outline as `PP12-T02-Results-[FirstInitialLastName]`.

Create a new presentation with a title slide title and subtitle of your choice for the customer satisfaction survey. Apply a design theme and then use the Word outline to create the additional slides. Ensure that all slides are formatted according to the PowerPoint theme rather than the Word outline. Save the presentation as `PP12-T02-BBQ-[FirstInitialLastName]`. Save a second copy, with the same name, in the 97-2003 format.

Create handouts in Word that display blank lines below each slide for note taking and comments for use by the Stormy staff before making the presentation public. Save the handout document as `PP12-T02-Handouts-[FirstInitialLastName]`. Store all files in the **PP2013 Lesson 12** folder.

Submit your final files based on the guidelines provided by your instructor.

Index

Index

Notes

Notes

Notes

Notes

Notes

Notes

Notes

Notes

Notes

Notes

Notes

Notes

Notes

Notes

Notes